Second Language
Vocabulary Acquisition

# THE CAMBRIDGE APPLIED LINGUISTICS SERIES

Series editors: Michael H. Long and Jack C. Richards

This series presents the findings of recent work in applied linguistics which are of direct relevance to language teaching and learning and of particular interest to applied linguists, researchers, language teachers, and teacher trainers.

*In this series:*

# Second Language Vocabulary Acquisition

## A Rationale for Pedagogy

*James Coady*
Ohio University

and

*Thomas Huckin*
University of Utah

 CAMBRIDGE
UNIVERSITY PRESS

PUBLISHED BY THE PRESS SYNDICATE OF THE UNIVERSITY OF CAMBRIDGE
The Pitt Building, Trumpington Street, Cambridge, United Kingdom

CAMBRIDGE UNIVERSITY PRESS
The Edinburgh Building, Cambridge CB2 2RU, UK
40 West 20th Street, New York, NY 10011–4211, USA
10 Stamford Road, Oakleigh, Melbourne 3166, Australia
Ruiz de Alarcón 13, 28014 Madrid, Spain
Dock House, The Waterfront, Cape Town 8001, South Africa

http://www.cambridge.org

First published 1997
Third printing 2000

Printed in the United States of America

Typeset in Sabon

Library of Congress Cataloging-in-Publication Data
Coady, James
Second language vocabulary acquisition : a rationale for pedagogy
/ James Coady, Thomas Huckin.
p. cm. – (The Cambridge applied linguistics series)
ISBN 0-521-56132-9. – ISBN 0-521-56764-5 (pbk.)
1. Language and languages – Study and teaching.  2. Second language
acquisition.  3. Vocabulary – Study and teaching.  I. Huckin, Thomas
N.  II. Title.  III. Series.
P53.9.C63  1996
418′.007 – dc20                                                    96-3115
                                                                      CIP

A catalog record for this book is available from the British Library

ISBN 0 521 56132 9 hardback
ISBN 0 521 56764 5 paperback

# Contents

# Contributors

Roann Altman, Ben-Gurion University of the Negev, Israel
Pierre J. L. Arnaud, Université Lumière, Lyons
James Coady, Ohio University, Athens
William Grabe, Northern Arizona University, Flagstaff
Jan H. Hulstijn, Vrije Universiteit, Amsterdam
Keiko Koda, Carnegie Mellon University, Pittsburgh, Pennsylvania
Batia Laufer, University of Haifa, Israel
Michael Lewis, LTP, Hove, England
Paul Nation, Victoria University of Wellington, New Zealand
Jonathan Newton, Victoria University of Wellington, New Zealand
Kate Parry, Hunter College of the City University of New York
T. Sima Paribakht, University of Ottawa, Ontario
Sandra J. Savignon, University of Illinois at Urbana-Champaign
Fredricka L. Stoller, Northern Arizona University, Flagstaff
Marjorie Wesche, University of Ottawa, Ontario
Lynne Yang, State University of New York, Buffalo
Cheryl Boyd Zimmerman, California State University, Fullerton

# Series editors' preface

The relative neglect of studies of vocabulary acquisition and related areas of lexical research in second language acquisition has often been commented on within the fields of language teaching and applied linguistics. Compared to work in grammar, phonology, and discourse studies, much less is known about the nature of the second language learners' lexicon. Yet adequate theories of L2 vocabulary acquisition and use are central to a wide range of issues in applied linguistics, including performance assessment, proficiency testing, curriculum development, and applied lexicography. Fortunately, since the mid-1980s there has been a renewed interest in the role of vocabulary in second language learning, and this has seen a growing body of empirically based studies of such issues as the nature of the bilingual lexicon, vocabulary acquisition, lexical storage, lexical retrieval, and use of vocabulary by second language learners.

*Second Language Vocabulary Acquisition* will be of great interest to those interested in current views on the nature of L2 vocabulary acquisition and approaches to L2 vocabulary teaching. It provides a useful introduction to the current state of theory and research, examines the topic of vocabulary learning and teaching from a number of perspectives, and presents a comprehensive range of papers that explore such issues as the nature of lexical competence, the measurement of vocabulary knowledge and growth, the role of vocabulary in L2 reading and listening, speaking and writing, the relations between L1 and L2 vocabulary, as well as pedagogical approaches to the teaching of vocabulary. Strategies employed by learners in processing vocabulary encountered in spoken and written discourse are illustrated, as are the cognitive skills involved in lexical comprehension.

As the papers in the book demonstrate, lexical competence is at the heart of communicative competence, and ways of measuring the size and nature of the L2 lexicon offer a challenge to researchers. A number of different research directions are illustrated throughout the book, including case studies, diary studies, introspection, and experimental studies. At the same time, the contributors explore applications of research and theory to a wide variety of issues in language education, including vocabulary teaching, language assessment, test construction, syllabus design, and materials preparation. The book will therefore be a valuable resource for researchers, teachers, and other language professionals interested in the nature of vocabulary in second language teaching and learning.

Michael H. Long
Jack C. Richards

# Acknowledgments

We offer thanks to the people who have helped us in so many ways. Primarily, we wish to thank the many contributors to this volume. Their patience and understanding during the production of the book were essential. We also wish to thank our editors at Cambridge – Mary Vaughn, Mary Carson, and Olive Collen – for their tireless work in helping in the preparation of the manuscript and in seeing it through to publication. Also, we appreciate the fact that Jack Richards encouraged us to attempt to publish this collection and supported us throughout. Finally, we are grateful to our wives, Miriam and Christiane, for their unflagging support and inspiration.

James Coady
Thomas Huckin

# PART I:
# SETTING THE STAGE

In recent years, second language vocabulary acquisition has become an increasingly interesting topic of discussion for researchers, teachers, curriculum designers, theorists, and others involved in second language learning. Part I provides a framework for the rest of the book by introducing the main dimensions of the topic: teaching techniques, testing principles, and learning processes. In so doing, it emphasizes those subtopics that have been given the most attention in the literature: (1) debates about different teaching methods, (2) the problem of how to test vocabulary knowledge in a valid yet practical way, (3) issues about the interrelationship of reading and word learning, in particular the effectiveness of contextual guessing, and (4) the role of detailed perceptual variables in the identification and misidentification of words. The range of topics runs from broad (e.g. general teaching approaches, global measures of lexical competence) to fine-grained (e.g., morphology, orthography).

Cheryl Zimmerman leads off with a historical survey of vocabulary teaching methods. Vocabulary is central to language, she notes, and words are of critical importance to the typical language learner. Nevertheless, researchers and teachers in the field of language acquisition have typically undervalued the role of vocabulary, usually prioritizing syntax or phonology as central to linguistic theory and more critical to language pedagogy. Zimmerman's chapter examines the position assigned to vocabulary within each of the major trends in language pedagogy, including the Grammar Translation Method, the Reform Movement, the Direct Method, the Reading Method and Situational Language Teaching, the Audiolingual Method, Communicative Language Approaches, the Natural Approach, and current proposals such as the Lexical Approach that stress the lexical nature of language and propose lexico-grammatical approaches to language instruction. The primary goals of each pedagogical approach are described and the implications for vocabulary instruction are examined; this includes the rationale for word selection, the perception of written versus spoken language, attitudes toward translation of target words or dictionary use, and examples of recommended word-learning strategies or exercises. The purpose of this survey is to build a better understanding of the past and to position future lexical pedagogy.

Vocabulary learning has long had a synergistic association with reading; each activity nourishes the other. But, as James Coady notes later in the book, it is not a simple, problem-free relationship. In Chapter 2, Batia Laufer discusses three lexical problems that may seriously impede reading comprehension in L2: (1) the problem of insufficient vocabulary, (2) misinterpretations of deceptively transparent words, and (3) inability to guess unknown words correctly. Drawing on a variety of studies, including her own, Laufer claims that by far the greatest lexical factor in good reading is the number of words in the learner's lexicon. A vocabulary of 3,000 word families or 5,000 lexical items is needed for general reading comprehension, as this would cover 90–95% of any text. Below this threshold, reading strategies become ineffective.

A large vocabulary is also claimed to solve the other two problems: deceptive transparency and guessing ability. Deceptively transparent words are words that look familiar to the learner even though they are unfamiliar. These are words with deceptive morphological structure (e.g. nevertheless = "never less"), idioms, false friends, words with multiple meanings, and "synforms" (e.g., cute/acute). Laufer argues that misinterpretations of such words are widespread among second language learners.

Guessing word meanings by use of contextual clues is far more difficult, according to Laufer, than is generally realized. Guessing can be impaired by any of the following factors: (*a*) nonexistence of clues, (*b*) lack of familiarity with the words in which the clues are located, (*c*) presence of misleading or partial clues, and (*d*) incompatibility between the reader's schemata and the text content. To consistently make good guesses, one should know about 98% of the words in a text. For this kind of coverage, one would generally need a sight vocabulary of about 5,000 word families (8,000 lexical items). Laufer concludes that a large sight vocabulary is indispensable to good L2 reading and vocabulary guessing.

Building a large sight vocabulary, however, requires accurate "sight," i.e., word perception. As Laufer notes in her discussion of synforms and words with deceptive morphological structure, many second language learners have trouble at this microscopic level of cognition. In Chapter 3, "The role of orthographic knowledge in L2 lexical processing," Keiko Koda addresses this problem. The major purpose of this chapter is to examine the ways in which L1 orthographic competence shapes L2 lexical processing. In an effort to clarify the nature of L2 vocabulary learning, the critical relationship between orthographic properties and processing mechanisms is first analyzed from a cross-linguistic perspective. Second, the cognitive consequences of L1 orthographies are examined through empirical L2 data. Finally, pedagogical implications are drawn from the current knowledge base on orthographic transfer.

Koda shows that there are strong connections between the L1

orthographic system and L2 processing. She argues that improved L2 vocabulary instruction therefore depends in part on a better understanding of this relationship and on its long-term impact on L2 processing. Second language reading and vocabulary instruction, she claims, should be individualized and it should be based more on L1 strategies than on L2 ones. Also, it should include explicit instruction, in particular orthographic properties of the target language.

# 1 Historical trends in second language vocabulary instruction

Cheryl Boyd Zimmerman

## Introduction

Vocabulary is central to language and of critical importance to the typical language learner. Nevertheless, the teaching and learning of vocabulary have been undervalued in the field of second language acquisition (SLA) throughout its varying stages and up to the present day. SLA researchers and teachers have typically prioritized syntax and phonology as "more serious candidates for theorizing" (Richards, 1976, p. 77), more central to linguistic theory, and more critical to language pedagogy. This chapter will seek to show how vocabulary has been viewed, researched, and presented throughout the history of SLA. The purpose of this survey is to build a better understanding of the past and to indicate likely developments in lexical pedagogy in the future.

## The Grammar Translation Method

The Grammar Translation Method was first introduced to teach modern languages in public schools in Prussia at the end of the eighteenth century. The primary goals of this method were to prepare students to read and write classical materials and to pass standardized exams (Howatt, 1984; Rivers, 1981). Like courses in classical Latin and Greek, this method used classical literature chosen for its intellectual content as materials; it was typically assumed that most students would never actually use the target language but would profit from the mental exercise. Students were provided detailed explanations of grammar in their native languages, paradigms to memorize, and bilingual vocabulary lists to learn; these prepared them for the regular task of translating long passages of the classics. Although the names of the Grammar Translation materials typically included the adjective "practical" (e.g., *The Practical Guide of the German Language* by T. H. Weisse), the word was not used to mean *useful* as we would use it today. Rather, it referred to the importance of *practice* (Howatt, 1984): Lessons typically consisted of a reading selection, two or three long columns of new vocabulary items with native-language equivalents, and a test (Rivers, 1981). Language skill was judged according to one's ability to analyze the syntactic structure, primarily to conjugate verbs.

It follows, then, that students using the Grammar Translation Method studied literary language samples that used primarily archaic structures and obsolete vocabulary. Students were exposed to a wide literary vocabulary (Rivers, 1981) that was selected according to its ability to illustrate grammatical rules, and direct vocabulary instruction was included only when a word illustrated a grammatical rule (Kelly, 1969). When vocabulary difficulties were addressed at all, their explanations depended largely on etymology. Latin and Greek roots or "primitives" were considered "the most accurate court of appeal on word meanings"; the ability to use etymology was respected as "one way of discovering truth" (Kelly, 1969, p. 30). The teaching of vocabulary was based on definition and etymology throughout the nineteenth century, at least in part because of the prevalent belief that the connection between etymon and derivative should be protectively preserved to avoid degeneration of the language. Bilingual word lists (*vocabularies*), used as instructional aids rather than as reference, were organized according to semantic fields and had been a normal part of grammars and readers since the mid-seventeenth century. During the period of Grammar Translation methodology, bilingual dictionaries became common as reference tools (Kelly, 1969). As more was understood about language families and the natural process of language change in the twentieth century, scholars began to emphasize the dangers of cognates, but this change in perspective was gradual.

The Grammar Translation Method was used well into the twentieth century as the primary method for foreign language instruction in Europe and the United States, but it had received challenges and criticism for many years. In the mid-1800s, the primary objection to the method was the neglect of realistic, oral language. This objection had implications for the role of vocabulary in language instruction. For example, the Frenchman François Gouin emphasized the acquisition of specific terms, especially of action words

. . . that could be physically performed as they were used. . . . Within these situations, students would act out very detailed sequences of appropriate actions in relation to objects, stating aloud exactly what they were doing with what. (Rivers, 1983, p. 116)

He introduced words in semantic fields in the interest of teaching a verb's collocations along with the verb, always emphasizing that "general terms are . . . terms of luxury, which the language can upon necessity do without" (Gouin, 1892, in Rivers, 1983, p. 116).

Another challenge came from Thomas Prendergast, who objected to archaic vocabulary lists; in his 1864 manual, *The Mastery of Languages, or, the Art of Speaking Foreign Tongues Idiomatically,* he listed the most common English words, based entirely on his intuitive judgment. This effort to rank vocabulary according to frequency was seen as one of many fleeting and rebellious methods that failed to perform what it promised and consequently "didn't significantly influence language teaching" (Sweet, 1899/1964, p. 2). Nevertheless, Prendergast's judgments were deemed surprisingly accurate when compared to the lists compiled systematically by Thorndike and Lorge in 1944: of a total of 214 words, 82% of Prendergast's words were among the first 500 most frequent words on the list of Thorndike-Lorge (Howatt, 1984). Prendergast's list was an important innovation because it came at a time when simplicity and everyday language were scorned and before it was normal to think in terms of common words.

## The Reform Movement

As already seen, although Grammar Translation dominated language teaching as late as the 1920s, it had been challenged on many fronts. In the 1880s its challengers had enough consensus and the intellectual leadership they needed from linguists such as Henry Sweet in England to establish the Reform Movement. Sweet insisted that previous reactions against Grammar Translation had failed because they were "based on an insufficient knowledge of the science of language and because they [were] one-sided" (Sweet, 1899/1964, p. 3). The Reformers emphasized the primacy of spoken language and phonetic training. *Fluency* took on a new meaning: the ability to accurately pronounce a connected passage and to maintain associations between a stream of speech and the referents in the outside world. The curriculum developed by Sweet is considered representative of the time (Howatt, 1984). His system began with the *Mechanical Stage,* where students studied phonetics and transcription, continued to the *Grammatical Stage,* where they studied grammar and very basic vocabulary, and then to the *Idiomatic Stage,* where they pursued vocabulary in greater depth. Stages four and five (*Literary* and *Archaic*) consisted of the study of philology and were reserved for university-level work. Sweet's lessons were based on carefully controlled spoken language in which lists of separated words and isolated sentences were avoided; only after thorough study of the complete text should grammar points or vocabulary items be isolated for instructional purposes.

Although language is made up of words, we do not speak in words, but in sentences. From a practical, as well as a scientific, point of view, the sentence is the unit of language, not the word. From a purely phonetic point of view words do not exist. (Sweet, 1899/1964, p. 97)

Perhaps the Reformers' most significant departure from the past in the area of vocabulary instruction was that words came to be associated with reality rather than with other words and syntactic patterns. To this end, vocabulary was selected according to its simplicity and usefulness. Sweet began to discuss the possibility of developing vocabulary lists based on statistical measures, though they were developed intuitively by consensus until the 1920s (Kelly, 1969). Sweet believed that practical words such as household items and articles of clothing were not only important to know, but also appropriately "dull and commonplace"; he warned that students might be distracted from learning by interesting materials (Howatt, 1984, p. 187).

# The Direct Method

The Direct Method, the best known of several "natural" methods introduced toward the end of the nineteenth century, benefited from the debate that ensued during the Reform Movement, though it wasn't considered grounded in linguistic theory by Sweet and other intellectual leaders (Richards & Rodgers, 1986). Its name came from the priority of relating meaning directly with the target language without the step of translation. Developed in the United States by Sauveur and made famous by Berlitz, the Direct Method stated that interaction was at the heart of natural language acquisition. Its proponents used the target language as the language of instruction in small, intensive classes consisting of carefully graded progressions of question and answer exchanges. Everyday vocabulary and sentences were used. Reading was taught throughout the course and was "developed through practice with speaking" (Larsen-Freeman, 1986). Criticisms against the Direct Method included its oversimplification of the similarities between L1 and L2 and its lack of consideration of the practical logistics of the public classroom (Richards & Rodgers, 1986).

In Sauveur's 1874 teacher's manual, *An Introduction to the Teaching of Living Languages without Grammar or Dictionary*, he proposed two principles of language teaching that dictated vocabulary selection and instruction. The first principle was that teachers were only to ask "earnest questions" that elicited answers in which the teacher had genuine interest. Second, questions needed to be connected to one another in "such a manner that one may give rise to another" to provide the learners with the opportunities to learn from context (Howatt, 1984, p. 201). The vocabulary was simple and familiar: the first few lessons of the Berlitz English course, for example, were based on objects in the classroom, clothing, and parts of the body, followed by *to be* and common adjectives (*big, small, thin, thick,* etc.) (Howatt, 1984, p. 206). Concrete vocabulary was explained with labeled pictures and demonstration, while abstract vocabulary was taught through the associating of ideas (Rivers, 1983; Richards & Rodgers, 1986). Charts and pictures were used during this period, first in the classroom and then in language textbooks. Objects were also used to demonstrate meaning, and the term *realia* or *realien* appears to have been adopted at this time (Kelly, 1969). Many traditionalists never adjusted to the Direct Method and criticized it for being trivial. It never was adopted in the ordinary schools of America or Europe, but gained an extensive following through private language facilities such as the Berlitz Schools (Howatt, 1984).

## The Reading Method/Situational Language Teaching

The 1920s and 1930s saw the birth of the Reading Method in the United States and Situational Language Teaching in Great Britain. The Reading Method was aimed primarily at the development of reading skills, a response in part to the 1929 Coleman report, which cited serious deficiencies in the foreign language reading skills of American students (Rivers, 1981). Similarly, in Great Britain, Michael West stressed the need to facilitate reading skill by improving vocabulary skills. Beginning with his thesis at Oxford in 1927 and continuing for more than forty years, he criticized direct methodologists for stressing the importance of speech without providing guidelines for selecting content:

The Primary thing in learning a language is the acquisition of a vocabulary, and practice in using it (which is the same thing as 'acquiring'). The problem is *what* vocabulary; and none of these 'modern textbooks in common use in English schools' have attempted to solve the problem. (West, 1930, p. 514)

He stated that foreign language learners did not have even a basic thousand-word vocabulary after three years of study, for three reasons: (1) their time was spent on activities that were not helping them speak the language; (2) they were learning words that were not useful to them; and (3) they were not "fully mastering" the words they were learning (West, 1930, p. 511). West's recommendation was to use word-frequency lists as the basis for the selection and order of vocabulary in student materials. In 1930 he recommended the use of Thorndike's word-frequency list; in 1953 West published *A General Service List of English Words*. Even though this list is old (the headwords have not changed since 1936), it is still considered the most widely used of high-frequency word lists. In fact, publishers and examining boards still quote West's 1953 list despite the existence of more updated lists compiled with the help of computer technology (Meara, 1980).

At the same time, British linguists H. E. Palmer and A. S. Hornby, considered leaders of the Situational Language Teaching movement, were influential both in the United States and in Great Britain; their initial aim was to develop a more scientific foundation for the oral methods made popular by direct methodologists. They believed language should be taught by practicing basic structures in meaningful situation-based activities; speech was the basis and structure that made speech possible. In their reaction to the ungraded speech imposed upon learners in the Direct Method, Palmer and Hornby stressed *selection, gradation,* and *presentation* of language structures (Richards & Rodgers, 1986, p. 33). Many language programs were published during this period, reflecting the perceived need for systematic gradation of language in language courses (Faucett, 1933; Ogden, 1930; Palmer, 1916, 1921, 1924). For the first time, vocabulary was considered one of the most important aspects of second language learning and a priority was placed on developing a scientific and rational basis for selecting the vocabulary content of language courses. The combined research of Palmer and Michael West led to the development of principles on vocabulary control; their attempts to introduce a scientific basis for vocabulary selection were the first efforts to establish principles of syllabus design in language teaching (Richards & Rodgers, 1990).

## The audio-lingual method

The audio-lingual method (or the structural approach, as it was called by its founders) was developed by American structural linguists during World War II, when governmental and institutional support was available for the teaching of foreign languages. Perceived by founder Charles Fries as a new approach to pedagogical grammar rather than as merely a new method, the audio-lingual method was originally used in the English Language Institute at the University of Michigan. Fries's 1945 *Teaching and Learning English as a Foreign Language* described the new approach as a practical interpretation of the "principles of modern linguistic science" (Fries, 1945, p. v). This approach suggested that most problems experienced by foreign language learners concern the conflict of different structural systems. With grammar or "structure" as its starting point and the belief that language learning is a process of habit formation, the audio-lingual method paid systematic attention to pronunciation and intensive oral drilling of basic sentence patterns. Students were taught grammatical points through examples and drills rather than through analysis and memorization of rules. The course, as proposed by Fries, consisted of three months of intensive study of the essentials of English structure.

With the major object of language teaching being the acquisition of structural patterns, vocabulary items were selected according to their simplicity and familiarity. New words were introduced through the drills, but only enough words to make the drills possible (Larsen-Freeman, 1986). The assumption seemed to be that the structural frames could be "fleshed out with words at a later stage when students were more certain of their lexical needs in particular situations" (Rivers, 1983, p. 118).

In Fries's 1945 text, he introduced the chapter on vocabulary learning by quoting Edward Sapir: "The linguistic student should never make the mistake of identifying a language with its dictionary" (Fries, 1945, p. 38). Fries suspected that language learners oversimplified the role of isolated words. He attributed the oversimplification of vocabulary issues to three false assumptions about the nature of language. First, it is falsely assumed that words have exact equivalents in different languages; Fries argued that the only words that convey exactly the same meaning from one language to another are highly technical words. Second, it is assumed that a word is a single meaning unit; in fact, Fries pointed out that English words usually have from fifteen to twenty meanings. The third false assumption is that each word has a "basic" or "real" meaning and that all other meanings are either figurative or illegitimate. Fries spent a considerable amount of time in this introductory document arguing against these false assumptions and illustrating the fact that words are linguistic forms: "symbols that derive their whole content and their limitations of meaning from the situations in which they are used" (Fries, 1945, p. 43).

It was thus suggested during this period that learning too much vocabulary early in the language learning process gives students a false sense of security. Wilga Rivers reflects this view in *Teaching Foreign Language Skills,* first published in 1968:

Excessive vocabulary learning early in the course gives students the impression that the most important thing about learning a language is accumulating new words as equivalents for concepts which they can already express in their native languages. They often fail to realize that meaning is expressed in groups of words and in combinations of language segments, and that the meaning of an individual word is usually difficult to determine when it is separated from a context of other words and phrases. Traditional vocabulary lists rarely provide contexts of this type. Students are thus unprepared to use the words they have learned as isolated units in any approximation to authentic communication. (Rivers, 1968/1981, p. 254)

She went on to recommend practice with morphological variations and syntactic structures using well-known vocabulary so that students would not be distracted from concentration on the target structures. She recommended that new vocabulary be introduced first in high-interest oral activities and that words be reused extensively in order to aid long-term retention. As will be seen shortly, Rivers altered this view in later publications.

Freeman Twaddell, a colleague of Fries, echoed Fries's concern that language learners often overvalue word knowledge and equate it with knowledge of the language; he suggested that teachers and theoreticians have reacted against learners' exaggeration of the role of vocabulary by downgrading it and have consequently overemphasized the role of grammar (1980). The ramifications of this view have been seen in curriculum and teaching materials that treat lexical items as the means by which to illustrate grammatical topics rather than as items with communicative value in themselves. Twaddell notes that the result is that, unlike L1 children who have more words than they can express in sentences, adult learners have "an infantile vocabulary and an adult mentality" (Twaddell, 1980, p. 442). His recommendation for addressing this problem is not to abandon the primacy of grammatical structures in the process of teaching a language, but rather to teach skills of compensation: "guessing word meanings and tolerating vagueness."

## Communicative language teaching

A major transition in linguistic theory was triggered by the publication of Noam Chomsky's *Syntactic Structures* in 1957. This work introduced the assumption that language is represented in the speaker's mental grammar by an abstract set of rules that is most clearly reflected in a speaker's unconscious intuitions about language, and least reflected in his or her conscious beliefs and statements about the use of language (Chomsky, 1965). Chomsky maintained that language existed in the individual quite apart from communicating needs, and labeled the internalized (unconscious) mental grammar of a language *competence,* and the actual use of it *performance.* At the same time, though, he paid little attention to the nature of language use in real communication. His work was a revolutionary reminder of the creativity of language and a challenge to the behaviorist view of language as a set of habits. In reaction against the Chomskyan notion of an autonomous linguistic competence, Dell Hymes introduced the concept of *communicative competence,* which, while not rejecting Chomsky's model, gave greater emphasis to the sociolinguistic and pragmatic factors governing effective language use. *Communicative competence* is defined as the internalized knowledge of the situational appropriateness of language (Hymes, 1972).

An essential insight that emerged from this period is that communicative competence incorporates linguistic competence in the sense of linguistic creativity and that language learning is quite different from the previously held model of habit formation. The result was a complete change in the direction for language instruction; the focus in language teaching changed to communicative proficiency rather than the command of structures. This shift has been manifested in communicative language teaching, a broad term used to refer to many specific methods. In general, communicative language teaching strives to "make communicative competence the goal of language teaching and to develop procedures for the teaching of the four language skills that acknowledge the interdependence of language and communication" (Richards & Rodgers, 1990, p. 66). Communicative methods have the common goals of bringing language learners into closer contact with the target language (Stern, 1981) and of promoting fluency over accuracy. Rivers described her perception of this shift in 1983 when she referred to the insufficiency of the *skill-getting* practices of the audio-lingual methods alone without the *skill-using* opportunities of real communication:

One failure in the past has been in our satisfaction with students who performed well in pseudo-communication. We have tended to assume that there would then be automatic transfer to performance in interaction (both in the reception and expression of messages). (Rivers, 1983, p. 43)

In the argument for fluency over accuracy, Rivers has exhorted language educators to pay more attention to words, considering carefully how to help learners communicate meaning, "even before they can express discriminatingly fifteen ways to ask that the door be opened" (Rivers, 1983, p. 120). Similarly, Widdowson (1978) has claimed that native speakers can better understand ungrammatical utterances with accurate vocabulary than those with accurate grammar and inaccurate vocabulary. Nevertheless, vocabulary has not been the focus of attention in communicative language research or methodology. Instead, attention has been turned more toward the appropriate use of communicative categories (cf. Van Ek, 1976; Wilkins, 1972), and toward language as discourse (cf. Widdowson, 1979).

The use of communicative categories began with British linguist David Wilkins's 1972 analysis of communicative meanings; his proposed categories subsequently became the basis for the communicative syllabi adopted by the Council of Europe. Wilkins demonstrated that there are two systems or categories of meaning involved in communication: notional categories (concepts such as *time, quantity, space,*) and functional categories (acts such as *requests, denials*) (Wilkins, 1972). It has been suggested that since notional and functional syllabi have been based on thematic and situational criteria, their content has been determined more by semantics than by syntax (Laufer, 1986). Nevertheless, little explicit attention has been given to vocabulary in either theoretical or methodological publications about notional and functional syllabi. Wilkins summarized his view of the role of vocabulary in language instruction directly in his 1974 work, *Second-Language Learning and Teaching:*

. . . the ability to refer to concrete and conceptual entities is as fundamental to language as is the capacity provided by the grammar to relate such entities to one another. Knowledge of a language demands mastery of its vocabulary as much as of its grammar. . . . Just as the grammatical meaning of a linguistic form can be established only by reference to the grammatical system of which it is a part, so lexical meaning is the product of a word's place in the lexical system. (Wilkins, 1974, pp. 19–20)

He suggests that the only way to master this lexical system is the same as that recommended to master the syntactic system: the learner must experience considerable exposure to the language.

This view that lexical systems of languages must be addressed in their complexity has also been suggested by the American linguist Edward Anthony:

A given referent is empirically bonded to more than one lexical word, and any one of such lexical units may be bonded to more than one referent. . . . A user of English is provided with culturally determined patterns of behavior which enable him to share his experience with others belonging to the same culture and subject to the same patterns of behavior. (Anthony, 1973, p. 13)

Anthony's suggestion for addressing the intricacy of lexical knowledge is to address words within their cultural context, to avoid oversimplification, and not to rely on translation as a factor in a teaching approach, a teaching methodology, or as a classroom technique. Communicative methods reflect these concerns in various ways, such as by basing course content on activities that are contextualized, by focusing on the discourse level rather than the sentence level, and by providing students with opportunities to develop strategies for interpreting and using the language as it is actually used by native speakers (Larsen-Freeman, 1986).

In the preparation of communicative materials, frequency counts have been largely displaced by subjective assessments of the usefulness of words (cf. Van Ek, 1976) because of several problems associated with frequency counts. Those who recommend the use of frequency lists suggest that the first 1,000 to 2,000 words make up a "beginner's vocabulary." However, the problems include the following: (1) the most important words for language learners do not always appear in the first or second thousand words (e.g., *stupid* and *behavior* do not appear in the first 3,000 words of Thorndike and Lorge's 1944 list); (2) the order of words in a frequency list does not always indicate the best order in which to teach words (e.g., *his* is the 74th word in one list and *hers* is the 4151st word; included in the first 1,000 words of Thorndike and Lorge's list are *issue* [*v*], *stock*, and *Chicago*); and (3) word-frequency lists disagree according to the types of texts being analyzed (Nation, 1990). As a result of such problems, word-frequency lists appear to contradict an underlying assumption of communicative approaches: Since vocabulary development occurs naturally in L1 through contextualized, naturally sequenced language, it will develop with natural, communicative exposure in L2.

## The Natural Approach

The Natural Approach is "similar to other communicative approaches being developed" during this period (Krashen & Terrell, 1983, p. 17), but it is based on its own set of hypotheses. Designed primarily to "enable a beginning student to reach acceptable levels of oral communicative ability in the language classroom" (Krashen & Terrell, 1983, p. 131), the Natural Approach is based on a theoretical model consisting of five hypotheses: (1) the Acquisition-Learning Hypothesis (the distinction between "natural" acquisition as seen in L1 and the formal learning that emphasizes conscious rules and error correction); (2) the Natural Order Hypothesis (that grammatical structures tend to be naturally acquired in a somewhat predictable order without artificial sequencing of input), (3) the Monitor Hypothesis (that conscious learning has the limited function of "monitoring" or editing language performance); (4) the Input Hypothesis (that language is acquired when input is in an interesting and relevant context that is slightly above one's current level of competence); and (5) the Affective Filter Hypothesis (that attitudinal factors are related to language acquisition; acquirers with a "low affective filter" – an optimal attitude – will be more receptive and more likely to interact with confidence). Natural Approach methodology emphasizes comprehensible and meaningful input rather than grammatically correct production.

It follows, then, that vocabulary, as a bearer of meaning, is considered by the Natural Approach to be very important to the language acquisition process:

Acquisition depends crucially on the input being comprehensible. And comprehensibility is dependent directly on the ability to recognize the meaning of key elements in the utterance. Thus, acquisition will not take place without comprehension of vocabulary. (Krashen & Terrell, 1983, p. 155)

The recommended teaching method for vocabulary, as for all aspects of language, emphasizes the importance of interesting and relevant input; student attention should be focused on the understanding of messages:

Just as a particular affective acquisition activity, for example, may entail the use of certain grammatical structures, the activity is not designed to "teach" that structure. The same is true of vocabulary; activities are not necessarily "vocabulary builders." Students' attention is not on vocabulary learning per se but on communication, on the goal of an activity. In this way, we encourage true vocabulary acquisition. (Krashen & Terrell, 1983, p. 156)

For students beyond the beginning levels, Krashen suggests that reading is the most efficient means by which to acquire new vocabulary

(Krashen, 1989; 1991; 1993a; 1993b). In short, Krashen's view is that free voluntary reading is the optimal form of comprehensible input; reading provides "messages we understand presented in a low-anxiety situation" (Krashen, 1993b, p. 23).

## Current and future perspectives on lexical issues

Lexicographical research begun in the 1980s reflected a perceived need for more accurate language description and marked a turning point for communicative syllabus design and language teaching. The Collins-Birmingham University International Language Database (COBUILD) Project is an extensive computer analysis based on a central corpus of twenty million words, designed to account for actual language use. The corpus primarily consists of written data and the project has generated a variety of dictionaries and course materials.

Three years before the 1987 publication of the first COBUILD dictionary, John Sinclair, the project's editor in chief, anticipated that computer processing of language text would lead to "a major reorientation in language description" that would necessitate major changes in language instruction:

The picture is quite disturbing. On the one hand, there is now ample evidence of the existence of significant language patterns which have gone largely unrecorded in centuries of study; on the other hand, there is a dearth of support for some phenomena which are regularly put forward in English. (Sinclair, 1985, p. 251)

This reorientation in language description has led many to rethink the nature of language and the role played by vocabulary. Work in corpus analysis and computational linguistics has led to considerable interest in the importance of large chunks of language, variously known as *lexical items, lexical phrases,* and *prefabricated units.* For example, in *Lexical Phrases and Language Teaching,* Nattinger and DeCarrico have systematically analyzed extensive samples of actual language to demonstrate a central role for multiword chunks (1992). They use lexico-grammatical units called *lexical phrases*[1] as the basis for analysis, asserting that pragmatic competence is determined by a learner's ability to access and adapt prefabricated "chunks" of language. Similarly, Michael Lewis refers to corpus lexicography along with other documentation of actual language

---

1 *Lexical phrases* are "chunks" of language of varying length that have an idiomatically determined meaning (e.g., *as it were, on the other hand, as X would have us believe,* etc.). The phrases have slots for various fillers (e.g., a *month* ago, a *year* ago) and are each associated with a particular discourse function (Nattinger & DeCarrico, 1992, p. 1).

use as the basis for his claim that lexical items[2] are central to language use and should be central to language teaching: "Language consists of grammaticalised lexis, not lexicalised grammar" (Lewis, 1993, p. 89). Lewis challenges the validity of a grammar-vocabulary dichotomy, demonstrating instead that language consists of multiword chunks; his pedagogical suggestions include an integration of the communicative approach with a focus on naturally occurring lexis.

The work of Sinclair, Nattinger, DeCarrico, and Lewis represents a significant theoretical and pedagogical shift from the past. First, their claims have revived an interest in a central role for accurate language description. Second, they challenge a traditional view of word boundaries, emphasizing the language learner's need to perceive and use patterns of lexis and collocation. Most significant is the underlying claim that language production is not a syntactic rule-governed process but is instead the retrieval of larger phrasal units from memory. This claim signals a departure from the post-Chomskyan focus on syntax as the basis for a speaker's internalized language knowledge, and holds considerable implications for future research and pedagogy.

## Conclusion

Theoretical priorities have changed throughout language teaching history, as reflected in the relative importance placed on pronunciation, grammar, reading, or conversing. Likewise, there have been contrasts in attitudes toward the use of formal versus colloquial language, toward memorization versus internalization of language forms, toward the gradation or sequencing of skills versus subjective assessments of the usefulness of structures or words, and toward language description. Until recently, however, there has been little emphasis placed on the acquisition of vocabulary; although the lexicon is arguably central to language acquisition and use, vocabulary instruction has not been a priority in second language acquisition research or methodology. It is hoped that the central role occupied by vocabulary in the reality of language learning will one day be reflected in the attention given to it in research and the classroom.

## References

Anthony, E. M. (1973). Towards a theory of lexical meaning: An essay. Unpublished manuscript, University of Pittsburgh, Department of General Linguistics.

2 A *lexical item* is defined as a word or word phrase that operates as a "socially sanctioned independent unit" that is used as a minimal unit for certain syntactic purposes (Lewis, 1993, p. 90).

Chomsky, N. (1957). *Syntactic structures.* The Hague: Mouton.

(1965). *Aspects of the theory of syntax.* Cambridge: MIT Press.

*Collins COBUILD Dictionary.* (1987). London: Collins Publishers.

Faucett, L. (1933). *The Oxford English course.* 4 vols. London: Oxford University Press.

Fries, C. C. (1945). *Teaching and learning English as a foreign language.* Ann Arbor: University of Michigan Press.

Howatt, A. P. R. (1984). *A history of English language teaching.* Oxford: Oxford University Press.

Hymes, D. (1972). On communicative competence. In J. B. Pride & J. Holmes (Eds.), *Sociolinguistics* (pp. 269–293). New York: Penguin.

Kelly, L. G. (1969). *Centuries of language teaching.* Rowley, MA: Newbury House.

Krashen, S. (1989). We acquire vocabulary and spelling by reading: Additional evidence for the input hypothesis. *Modern Language Journal, 73*(4), 440–464.

(1991). The input hypothesis: An update. In J. Alatis (Ed.), *Georgetown University Round Table on Languages and Linguistics* (pp. 427–431). Washington, DC: Georgetown University Press.

(1993a). The case for free voluntary reading. *Canadian Modern Language Review, 50*(1), 72–82.

(1993b). *The power of reading.* Inglewood, CA: Libraries Unlimited.

Krashen, S., & Terrell, T. (1983). *The natural approach: Language acquisition in the classroom.* Oxford: Pergamon.

Larsen-Freeman, Diane. (1986). *Techniques and principles in language teaching.* New York: Oxford University Press.

Laufer, B. (1986). Possible changes in attitude towards vocabulary acquisition research. *International Review of Applied Linguistics, 24*(1), 69–75.

Lewis, M. (1993). *The lexical approach: The state of ELT and a way forward.* Hove, England: Language Teaching Publications.

Mackey, W. F. (1971). *Language teaching analysis.* Bloomington: Indiana University Press.

Meara, P. (1980). Vocabulary acquisition: A neglected aspect of language learning. *Language Teaching and Linguistics: Abstracts, 13*(4), 221–247.

Nation, I. S. P. (1990). *Teaching and learning vocabulary.* New York: Newbury House.

Nattinger, J. R., & DeCarrico, J. S. (1992). *Lexical phrases and language teaching.* Oxford: Oxford University Press.

Ogden, C. K. (1930). *Basic English: A general introduction with rules and grammar.* London: Kegan, Paul, Rench and Trubner.

Palmer, H. E. (1916/1968). *The scientific study and teaching of languages.* London: Harrap. Republished by Oxford University Press, 1968, edited by D. Harper.

(1921). *The oral method of teaching language.* Cambridge: Heffer.

(1924). *A grammar of spoken English, on a strictly phonetic basis.* Cambridge: Heffer.

Prendergast, T. (1864). *The mastery of languages, or, the art of speaking foreign tongues idiomatically.* London: R. Bentley.

Richards, J. (1976). The role of vocabulary teaching. *TESOL Quarterly, 10*(1), 77–89.

Richards, J., & Rodgers, T. S. (1986). *Approaches and methods in language teaching: A description and analysis.* New York: Cambridge University Press.

Rivers, W. M. (1968/1981). *Teaching foreign language skills* (2d ed.). Chicago: University of Chicago Press.

(1983). *Communicating naturally in a second language: Theory and practice in language teaching.* New York: Cambridge University Press.

Sauveur, L. (1874). *An introduction to the teaching of living languages without grammar or dictionary.* Boston: Schoenhof & Moeller.

Sinclair, J. (1985). Selected issues. In R. Quirk & H. G. Widdowson (Eds.), *English in the world* (pp. 248–254). Cambridge: Cambridge University Press.

Stern, H. H. (1981). Communicative language teaching and learning: Toward a synthesis. In J. E. Alatis, H. B. Altman, & P. M. Alatis (Eds.), *The second language classroom: Directions for the 1980s* (pp. 131–148). New York: Oxford University Press.

Sweet, H. (1899/1964). *The practical study of languages: A guide for teachers and learners.* London: Oxford University Press.

Thorndike, E. L., & Lorge, I. (1944). *The teacher's word book of 30,000 words.* New York: Teachers College, Columbia University.

Twaddell, F. (1980). Vocabulary expansion in the TESOL classroom. In K. Croft (Ed.), *Readings on English as a second language* (2d. ed.) (pp. 439–457). Cambridge: Winthrop.

Van Ek, J. A. (1976). *The threshold level for modern language learning in schools.* London: Longman.

West, M. (1930). Speaking-vocabulary in a foreign language. *Modern Language Journal, 14,* 509–521.

(1953). *A general service list of English words.* London: Longman, Green and Co.

Widdowson, H. G. (1978). *Teaching language as communication.* Oxford: Oxford University Press.

(1979). Directions in the teaching of discourse. In C. J. Brumfit & K. Johnson (Eds.), *The communicative approach to language teaching* (pp. 49–60). Oxford: Oxford University Press.

Wilkins, D. (1972). *Linguistics in language teaching.* London: Edward Arnold.

(1974). *Second-language learning and teaching.* London: Edward Arnold.

# 2 The lexical plight in second language reading

*Words you don't know, words you think you know, and words you can't guess*

Batia Laufer

## Introduction

No text comprehension is possible, either in one's native language or in a foreign language, without understanding the text's vocabulary. This is not to say that reading comprehension and vocabulary comprehension are the same, or that reading quality is determined by vocabulary alone. Reading comprehension (both in L1 and in L2) is also affected by textually relevant background knowledge and the application of general reading strategies, such as predicting the content of the text, guessing unknown words in context, making inferences, recognizing the type of text and text structure, and grasping the main idea of the paragraph. And yet, it has been consistently demonstrated that reading comprehension is strongly related to vocabulary knowledge, more strongly than to the other components of reading. Anderson and Freebody (1981) survey various studies (correlational, factor analyses, readability analyses) that show that the word variable is more highly predictive of comprehension than the sentence variable, the inferencing ability, and the ability to grasp main ideas. Beck, Perfetti, and McKeown (1982), Kameenui, Carnine, and Freschi (1982), and Stahl (1983) have demonstrated that an improvement in reading comprehension can be attributed to an increase in vocabulary knowledge.

A similar picture of vocabulary as a good predictor of reading success emerges from second language studies. Laufer (1991a) found good and significant correlations between two different vocabulary tests (the *Vocabulary Levels Test* by Nation [1983a] and the *Eurocentres Vocabulary Test* by Meara and Jones [1989]) and reading scores of L2 learners. The correlations were .5, significant at the level of p < .0001, and .75, significant at the level of p < .0001, respectively. Even higher correlations are reported by Koda (1989) between vocabulary (tested by a self-made test) and two reading measures, cloze and paragraph comprehension. These correlations are .69, p < .0002 and .74, p < .0001. Coady, Magoto, Hubbard, Graney, and Mokhtari (1993) conducted two experiments that showed that increased proficiency in high-frequency vocabulary also led to an increase in reading proficiency. Vocabulary materials were so successful that in the second experiment, no control group, which was to be taught without the materials, could be set up, since all the students wanted to use them.

Syntactic complexity, on the other hand, was found not to affect the level of reading comprehension. Ulijn and Strother (1990) claim that 'while a complete conceptual and lexical analysis may be necessary for reading comprehension, a thorough syntactic analysis is not' (p. 38). As for the effect of general reading strategies on L2 reading, the current view is that since reading in L2 is both a reading problem and a language problem, 'some sort of threshold or competence ceiling has to be attained before existing abilities in the first language can begin to transfer' (Alderson, 1984, p. 20). In other words, even if a reader has good metacognitive strategies, which he or she uses in L1, these will not be of much help in L2 before a solid language base has been reached. This conclusion is borne out by empirical evidence. Perkins, Brutten, and Pohlmann (1989) tested Japanese learners of English on various components of reading in L1 and L2 and then related the correlations (between L1 reading and L2 reading scores) to the TOEFL scores of the learners. The authors suggest, albeit cautiously, that the threshold of L2 competence is reflected in the score interval of 375–429 on the TOEFL test. In other words, this interval indicates the lowest level at which reading in L2 can be expected to start resembling reading in L1.

Since language threshold is essential for comprehension, an important question is, therefore, what the nature of this threshold is. According to Ulijn (1984), Ostyn and Godin (1985), Ostyn, Vandecasteele, Deville, and Kelly (1987), and Ulijn and Strother (1990), indispensable conditions for reading in L2 are understanding the text's words and the knowledge of its subject matter. Laufer and Sim (1985a, 1985b) found that, in interpreting texts, students tend to regard words as main landmarks of meaning. Background knowledge is relied on to a lesser extent, and syntax is almost disregarded. Haynes and Baker (1993) too came to the conclusion that the most significant handicap for L2 readers is not lack of reading strategies but insufficient vocabulary in English. What these studies indicate is that the threshold for reading comprehension is, to a large extent, lexical. Lexical problems will, therefore, hinder successful comprehension. Intuitively, most people associate lexical problems in comprehension with nonfamiliarity with words in the text. This is certainly a major obstacle, which I will discuss and refer to as 'words you don't know'. However, in addition to the phenomenon of noncomprehension, the learner will often experience miscomprehension of certain words that look familiar even though they are unknown. Since meaning is, to some extent, in the eye of the beholder, the problem of 'pseudofamiliar' words will be discussed as well. It will be referred to as 'words you think you know'. The third major lexical obstacle in comprehension is connected with guessing, or rather the nonguessing, of unknown words. Since lexical guessing is often suggested as a remedy for a limited vocabulary, I consider it important to put guessing in a proper perspective by showing why this strategy does not always work. This will be discussed in the section titled 'words you can't guess'.

## Words you don't know

### The below-threshold syndrome

When an L2 reader with an insufficient vocabulary is trying to interpret an authentic text (and such texts are not usually written for people with limited vocabularies), he or she will normally be unable to apply effective reading strategies used in L1. In an exceptional case, where a strategy can be used, the text may, nevertheless, remain unclear. Let us take the example of grasping the main idea of a paragraph. Before deciding which information in the paragraph is main, which is peripheral, and which can be discarded, it is necessary to understand the information itself. Otherwise, the discarded information will be that which is not understood properly, whether it happens to be important in the text or not (Laufer & Sim, 1985b). An example of a strategy that can be applied without much vocabulary understanding is noticing the text structure. With the help of discourse markers and words like 'claim', 'argument', 'evidence', 'opposing view', 'position, reconcile', the reader can notice that the text structure consists of a writer's making a claim, giving some supporting arguments, contrasting them with some counterarguments, and synthesizing the contradictory claims. The question is, however, how useful this strategy is if, because of insufficient vocabulary, the reader is left without understanding, or with a rather fuzzy idea of what the claim is, which arguments are supporting it, whether the conclusion follows from the discussion, and what the conclusion is.

The threshold vocabulary readers need in order to transfer their L1 reading strategies is what is commonly referred to as sight vocabulary – words whose forms and common meanings are recognized *automatically,* irrespective of context. I would not include in the threshold vocabulary words that are slightly familiar in a particular context, or new words whose meaning can be inferred from context, as both would require conscious attention during reading, or what Schneider and Shifrin (1977) call controlled processing. Since the amount of information that can be cognitively manipulated at one point of time by controlled processing is limited, focussing on slightly or completely unfamiliar words will take up some cognitive capacity that would otherwise be used for higher-level processing of the text. Automatic recognition of a large vocabulary, or a large sight vocabulary, on the other hand, will free one's cognitive resources for (1) making sense of the unfamiliar or slightly familiar vocabulary and (2) interpreting the global meaning of the text. (For a theory of human language processing and its relation to reading, see Schneider and Shifrin, 1977, and Coady et al., 1993, respectively.) For example, if a reader's cognitive effort is directed at deciphering information at phrase and sentence level, i.e., at trying to recognize the unfamiliar words, he or she will have difficulty with noticing the relationship between paragraphs. By the time the end of paragraph two is reached, he or she may have forgotten what paragraph one was all about and therefore be unable to make the connection between the two.

## The threshold vocabulary

An important question relating to the issue of threshold vocabulary is how many words one must know (be able to recognize automatically irrespective of context) in order to be able to use the higher level processing strategies with success. Before answering this question, we will clarify the term 'word' as it is used in this paper. Different unrelated items of meaning are considered as different words, e.g., 'bank', 'pupil'. An idiom that forms one unit of meaning is one word, e.g., 'break a leg' = succeed. Inflexional forms of the same unit of meaning are not different words, but one word, e.g., 'bring, brought, brings, bringing'. Differences of opinion exist as to whether derivatives of a word, e.g., 'man, manly, unmanly, manhood,' are one word or separate words. Here we adopt Nation's (1983b) definition of a 'word' as a word family (including all the derivatives), but in the forthcoming statements of figures, we will present the numbers in word families and in lexical items (without the derivatives).

Let us now return to the question of the number of words readers must have in their sight vocabulary. In a study by Laufer (1991a), ninety-two adult students of EFL were tested on vocabulary level and reading comprehension. The subjects were divided into five different vocabulary levels: those whose vocabulary was below 2,000 word families, those with 2,000, those with 3,000, those with 4,000, and those with 5,000. The reading scores of these five groups were then compared. The difference between the means was found to be significant at the transition from the 2,000 to the 3,000 vocabulary level. The reading scores of the 4,000 level learners were higher than those of the 3,000 level learners, but not significantly so. The same was true for the 5,000 level vis-à-vis 4,000 and 5,000 vis-à-vis 3,000. The differences in the reading scores were not significant. This suggests that the turning point of vocabulary size for reading comprehension is about 3,000 word families. If we represented the same number (3,000 word families) in terms of lexical items, the result would be $3{,}000 \times 1.6 = 4{,}800$ (for the conversion formula, see Nation [1983a]). The level at which good L1 readers can be expected to transfer their reading strategies to L2 is 3,000 word families, or about 5,000 lexical items. Until they have reached this level, such transfer will be hampered by an insufficient knowledge of vocabulary. A regression analysis was carried out to check how an increase in vocabulary quantity related to the improvement in reading. The analysis showed that an increase in 1,000 words resulted in an increase of 7% on a comprehension test. Thus, if we tried to predict the relationship between vocabulary increase and comprehension increase, we might expect a knowledge of 3,000 word families (5,000 lexical items) to result in a reading score of 56% (the minimum passing grade on reading tests in the students' institution at the time of the experiment), a knowledge of 4,000 (6,400 lexical items) in 63%, 5,000 (8,000 lexical items) in 70%, 6,000 (9,600 lexical items) in 77%, and so on. These figures are correct if the progress in reading vis-à-vis vocabulary size is always linear. It is possible, however, that when the learner reaches a certain vocabulary level, progress in the reading score will decrease and finally level off.

Even if the results are not conclusive for all vocabulary levels, they provide, nevertheless, a general idea of how reading progresses above the threshold level of 3,000 word families and what vocabulary size should be aimed at for different reading levels. If the optimal reading score is considered to be, for example, 70%, then the vocabulary size to aim for will be 5,000 word families; if 63% is taken as a passing score, then 4,000 will suffice.

Further support for 3,000 word families as the lexical threshold is found in Laufer (1992). Adult learners were compared on their vocabulary level, reading comprehension in EFL, and general academic ability, which included a reading in L1 component. (The General Academic Ability score and the EFL reading score were taken from the university psychometric entrance test.) It was shown that learners below the 3,000 vocabulary level (5,000 lexical items) did poorly on the reading test regardless of how high their academic ability was. In other words, even the more intelligent students who are good readers in their native language cannot read well in their L2 if their vocabulary is below the threshold.

In terms of text coverage, i.e., the actual percentage of word tokens in a given text understood by a reader, the 3,000 word families are reported to provide a coverage of between 90% and 95% of any text (for surveys of frequency counts, see Nation, 1983a and 1900). The figure claimed to be necessary for text comprehension is 95% of text coverage (Deville, 1985; Laufer, 1989b). Thus, both earlier frequency counts and later empirical studies of L2 vocabulary and reading suggest a similar vocabulary minimum, which is 3,000 word families, or 5,000 lexical items. As mentioned before, the higher the comprehension level expected, the larger the vocabulary should be.

# Words you think you know

## Deceptive transparency

So far we have discussed one aspect of the lexical plight in L2 reading – words one does not know, or, more precisely, words the reader knows he or she does not know. In addition to these, there are other words that are not even recognized as unfamiliar by the reader. These words are deceptively transparent, i.e., they look as if they provided clues to their meaning. For example, *infallible* looks as if it were composed of in+fall+ible and meant 'something that cannot fall'; *shortcomings* looks like a compound of 'short' and 'comings', meaning 'short visits' (these are actual misinterpretations provided by students). Huckin and Bloch (1993) found similar types of misinterpretations. They refer to the deceptively transparent words as cases of 'mistaken ID'. The deceptively transparent words (hence DT words) seem to fall into one of five distinct categories.

## Words with a deceptive morphological structure

These are words that look as if they were composed of meaningful morphemes. Thus, *outline* was misinterpreted as 'out of the line', *nevertheless* as 'never less', *discourse* as 'without direction'. The learner's assumption here was that the meaning of a word equalled the sum of meanings of its components. This assumption is correct in the case of genuinely transparent words, but not when the 'components' are not real morphemes.

## Idioms

*Hit and miss, sit on the fence, a shot in the dark, miss the boat* were translated literally, word by word. The learner's assumption in the case of idioms was similar to that of deceptive transparency, i.e., the meaning of the whole was the sum of the meanings of its parts.

## False friends

*Sympathetic* was interpreted as 'nice' (Hebrew 'simpati'); *tramp* as 'lift' (Hebrew 'tremp'); *novel* as 'short story' (Hebrew 'novela'). The mistaken assumption of the learner in this case was that if the form of the word in L2 resembled that in L1, the meaning did so too.

## Words with multiple meanings

It often happens that students know one meaning of a polyseme or a homonym and are reluctant to abandon it even when, in a particular context, its meaning is different. For example, *since* was interpreted as 'from the time when' though it meant 'because'; *abstract* as 'not concrete' instead of 'summary'; *state* as 'country' instead of 'situation'. The mistaken assumption of the learner in this case was that the familiar meaning was the *only* meaning.

## 'Synforms' (similar lexical forms)

The largest category of DT words is that of 'synforms', pairs/groups of words that are similar in form. (For criteria of synform similarity, classification of synforms, and discussion of the problems they raise, see Laufer, 1988 and 1991b.) Generally speaking, some synforms are similar in sound (cute/acute, available/valuable, conceal/cancel, price/prize); some are morphologically similar (economic/economical, industrious/industrial, reduce/deduce/induce).

Synformic confusions may have two sources: The learner might have learnt one word of the pair/group, but since its representation in the memory is insecure or defective, a similar word that shares most of its formal features might look identical to it. Or, the learner might have studied both synforms but since the knowledge of both is insecure, he or she is not sure which word form is associated with which meaning. Whatever the reason, the result is to misinterpret one synform as its counterpart.

## Deceptive transparency and reading comprehension

Laufer (1989a) studied students' interpretations of various DT words in text context. The results were as follows: (*a*) errors of word understanding were more frequent with DT words than with non-DT ones; (*b*) students were less aware of their ignorance with DT words than with non-DT ones; (*c*) there was a significant correlation between reading comprehension and learners' awareness of unknown DT words. Correlations do not necessarily show cause-effect relationships between the variables. Nevertheless, I will try to argue for such a relationship between reading and awareness of DT words.

When a foreign learner does not understand a word in a text, he or she has the following options: ignore it (if it is considered unimportant), look it up in a dictionary, ask someone who knows its meaning, or try to guess it from context. But an attempt to guess (regardless of whether it is successful or not) presupposes awareness on the part of learners that they are facing an unknown word. If such awareness is not there, no attempt is made to infer the missing meaning. This is precisely the case with deceptively transparent words. (See also Huckin and Bloch, 1993.) Learners think they know them and assign the wrong meaning to them, distorting the immediate context in this way. But this may not be the end of the distortion process. The misinterpreted words will sometimes serve as clues for guessing words that the learner recognizes as unknown, which may lead to larger distortions. Graphically, the process can be represented in the following manner: unawareness of ignorance of DT words → misinterpretation of DT words → distortion of immediate context → using distorted context for further interpretation → distortion of larger context.

Here is an example of a distorted sentence resulting from misinterpretation of three words. The original sentence was: 'This nurturing behaviour, this fending for females instead of leaving them to fend for themselves, may take many different forms'. *Nurturing* was confused with 'natural', *fending* with 'finding', *leaving* with 'living'. The result was the following: 'Instead of living natural life, natural behaviour, females and children find many different forms of life'. For more examples of similar misinterpretation, see Laufer and Sim (1985b).

The suggested cause-effect relationship between awareness of DT words and reading comprehension can therefore be explained as follows: A better awareness of DT words is necessary for attempting to find their meaning. Such an attempt will result in a larger number of correctly interpreted words. These will in turn reduce the density of unknown words. Such reduction will result in an increase in contextual clues that are necessary for understanding additional new words. This understanding will increase the total number of correctly interpreted words. A larger number of known words will be an asset to global comprehension of the text.

## Words you can't guess

The third lexical problem in L2 reading can occur when the reader is trying to guess unknown words, more precisely words that have been recognized as unfamiliar (as opposed to DT words, which are not recognized as such). The importance of guessing has been widely discussed (Liu Na & Nation, 1985; Nation & Coady, 1988; Van Parreren & Schouten-van Parreren, 1981, and many others). I do not contest the value of the guessing activity as such or the fact that it takes place. What I find hard to accept is taking for granted that guessing in L2 is indeed possible with most unknown words and that successful guessing depends mainly on the learner's guessing strategies. This seems to be a naive belief since a variety of factors will interfere with the guessing attempts of the reader.

## Nonexistent contextual clues

Looking for contextual clues for the unknown word will not help if the clues are not there to be exploited. One cannot as a rule rely on contextual redundancy since there is no guarantee that a given context is redundant enough to provide clues to precisely those words that are unknown to the reader. Kelly (1990) collected a random sample of unknown words from two Italian books and tried to guess their meanings from context. His lack of success, together with a similar experience with students, led him to believe that 'unless the context is very constrained, which is a relatively rare occurrence, or unless there is a relationship with a known word identifiable on the basis of form and supported by context, there is little chance of guessing the correct meaning' (p. 203). Bensoussan and Laufer (1984) found that in a fairly standard passage of academic prose, out of seventy words that the learners were asked to guess, clear contextual clues could be found only for thirteen words. This may not be the case with other texts. Some may provide more clues, others even less. But the basic assumption, that a text will provide clues to unknown words, is overoptimistic.

## Unusable contextual clues

The word guessability problem can occur in spite of the existence of clues. If the clues to the unknown word happen to be in words that are themselves unfamiliar to the reader, then, as far as the reader is concerned, the clues do not exist since they simply cannot be used. Let us look at the example mentioned previously: 'This nurturing behaviour, this fending for females instead of leaving them to fend for themselves, may take many different forms'. If 'nurture' is unknown and we are looking for a clue to its meaning, it is right there in the sentence – 'fending for someone', 'not leaving someone to fend for himself'. But what if 'fend' is also unknown? The learner may be lucky enough to recognize *nurture* and *fend* as unknown words (instead of confusing them with 'nature' and 'find', as described earlier), but since each of the words serves as a clue for the other, the two words will remain unguessable from context. Here is another example from our study: 'unless they accept, by specification or by implication, that the nature of man . . .' A reader trying to guess *implication* can notice that it is contrasted with *specification* and is therefore its opposite. This strategy will lead to a correct guess only if the meaning of *specification* is known. If it is not, the meaning of its opposite will remain a mystery.

It is precisely because clues that appear in unfamiliar words cannot be exploited that the density of unknown words in a text is of crucial importance to successful guessing. We do not have a definite answer as to the optimal ratio of unknown to known words in a text. I suggested earlier that a minimum of 95% text coverage, which is achieved by 3,000 word families, will lead to the transfer of reading strategies (including successful guessing). One should not forget that learners with such coverage received the minimum passing grade on the comprehension test. Hirsh and Nation (1992) discuss a different type of reading, which is easier and more fluent – reading for pleasure. Such reading, they argue, requires a higher lexical text coverage – a coverage of 98%. The remaining 2% can easily be guessed. To achieve a coverage of 98%, the learner needs to know about 5,000 word families, or 8,000 lexical items, according to Nation (1990). Whether one reads for pleasure (with 98% of coverage), or for bare necessity (with 95% of coverage), familiarity with a large number of words is a prerequisite for successful guessing.

## Misleading and partial clues

We saw earlier that the deceptively transparent words tend to look familiar to the reader even though they make no sense in context. Familiar form makes it look right, thus overriding contextual clues (see also Haynes, 1984; Huckin and Bloch, 1993). But there are words recognized as unfamiliar by the reader and guessed incorrectly, or at best imprecisely, because the clues are misleading. Some of Kelly's (1990) Italian examples illustrate the point. The unknown words are in italics, the English translations in parentheses.

E dappertuto si beveva, si cantava, si ballava, *si rissava*. (And everywhere people were drinking, singing, dancing, brawling.) The unknown word was understood as 'enjoying themselves' instead of 'brawling' as the interpretation fitted the context of drinking, singing, dancing.

. . . scaldava le sue membra *intirizzite* (he warmed his numb limbs). *Intirizzite* was interpreted as 'frozen/cold' instead of 'numb' as it seemed sensible that someone would warm his 'cold' limbs. For more inadequacies of contextual clues, see Stein (1993).

Context may not necessarily be misleading. It can provide partial clues that will help the reader to arrive at a general word meaning. Here is an example from Clarke and Nation (1980). 'Typhoon Vera killed or injured 28 people and *crippled* the seaport city of Kellung'. *Crippled* can be understood as 'damaged, destroyed' since a typhoon will have some kind of negative influence upon a city. In some texts it may be sufficient to arrive at the general or approximate meaning of words in order to understand the passage. But how safe is it to rely on approximations in a legal or medical text? It is all too easy and tempting to say, 'The word looks right in context, so it presumably means what I think it means'. What looks right may be wrong; and reliance on what is more or less right may sometimes produce an irresponsible interpretation.

## Suppressed clues

One of the factors that contribute to successful guessing is the reader's background knowledge of the subject matter of the text, or content schemata. Inferences are drawn from the text on the basis of the reader's expectations of certain content. Since 'reading is a psycholinguistic guessing game' (Goodman, 1967), the successful players should, among other things, draw on their experiences and concepts. This strategy may work quite well, except when the reader's expectations and concepts are different from those of the author of the text. Readers tend to disregard information that, according to their world view, seems unimportant, add information that 'should' be there, and focus their attention on what, in their opinion, is essential (Steffensen & Joag-Dev, 1984). So strong is the effect of background knowledge that it overrides lexical and syntactic clues. In an experiment by Laufer and Sim (1985b), students were given a passage where the author (Margaret Mead) discussed biological differences between men and women, and clearly implied that boys and girls should get a different education. Some learners, however, insisted that the author was advocating the same education for both sexes. From interviews it became clear that the students were using their knowledge of the world, which was that nobody today would dare to suggest different education for men and women, certainly not a woman author. When a biased opinion of this kind is introduced into the interpretation, individual unknown words will be taken to mean whatever suits the reader's own notion of what the text says. If there are clues in context that would suggest a different interpretation, they can easily be suppressed.

## Summary and conclusion

In this essay, I have discussed three lexical problems that may seriously impede reading comprehension in L2: (1) the problem of insufficient vocabulary, (2) misinterpretations of deceptively transparent words, and (3) inability to guess unknown words correctly. I will recapitulate my arguments starting with the third issue. A learner who has been taught guessing strategies will not automatically produce correct guesses. The following factors, which are beyond the reader's control, will affect guessing.

1. Availability of clues. It cannot be taken for granted that clues are present in the text and need only to be discovered by the reader. They may be there, or they may not be there.
2. Familiarity with the clue words. Mere availability of clues does not mean that they can be used by the reader. To be used, the clue-containing words have to be understood. A high density of unknown words will reduce the usability of clues as there will be a higher probability that words that explain each other will be unfamiliar.
3. Presence of misleading clues. Not everything that looks right in context is necessarily right. Yet the learner who has been taught that there is no need to understand the precise meaning of words may remain satisfied with whatever makes sense in the context, whether it is right or wrong.
4. Compatibility between the reader's schemata and the text content. If the two are different, the reader may impose his or her interpretation on the text and try to understand individual words in a way that will fit the global meaning, suppressing the clues that suggest a different interpretation.

One of the factors that overrides contextual clues is deceptive transparency of words. Words that look familiar will be interpreted to mean what the learner thinks they mean. These are words with a deceptive morphological structure, idioms, false friends, words with multiple meanings, and synforms. Since learners are unaware of their ignorance of the DT words, they will stick to the false meanings and may use them as clues to guessing other words. When this happens, both the immediate context of the DT word and the larger context are distorted. Readers with lower awareness of DT words also score lower on reading comprehension tests.

By far the greatest lexical obstacle to good reading is insufficient number of words in the learner's lexicon. Lexis was found to be the best predictor of success in reading, better than syntax or general reading ability. Whatever the effect of reading strategies is, it is short-circuited if the vocabulary is below the threshold, i.e., below the minimum of 3,000 word families, or 5,000 lexical items.

A large sight vocabulary is also an answer to the other two problems: deceptive transparency and guessing ability. The larger the vocabulary, the fewer the words that will look deceptively transparent to the learner and the fewer the DT errors that will be made. A large vocabulary will provide a good lexical coverage of a text (3,000 word families, or 5,000 lexical items cover about 95% of text). The higher the coverage, the lower the density of unknown words. When the density is low, there is a good chance of finding clues to the unknown words. There is also less cognitive capacity involved in lower-level processing. As more clues are made available, the better guessing becomes. As less cognitive capacity is invested in decoding words, more of it is available for higher-level processing.

In this discussion of the lexical plight in L2 reading I have tried to show how indispensable good vocabulary knowledge is to reading. Reading may well be a psycholinguistic guessing game. But words are the toys you need to play it right.

## References

Alderson, J. C. (1984). Reading in a foreign language: A reading problem or a language problem? In J. C. Alderson & A. H. Urquhart. London: Longman (Eds.), *Reading in a foreign language* (pp. 1–27).

Anderson, R. C., & Freebody, P. (1981). Vocabulary and knowledge. In J. T. Gutrie (Ed.), *Comprehension and teaching: Research review* (pp. 77–117). Newark, DE: International Reading Association.

Beck, I. L., Perfetti, C. A., & McKeown, M. G. (1982). Effects of text construction and instructional procedures for teaching word meanings on comprehension and recall. *Journal of Educational Psychology, 74,* 506–521.

Bensoussan, M., & Laufer, B. (1984). Lexical guessing in context in EFL reading comprehension. *Journal of Research in Reading, 7,* 15–32.

Clarke, D. F., & Nation, I. S. P. (1980). Guessing the meanings of words from context: Strategy and techniques. *System, 8,* 211–220.

Coady, J., Magoto, J., Hubbard, P., Graney, J., & Mokhtari, K. (1993). High frequency vocabulary and reading proficiency in ESL readers. In T. Huckin, M. Haynes, & J. Coady (Eds.), (pp. 217–228). Norwood, NJ: Ablex.

Deville, G. (1985). Measuring a FL learner's lexical needs. Paper presented at the fifth LSP Symposium, Louvain, Belgium.

Goodman, K. S. (1967). Reading: A psycholinguistic guessing game. *Journal of the Reading Specialist, 6,* 126–135.

Haynes, M. (1984). Patterns and perils of guessing in second language reading. In J. Handscombe, R. A. Orem, & B. P. Taylor (Eds.), *On TESOL 83* (pp. 163–176). Washington, DC: TESOL.

Haynes, M., & Baker, I. (1993). American and Chinese readers learning from lexical familiarization in English texts. In T. Huckin, M. Haynes, & J. Coady (Eds.), *Second language reading and vocabulary acquisition* (pp. 130–152). Norwood, NJ: Ablex.

Hirsh, D., & Nation, P. (1992). What vocabulary size is needed to read unsimplified texts for pleasure? *Reading in a foreign language, 8*(2), 689–696.

Huckin, T., & Bloch, J. (1993). Strategies for inferring word-meanings in context: A cognitive model. In T. Huckin, M. Haynes, & J. Coady (Eds.), *Second language reading and vocabulary acquisition* (pp. 153–180). Norwood, NJ: Ablex.

Kameenui, E. J., Carnine, D. W., & Freschi, R. (1982). Effects of text construction and instructional procedures for teaching word meanings on comprehension and recall. *Reading Research Quarterly, 17,* 367–388.

Kelly, P. (1990). Guessing: No substitute for systematic learning of lexis. *System, 18,* 199–207.

Koda, K. (1989). The effects of transferred vocabulary knowledge on the development of L2 reading proficiency. *Foreign Language Annals, 22,* 529–540.

Laufer, B. (1988). The concept of 'synforms' (similar lexical forms) in vocabulary acquisition. *Language and Education, 2*(2), 113–132.

(1989a). A factor of difficulty in vocabulary learning: Deceptive transparency. *AILA Review, 6 (Vocabulary acquisition),* 10–20.

(1989b). What percentage of lexis is essential for comprehension. In C. Lauren & M. Nordman (Eds.), *From humans thinking to thinking machines* (pp. 316–323). Clevedon, UK: Multilingual Matters.

(1991a). How much lexis is necessary for reading comprehension? In P. J. L. Arnaud & H. Béjoint (Eds.), *Vocabulary and applied linguistics* (pp. 126–132). Basingstoke: Macmillan.

(1991b). *Similar lexical forms in interlanguage.* Tübingen: Gunter Narr Verlag.

(1992). Reading in a foreign language: How does L2 lexical knowledge interact with the reader's general academic ability? *Journal of Research in Reading, 15,* 95–103.

Laufer, B., & Sim, D. D. (1985a). Measuring and explaining the threshold needed for English for Academic Purposes texts. *Foreign Language Annals, 18,* 405–413.

(1985b). Taking the easy way out: Nonuse and misuse of contextual clues in EFL reading comprehension. *English Teaching Forum, 23*(2), 7–10, 22.

Liu, Na, & Nation, I. S. P. (1985). Factors affecting guessing vocabulary in context. *RELC Journal, 16,* 35–42.

Meara, P., & Jones, G. (1989). *Eurocentres vocabulary test 10 KA.* Eurocentres, Zurich.

Nation, I. S. P. (1983a). *Learning and teaching vocabulary.* NZ: Wellington, Victoria University.

(1983b). Testing and teaching vocabulary. *Guidelines, 5* (RELC supplement), 12–24.

(1990). *Learning and teaching vocabulary.* New York: Newbury House.

Nation, P., & Coady, J. (1988). Vocabulary and reading. In R. Carter & M. McCarthy (Eds.), *Vocabulary and language teaching* (pp. 97–110). London: Longman.

Ostyn, P., & Godin, P. (1985). RALEX: An alternative approach to language teaching. *Modern Language Journal, 69,* 346–353.

Ostyn, P., Vandecasteele, M., Deville, G., & Kelly, P. (1987). Towards an optimal programme of FL vocabulary acquisition. In A. M. Cornu, J. Vanparijs, M. Delaheye, & L. Baten (Eds.), *Beads or bracelet? How do we approach LSP?* (pp. 292–305). Oxford: Oxford University Press.

Perkins, K., Brutten, S. R., & Pohlmann, J. T. (1989). First and second reading comprehension. *RELC Journal, 10*(2), 1–9.

Schneider, W., & Shifrin, H. M. (1977). Controlled and automatic human information processing: I. detection, search and attention. *Psychological Review, 84,* 1–66.

Stahl, S. (1983). Differential word knowledge and reading comprehension. *Journal of Reading Behaviour, 15,* 33–50.

Steffensen, M. S., & Joag-Dev, Ch. (1984). Cultural knowledge and reading. In J. C. Alderson & A. H. Urquhart (Eds.), *Reading in a foreign language* (pp. 48–61). London: Longman.

Stein, M. J. (1993). The healthy inadequacy of contextual definition. In T. Huckin, M. Haynes, & J. Coady (Eds.), *Second language reading and vocabulary acquisition* (pp. 203–216). Norwood, NJ: Ablex.

Ulijn, J. M. (1984). Reading for professional purposes: Psycholinguistic evidence in a cross-linguistic perspective. In A. K. Pugh & J. M. Ulijn (Eds.), *Reading for professional purposes* (pp. 66–81). London: Heinemann.

Ulijn, J. M., & Strother, J. B. (1990). The effect of syntactic simplification on reading EST texts as L1 and L2. *Journal of Research in Reading, 13*, 38–54.

Van Parreren, C. F., & Schouten-van Parreren, M. C. (1981). Contextual guessing: a trainable reader strategy. *System, 9*, 235–241.

# 3 Orthographic knowledge in L2 lexical processing

## A cross-linguistic perspective

Keiko Koda

## Introduction

During the last decade, there has been a growing interest in vocabulary acquisition among second language (L2) researchers. The research stockpile has expanded in scope and complexity at a remarkable rate for the brief period of time. Despite the increasing number of empirical studies, however, relatively little attention has been given to orthographic considerations. In view of the major gains in L2 vocabulary research, the gap has become problematic.

Conceivably, the minimal concern with orthographic knowledge may stem from the predominance of top-down approaches to L2 reading research over the last decade. More than 60% of the empirical research between 1974 and 1988 reflected this perspective (Bernhardt, 1991). As a consequence, scant work had been done on lower-level verbal processing mechanisms until very recently, and the role and function of orthographic knowledge remain largely unexplored.

There are compelling reasons, however, to believe that orthographic knowledge plays a critical part in L2 reading, particularly in lexical processing. Current L2 vocabulary studies, for example, consistently demonstrate that the ability to utilize context in inferring the meaning of unknown words is highly correlated with reading proficiency (e.g., Chern 1993; Haynes, 1984). And, even more important, the failure to use context for lexical inference is, in many cases, attributable to word misidentification (Huckin & Bloch, 1993). When L2 learners mistakenly assume they know a word, they tend to ignore various contextual clues that highlight the semantic incongruity resulting from the misidentification. But of greatest significance, many identification errors result from insufficient information derived from orthographic processing (e.g., Holmes & Ramos, 1993; Huckin & Bloch, 1993; Laufer, 1988). Thus, inefficient orthographic processing can lead not only to inaccurate lexical retrieval, but to poor comprehension as well.

Further support for the importance of orthographic contribution can be found in the L1 word recognition research. Of late, a renewed interest

35

in word recognition has evolved. Contemporary studies, for example, suggest that poor readers generally are inefficient in retrieving lexical information from printed texts (e.g., Perfetti, 1985, 1991; Stanovich, 1988, 1991). Similarly, eye-movement research consistently indicates that the vast majority of words – both content and functional – receive direct visual fixation even when they occur in a rich context (e.g., Balota, Pollatsek, & Rayner, 1985; Just & Carpenter, 1987). Moreover, the absence of even one letter in a word may impair reading speed considerably (e.g., McConkie & Zola, 1981; Rayner & Bertera, 1979). These findings make it plain that reading is dependent on visual information contained in the text to a far greater degree than has been assumed in top-down models. It is for these reasons that the importance of orthographic knowledge has become widely acknowledged among L1 researchers.

In an effort to clarify the nature of orthographic knowledge and its specific function in L2 contexts, this chapter examines the ways in which L1 orthographic competence shapes L2 lexical processing. Inasmuch as previous research findings suggest that (1) L2 learners' multiple sets of linguistic knowledge and processing skills interact during L2 comprehension (Koda, 1993c), and (2) prior orthographic experience has a strong impact on the development of L2 lexical processing skills and strategies (e.g., Brown & Haynes, 1985; Green & Meara, 1987; Koda, 1988, 1990), the present analysis was performed from a cross-linguistic perspective. An understanding of language transfer, therefore, is central to the discussion.

## Language transfer

Language transfer has long been one of the central concerns in L2 research. Transfer concepts originated in the Contrastive Analysis (CA) hypothesis, which was widely accepted in the 1950s and 1960s. The CA hypothesis – deeply rooted in behaviorism – contends that the principal barrier to L2 acquisition stems from interference factors created by the L1 system. In this behavioristic view of learning, L1 was regarded as the primary source of confusion.

In the late 1960s, as a result of Chomskyan influence, a new perspective on language learning emerged, and L2 learning began to be regarded as an active process wherein the learner consciously constructs and tests hypotheses about the target language against available linguistic data. In this newer perspective, L1 is viewed as the critical basis for learning the new linguistic system rather than as an interfering effect.

This definitive transition in language learning theories has given rise to particular trends in language transfer research. As a case in point, the growing attention given to transfer phenomena in recent years stems from an unprecedented interest in cross-linguistic variance in language acquisition and processing. L1 researchers have been attracted, among other things, by recent linguistic postulations contending that languages vary in specific values along the grammatically central dimensions of their organization. According to this view, children are endowed with a set of universal principles, or parameters, each of which has a predetermined set of possible values, which must, therefore, be set at the correct value for the language. This parametric postulation thus provides a plausible explanation for cross-linguistic variations in L1 acquisition (Hyams, 1986, 1987; Lust, 1987; Solan, 1987).

In addition, experimental psychologists are now challenging language processing theories based on data obtained exclusively from English-speaking subjects. Cross-linguistic studies on sentence processing, for example, consistently demonstrate that the cognitive strategies involved in sentence comprehension and production are heavily constrained by the linguistic properties specific to each language (e.g., Bates & MacWhinney, 1989; Bates, McNew, MacWhinney, Devescovi, & Smith, 1982; Kail, 1989), and, importantly, that cross-linguistic variations in processing procedures are consistent with the predictions that could be derived from the morphosyntactic structure of subjects' respective languages. Similarly, child language studies demonstrate that children cannot systematically deal with linguistic forms that contradict their perceptions of the prototypical sentence structure of their native languages (e.g., Berman, 1986; Hakuta 1982; Slobin, 1985; Slobin & Bever, 1982). This suggests, obviously, that children are sensitized to the specific features of their language very early in their development. Such linguistic conditioning serves not only to shape cognitive strategies appropriate to the language, but also to help regulate their perception and interpretation of linguistic input. Cross-linguistic studies imply, in short, that the linguistic features essential to sentence comprehension and production vary from language to language, and, significantly, that specific processing skills and strategies are developed to capitalize on essential linguistic information provided by the language.

Consequently, the conception of language transfer emerging from the language-specific perspective yields a powerful framework through which individual differences in L2 processing can be analyzed and explained. Since processing mechanisms are language specific, the presumption that L2 learners are heavily dependent on their L1-based processing mechanisms would account for qualitative processing behavior differences among L2 learners from different linguistic backgrounds. Moreover, the transfer theories could also explain differences among L2 learners from different linguistic backgrounds. Moreover, the transfer theories could also explain differences in processing efficiency, and possibly the resultant variance in performance outcomes. Because typologically, some languages are more similar than others, the linguistic distance between a learner's L1 and L2 varies widely among individuals. Presumably, then, the degree of linguistic property similarity in the learner's two languages is highly correlated with that in processing procedures. It follows, therefore, that the use of L1 processing mechanisms that are typologically similar will result in better and more efficient performance. Hence, this framework provides a partial explanation of quantitative differences in performance among L2 learners with related and unrelated L1 backgrounds, as well as varying rates of L2 acquisition among different L1 groups. Language transfer is, in fact, evident in various aspects of linguistic and metalinguistic elements in both oral and written forms of L2 production and comprehension: for example, morphosyntactic systems (e.g., Gundel & Tarone, 1983; Hakuta, 1976; Rutherford, 1983, Yanco, 1985; Zehler, 1982), communicative strategies (e.g., Cohen, Olshtain, & Rosenstein, 1986; Olshtain, 1983; Scarcella, 1983), and pragmatics (e.g., Irujo, 1986). Recent L2 empirical studies, moreover, suggest that the orientation generated by L1 linguistic features not only influences L2 acquisition (e.g., Flynn, 1987, 1989; Gass, 1989; Gass & Schachter, 1989; Phinney & White, 1987; White, 1989; see also Odlin, 1989, for a thorough overview of the topic), but also constrains the cognitive procedures used in L2 processing (e.g., Brown & Haynes, 1985; Kilborn & Ito, 1989; Koda, 1988, 1990, 1993c; McDonald, 1987; Tzeng & Wang, 1983).

## Framework for cross-linguistic analysis

Earlier research findings suggest that (1) lower-level processing plays a significant role in reading comprehension; (2) qualitatively different mechanisms are involved in the linguistic processing of different languages; and (3) L1-based skills and strategies are transferred at various L2 processing levels. Consequently, there is reason to believe, first, that orthographic knowledge makes a more central contribution to L2 reading comprehension, particularly lexical processing, than previously has been assumed; second, that different orthographic properties generate qualitatively distinct processing procedures for word recognition in different languages; and third, that L2 word recognition processing mechanisms are heavily constrained by the learner's L1 orthographic properties. Within the transfer framework, presumably, we can further expect that L1 orthographic knowledge, coupled with other factors, contributes to individual variations in L2 processing behaviors.

To help clarify the specific effects of L1 orthographic knowledge on L2 lexical processing, an examination of the ways such knowledge shapes and limits the cognitive procedures involved in L2 word recognition might be useful. Consequently, the specific purposes of this chapter are threefold: (1) to analyze the critical relationship between orthographic properties and processing mechanisms across languages; (2) to examine the cognitive consequences of L1 orthographies through empirical L2 data; and (3) to draw pedagogical implications from the current knowledge base on orthographic transfer. Hopefully, the discussion will promote a better understanding of processing variations induced by the orthographic properties of different languages, and their long-term impact on L2 processing, and – in so doing – provide a basis for enhancing the effectiveness of L2 vocabulary instruction. In the first sections that follow, three major orthographic systems are described, and then the cross-linguistic variations in orthographic processing are discussed. Next, the L1 orthographic impact on L2 processing is explored in empirical data from current L2 reading research. And, finally, pedagogical implications are drawn and specific recommendations outlined for L2 reading pedagogy in general, and vocabulary instruction in particular.

## Different orthographic systems

Three major orthographic systems – logographic, syllabic, and alphabetic – presently are used in languages. In the first, logography, one graphemic unit usually represents the meaning and the sound of an entire word or morpheme. Because of the one-to-one correspondence between graphemic representation and meaning, learning to read in a logography seemingly is simplified when a limited number of characters must be processed. In reality, however, the logographic reader must know as many signs as there are words and morphemes in the spoken language. In Japan, as an illustration, children are required to learn 996 Kanji (Japanese logography) characters during the 6 years of elementary school, and an additional 949 characters during the 3 years of junior high school (Japanese Ministry of Education, 1982). Japanese children hence learn approximately 2,000 characters during their nine years of compulsory education.

In the second system, syllabary, each graphemic unit represents a syllable. Since languages usually have fewer syllables than morphemes, syllabaries embody spoken language with fewer symbols than do logographies. Another Japanese example can be used since the language utilizes two syllabaries as well as a logographic system. Each Japanese syllabary consists of 46 basic letters and two forms of diacritic marks, which can be added to 20 of the basic letters to represent 25 voiced syllables. The total number of symbols for each type of syllabary (Kana) is 71 – which is obviously far smaller than the number of symbols in the logography (Kanji).

The third orthographic system is alphabetic, in which the unit of representation is the phoneme. Since the symbol-to-sound correspondence in the alphabet is reduced to the smallest sound unit (phoneme), a smaller number of symbols is needed to transcribe spoken language (Gelb, 1963; Goody, 1968). It has been argued, therefore, that the alphabetic system increases learnability and makes literacy accessible to a wider public (Olson, 1975, 1977).

Given that the fundamental difference in the three major orthographic systems exists in the type of phonological information provided by a single graphemic unit, it seems reasonable to argue that the most salient distinction in word recognition mechanisms should be found in the process of obtaining a phonological code from the graphemic representation, or phonological processing. Consequently, cross-linguistic variations in phonological processing are discussed in the following section.

## Cross-linguistic variations in phonological processing

Although the most widely recognized goal of word recognition is retrieval of context-appropriate meaning, many theorists agree that phonological processing is no less important than semantic analysis, as well as an obligatory process, irrespective of the orthographic system used (e.g., Henderson, 1984; Tzeng & Wang, 1983). It has also been suggested that the phonological code facilitates visual – as well as semantic – processing of orthographically unfamiliar words (e.g., Doctor & Coltheart, 1980; Forster & Chambers, 1973). A dominant function of the phonological code, nonetheless, is to facilitate information storage in working memory (e.g., Kleiman, 1975; Levy, 1975). A number of studies have demonstrated that phonological encoding is more effective and durable than visual encoding for information register in working memory not only in English (e.g., Baddeley, 1966; Conrad, 1964) but also in logographic Chinese (e.g., Mou & Anderson, 1981; Yik, 1978; Zhang & Simon, 1985).

Importantly, the cognitive mechanism involved in phonological processing is directly related to phonological recodability. Phonological recodability has to do with how systematically phonological information can be retrieved from the graphemic representation. Two elements are critical: (1) the basic unit of orthographic representation (i.e., a linguistic unit – e.g., morpheme, phoneme, syllable – corresponding to individual symbols), and (2) the regularity of symbol-to-sound correspondence.

First, based on the basic unit of representation, three major orthographies presently used in various languages can be divided into two orthographic types: logography and phonography. Different phonological processing mechanisms can be expected between the two types. In phonography, for example, each graphemic unit is associated with a segment of phonological information, such as phoneme in the alphabet and syllable in the syllabary. In order to obtain a phonological code, therefore, segmental information must be analyzed and assembled together in one way or another – such as grapheme-to-phoneme translation and lexical analogy, typical of alphabetic readers (e.g., Glushko, 1979; Henderson, 1985; Patterson & Morton, 1985).

In contrast, in logography, the basic unit of representation is a morpheme, wherein a one-to-one correspondence is established between the single graphemic unit and a phonological code of an entire word or morpheme. It is claimed, therefore, that phonological processing in logography involves an all-or-nothing process (Gleitman, 1985; Gleitman & Rozin, 1977). Although it is often claimed that many logographic symbols have a radical that provides phonological information, the phonetic radical itself is an independent character. The radical, therefore, cannot provide adequate information until its phonological code is first retrieved. In short, phonological processing in logography occurs virtually without the need for phonetic representation (Gleitman, 1985; Mann, 1985).

A number of empirical studies have, in fact, shown that distinctive mechanisms are utilized for phonological processing in logographies and phonographies (e.g., Frost et al., 1987; Saito, Inoue, & Nomura, 1979; Sasanuma, 1984; Turvey, Feldman, & Lukatela, 1984; Tzeng & Wang, 1983). It has been reported, for example, that recall of logographic words is correlated with both linguistic (spoken nonsense words) and nonlinguistic (visual nonsense designs) memory, while recall of alphabetic and syllabic words correlates only with linguistic memory (Mann, 1985).

Similarly, strong evidence supporting the probability that different mechanisms mediate phonological processing between the two orthographic types can be found in experimental and clinical studies conducted with Japanese subjects. The use of multiple orthographies (logographic Kanji and syllabic Kana) in Japanese allows intra-individual comparisons of processing mechanisms involved in the two contrasting types of scripts. Experimental studies, for example, demonstrate that phonological interference has differential effects on Kanji and Kana processing (Saito, 1981; Saito, Inoue, & Nomura, 1979); and also that a clear difference exists in visual processing patterns between the two types of scripts (Hatta, 1978). More convincingly, clinical observations of Japanese aphasics have revealed that two forms of Japanese aphasic patients (those with either a Kana or a Kanji impairment) have lesions in different areas of the brain (Sasanuma, 1974a, 1974b, 1975, 1984).

Regularity of symbol-to-sound correspondence is another factor directly contributing to phonological recodability. Diverse processing mechanisms are likely, therefore, when phonographic orthographies vary in the regularity of their grapheme-phoneme correspondence. Coltheart (1984), for example, identifies three properties by which alphabetic orthographies can be classified: (1) regularity of one-to-one correspondence, (2) regularity of phonemic assignment, and (3) regularity of graphemic assignment.

First, the regularity of one-to-one correspondence refers to the extent to which a systematic relationship is established between a single graphemic unit and a single phoneme. In English, for example, this regularity is violated when one phoneme is assigned to two graphemic units, as seen in digraphs – such as *gh* corresponding to the phoneme /f/ as in *laugh;* and *ck* corresponding to the phoneme /k/ as in *kick*. Second, the regularity of phonemic assignment implies that a particular letter does not fulfill more than one phonemic assignment. Again, to use English as an example, one graphemic unit often serves several phonemic purposes. One graphemic unit, the letter *b*, for instance, is pronounced /b/ in *boy*, but is silent in *debt*. As another illustration, the letter *i* is pronounced /i/ in *give*, but /ai/ in *five*. Third, the regularity of graphemic assignment has to do with a systematicity in which a single phoneme is symbolized by a single graphemic representation. Note, as a case in point, that the phoneme /s/ can be represented either by the letter *c* or *s*, as in *cite* and *site*.

It is, then, conceivable, that in phonologically higher regular orthographies, such as Serbo-Croatian and Spanish, phonological and orthographic processing occur in completely parallel fashion, and the phonological processor never lags behind in generating its output. Empirical data from Serbo-Croatian subjects seem to suggest this to be the case, by demonstrating that a phonological code is, of necessity, obtained prior to lexical access (Turvey, Feldman, & Lukatela, 1984).

The representational properties in individual orthographies are thus directly related to phonological recodability, which, in turn, accounts for phonological processing variations in different types of orthographies. The clear implication is that L1 literacy experience with a particular writing system provides a basis for establishing processing mechanisms suitable for that system.

## L1 orthographic impact on L2 word recognition

A number of SLA studies confirm that various aspects of linguistic and metalinguistic knowledge, as well as their corresponding processing procedures, are transferred from L1 in both oral and written forms of L2 production and comprehension (e.g., Gass, 1987; Gass & Selinker, 1983; Kellerman & Sharwood Smith, 1986; Kilborn & Ito, 1989; Sasaki, 1991). We can, therefore, safely assume that L2 readers bring their L1 orthographic knowledge and processing mechanisms to bear on L2 word recognition.

As a case in point, Green and Meara (1987) examined visual processing strategies for letter searching in both L1 and L2. Their subjects included three groups of ESL learners with Roman-alphabetic (Spanish), non-Roman alphabetic (Arabic), and nonalphabetic (Chinese) L1 backgrounds. They found that (1) the three groups utilized different visual processing strategies when pursuing the search task in their L1s, and (2) when performing the task in their L2, all subjects used visual search strategies remarkably similar to those used in their respective L1s. The researchers, therefore, contend that L1 writing systems have profound and long-lasting effects on the way L2 linguistic materials are processed. In a subsequent experiment, Ryan and Meara (1991) compared the ability of Arabic and non-Arabic ESL learners, in a lexical matching task, to detect missing vowels and found that Arabic subjects were considerably slower and less accurate than non-Arabic ESL learners. The researchers attributed the results to the fact that "modern Arabic writing does not normally represent short vowels" (p. 533), and that Arabic learners' heavy L1 reliance on consonants is transferred to their L2 lexical processing. The findings thus confirm the earlier contention that L1 orthography has a long-lasting impact on L2 processing.

Further support for processing transfer has been provided by the research investigating phonological processing among ESL learners with contrasting L1 orthographic backgrounds. In a series of experiments, Koda (1988, 1990) compared phonological recoding strategies used by ESL learners with phonographic (Arabic and Spanish) and logographic (Japanese) L1 backgrounds. Her data demonstrated that when phonological information is masked in the visual configuration, the performance of alphabetic L1 readers is seriously impaired. Interestingly, however, phonological inaccessibility has virtually no effect on logographic L1 readers, suggesting that their processing is heavily dependent on L1-based processing mechanisms – mechanisms that do not require the direct analysis of visually accessible phonological information visually accessible in the graphemic representation. The findings thus confirm Green and Meara (1987), who conclude that L2 learners from varying L1 orthographic backgrounds utilize distinctive L2 processing strategies.

Similar results have been obtained in other recent studies through cross-linguistic experiments involving logographic (Chinese and Japanese) and non-Roman alphabetic (Arabic) ESL learners (Koda, 1988; Gairns, 1992). Comparing lexical-decision performance under two forced-choice conditions, wherein either orthographic or phonological cues were removed, the researchers found that both ESL groups performed better when orthographic, rather than phonological, cues were available; and also that the performance of logographic subjects declined far more sharply than that of Arabic learners when orthographic, or visual, cues were blocked. These results indicate that the extent to which ESL readers utilize phonological and orthographic cues varies widely, and importantly, that phonographic L1 readers rely on phonological cues far more than logographic L1 readers. Hence, the cross-linguistic data again attest to L1 orthographic impact on L2 processing, further confirming language transfer during L2 lexical processing.

From another perspective, Brown and Haynes (1985) examined the effects of L1 reading experience on L2 component skills development among Arabic, Spanish, and Japanese ESL learners. The data revealed that while Japanese subjects were superior to the other groups in visual discrimination, this advantage was not sustained in a visual-to-sound translation task, again confirming that L1 reading is a significant force in molding L2 processing mechanisms. Interestingly, Brown and Haynes also found that listening and reading comprehension ability correlated differently in logographic (Japanese) and phonographic (Arabic and Spanish) groups. While reading and listening abilities were highly correlated among Arabic and Spanish subjects, only a negligible relationship existed in their Japanese counterparts. The implications, seemingly, are (1) that L1 orthographic experience interacts in highly complex fashion with the cognitive and linguistic requirements in processing, and therefore (2) that qualitatively different developmental processes evolve among L2 learners from divergent L1 backgrounds.

In recent years, moreover, research on beginning English readers consistently has suggested that a particular form of metalinguistic sensitivity, phonemic awareness, is directly related to phonological processing skills in alphabetic languages (e.g., Bradley & Bryant, 1983; Liberman, Shankweiler, Fischer, & Carter, 1974). Phonemic awareness refers both to the metalinguistic insight that words can be segmented into sequences of phonemes and to the ability to separate the internal structure of a word into its phonemic constituents. Longitudinal studies repeatedly show that phonemic awareness is a reliable predictor of subsequent reading achievement in both primary grades (e.g., Bryant, Maclean, & Bradley, 1990; Juel, Griffith, & Gough, 1986) and secondary grades (e.g., Byrne, Freebody, & Gates, 1992; Juel, 1988). And, of greater importance, it has been noted that phonemic awareness and literacy experience are mutually enhancing through a reciprocal relationship (e.g., Bowey & Francis, 1991; Perfetti, Beck, Bell, & Hughes, 1987).

This reciprocity has major implications for L2 (ESL in particular) reading development. To wit, if, indeed, a high level of phonemic awareness results from experiential exposure to alphabetic script, an assumption can be made that readers with nonalphabetic L1 backgrounds are seriously handicapped. Since nonalphabetic readers do not engage in phonological processing at the phonemic level, they are unlikely to develop phonemic sensitivity to the same extent as alphabetic L1 readers. Further, because of their limited phonemic awareness, we can hypothesize that nonalphabetic L1 readers may experience considerable difficulty in mastering English phonological processing skills.

Koda (1993a) empirically tested this hypothesis with two groups of ESL readers from non-Roman alphabetic (Korean Hungle) and nonalphabetic (Chinese) L1 backgrounds. The groups were compared on phonemic awareness, phonological processing skills, and text comprehension ability. The results further complicate an already complex picture: First, the two groups did not differ in their ability either to distinguish English phonemes or to process single phonemes; second, Korean learners outperformed Chinese in phonemic tasks requiring the simultaneous manipulation and analysis of multiple phonemes; third, virtually no differences existed in the groups' text comprehension ability; and fourth, phonemic awareness, phonological skills, and reading comprehension were closely interconnected among Korean ESL learners, but no such relationships were found among Chinese. The data thus demonstrate that while prior alphabetic experience appears to enhance L2 phonemic analysis skills, the absence of such experience has little impact on reading comprehension. Moreover, the fact that the three variables – phonemic awareness, phonological processing skills, and reading comprehension – correlated differently between the two ESL groups indicates that Korean and Chinese ESL learners utilize phonemic analyses to differential degrees during phonological processing and reading comprehension. This, in turn, explains why Chinese ESL subjects, despite limited alphabetic experience in L1, perform far better on reading comprehension than might have been predicted – i.e., their phonological processing required phonemic analyses to a much less extent than the Koreans'. These outcomes suggest that the degree of prior alphabetic experience leads to qualitative differences in the reading process, but not to quantitative differences in performance. There is, thus, additional support for the notion that diverse L1 reading backgrounds are directly related to processing variations in L2 reading.

# Summary and implications

To summarize, three major orthographic systems – logography, syllabary, and alphabet – differ in two critical dimensions: (1) the basic unit of representation and (2) the regularity in symbol-to-sound correspondence. Both dimensions not only differentiate orthographic systems, but determine their phonological recodability in each system. The phonological recodability, in turn, is directly responsible for procedural variations in the phonological processing of the orthographies.

Similar processing variations are also observable in L2. Recent word recognition research consistently shows that qualitatively different processing procedures are used in the visual scanning and phonological recoding of L2 readers with different L1 orthographic backgrounds. And, of greatest significance, differences in L2 word recognition patterns are linked with specific properties in the learner's L1 orthographic system. The empirical data thus suggest that there are strong connections between the L1 orthographic system and L2 processing procedures.

Consequently, several recommendations can be made for L2 vocabulary instruction. First, given that L2 readers utilize their L1-based strategies, and that some languages relate more closely in orthographic properties to the target language than others, we can logically assume that beginning L2 readers, because of their varying orthographic backgrounds, develop processing skills at different rates. Therefore, when L2 teachers, through simple linguistic analyses, become aware of similarities and differences between students' L1 and L2, they can anticipate the difficulties their students may encounter in learning to read a new language, but provide guidance in surmounting processing problems. In addition, L2 reading instruction can be individualized, at least in part, so as to accommodate particular students' needs. Individualized programs, moreover, can be facilitated through recent new technologies for language learning (e.g., CALL, interactive video), as well as through extended outside reading programs.

Second, since diverse L1 reading experiences engender qualitatively different processing mechanisms among L2 readers, it would seem that direct strategy instruction would be extremely beneficial in helping learners develop effective verbal processing skills. Gairns (1992) conducted an exploratory study directly addressing this issue. Contrary to prediction, her results indicated that explicit L2-based strategies instruction produces little improvement in reading performance, and in some cases even results in a slight decline. The reading performance of L2 readers, however, improved considerably with instruction related to their L1-based strategies. These findings make it plain that strategy choice cannot be explained solely on the basis of linguistic features. Other factors must be involved in the selection process. Conceivably, for example, cognitively mature L2 learners select – in their metacognitive efforts to improve processing efficiency – processing strategies based on what they intuitively perceive as effective. If, indeed, such attempts occur during L2 processing, we cannot assume the effectiveness of arbitrary strategy instruction based on prespecified skills. L2 teachers, instead, should avoid predetermined assumptions regarding the long-term utility of mandatory strategy usage. Since students are autonomous in selecting processing procedures, they may, logically or illogically, for good reasons or bad, choose to resist a specified strategy. Consequently, teachers should, through careful monitoring, remain alert to quantitative and qualitative changes in students' progress, and make appropriate adjustments and modifications as they become necessary.

Finally, familiarizing students with the function of particular orthographic properties in the target language would be extremely beneficial. It has been reported that L2 learners of Japanese from non-logographic backgrounds are reluctant to use Kanji in written composition because of uncertainty about the system (Koda, 1993b). Explicit instruction on L2-specific orthographic and other linguistic functions may help students develop a cognitive grasp of the ways such features facilitate the reading. A clear understanding of specific linguistic function should lead to a higher motivation for learning and using those particular features, which, in turn, may result in improved skills. Thus, explicit instruction may offer advantages, both in providing a conceptual organization for the linguistic system and in promoting its mastery.

## References

Baddeley, A. D. (1966). Short term memory for word sequences as a function of acoustic, semantic, and formal similarity. *Quarterly Journal of Experimental Psychology, 18*, 362–365.

Balota, D., Pollatsek, A., & Rayner, K. (1985). The interaction of contextual constraints and parafoveal visual information in reading. *Cognitive Psychology, 17*, 364–390.

Bates, E., & MacWhinney, B. (1989). Functionalism and the competition model. In B. MacWhinney & E. Bates (Eds.), *The crosslinguistic study of sentence processing* (pp. 3–73). Cambridge: Cambridge University Press.

Bates, E., McNew, S., MacWhinney, B., Devescovi, A., & Smith, S. (1982). Functional constraints on sentence processing: A cross-linguistic study. *Cognition, 11*, 245–299.

Berman, R. (1986). A crosslinguistic perspective: Morphology and syntax. In P. Fletcher & M. Garman (Eds.), *Language acquisition: Studies in first language development* (2d ed.) (pp. 429–447). Cambridge: Cambridge University Press.

Bernhardt, E. B. (1991). *Reading development in a second language*. Norwood, NJ: Ablex.

Bowey, J. A., & Francis, J. (1991). Phonological analysis as a function of age and exposure to reading instruction. *Applied Psycholinguistics, 12*, 91–121.

Bradley, L., & Bryant, P. E. (1983). Categorizing sounds and learning to read – a causal connection. *Nature, 301*, 419–421.

Brown, T., & Haynes, M. (1985). Literacy background and reading development in a second language. In T. H. Carr (Ed.), *The development of reading skills* (pp. 19–34). San Francisco: Jossey-Bass.

Bryant, P. E., Maclean, M., & Bradley, L. L. (1990). Rhyme, language, and children's reading. *Applied Psycholinguistics, 11*, 273–252.

Byrne, B., Freebody, P., & Gates, A. (1992). Longitudinal data on the relations of word-reading strategies to comprehension, reading time, and phonemic awareness. *Reading Research Quarterly, 27,* 140–151.

Chern, C. L. (1993). Chinese students' word-solving strategies in reading in English. In T. Huckin, M. Haynes, & J. Coady (Eds.), *Second language reading and vocabulary learning* (pp. 67–85). Norwood, NJ: Ablex.

Cohen, A. D., Olshtain, E., & Rosenstein, D. S. (1986). Advanced EFL apologies: What remains to be learned? *International Journal of the Sociology of Language, 62,* 51–74.

Coltheart, M. (1984). Writing systems and reading disorders. In L. Henderson (Ed.), *Orthographies and reading: Perspectives from cognitive psychology, neuropsychology, and linguistics* (pp. 67–80). Hillsdale, NJ: Lawrence Erlbaum.

Conrad, R. (1964). Acoustic confusion in immediate memory. *British Journal of Psychology, 55,* 75–84.

Doctor, E. A., & Coltheart, M. (1980). Children's use of phonological encoding when reading for meaning. *Memory & Cognition, 8,* 195–204.

Flynn, S. (1987). *A parameter-setting model of L2 acquisition: Experimental studies in anaphora.* Hingham, MA: Kluwer.

(1989). The role of the head-initial/head-final parameter in the acquisition of English relative clauses by adult Spanish and Japanese speakers. In S. M. Gass & J. Schachter (Eds.), *Linguistic perspectives on second language acquisition* (pp. 89–108). Cambridge: Cambridge University Press.

Forster, K. I., & Chambers, S. M. (1973). Lexical access and naming time. *Journal of Verbal Learning and Verbal Behavior, 12,* 627–635.

Frost, R., Katz, L., & Ben, S. (1987). Strategies for visual word recognition and orthographic depth: A multilingual comparison. *Journal of Experimental Psychology: Human Perception and Performance, 13,* 104–115.

Gairns, B. (1992). Cognitive processing in ESL reading. Master's thesis, Ohio University, Athens, OH.

Gass, S. (1987). The resolution of conflicts among competing systems: A bidirectional perspective. *Applied Psycholinguistics, 8,* 329–350.

(1989). How do learners resolve linguistic conflicts? In S. Gass & J. Schachter (Eds.), *Linguistic perspectives on second language acquisition* (pp. 183–199). Cambridge: Cambridge University Press.

Gass, S., & Schachter, J. (Eds.). (1989). *Linguistic perspectives on second language acquisition.* Cambridge: Cambridge University Press.

Gass, S., & Selinker, L. (Eds.). (1983). *Language transfer in language learning.* Rowley, MA: Newbury House.

Gelb, I. J. (1963). *A study of writing.* Chicago: University of Chicago Press.

Gleitman, L. R. (1985). Orthographic resources affect reading acquisition – if they are used. *Remedial and Special Education, 6,* 24–36.

Gleitman, L. R., & Rozin, P. (1977). The structure and acquisition of reading I: Relation between orthographies and the structure of language. In A. S. Reber & D. L. Scarborough (Eds.), *Toward a psychology of reading: The proceedings of the CUNY conference* (pp. 1–5). Hillsdale, NJ: Lawrence Erlbaum.

Glushko, R. J. (1979). The organisation and activation of orthographic knowledge in reading aloud. *Journal of Experimental Psychology: Human Perception and Performance, 5,* 674–691.

Goody, J. (1968). Introduction. In J. Goody (Ed.), *Literacy in traditional societies* (pp. 1–26). Cambridge: Cambridge University Press.

Gough, P. B. (1983). Context, form, and interaction. In K. Rayner (Ed.), *Eye movements in reading: Perceptual and language processes* (pp. 203–211). New York: Academic Press.

Green, D. W., & Meara, P. (1987). The effects of script on visual search. *Second Language Research, 4,* 102–117.

Gundel, J. K., & Tarone, E. E. (1983). Language transfer and the acquisition of pronominal anaphora. In S. Gass & L. Selinker (Eds.), *Language transfer in language learning* (pp. 281–296). Rowley, MA: Newbury House.

Hakuta, K. (1976). A case study of a Japanese child learning English as a second language. *Language Learning, 26,* 321–351.

(1982). Interaction between particles and word order in the comprehension and production of simple sentences in Japanese children. *Developmental Psychology, 18,* 62–76.

Hatta, T. (1978). Recognition of Japanese Kanji and Hirakana in the left and right visual fields. *Japanese Journal of Psychology, 20,* 51–59.

Haynes, M. (1984). Patterns and perils of guessing in second language reading. In J. Handscombe, R. A. Orem, & B. P. Taylor (Eds.), *On TESOL '83* (pp. 163–176). Washington, DC: TESOL.

Henderson, L. (1985). Issues in the modeling of pronunciation assembly in normal reading. In K. E Patterson, J. C. Marshall, & M. Colthear (Eds.), *Surface dyslexia* (pp. 459–508). Hillsdale, NJ: Lawrence Erlbaum.

(Ed.). (1984). *Orthographies and reading: Perspective from cognitive psychology, neuropsychology and linguistics.* Hillsdale, NJ: Lawrence Erlbaum.

Holmes, J., & Ramos, R. G. (1993). False friends and reckless guessers: Observing cognate recognition strategies. In T. Huckin, M. Haynes, & J. Coady (Eds.), *Second language reading and vocabulary learning* (pp. 86–108). Norwood, NJ: Ablex.

Huckin, T., & Bloch, J. (1993). Strategies for inferring word meaning in context: A cognitive model. In T. Huckin, M. Haynes, & J. Coady (Eds.), *Second language reading and vocabulary learning* (pp. 153–180). Norwood, NJ: Ablex.

Hyams, N. (1986). *Language acquisition and the theory of parameters.* Dordrecht, NL: Reidel.

(1987). The theory of parameters and syntactic development. In T. Roeper & E. Williams (Eds.), *Parameter setting* (pp. 1–22). Boston, MA: Dordrecht Reidel.

Irujo, S. (1986). Don't put your leg in your mouth: Transfer in the acquisition of idioms in a second language. *TESOL Quarterly, 20,* 287–304.

Juel, C. (1988). Learning to read and write: A longitudinal study of fifty-four children from first through fourth grade. *Journal of Educational Psychology, 80,* 437–447.

Juel, C., Griffith, P. L., & Gough, P. B. (1986). Acquisition of literacy: A longitudinal study of children in first and second grade. *Journal of Educational Psychology, 78,* 243–255.

Just, M. A., & Carpenter, P. A. (1980). A theory of reading: From eye fixation to comprehension. *Psychological Review, 87,* 329–354.

(1987). *The psychology of reading and language comprehension.* Boston, MA: Allyn & Bacon.

Kail, M. (1989). Cue validity, cue cost, and processing sentence comprehension in French and Spanish. In B. MacWhinney and E. Bates (Eds.), *The crosslinguistic study of sentence processing* (pp. 77–117). Cambridge: Cambridge University Press.

Kellerman, E., & Sharwood Smith, M. (1986). *Crosslinguistic influence in second language acquisition.* Oxford: Pergamon Press.

Kilborn, K., & Ito, T. (1989). Sentence processing strategies in adult bilinguals. In B. MacWhinney and E. Bates (Eds.), *The crosslinguistic study of sentence processing* (pp. 257–295). Cambridge: Cambridge University Press.

Kleiman, G. M. (1975). Speech recording in reading. *Journal of Verbal Learning and Verbal Behavior, 14,* 323–339.

Koda, K. (1988). Cognitive process in second language reading: Transfer of L1 reading skills and strategies. *Second Language Research, 4*(2), 133–156.

(1990). The use of L1 reading strategies in L2 reading: Effects of L1 orthographic structures on L2 phonological recording strategies. *Studies in Second Language Acquisition, 12*(4), 393–410.

(1993a). The role of phonemic awareness in L2 reading. Paper presented at the meeting of AAAL, Atlanta, April.

(1993b). Task-induced variability in FL writing: Cross-linguistic perspectives. *Foreign Language Annals, 16,* 332–346.

(1993c). Transferred L1 strategies and L2 syntactic structure in L2 sentence comprehension. *Modern Language Journal, 77,* 491–500.

Laufer, B. (1988). The concept of 'synforms' (similar lexical forms) in vocabulary acquisition. *Language and Education, 2,* 113–132.

Levy, B. A. (1975). Vocalization and suppression effects in sentence memory. *Journal of Verbal Learning and Verbal Behavior, 14,* 304–316.

Liberman, I. Y., Shankweiler, D., Fischer, F. W., & Carter, B. (1974). Explicit syllable and phoneme segmentation in the young child. *Journal of Experimental Child Psychology, 18,* 201–212.

Lust, B. (1987). *Studies in the acquisition of anaphora.* Hingham, MA: Kluwer Academic Publishing.

Mann, V. A. (1985). A cross-linguistic perspective on the relation between temporary memory skills and early reading ability. *Remedial and Special Education, 6,* 37–42.

McConkie, G. W., & Zola, D. (1981). Language constraints and the functional stimulus in reading. In A. M. Lesgold & C. A. Perfetti (Eds.), *Interactive processes in reading* (pp. 155–175). Hillsdale, NJ: Lawrence Erlbaum.

McDonald, J. L. (1987). Sentence interpretation in bilingual speakers of English and Dutch. *Applied Psycholinguistics, 8,* 379–415.

Mou, L. C., & Anderson, N. S. (1981). Graphemic and phonemic codings of Chinese characters in short-term retention. *Bulletin of the Psychonomic Society, 17,* 255–258.

Odlin, T. (1989). *Language transfer: Cross-linguistic influence in language learning.* Cambridge: Cambridge University Press.

Olshtain, E. (1983). Sociocultural competence and language transfer: The case of apology. In S. Gass & L. Selinker (Eds.), *Language transfer in language learning* (pp. 232–249). Rowley, MA: Newbury House.

Olson, D. R. (1975). Book review. [Review of *Towards a literacy society*]. *Proceedings of the National Academy of Education, 2,* 109–178.

(1977). From utterance to text: The bias of language in speech and writing. *Harvard Educational Review, 47,* 257–281.

Patterson, K. E., & Morton, J. (1985). From orthography to phonology: An attempt at an older interpretation. In K. E. Patterson, J. C. Marshall, & M. Coltheart (Eds.), *Surface dyslexia* (pp. 331–359). Hillsdale, NJ: Lawrence Erlbaum.

Perfetti, C. A. (1985). *Reading ability.* New York: Oxford University Press.

(1991). Representations and awareness in the acquisition of reading competence. In L. Rieben & C. A. Perfetti (Eds.), *Learning to read* (pp. 33–46). Hillsdale, NJ: Lawrence Erlbaum.

Perfetti, C. A., Beck, I., Bell, L., & Hughes, C. (1987). Phonemic knowledge and learning to read are reciprocal: A longitudinal study of first grade children. *Merrill-Palmer Quarterly, 33,* 283–319.

Phinney, M., & White, L. (1987). The pro-drop parameter in second language acquisition. In T. Roeper & E. Williams (Eds.), *Parameter setting* (pp. 221–246). Boston, MA: Dordrecht Reidel.

Rayner, K., & Bertera, J. H. (1979). Reading without a fovea. *Science, 206,* 468–469.

Rutherford, W. E. (1983). Language typology and language transfer. In S. Gass & L. Selinker (Eds.), *Language transfer in language learning* (pp. 358–370). Rowely, MA: Newbury House.

Ryan, A., & Meara, P. (1991). The case of invisible vowels: Arabic speakers reading English words. *Reading in a Foreign Language, 7*(2), 531–540.

Saito, Y. (1981). The effects of article deletion in English on the cognitive process reflected in the eye movements and metacognitive awareness of native readers and Japanese readers of English: An eye-tracking study. Paper presented at the annual meeting of National Reading Conference, Austin, TX, December.

Saito, H., Inoue, M., & Nomura, Y. (1979). Information processing of Kanji (Chinese characters) and Kana (Japanese characters): The close relationship among graphemic, phonemic, and semantic aspects. *Psychologia, 22,* 195–206.

Sasaki, Y. (1991). English and Japanese interlanguage comprehension strategies: An analysis based on the competition model. *Applied Psycholinguistics, 12* 47–73.

Sasanuma, S. (1974a). Impairment of written language in Japanese aphasics: Kana vs. Kanji processing. *Journal of Chinese Linguistics, 2,* 141–157.

1974b. Kanji vs. Kana processing in alexia with transient agraphia: A case report. *Cortex, 10,* 89–97.

(1975). Kana and Kanji processing in Japanese aphasics. *Brain and Language, 2,* 369–383.

(1984). Can surface dyslexia occur in Japanese? In L. Henderson (Ed.), *Orthographies and reading: Perspectives from cognitive psychology, neuropsychology, and linguistics* (pp. 43–56). Hillsdale, NJ: Lawrence Erlbaum.

Scarcella, R. C. (1983). Discourse accent in second language performance. In S. Gass & L. Selinker (Eds.), *Language transfer in language learning* (pp. 306–326). Rowley, MA: Newbury House.

Slobin, D. I. (1985). Crosslinguistic evidence for the language-making capacity. In D. I. Slobin (Ed.), *The crosslinguistic study of language acquisition* (pp. 1157–1249). Hillsdale, NJ: Lawrence Erlbaum.

Solan, L. (1987). Parameter setting and the development of pronouns and reflexives. In T. Roper & E. Williams (Eds.), *Parameter setting* (pp. 189–200). Boston, MA: Dordrecht Reidel.

Sridhar, S. N. (1989). Cognitive structures in language production: A crosslinguistic study. In B. MacWhinney & E. Bates (Eds.), *The crosslinguistic study of sentence processing* (pp. 209–224). Cambridge: Cambridge University Press.

Stanovich, K. E. (1988). The language code: Issues in word recognition. In S. R. Yussen & M. C. Smith (Eds.), *Reading across the life span*. New York: Springer-Verlag.

   (1991). Changing models of reading and acquisition. In L. Rieben & C. A. Perfetti (Eds.), *Learning to read* (pp. 19–32). Hillsdale, NJ: Lawrence Erlbaum.

Turvey, M. T., Feldman, L. B., & Lukatela, G. (1984). The Serbo-Croatian orthography constrains the reader to a phonologically analytic strategy. In L. Henderson (Ed.), *Orthographies and reading: Perspectives from cognitive psychology, neuropsychology, and linguistics* (pp. 81–90). Hillsdale, NJ: Lawrence Erlbaum.

Tzeng, O. L. J., & Wang, W. S.-Y. (1983) The first two R's: The way different languages reduce speech to script affects how visual information is processed in the brain. *American Scientist, 71,* 238–243.

White, L. (1989). *Universal grammar and second language acquisition.* Philadelphia, PA: J. Benjamins.

Yanco, J. J. (1985). Language contact and grammatical interference: Hausa, Zarma in Niamey, Niger. *Studies in African Linguistics, 9,* 318–322.

Yik, W. F. (1978). The effects of visual and acoustic similarity on short-term memory for Chinese words. *Quarterly Journal of Experimental Psychology, 30,* 487–494.

Zehler, A. M. (1982). Reflection of first-language-derived processes in second-language acquisition. *DAI, 43,* 3054A.

Zhang, G., & Simon, H. A. (1985). STM capacity for Chinese words and idioms: Chunking and acoustical loop hypothesis. *Memory and Cognition, 13,* 193–201.

# PART II:
# CASE STUDIES

Case studies can be helpful in "bringing to life" some of the complexity and individual variation involved in vocabulary learning. Part II presents detailed portraits of four adult second language learners struggling to build up their word knowledge in English, Hebrew, and Portuguese. Of special interest is the fact that two of the studies are "self-portraits," with the authors describing their own efforts to build their second language vocabulary. If any objectivity is sacrificed in this effort, it is more than compensated for by the unusually high level of self-awareness provided by the investigators.

The first chapter in Part II, Kate Parry's "Vocabulary and comprehension: Two portraits," presents two case studies of advanced ESL students handling the vocabulary encountered in introductory anthropology texts. The students made lists of the words they found difficult, tried to guess the meaning of these words, recorded think-aloud protocols while reading a passage, and translated a portion of this passage into their first languages (Greek and Korean, respectively). These data are analyzed and the differences between the two students are discussed. Parry suggests that the two students used quite different reading strategies with the Greek speaker adopting the holistic approach and the Korean speaker an analytic one. Since neither approach was fully satisfactory, she concludes that ESL teachers should spend more class time on metacognition, discussing pros and cons of different vocabulary-learning strategies according to particular circumstances and purposes.

The next chapter, by Roann Altman, describes a six-year case study of an English-speaking learner (the author herself) of Hebrew, focusing on verbs and emphasizing *productive* vocabulary use. Altman argues that successful productive vocabulary use is best facilitated by (1) morphophonological regularity and (2) phonological input to the learning process. "Once the underlying morphophonological pattern had been extracted from all the instances perceived," she writes, "a threshold was reached wherein the pattern could then be applied to the whole array of roots (whose meaning was known) and thus result in a significant increase in production." Altman as learner passed through five distinct stages of development beginning with the most morphologically regular forms and ending with the least regular ones. Unanalyzed wholes were learned before analyzed ones. Her production was improved by good teaching, oral input, and metacognitive awareness of input. One of the strongest triggers for such awareness was the *need to produce* in the language. Encountering the language in multiple situations also helped. Combined, these elements created a "confluence of opportunity" for the learner, and repeated use led to automaticity.

Part II concludes with William Grabe and Fredricka L. Stoller's description of a five-month case study that explored the extent to which extensive newspaper reading, without formal instruction but with the aid of a bilingual dictionary, would allow the first author to develop his vocabulary and his reading ability in Portuguese as a second language. The authors were particularly interested in the relationship between reading development and (*a*) vocabulary acquisition, (*b*) general comprehension processing, and (*c*) overall L2 language acquisition. The main sources of data evaluated were front pages of newspapers and corresponding look-up vocabulary lists generated by the subject of the study, the journal entries he kept, and a battery of objective tests (i.e., vocabulary, reading comprehension, listening comprehension, and cloze tests).

Results indicate that the learner (Grabe) made dramatic progress in vocabulary knowledge, reading comprehension, and listening comprehension. Indeed, there seemed to be a synergistic relationship among these three skill areas. Newspapers proved to be very appropriate texts for reading, although they also had some genre-based limitations associated with them. Dictionary use was found to be especially helpful, providing the learner with a psychologically valuable "accuracy anchor" and encouraging more complete learning. Conversely, recognition of semantic fields and knowledge of grammar were found to be relatively unimportant in the vocabulary learning process. The authors conclude that extensive reading is a very effective way to develop vocabulary knowledge and other language abilities over time.

# 4 Vocabulary and comprehension
## Two portraits

Kate Parry

Many colleges and universities in the United States admit large numbers of international or immigrant students whose proficiency in English is quite limited. Such students are usually required to take a language test, and if they do not do well, they have to enroll in courses in English as a second language (ESL). Only after passing these are they allowed, in many colleges, to proceed with regular courses and complete their degrees. By this time, they are, presumably, at an advanced stage of language learning: They have control of the main grammatical structures of English, and they know a good deal of vocabulary. But as they embark on courses designed for native speakers, they are bound to come across many words that are new to them, both the specialized terms of particular academic fields and the enormous numbers of nonspecialized but nonetheless infrequent words that characterize English academic prose (Hofland & Johansson, 1982; Kucera & Francis, 1967). These words are not taught in language classes – as Nation (1990) points out, it is neither practicable nor productive to try to teach them – and the nonspecialized ones are not taught in content classes either; so the students must deal with them on their own. The question is, How do they do this? And can language teachers help them, before they leave ESL classes, to develop more appropriate strategies?

My approach to these questions has been through case studies of individual students who had been through the ESL sequence at Hunter College of the City University of New York, and who were, at the time I studied them, enrolled in Introductory Anthropology, one of the college's

The research on which this article is based was supported by grant number 668415 from the PSC-CUNY Research Award Program of the City University of New York, and material was first presented in 1991 at the 25th Annual TESOL Convention as part of a colloquium titled "Research Issues in L2 Vocabulary." I am grateful to TESOL for the opportunities its conventions have provided for presenting my ideas on vocabulary acquisition, and to the editors of this volume for encouraging me to develop these ideas. I would also like to thank Dimitri and Ae Young, without whose cooperation the research would have been impossible; Agathi Raptu and Joo-Eun Ju for their help in translating the Greek and Korean data; Franklyn Horowitz for making an independent assessment of the students' glosses; and my colleagues at Hunter College, in both the English and the Anthropology Departments, for their help in carrying out the project.

distribution requirement courses. The two students whose portraits are drawn here are a Greek Cypriot man called Dimitri and a Korean woman called Ae Young (the names are fictitious). Both took the anthropology course in the fall of 1988, having successfully completed the highest of the college's ESL courses the previous spring; and, before coming to Hunter, both had completed a high school education in their own country. This latter point is important, because I wanted students for this study who would have a sufficiently wide vocabulary in their first language to demonstrate, by translation, the accuracy of their understanding of the English words with which they were now dealing.

Once I had identified the students and secured their agreement to participate in the project, my method was to give them, first, a standard vocabulary test (I used the vocabulary section of the Michigan Test of English Language Proficiency) and then to ask them to keep lists of any words that they encountered in their anthropology textbook that caused them "difficulty." (The textbook in question was *Cultural Anthropology: A Contemporary Perspective* by Roger M. Keesing [1981].) The entry for each word included the page reference (so that I could identify the context), the student's guess as to the word's meaning, and a record of the dictionary definition if the student chose to look it up. Then, after the students had been making these lists for about 6 weeks, each made a similar one, based on another anthropology text (it was an extract from an article entitled "African and Afro-American Family Structure" by Niara Sudarkasa [1982], thinking aloud as they did so. Two weeks after making these think-aloud protocols, the students translated into Greek or Korean, respectively, two paragraphs of the text on which the protocols had been based. Finally, at the end of the term, by which time the students had completed several more lists on their own, each of them did a test based on his or her own lists. This test consisted of every fifth word that the student in question had recorded, and it was presented in two stages: First, the words were shown in isolation, and the student was asked to write down the meanings of any that he or she could remember; then each word was shown in the context of the single sentence in which the student had first noted it, and, again, the student was asked to write down what each word meant. Throughout, the students were invited to use their first languages for the expression of meaning; and then all the first language glosses, as well as the translations, were put back into English by informants who were native speakers of Greek and Korean, respectively, and who were also extremely proficient speakers of English.

This procedure provided, first, a broad, though necessarily incomplete, view of each student's vocabulary and of its development through the anthropology course and, second, a detailed, though also incomplete, picture of the students' strategies as they dealt with the new vocabulary and of the accuracy with which they were thereby interpreting the text.

TABLE I. COMPARISON OF DATA PRODUCED BY TWO STUDENTS

|  | Dimitri | Ae Young |
|---|---|---|
| 1. Pretest | | |
| Score | 58% | 63% |
| 2. Work based on textbook | | |
| Words read | 72,000? | 7,500? |
| Words listed | 91 (0.1%?) | 119 (1.6%?) |
| # "relatively frequent" | 8 (9%) | 36 (31%) |
| Words glossed | 83 (91%)* | 116 (97%)* |
| "Correct" | 20 (22%)* | 14 (12%)* |
| "Partly correct" | 35 (39%)* | 44 (37%)* |
| "Incorrect" | 27 (30%)* | 58 (49%)* |
| 3. Posttest | | |
| Stage 2: # glosses given | 1/19 (5%) | 7/24 (29%) |
| Stage 2: # glosses given | 18/19 (95%) | 19/24 (79%) |
| "Correct" | 2/19 (11%) | 6/24 (25%) |
| "Partly correct" | 3/19 (17%) | 9/24 (38%) |
| "Incorrect" | 13/19 (68%) | 4/24 (17%) |

*Percentages are of total number of words listed.

The broad view is summed up in Table 1, which shows how the students did, first, on the pretest, second, on the lists that they made on the basis of the textbook, and, third, on the posttest.

There are obvious difficulties in reducing this kind of information to figures, as is suggested here by the use of question marks and quotation marks. To begin with, I cannot be sure of the total number of words read by each student: The figures given here are an estimate based on the number of pages they claimed to have covered, but there is no certainty that they read everything that was on each page. Second, the assessment of the glosses is necessarily subjective, being based on my own judgment after discussion with my informants (see Parry, 1993b for how the decisions were reached); thus the figures can be taken only as a general indication, and only the broadest differences can be considered significant.[1]

Nevertheless, the figures are useful for purposes of comparison, and they suggest a contrast that is indeed striking. Although the two students were putatively at the same level, in terms of both their status in relation to the college's English language program and the scores they obtained on the Michigan vocabulary test, they seem, by all the other indicators, to

1 I did, however, have a colleague assess the glosses (or their back-translations) independently, and we reached 77% agreement on Dimitri's and 84% on Ae Young's. I should add that my colleague's classifications were consistently less stringent than mine (see Parry, 1991).

differ greatly in proficiency. To judge from his lists, Dimitri is by far the stronger of the two: He read much more, he found fewer words to be difficult, only a small proportion of those words were "relatively frequent" – which I defined as appearing ten or more times in the frequency counts of both Kucera and Francis (1967) and Hofland and Johansson (1982) – and he was relatively successful in guessing the meanings of the words he did not know. Ae Young, by contrast, read very little (much less, indeed, than any of the four students that I have studied) and claimed she had difficulty with a much higher percentage of the words; of these a larger proportion were "relatively frequent," and her guesses as to the meanings of the difficult words were "incorrect" nearly half of the time.

When we look at the posttest scores, however, the position is reversed: Ae Young seemed to have quite a good memory for the words she had recorded, recognizing nearly a third (29%) of those sampled when she saw them in isolation, and defining more than half (25% plus 38%) with some degree of accuracy when she saw them in their original single-sentence context. Dimitri's performance, by contrast, was abysmal: he apparently only recognized one of the nineteen words that he was given in isolation, and, when he was given the single-sentence context for each, he was still able to produce only five definitions (28%) that were even partly correct. We are thus presented with a conundrum: Dimitri would seem, from his lists, to have a wider vocabulary than Ae Young, but how could he have acquired it if his memory for what he learns is so bad? Ae Young would seem, from her posttest, to be relatively good at learning new words, but if so, why does she not do better on her lists? The answer suggested by their protocols and translations is that they employed quite different strategies, which are effective in different ways and for different kinds of comprehension.

Now let us look at the detailed picture that is given us by the protocols. Figures 1 and 2 show the words the students listed when they read the protocol passage, together with their glosses (the glosses that have been translated back from Greek or Korean are in italics). Also shown are my own classifications of these glosses in terms of accuracy. When these lists are analyzed in the same way as those made by the students when they were reading the textbook on their own, they produce comparable results. The figures are given in Table 2.

Ae Young recorded much the same proportion of the total number of words read as she did when working on her own (1.4% as compared to 1.6%). Dimitri recorded a rather higher proportion (0.6% as compared to 0.1%) – a difference that can probably be accounted for by the fact that my observing him made him self-conscious – but he still recorded many fewer words than did Ae Young. As for the accuracy of the glosses, while the numbers are too small and the classifications too uncertain for

| Original word | Gloss | Classification |
|---|---|---|
| matrilineage | males and females have common female ancestor | partly correct |
| uterine | *half-brother or sister* | partly correct |
| paternally | from the father race | partly correct |
| deities | — | — |
| solely | only, exclusively | correct |
| consanguineal | — | — |
| reckoned | it is common between the two groupping | incorrect |
| bilaterally | by both parents | partly correct |
| perpetuity | exists one upon the other | incorrect |
| domiciled | the family whose sister and daughters after mariage ar movinging to their husbands compounds | incorrect |
| indigenous | the lineage betweeen males ad femals or husbands ad wives was strict | incorrect |

*Figure 1  Dimitri's glosses for protocol text.*

---

| Original word | Gloss | Classification |
|---|---|---|
| uterine | cousins whos mothers are sister | correct |
| sired | born | correct |
| paternity | standard example | incorrect |
| precolonial | before whole city separated into many pieces | partly correct |
| entity | *fixed property* | incorrect |
| allocation | something given | partly correct |
| deities | roll or function | incorrect |
| mandate | *accomplish* | incorrect |
| alliance | help | partly correct |
| customary | custom | partly correct |
| rudimentary | opposite elementary | incorrect |
| sibling | brothers and sisters | correct |
| filiation | — | — |
| bilaterally | through both parents | partly correct |
| discrete | *each other do not open their minds* | incorrect |
| overlapping | care about too much | incorrect |
| marital | about marriage | correct |
| transresidential | movable residense | partly correct |
| perpetuity | permenante period | correct |
| affiliation | ascendant | incorrect |
| labyrinthine | extended | partly correct |
| domiciled | wihout wives | incorrect |
| severance | — | — |
| indigenous | not open | incorrect |
| analogous | something to opposite | incorrect |

*Figure 2  Ae Young's glosses for protocol text.*

TABLE 2. PERFORMANCE OF TWO STUDENTS ON PROTOCOL TEXT

|  | *Dimitri* | *Ae Young* |
|---|---|---|
| Words read | c. 1,800 | c. 1,800 |
| Words listed | 11 (0.6%) | 25 (1.4%) |
| Words glossed | 9 (82%)* | 23 (92%)* |
| "Correct" | 1 (9%)* | 5 (20%)* |
| "Partly correct" | 4 (36%)* | 7 (28%)* |
| "Incorrect" | 4 (36%)* | 11 (44%)* |

*Percentages are of total number of words listed.

the percentages given here to carry much weight, there are two interesting points to note: First, on the protocol passage, as on the textbook, both students produced more glosses that were at least "partly correct" than ones that were clearly "incorrect," and, second, Ae Young produced significantly more "incorrect" ones than did Dimitri.

What I want to emphasize here, however, is not so much the relative accuracy of the students' guesses as the different ways in which they arrived at them. Simply by looking at the lists, we can see a significant difference in the two students' styles: when Dimitri glosses a word, he tends not to isolate it, but to interpret the larger unit in which it appears, whereas Ae Young is more likely to give as a gloss a single word or phrase that could be substituted for the one in question. For example, the word *indigenous* appears in this context:

Divorce was not common in *indigenous* African societies.

Dimitri, in glossing it as "the lineage between males ad femals or husbands ad wives was strict," seems to have paraphrased the whole sentence, as he understood it; and his glosses for *matrilineage, reckoned, perpetuity,* and *domiciled* share this characteristic. Ae Young, by contrast, in glossing *indigenous* as "not open," seems to have been thinking of the word on its own and even to have analyzed its constituent parts (*in-* as "not" and *-digenous* as "open"); and there is evidence from her protocol that she did the same thing with *pre-colonial, bi-laterally, dis-crete, over-lapping,* and *trans-residential.* Only in the case of *uterine,* for which she guessed "cousins whos mothers are sister," do we see reflected in her gloss her interpretation of the whole phrase in which the word appears (the phrase is "children of uterine sisters," so, as an interpretation of the whole, her gloss is quite accurate).

It may therefore be possible to characterize Dimitri's style as "holistic," in contrast to Ae Young's, which is "analytic" (Van Daalen-Kapteijns & Elshout-Mohr, 1981); or, alternatively, they can be thought of as "top-down" and "bottom-up" (see Parry, 1993a). This impression is confirmed by the general strategies shown by the two students in the think-aloud protocol. Dimitri, when asked to read the passage and gloss the difficult words in the same way as he usually did when making his lists, read the whole text straight through, marking the words as he went, but spending little time thinking about them. Then he read through the passage again, this time stopping to write each word down and work out its meaning; after a minute or two of thought, he wrote down his gloss (except in the cases of *deities* and *consanguineal*) and proceeded to look the word up in the dictionary. This last step took him a surprisingly long time – he seemed not to be sure of alphabetical order, and on at least two occasions wasted time by scanning the wrong pages – but once he had found the word he worked quickly: He looked at the definitions offered, selected the one he thought most appropriate, wrote it down, and went straight on with reading the passage. Ae Young, by contrast, read the passage only once, stopping and working on each word as she came to it. In each case she spent a long time trying to work out the word's meaning, and then, when she had written her gloss, she turned to the dictionary. She was much more efficient than Dimitri at finding the word, but once she had recorded the definition, she did not go straight on; instead, she went back to the context, reconstructing her interpretation in the light of the definition she had found.

These differences between the two students can best be illustrated by comparing what they said about a couple of the words that they both found difficult. One of these was *deities*, which appears in this context:

Although it is beyond the scope of this paper to discuss all the functions of lineages in African societies, suffice it to say that where they existed in precolonial times, they were landholding corporate entities charged with the allocation of land, titles, and other properties among their members. In virtually all cases, lineages were identified with particular ancestral homelands; in some instances, they had special *deities* as well. Although there have been some changes in the function of lineages in contemporary Africa, where they exist they are still a vital part of the social structure. Ultimately, because of the actual and fictive links that connect the living members to the founding ancestor, lineages were and are the kin groups that signify and symbolize social continuity in African societies.

On his first reading of the passage Dimitri stopped at *deities* and marked it, repeating it once as he did so. He commented that he did not know it and then went on reading. The second time around he stopped again when he came to the word, commented briefly "that word," and reread the sentence in which it appeared. He did not, however, come up with any guess as to its meaning, but simply said "I'll have to look that word," and began looking through the dictionary. When he found it, he read the first definition, making a miscue at first, but correcting himself: " 'The state of being good – the state of being god.' " He paused and then suggested an interpretation: "Which means something that is special to them." But he seemed not to be happy with this, for he read over the sentence again, substituting the words *state of being god* for deities. "No," he said, "I think – it doesn't look right, this one," and, reading from the dictionary again, " 'the state of being god, divine, natural, a god of – or goddess – deity," but he left the definition, *state of being god,* written down and went on with the passage.

When Ae Young came to the same point – which took her a long time, for she had to stop and work on *precolonial, entities,* and *allocation* as well – she repeated the word, as had Dimitri, and then said, writing as she did so, "They had special deities. Deities as well. Mm." Then she reread the sentence and went on reading to the end of the paragraph. At that point she stopped: "OK, then. Deities. They had special – I think it's related to the word homeland. So, um." She read the sentence again, and rejected this hypothesis – "No, it's not about homeland" – and, having read the sentence yet again, came up with another: "It means – they had special deities – is it like – identification?" She read the sentence once more, and then went back to the beginning of the paragraph, reading one sentence beyond the problematic word. This generated yet another hypothesis: "I think it's like – um – something they have to do, I mean, some – some respons – some responsibility for – I mean, some role, role? Function?" And this was what she wrote down. Of course, when she looked it up, she found something quite different, and registered her surprise: " 'The rank or nature of a god or a – special? OK – supreme being, god?' Oh? OK," and she looked at the context in which she had found the word again. It took her a little time to work it out, but then she saw what it meant: "OK, so it means they are own god like special home god. Or – supreme beings. Something they delivering – like, oh, OK. It means so they have their special – gods as well as ancestral homelands." At that point she wrote down the definition.

It is hardly fair to Dimitri to illustrate his strategy only with a word on which he did not even attempt a guess. So let us consider what he did with *domiciled,* a word both students glossed, but neither of them correctly. It appears in this context:

Although African extended families tend to be large, labyrinthine groupings, for illustrative purposes an extended family occupying a single compound in a patrilineal society . . . might be diagrammed as a group of brothers, their wives, their adult sons and grandsons and their wives, and any unmarried children in the group. . . . The married daughters and sisters of the adult males would be resident in the compounds of their husbands. Thus, the consanguineal core of the *domiciled* extended family consists of the adult males and their unmarried children.

On his first reading, Dimitri commented only briefly on the word: "Domiciled – that kind of family? I think domiciled, that's the consanguineal core of that kind of family – of that family." Then he went on reading. The second time around he gave it a bit more attention, first going back to the beginning of the previous sentence and rereading from "The married daughters" to "their unmarried children," and then quite quickly coming up with a hypothesis: "Domiciled extended families – the families whose – oh – daughters and sisters are when they get married they are moving to their husband's compound." The guess is not correct, of course, but it is clearly motivated by the text, and also, probably, by what he had been taught in anthropology about patrilocal as opposed to matrilocal societies. So he wrote the guess down and went straight to the dictionary. There (after much flipping through pages) he found "Customary dwelling place, home residence, law one's fixed place of dwelling where one tends to reside more or less permanently," and it is evident from the fact that he both read and wrote down the word *law* as a continuous part of the dictionary definition that not only was he unaware of the conventions by which dictionaries indicate specialist terms, but he was not really using the information that he had looked up. On the contrary, he just went on, making no apparent attempt to incorporate the definition into his interpretation of the text.

Ae Young, however, with *domiciled* as with *deities,* showed a much more thorough processing of the word. First she went back, as had Dimitri, to the beginning of the previous sentence and read down to "their unmarried children." Then she repeated again, " 'Domiciled extended family consists of the adult males and their unmarried children' " and commented: "Adult males. Just males. Not females. So, domiciled. Oh – domiciled. It's, um, means – oh. It means without wives? Like, domiciled – Consangui – it means the blood, right? Blood relatives. Only – males and their unmarried children. . . . if they do have their wives, then they will have their – no, if they marry, then they are living out. Domiciled extended family. Why no wives? Without wives? [she wrote the gloss down at this point] I don't – I – I don't think so." At this point she looked in the dictionary, and, as with *deities,* found quite a different interpretation: "OK. No. No. It's just a dwelling place, home. Domiciled. Do-mi-ciled. OK, so it's not about the wives. It's about – OK, if it's just a home, then, that mean 'Thus the consanguineal core of the domici – ' Oh, the *core,* so it's the – it's because of the blood, OK 'of the adult males and their unmarried children.' OK."

The patterns shown in these two examples were repeated throughout the two protocols. Dimitri stopped for 11 words, and he spent an average of 193 seconds working on each; but over half of that time was spent looking at the dictionary, and only 90 seconds (47%) were spent working out his own interpretation of the word in the context. Ae Young, on the other hand, stopped for 25 words, and spent an average of 183 seconds working on each one; of this time, only 37 seconds (20%) were spent looking in the dictionary, while 146 seconds (80%) were spent either trying to guess the word's meaning or reconstructing her interpretation of the text once she had looked it up. Moreover, in working with each word, Ae Young repeated it, on average, no fewer than fifteen times, in contrast to Dimitri, whose repetitions of his "difficult" words (including his second reading of the whole text) averaged only eight.

This analysis of the protocol goes a long way toward explaining the figures presented earlier. Dimitri's holistic, or top-down, approach is obviously much faster than Ae Young's analytic, more bottom-up, one, and this would explain why he read so much more through the term than she did.[2] It also explains why he recorded fewer words as "difficult": if he consistently reads a lot more than she does, he is indeed likely to know more words, simply from having been exposed to them, and this must be particularly true of relatively frequent ones. Ae Young's analytic approach, on the other hand, makes her reading painfully slow; consequently, she does not read much, and so she encounters fewer words altogether, and the more frequent ones less often, than does Dimitri. Those words that she does encounter, however, she works over so thoroughly that she has a relatively good chance of remembering them when she is tested on them within a period of a few weeks. As for the "incorrect" glosses, Ae Young's relatively high proportion of these can be explained partly by her willingness to write down guesses that she really thought might be wrong – as we have seen in the case of "without wives" for *domiciled;* thus the misinterpretation that such a guess represents may often be only provisional, and the fact that she reconstructs her interpretation after finding the dictionary definition suggests that any misinterpretation she does make is soon corrected.

Indeed, when we look at the translations that the students both did, we can see that Ae Young's strategy produced, at least in this case, significantly more accurate comprehension than Dimitri's. The two paragraphs used for this task were taken from the protocol text and outlined the differences between the *lineage* and the *extended family*. The first sentence reads like this:

It is important to understand the differences between the lineage and the extended family in African kinship, for although the two groupings are closely related, they are not the same.

Dimitri's translation, translated back into English, is this:

It is important to understand the differences among the two types of families existing on African land; however the two categories are very closely related but they are not exactly the same.

2 There is also the fact that Ae Young had, apparently, to spend a great deal of time working in her family's store.

So far, so good, it seems; only note that he has expressed *kinship* as "land," and he has made no terminological distinction between *lineage* and *extended family*, subsuming them instead under the general phrase "two kinds of family." Ae Young's translation of the sentence reads less well:

It is important to understand the difference of human relationship between blood ties and extended family in Africa. Because two groups are not same, even though they are closely related.

But she has included the notion of "kinship" as "relationship," and she does employ separate terms for *lineage* and *extended family* – although the expression translated back as "blood ties" is not an exact equivalent for the former.

The second sentence of the translation passage constitutes an explication of the point made in the first one:

From what I have said so far, it should be apparent first of all that extended families are based on marriage and descent, whereas lineages are based solely on descent.

Dimitri's translation, as with the previous sentence, begins with remarkable accuracy – but then something goes badly wrong:

From what I have said so far it is possible to understand that the two family categories are based on the institution of marriage and on the classification from which they come from, with which I mean from which family the two persons are from.

Again, the distinction between *lineage* and *extended family* is lost, subsumed in the more general "two family categories," and the final clause, which presents a distinctive feature of the lineage as a social construct, is completely misinterpreted. Contrast Ae Young's translation of this sentence, which, though increasingly peculiar, does show a grasp of the basic distinction:

My saying so far represents that while preferentially extended family is based on marriage and offsprings, blood tie is based on offsprings only.

In the next sentence, both students seem to get lost. It reads like this:

It is important to realize also that the living adult members of a lineage form the core of consanguineal ("blood") relatives around whom the extended family is built.

Dimitri again loses the distinction between *lineage* and *extended family*, and apparently makes up for his loss of comprehension by producing another explanatory clause that is pure invention:

It is very essential to understand that men from one family are connected to the institution which depends on the blood type with this I mean that all individuals coming from one family, their blood has something common.

Ae Young, by contrast, keeps the distinction, and recognizes all the other lexical elements in the sentence; but she seems to have little understanding of how they fit together:

It is also important to recognize that extended family is composed of live adults of blood ties centering blood relatives.

Finally, in the last sentence of the paragraph, Dimitri demonstrates how fundamental his failure to understand *lineage* is. The sentence is as follows:

Furthermore, as Uchendu notes, even in those African societies where corporate lineages are absent or exist only in rudimentary form, the extended families are still based around consanguineal cores, that is, persons linked by parent-child and/or sibling ties.

Dimitri's translation of this sentence suggests that he is at this point thinking of *lineage* as "marriage":

Also, as Uchendu has written, these African societies in which the institution of marriage is not so strong, if is existing only the very light type, these families rely on the institution of blood connection and that individuals are connected, for example like a father and son.

Perhaps what has happened here is a case of what Huckin and Bloch call "mistaken ID" (1993); Dimitri could be confusing *lineage* with linkage, an interpretation also suggested by his gloss for *indigenous* (see Figure 1). Be that as it may, the problem is a serious one: *Lineage* is a key word in this text, and Dimitri obviously does not know it. Worse still, he does not know that he does not know it, so that he does not even develop a hypothesis as to its meaning in the various sentences in which it appears. Thus, despite his holistic approach to text, he totally misses the main point. Ae Young, on the other hand, does get the main point, though her expression of it is very peculiar (my Korean informant assures me that it is quite as peculiar in Korean as it is in English). Her translation of the last sentence of the paragraph is this:

Moreover, as Wenchedoo mentioned, even in African society in which cooperative blood tie does not exist or exist in fundamental forms, extended family is still based on the relationship between parents and offsprings of blood relatives.

If we remember that she is using "blood tie" for *lineage,* her translation does bear some resemblance to the intended sense.

For the remaining four sentences of the translation, the story is the same: Dimitri alternates between interpreting *lineage* as a "category" of family, or as an "institution" (though he does not again suggest specifically "marriage"); Ae Young keeps her interpretation of the word as "blood tie" stable, and maintains the distinction between it and *extended family.* The consequence is that while Ae Young keeps more or less on track, Dimitri goes badly off it, so much so that his translation makes little sense at all.

Dimitri got a C for his anthropology course, and if his performance in the protocol and translation tasks is typical, this C is not surprising. Yet he must have been surprised by it, and disappointed too. After all, he did all the reading for the course and attended most of the lectures, as well as doing all the additional work for me, and, judging from the fluency with which he read the protocol passage and wrote the translation, he seemed to have little sense that anything was wrong. Indeed, in the earlier stages of learning the language, when he was dealing with texts that were simpler in content and used less infrequent vocabulary, I suspect that nothing very much was wrong: At that stage his holistic strategy would have paid off, for he was, as we have seen, successful at guessing word meanings from context, and vocabulary items that are encountered quite frequently are probably best learned in this way (cf. Saragi, Nation, & Meister, 1978). But specialized academic terms have to be understood with some precision, and so do many of the nonspecialized but infrequent words that are used to explain them: Dimitri's strategy of looking for a broad general picture, and being satisfied with interpretation at the level of sentence or phrase rather than of individual words, is simply not exact enough for these purposes. Dimitri needs to learn something from Ae Young, it seems, about how to isolate problematic words and to analyze their contribution to the context.

On the other hand, Ae Young did not do so well either. She got a B, but her instructor said it was a weak one, her average score on her exams falling only just above the boundary between B and C. Moreover, she read very little of the text, which means that she never encountered many of those words that are used only once in it, and, still more serious, she did not encounter as many times the words that are used more frequently. If this was how she was reading throughout her ESL courses, it is not surprising that she completed the last one with an apparently rather narrow vocabulary. She would have done better, when reading simpler texts, to follow a strategy more like Dimitri's, and, indeed, such a strategy would probably help her to speed up even on texts as difficult as this.

Unfortunately, Dimitri and Ae Young have both completed their language courses, so it is unlikely that anyone will help them to develop new strategies: Dimitri may well continue to get Cs without knowing why, and Ae Young may continue to find the assigned reading for her courses an intolerable burden. The students who are at present in our classes may, however, benefit from Dimitri's and Ae Young's experience. These two portraits show a marked difference between holistic and analytic approaches to vocabulary, and demonstrate that both approaches are necessary but that neither is appropriate at all times. The implication is that students need to develop flexibility. This should be the focus of vocabulary teaching at the higher levels of language learning: We need to discuss strategies in our classes and to devise exercises that will help students not only to learn specific words but also to approach vocabulary in different ways. It is vital, above all, that students find out, and show us, what kind of learners they are; with that information we can advise them appropriately, and, still more important, they will be better able to help themselves.

## References

Hofland, K., & Johansson, S. (1982). *Word frequencies in British and American English*. Harlow, England: Longmans.

Huckin, T., & Bloch, J. (1993). Strategies for inferring word-meanings in context: A cognitive model. In T. Huckin, M. Haynes, & J. Coady (Eds.), *Second language reading and vocabulary acquisition* (pp. 153–180). Norwood, NJ: Ablex.

Keesing, R. M. (1981). *Cultural anthropology: A contemporary perspective*. New York: Holt, Rinehart & Winston.

Kucera, H., & Francis, W. N. (1967). *Computational analysis of present-day American English*. Providence, RI: Brown University Press.

Nation, I. S. P. (1990). *Teaching and learning new vocabulary*. New York: Newbury House.

Parry, K. J. (1991). Building a vocabulary through academic reading. *TESOL Quarterly, 25*(4), 629–653.

(1993a). The social construction of reading strategies: New directions for research. *Journal of Research in Reading, 16*(2), 148–158.

(1993b). Too many words: Learning the vocabulary of an academic subject. In T. Huckin, M. Haynes, & J. Coady (Eds.), *Second language reading and vocabulary acquisition* (pp. 109–129). Norwood, NJ: Ablex.

Saragi, T., Nation, I. S. P., & Meister, G. F. (1978). Vocabulary learning and reading. *System, 6*(2), 72–78.

Sudarkasa, N. (1982). African and Afro-American family structure. In J. B. Cole (Ed.), *Anthropology for the eighties* (pp. 132–160). New York: Free Press.

Van Daalen-Kapteijns, N., & Elshout-Mohr, M. (1981). The acquisition of word meaning as a cognitive learning process. *Journal of Verbal Learning and Verbal Behavior, 20*, 386–399.

# 5 Oral production of vocabulary
## A case study

### Roann Altman

Despite general consensus as to the importance of the lexicon as an area for investigation, the research itself has taken many different paths. Nation, for example, in his review of the literature (1982), emphasized the following issues in vocabulary instruction: (1) whether vocabulary should be taught directly, (2) guidelines for instruction, and (3) the relative efficacy of techniques depending on whether the goal was receptive or productive learning. Gass (1987) presented research on the nature of the lexicon itself: (1) the nature of the learning of the lexicon, (2) lexical organization, and (3) lexical use. Carter's introduction in Nation and Carter (1989) offered an overview in terms of (1) quantity, (2) processing, (3) evaluation, (4) difficulty, and (5) development. And Huckin, Haynes, and Coady (1993) have most recently chosen to focus on the intimate connection between vocabulary acquisition and reading. The research presented here focuses on the *process* of vocabulary acquisition in the second or foreign language context.

## Background

In order to be able to focus on questions concerning the process of vocabulary acquisition, an applied study was determined to be more appropriate than an experimental study because it would allow the research to be conducted in natural learning situations, with minimal researcher intervention (Firestone & Dawson, 1988).

Because I was myself at the stage of learning a language where I had passed the initial focus on grammar and was beginning to turn my attention to the task of vocabulary acquisition, I decided to use myself as subject in a longitudinal case study of the process of vocabulary acquisition.[1]

The author would like to thank Andrew Cohen, Dick Schmidt, Jim Coady, Yishai Tobin, Elda'a Weizman, and Lewis Glinert for comments on various versions of this chapter (first presented as a paper at AILA 1990 and later revised for TESOL 1991). All errors of interpretation, however, rest with the learner/researcher.
1 Granted, bias can result from the researcher-as-subject paradigm. Nevertheless, it was felt that the advantage of constant presence of self-as-researcher over an extended period of time during the language learning process was a benefit that could not be matched by any other approach.

The language I was studying was Hebrew, a language that presents a particular challenge for a native English speaker. Not only is it a non-Indo-European language (and thus most of its vocabulary is not cognate with English), but it is written with a non-Roman alphabet – thus precluding easy visual recognition of even those words that may have had a Latin base.

The general research questions posed at the beginning of the study were:

1. To what can successful productive vocabulary use be attributed?
2. What particular stages in development can be identified?
3. How can vocabulary production be made more successful?

## Hebrew

Hebrew, a Semitic language, is characterized by words being related to each other through common consonantal roots; that is, most words are composed of a root of usually three consonants, and morphological variations (e.g., plurals, nominal compounds) are formed primarily by patterns of internal vowel alternation and affixation (vowels and consonants). Such patterning is particularly evident in the verb system, where seven related forms, each usually with a different meaning, are derived from one triconsonantal root. Nouns, adjectives, and adverbs are often similarly patterned. A sample root in all seven forms – each one called a *binyan* (meaning *structure*) – can be seen in Figure 1.²

The three-consonant root for this verb is *k-t-b,* where the stops *b* and *k* alternate with the fricatives *v* and *x* in accordance with morphophonemic rules. While the *binyanim* are basically grammatical categories, their intimate connection with the semantics of the verb is evident particularly in *piel* (intensive), *hitpael* (reflexive/reciprocal), and *hifil* (causative), where a switch to a different *binyan* results in an alteration to the basic meaning. The fact that the form of the verb in Hebrew includes more semantic meaning than just the meaning of the three-consonant root is what makes the verb system such a rich source of data for vocabulary

2 The semantic functions listed in Figure 1 are not as clear as they appear to be. Although so taught during the early stages of language learning, it becomes evident, even to the learner, that *nifal* (P2) is not just passive but can also be a regular intransitive verb (e.g., *nixnas* – enter), and that *hitpael* (P4) can also be something other than reciprocal or reflexive (e.g., *hitkabel* – BE received, a middle verb [Berman, 1982]). Because of the complexity of the system, the expanded range of semantic possibilities is rarely presented to Hebrew language learners. It is, on the other hand, a subject central to courses on Hebrew linguistics and a frequent topic at conferences on Hebrew language teaching. As a result of the complexity, the full system may never be fully transparent to most adult second language learners.

| English | Binyan[a] | Semantic function | Hebrew[b] |
|---|---|---|---|
| write | paal (P1)[a] | regular active | katav |
| BE written | nifal (P2) | passive P1 | nixtav |
| engrave | piel (P3) | active; intensive P1 | kitev[c] |
| correspond | hitpael (P4) | reflexive/reciprocal[d] | hitkatev |
| dictate | hifil (P5) | causative P1 | hixtiv |
| written (participle) | pual (P6)[e] | passive P3 | katuv |
| BE dictated | hufal (P7)[e] | passive P5 | huxtav |

[a]Each of the *binyan* patterns has a name based on the three-consonant root for verb – p-ʂ-l, incorporated with the vowel patterns representative of that *binyan*. These forms are each stressed on the first syllable.

[b]In accordance with dictionary listings, the verbs in Hebrew are given in their third person past form, though in actuality they can appear in any person, number or tense. Unlike *binyan* names, they mostly receive syllable-final stress.

[c]Infrequent form for this particular root.

[d]Although Berman lists the main function for *hitpael* as middle P3 (i.e., accusative/ergative), I retain the more traditional designation of reflexive/reciprocal as these are the functions first produced in this *binyan* by learners, and the functions listed in the textbook from which the language was first learned (Uveeler & Bronznick, 1980).

[e]Not included in Berman (1978).

*Figure 1   Sample root in seven major* binyanim *(adapted from Berman, 1978, 1982).*

acquisition. Learners must learn not only the meaning of each root but also the meaning of the *binyan* itself. Of course, once each of these basic *binyan* patterns is learned (the first five predominating during the early stages of learning), the full semantic meaning of any verb can be determined if the meaning of the consonantal root is known. Similarly, production of the full range of verb forms is facilitated because one need only plug consonantal roots in to the acquired vowel patterns of any *binyan*.

Studying the acquisition of verbs as a lexical item makes it possible to focus on a restricted subset of the vocabulary of the language yet gain insight into the acquisition of a system with complex morphophonemic rules. Results from the focus on the verb could also be generalized to other subsets of vocabulary in Hebrew – particularly the noun, but also adjectives and adverbs – because of the similar way in which the lexicon is constituted. The same three-consonant roots often appear in the other parts of speech, and, in the noun particularly, there are patterns called *mishkalim*, which are similar to the *binyanim* for the verb. To the root may be added any combination of prefixes and suffixes that carry meaning in and of themselves and may also affect internal vowel patterns.

## Context of the study

This study spans a period of approximately 6 years of language learning in both naturalistic and formal settings. The 700 hours of formal language instruction during the first 4 years was almost evenly divided between the foreign language context (i.e., university learning at an American university) and the second language context in Israel. The final 2 years consisted of entirely naturalistic learning in Israel.

This study is unusual among second language diary studies in (1) the length of time for which the diary was kept (more than 6 years), (2) the breadth of the study (formal as well as informal learning, second as well as foreign language, all skills, all aspects of language), (3) the focus of the study (vocabulary acquisition, particularly the verb), and (4) the corroboration of its content through the analysis of language production data.

# Method

## Description of the subject

This longitudinal case study consisted of a single subject learning Hebrew as a second and foreign language. The subject was a language major in both high school and college and had a background in several other languages prior to this intensive Hebrew learning situation.[3] The language learning history is summarized in Figure 2.

In essence, Hebrew was the fourth language learned after the three Romance languages Spanish, French, and Italian. Almost all learning of the Romance languages was undertaken in the foreign language context.[4] In contrast, Hebrew language learning was primarily foreign language learning for the first three years, with a switch to informal learning in the natural context for the last three years. This combination of formal and informal learning and extensive residence abroad resulted in Hebrew becoming the strongest spoken foreign language.[5]

3 Hebrew was actually the first foreign language I had been exposed to (at the age of 12) where I learned how to read (i.e., decode) and could understand a limited number of vocabulary items. Production was virtually nil.

4 Of special note is the fact that Spanish is the only language studied solely formally in which advanced proficiency could be said to have been achieved – and this only because of the fact that, ten years after the termination of formal study, a year was spent working in Spain.

5 Although I can barely speak Spanish now, I still feel that my *competence* in Spanish is better than it is in Hebrew. This loss of ability in a formerly stronger language has been noted as well, for example, by Rivers (1979).

| Language | Age at first encounter | Nature of encounter<br>Formal class/Informal natural | Proficiency[a]<br>L S R W |
|---|---|---|---|
| Spanish | 12 | public school 6 years<br>college 4 years | Spain 1 year<br>(age 31) | ACTFL Advanced<br>L>R>S>W |
| French | 15 | public school 3 years<br>college 4 years | briefly as tourist | ACTFL Intermediate<br>R>L>S>W |
| Italian | 20 | college 2 years | briefly as tourist | ACTFL Novice<br>R>L>S>W |
| Russian | 31 | adult ed. 20 hours | — | 0 |
| Portuguese | 32 | — | briefly as tourist | R>L |
| Arabic | 35 | adult ed. 20 hours<br>college 1/2 year | — | 0 |
| Japanese | 38 | adult ed. 40 hours | — | 0 |
| Hebrew | 37 | adult ed. 1 year<br>college FL 2 years<br>intensive ulpan[b] 3 months<br>college SL 2 months | Israel 3 years<br>(age 41) | ACTFL Advanced<br>L>S>R>W |

[a]Proficiency level is based on the ACTFL scale developed by the American Council on the Teaching of Foreign Languages (1986).
[b]Ulpan is the name given to the intensive language-learning program offered in Israel to promote rapid learning of Hebrew by new (adult) immigrants.

Figure 2 *Language learning history of the learner/researcher.*

## Journal entries

Throughout the language learning experience – as often as possible and as consistently as possible – an attempt was made to write down thoughts regarding language learning.

There were three basic types of entries:

1. Specific and detailed about a particular language item or situation
   a. Notes in margins of language materials (e.g., books, newspapers, class notes, tests)
   b. A minijournal of specific perceptions (usually difficulties) in listening and speaking
   c. Entries regarding specific incidents (e.g., language production or processing difficulties; reactions to data elicitation instruments)
2. More general and retrospective about language production or processing or the teaching-learning environment
3. Pretheoretical focusing on issues of language learning, language teaching, cognition, and the organization of knowledge

## Data elicitation instruments

The objective measures used to supplement the introspective journal data were language elicitation instruments:

1. *Oral storytelling.* An audio-taped oral recounting of the Pear Film – a 7-minute, silent film that has served as the elicitation instrument for numerous language analysis and language learning studies (see Chafe, 1980, for example).
2. *Oral storytelling in written form.* A written story based on a series of six pictures appearing in a popular composition book. (The written data have been included because the writing was nothing more than a putting down on paper of an oral story.)
3. *Oral interview.* An audio-taped interview between myself and a native speaker of the language (either a current or a former teacher).

As it was quite possible that these data elicitation instruments (particularly the oral storytellings) might be constraining the type of verbs produced because of the restricted contexts, it was decided to add a measure that would be less restricted in scope and might also provide evidence of verb production in formal contexts. Thus, at the end of 5½ years, the following was added:

4. *Formal lecture.* An audio-taped lecture I gave on the topic of language learning to directors of intensive Hebrew language programs. (I outlined the lecture in Hebrew in advance and delivered it basically extemporaneously, referring to the outline only for the order of ideas.)

Since even the formal lecture presented a context that was restrictive in its own right (i.e., by topic of lecture chosen), I was concerned that I would still not be getting a true picture of my overall verb-production ability. It would have been ideal to keep track of all new instances of verbs I produced, given that I, as researcher, was always present during learning, and I was keeping a journal of my language learning. This, however, was impossible in reality, because spoken language goes by so quickly, items produced are not always held in short-term memory long enough for post hoc recording, and it is not always possible to communicate and write at the same time. However, since I often found myself checking what I knew or didn't know – by marking items as known productively, I therefore decided to assess my knowledge (both receptive and productive) of a core set of verbs in the language via a fifth data elicitation instrument:

5. *Self-assessment.* A categorization of some 800 verbs from a popular verb book (Tarmon & Uval, 1978) into five categories ranging from full productive use to unknown.

## Data collection

The first three data elicitation instruments (storytellings and oral interview) were administered at four different times over a 1½ year period – the first time after 300 hours of formal instruction, the subsequent times after approximately every 100 hours of formal instruction (or after one year if 100 hours had not been achieved). The lecture was taped at the end of 5½ years of learning.

The verbs produced during each administration of the three elicitation instruments and the formal lecture were listed in Roman orthography. Since the purpose of the study was to document vocabulary learning and not grammatical accuracy, all verbs were converted to their base dictionary form, that is, third person masculine singular past. For the self-assessment, administered at the end of 5½ years and again 6 months later, an alphabetical list of 816 Hebrew verbs (with their English equivalents) was reviewed and a number from 1 to 5 was noted next to each one:

1. produce – often/correctly
2. produce – lately/rarely/unstably
3. recognize – always/usually
4. recognize – sometimes/unstably
5. don't recognize[6]

6  This coding is similar to the Vocabulary Knowledge Scale (VKS) developed independently by Wesche and Paribakht (1993) but differs from it in that (1) the highest proficiency is assigned a 1 rather than a 5, and (2) there are two possible categories for assessing production rather than one.

## Data analysis

Three different types of analysis were conducted. For the multiple administrations of the three tasks, the number of verbs appearing in the baseline administration (after approximately 300 hours of instruction) were counted and compared with the number of verbs appearing in each successive administration. The new verbs produced at each successive administration were then analyzed to see if their production could be accounted for. The verbs produced in the lecture were compared to all those verbs produced previously and then further analyzed as to their indication of language development. For the self-assessment, the number of verbs falling into each of the five categories was tallied and then a percent was calculated for each proficiency category.

# Results

## Oral storytellings and interview

The results from the three data elicitation tasks administered at four different times over a 1 ½-year period are summarized in Table 1. As can be seen, several new tokens appeared at each successive administration. Nevertheless, the question was how to account for their appearance in production. Had they been explicitly taught? Had they appeared frequently in the input? In order to answer these questions, the journal entries were reviewed for the period of time immediately preceding each of the data elicitation administrations in order to ascertain if any record existed that related to each of the items. The results are summarized in Table 2.

Four types of sources of production were identified: *General* means that they appeared in class notes; *working* means that there were notes or journal entries indicating that the verb was either needed for a particular situation or was being worked on in some way; *interview* means that the verb appeared in the interviewer's preceding turn; and *topic* means that it was a verb central to a discussion or composition topic on which a great deal of class time had been spent. As can be seen, about half of the fifty-one new verbs can be accounted for directly in the written journal data.

In order to try to account for the appearance of the other half of the verbs, the tokens were analyzed according to the *binyan* to which they belonged. A summary of the data appear in Table 3.

The first column of data includes the total number of all new verbs added during test administrations 2–4. On the surface, there appears to

TABLE I. NUMBER OF NEW VERB TOKENS PRODUCED DURING
SUCCESSIVE ADMINISTRATIONS OF A SET OF THREE
ELICITATION DEVICES

| *Administration* | | |
|---|---|---|
| 1 | June 1988 | 51 |
| 2 | August 1988 | 20 |
| 3 | June 1989 | 13 |
| 4 | January 1990 | 18 |

TABLE 2. SOURCE OF VERBS PRODUCED ACCORDING TO JOURNAL ENTRIES

| *Data elicitation admin. no.* | *No. of new verbs* | *Sources in input* | | | | *Total reflexes accounted for* |
|---|---|---|---|---|---|---|
| | | *General* | *Working* | *Interview* | *Topic* | |
| 2 | 20 | 3 | 2 | 2 | 3 | 10 |
| 3 | 13 | 1 | 0 | 2 | 1 | 4 |
| 4 | 18 | 6 | 4 | 1 | 0 | 11 |
| | 51 | | | | | 25 |

TABLE 3. SUMMARY OF VERBS PRODUCED BY *BINYAN*

| *Binyan*[a] | *New verbs (administrations 2–4)* | | *Baseline verbs (Administration 1)* | | *Child L1 data Berman (1982, p. 178)* | |
|---|---|---|---|---|---|---|
| | # | % | # | % | # | % |
| P1 | 17 | 33.3 | 34 | 66.7 | — | 66.5 |
| P2 | 4 | 7.8 | 2 | 3.9 | — | 3.0 |
| P3 | 14 | 27.5 | 6 | 11.8 | — | 9.0 |
| P4 | 2 | 4.0 | 4 | 7.8 | — | 6.5 |
| P5 | 14 | 27.5 | 5 | 9.8 | — | 13.5 |
| | 51 | 100.0 | 51 | 100.0 | 1,049 | 98.5[b] |

[a]As established by Berman (1978), the numbers refer to the *binyan* categories as follows: P1 = *paal*, P2 = *nifal*, P3 = *piel*, P4 = *hitpael*, P5 = *hifil*.
[b]Berman notes that the total does not equal 100% because of the inclusion of participial forms that could be considered either verbs or adjectives.

be nothing unusual: approximately equal instances of P1 (*paal*), P3 (*piel*), and P5 (*hifil*). Nevertheless, this distribution differs radically from that of the baseline data (middle column), where it can be seen that most verb reflexes appeared in P1 (*paal*) – almost 67% – with very few in P2 (*nifal*). Which distribution more accurately reflects the distribution of verb forms in normal language production? To what can the more irregular distribution be attributed?

A look at the distribution of verbs produced by children learning Hebrew as a first language (Berman, 1982) shows a remarkable similarity to the verbs produced during the baseline administration. That means that, if the percentages in the middle and right columns of data are representative of developing language use, then the percentages in the left column of the table are clearly deviant. Although most new verbs added are also P1 (*paal*), they do not predominate. Also, the P2 (*nifal*), P3 (*piel*), and P5 (*hifil*) *binyanim* are overrepresented here, with two to three times as many reflexes as in the baseline data.

How can this overrepresentation of tokens from particular *binyanim* in the data be accounted for? Referring back to the extensive journal entries, it was found that many times during the periods under investigation there had been a focus of instruction on two of the *binyanim* – particularly P2 (*nifal*) and P5 (*hifil*). They seemed to form the core of the teaching curriculum (at least as far as the verbs were concerned) for students at this level of proficiency. A particular note made on 9/19/89 showed how the presentation of the root *r-sh-m* in all possible *binyanim* in the infinitive and third person masculine singular past helped me to sort out the difference between *nifal* and *hifil*.[7] I noticed the morphophonological differences (*capitalized*): NIfal – *lehErAshem* (actually an irregular morphophonemic form due to the problematic consonant *r*)[8] and *hiFIL* – *lehArshIm*. This focus on *nifal* and *hifil* carried over into the work being done individually on the language, whereby I would underline or circle verbs appearing in the easy Hebrew newspaper that belonged to these two *binyanim*.

The journal entries of this time period also indicate that, eager to sort these forms out in my mind, I had asked my teacher at the ulpan if stories

---

7   The absence of a clear model can lead to confusion, as it did during my first year of instruction where the teacher used the same three-consonant root (*k-n-s*) as the model for both P2 (*nifal*) and P5 (*hifil*) – which were easily confused because the first root consonant of the infinitive (*le-*) of each begins with the same sound /h/: *lehikanes* and *lehaxnis*. The problem did not get sorted out until I began looking words up extensively in the dictionary and found that the third person male singular past dictionary entry form was different for each: *nixnas* and *hixnis*, respectively.

8   Some verb forms in Hebrew are irregular due to the appearance of a problematic consonant in one of the letters of the verb root (viz., a guttural or a silent consonant) or the formulation of a verb in a different *binyan* for particular forms.

could be told in which these forms were prominently featured. The results of this request were noted at the time.

9/24/89   Got special lesson, as requested, on *nifal*. Then got special lesson on *hitpael* (not requested). Requested *hifil* but teacher made a face and said it's not used much.[9]

The request was partially honored by the teacher's providing us with a written story featuring P2 (*nifal*). This was not fully satisfactory, however, since my request for *hifil* was discounted and the input received on *nifal* was written. Apparently, I was searching for an oral model: I wanted to *hear* the story with all verbs in *nifal* and not just see them. I wanted a different exposure to the forms, a sort of oral input that would bring to life the forms presented by most teachers in the traditional way – i.e., in written paradigms.

This realization of the importance of the oral model led to the hypothesis that production of verb forms in the data elicitation tasks that did not have an apparent source in the journal entries was most likely due to the successful internalization of a morphophonological model; that is, once the consonantal verb root for a particular semantic meaning had been learned, then the root was applied to the appropriate *binyan* pattern and a new form was produced. The special attention placed on these newer *binyanim* in the classroom, particularly the reinforcing of forms orally through repetition and explanation, helped in the acquisition of a morphophonological pattern that could be generalized to new roots.

Examples of verbs produced during the new administrations that were likely to have been produced as the result of generalizing to a morphophonological model appear in Figure 3.

The overrepresentation in the data of P3 (*piel*) – the third of the *binyanim* with more items than in normal, developmental speech – might be attributed to the fact that it is next in the sequence of *binyanim* following P1 (*paal*) in terms of frequency and/or ease of learning. It is also equally likely, however, that an overdose of oral input with it was received from a linguistics class attended at the time, in which much of the discussion had focused on the use of P3 (*piel*) as the dominant force in verbal innovations in modern-day Hebrew.

In sum, the data elicitation instruments of film and picture-based, oral storytelling and an oral interview elicited a range of verbs. The journal entries provided explanations for the occurrence of these verbs, first by tracing prior encounters in the input and then by identifying factors that could account for apparent anomalies in the data. A comparison of baseline data with subsequent data revealed stages in acquisition: More common forms appeared first followed by less common forms as a result of

9 According to Berman (1982), however, *hifil* is a rather productive *binyan*.

| P1 paal | P3 piel | P5 hifil |
|---------|---------|----------|
| ana | bikesh | hexin |
| tafas | shina | hexlit |
| shaal | sixek | himshix |
| asaf | mile | hipil |
| kaas | miher | hidgish |
| nasa | tirgem | hisbir |
| pana | | |
| xazar | | |
| zaz | | |
| axal | | |
| shaxav | | |
| shavar | | |

*Figure 3    Verbs produced in accordance with morphophonological model.*

instruction and/or intensive exposure; more basic forms appeared first followed by more derived forms (e.g., passive, causative). Inasmuch as the data were derived from informal spoken sources, certain forms such as passives and participles were noticeably lacking, as was a wide range of verbs that would normally be present only in more formal discourse. This gap in the data was partially filled by the analysis of verbs produced as part of a formal lecture.

## Formal lecture

The formal lecture on language learning given to ulpan directors provided an opportunity to analyze verbs produced under entirely different circumstances. Success of production now had to be investigated not just in terms of the nature of the items produced (i.e., which *binyan* was involved) but also in terms of the relative overall success of verb production in a formal lecture context vis-à-vis an informal conversation-like context.

The general pattern of verbs produced during the spontaneous lecture based on notes is documented in Table 4. As can be seen from the data in Table 4, 202 verbs were produced in 18 minutes. On the one hand, this might be considered successful in terms of overall quantity of output, with an average of 11 verb tokens produced each minute. On the other hand, closer analysis shows that (1) only 54 different types are produced (in effect an average of only 3 types per minute); (2) only 14 of the 54 tokens were new since the previous administration of the data elicitation

TABLE 4. VERBS PRODUCED DURING LECTURE

| |
|---|
| Total number of verb tokens   202 |
| Total number of verb types   54 |
| Token-type ratio   202:54 |
| New tokens   14 |
| 8/54 types (15%) account for 106/202 tokens (53%) |

TABLE 5. EIGHT MOST FREQUENT VERB TOKENS IN LECTURE[a]

| | |
|---|---|
| *there is/there are* | 27 |
| *do/make* | 19 |
| *say* | 27 |
| *there was/were* | 11 |
| *study/learn* | 11 |
| *speak* | 9 |
| BE *able* | 8 |
| BE *possible*[b] | 8 |

[a]The next most common types were *need* (6), *think* (6), *take* (6), *know information* (5), and *know people* (4).
[b]BE *possible* is considered an impersonal verb for purposes of analysis.

instruments a year and a half earlier; and (3) a small number of verbs (N = 8 or 15%) account for over half the tokens (N = 106). These 8 types and their respective number of tokens can be seen in Table 5.

The lack of diversity in tokens produced, and the concentration of production in a very few tokens, can be explained quite easily by the nature of the task: The lecture had not been written out in advance; it was the first formal lecture being given in Hebrew; and the audience consisted of Hebrew language teaching professionals. Under the circumstances, then, it is not surprising that the output was restricted.

While delivering the lecture, I was well aware of the limited variety in the verb tokens because of my frequent recourse to English. At one point in the lecture, the students helped provide a word that I had first said in English. Yet I was simply unable to incorporate this new form into the lecture. The verb was causative *hifil,* and although I knew very well that the third person masculine singular past form was *heemid,* I was unable to adjust to the infinitive (*le-*) form, which required *lehaamid* due to a problematic first letter in the verb (*ayin*).

Of the fourteen forms that were new since the earlier data elicitation tasks, four belonged to a brand new *binyan* – *pual* (P6), the passive equivalent of *piel* (P3). The forms produced are listed in Table 6. In the

82    *Roann Altman*

TABLE 6. INSTANCES OF *PUAL* FORMS USED

| *mebusas** | 3 | based on |
|---|---|---|
| *medubar* | 1 | speaking of |
| *mefursam* | 3 | famous |
| *mekubal* | 1 | accepted |

*Apparently, the /b/ should really be /v/. Because of normal alternation in the language between /b/ and /v/, it is not surprising that the /b/ was retained here.

present tense, they are participles functioning as adjectives. They are included here because of their verbal nature.[10]

The rather sudden appearance of these forms at this stage of production can be accounted for quite easily. First of all, these are virtually the only forms produced in this *binyan:* no other verbs; no other tenses. As such, they were apparently produced as unanalyzed wholes, except for frequent appropriate person and number agreement; for example, third person feminine singular *mebuseset,*[11] *meduberet;* third person masculine plural *mefursamim;* third person feminine plural *mekubalot.* At times the third person masculine singular form was overgeneralized; for example, *mekubal* should have been *mekubelet.* The general success in number and gender agreement is most likely due to a high level of monitoring during delivery of the lecture. In one case, however, when the intended meaning needed to be *was received* (feminine), the past tense of TO BE was erroneously used with the present tense *pual* form, *hayta mekubelet.*[12]

The appearance of these unanalyzed passive forms in *binyan pual* had its source in earlier language encounters, as recorded in journal entries beginning November 1989:

11/2/89   Something changed this week RE my "knowledge" of the Hebrew language. . . . Why hadn't I learned the forms [for the passive]?

10 Since I ceased formal learning just at the point when the two passive *binyanim* would have been introduced, I do not remember ever hearing that the present tense forms of these verbs function as adjectives. I came to this conclusion based on my analysis of the data for this research. My induction has since been verified as correct.
11 This form actually should have been *mevuseset:* The *b/v* alternation, historically allophonic, is phonemic in modern Hebrew.
12 This is obviously incorrect, though I am not sure I know how it should be expressed. All that comes to mind is that a different *binyan* must be used: *hitkabla* (*hitpael*).

. . . If it hadn't been for the test items this week, I might not even have realized that it was something I had so little control over. . . . Just have received verb chart from ulpan. Aha! *Nifal* is the passive of *paal* – which is why it's the first passive we did; *pual* is the passive of *piel; hufal* is the passive of *hifil.* Now it's beginning to fall into place.

11/2/89   Earlier in the week I had been writing a letter in Hebrew and I wanted to say *I was surprised* but couldn't figure out how to form it, feeling, however, it was something like *\*hufta'a.* After doing the exercise, I found out it was more like *hufta'ati* – that the passive is formed in all three tenses.

11/2/89   But the revelation came today while I was in [secretary's] office and she was on the phone and she said: *Is it familiar/known to you [mukar lexa]?* What is so interesting about this form of the passive is that it appears in the spoken language and it is a passive form – something for which we would never use a passive in English. . . . Later, when speaking with friend, I needed to know if he was familiar with something, and immediately thought of *Is it familiar/known to you [mukar lexa]?* and said it.

12/21/89   Needed to use that – *I was invited [huzmanti]* – when speaking with [friend], but because she's a teacher, checked to be sure it was OK. Of course – and she was pleasantly surprised I used it correctly.

1/4/90   A sympathetic listener explained the passive form *capable [mesugal]* – which then came up the following day.

1/10/90   I asked [Hebrew language professional] if [something I had said] was OK. . . . He said yes, they say it now. I asked if it was *accepted [mekubal].* He said yes – thus also acknowledging my attempts at the passive.

5/12/90   Notice difficulty producing passive. *Students with low scores are not accepted here.* Had received *mitkabel* from interlocutor; so is it *\*nitkablu* or *\*nitkablim?*

7/6/91   During conference on Hebrew language, paid attention to passives produced and wrote them down. Had trouble distinguishing *nifal* [passive of most common *binyan paal*] from other forms that seem more adjectival in nature.

Since the journal entries referred to *pual* forms more often than they did to *hufal* forms, it is not surprising that the lecture data did not include any *hufal* forms. The entry of 7/6/91 points to the confusion resulting from the knowledge that *pual* and *hufal* were passives: They didn't look like the classic *nifal* passive because they usually appeared in the present tense, where they were actually participles and thus adjectival in nature.

| Date | Hebrew word | Translation | Binyan | Active correlate | |
|---|---|---|---|---|---|
| 9/88 | muzmanim | invited | hufal | P5 | hifil |
| 12/88 | mefuzarim | spread out | pual | P3 | piel |
| 2/89 | mushlam | perfect | hufal | P5 | hifil |
| 4/89 | mukdash | dedicated | hufal | P5 | hifil |
| | mugeshet | presented | hufal | P5 | hifil |
| 5/89 | mefutaxat | developed | pual | P3 | piel |
| | mefuzar | spread out | pual | P3 | piel |
| | meruce | satisfied | pual | P3 | piel |
| | menutak | cut-off | pual | P3 | piel |
| 11/89 | meudkan | updated | pual | P3 | piel |
| 1/90 | munaxim | resting | hufal | P5 | hifil |
| | mushpaat | influenced | hufal | P5 | hifil |
| | musmaxim | reliable | hufal | P5 | hifil |
| | mukdashot | dedicated | hufal | P5 | hifil |
| | mesugal | capable of | pual | P3 | piel |
| 3/90 | muznax | neglected | hufal | P5 | hifil |

*Figure 4    Early noticings of* pual/hufal *forms in the input.*

A list of the passive-form items noticed in input from as early as September 1988 can be seen in Figure 4. In all cases, the present tense, adjectival forms were the ones that were noticed. There is no way to know if these roots did not appear in any other tense in the data or if they just were not recognized as belonging to the same *binyan*. These forms had been noticed primarily because of their salience, all beginning with /m/. The fact that all the forms listed were present tense and adjectival led me to think that they are verblike only when they are not in the present tense.[13]

In sum, the production of the passive forms in *pual* during the lecture was triggered by the more formal nature of the task. This task also provided further insight into the stages of verb production in Hebrew; i.e., passive forms are produced subsequent to active forms. Confusion caused by the fact that what is traditionally called a passive form is actually a participle functioning as an adjective is likely to result in continued focus on these forms until clarification is achieved.

13 This has been verified as correct. I have avoided seeking a more exact grammatical explanation for this phenomenon in order to maintain my status as learner, without too much interference from me the researcher.

## Self-assessment

Despite the overall success of the storytelling, interview, and lecture as data elicitation devices, the lack of examples of a wide range of verbs made it impossible to further characterize stages in the development of the Hebrew verb. In order to compensate for the limited variety of the spontaneously elicited data, a self-assessment task of a preselected set of verbs was administered. The total number of items appearing in each proficiency category at each test administration (July and December 1991) can be seen in Table 7. As of July 1991, a total of about 37% of the verbs fell into the two productive categories (1 & 2), while 41% fell into the two receptive categories (3 & 4). By December 1991, however, there was a shift of approximately 30 items from category 3 (recognize – always) to category 2 (produce – unstably), so that now 43% of the verbs could be considered productive and 36% receptive.

To what can this major shift from reception to production be attributed? A clue might be found in a journal entry from shortly before the December self-assessment:

10/8/91   Feel a spurt, upsurge in production. Don't know what to attribute it to. Fluency – lots faster; new vocabulary – lots of practice with much vocabulary/verbs and in different forms.

Apparently, after some time spent increasing receptive knowledge of the language, some sort of threshold had been reached that allowed initial production of vocabulary – particularly verbs, albeit hesitatingly and unstably. Three years of formal classroom learning had been followed by two years' residence in the country accompanied by additional classroom learning. Notes had been made of forms that were noticed. The morphophonological patterns of most of the more common *binyanim* had apparently been internalized so that new verbs could be formed by inserting new semantic roots into the model as needed. In the self-assessment from 12/91, the verbs listed in Figure 5 advanced to category 1 (produce often/correctly).

Insights about vocabulary production can also be gathered by looking at instances of less-than-successful production. Analysis of several of the verbs rated as level 3 (i.e., recognize – usually) that failed to show improvement over the six-month testing period reveals that, apart from the lack of need to have used some of these verbs, some of them posed morphophonological difficulties in their formation. Examples include verbs such as *AfA, hivrIY, kafA* – each with at least one problematic root letter (*capitalized*), and easily confused pairs such as *hoda/hodiya*.

This self-assessment on a predetermined corpus of verbs resulted in a broader focus on overall verb competence (i.e., receptive versus produc-

TABLE 7. SELF-ASSESSMENT OF 816 HEBREW VERBS

|  | July 1991 | | December 1991 | |
|---|---|---|---|---|
|  | # | % | # | % |
| 1 produce – often/correctly | 211 | 25.8 | 224 | 27.5 |
| 2 produce – lately/rarely/unstably | 90 | 11.0 | 126 | 15.4 |
| 3 recognize – always/usually | 203 | 24.9 | 172 | 21.1 |
| 4 recognize – sometimes/unstably/ in context | 133 | 16.3 | 120 | 14.7 |
| 5 do not recognize | 179 | 21.9 | 174 | 21.3 |
|  | 816 | 100% | 816 | 100% |

| P1 | *paal* | yacar, yashan, shaxav |
|---|---|---|
| P2 | *nifal* | nixshal, nikba |
| P3 | *piel* | seyrev |
| P4 | *hitpael* | hitkadem, hitkasher |
| P5 | *hifil* | higdil |
| P6 | *pual* | dubar, sudar |
| P7 | *hufal* | huxan, huzman |

*Figure 5    Verbs produced often/correctly by second self-assessment.*

tive ability) rather than on individual verbs or *binyanim*. Improvement, or lack thereof, over time could further be explained by referring to the journal entries.

## Journal

The introspective journal entries served two basic functions. First, they supported the data produced by the elicitation tasks described earlier by helping to account for successful or less-than-successful production. Second, they served as primary language data themselves, helping to delineate the stages of learning of the verbs in Hebrew. It is the results of this second function that will now be presented.

Learner attitudes expressed in the journal entries were indicative of stages of acquisition: Positive entries indicated stages already passed; negative entries indicated areas being worked on. Lack of entries in a particular area usually meant that it did not pose any problem (i.e., well learned, not an issue) or had not yet entered the learner's awareness (i.e., beyond current level of competence). The journal entries analyzed for this study indicate approximately three major stages in the acquisition of the Hebrew verb.

The first, most basic stage occurred during the first year of learning, when a basic vocabulary and extensive instruction in the first, most common *binyan*, P1 (*paal*), was received.

4/3/88   I certainly know a lot more vocabulary now and am a bit more fluent with verbs and basic structures. But there's a trapped feeling inside that I can't speak. . . . Having studied for 1½ years at the university, I have gained quite a bit of knowledge about Hebrew, and can understand and produce some – but still don't feel comfortable with the language. I still feel outside it; it doesn't feel like mine, like I own it.

6/27/88   Verbs are floating around; glad teacher attached them now [by giving visual chart relating passive to active *binyanim*]; now much clearer but will we again focus only on the first three *binyanim* [i.e., active]?

During this time, a great many introspective entries dealt with particle confusion (specific particles are required following certain verbs) and difficulties formulating the future. But a year later, at the end of the fourth year of learning, a new stage seems to have been reached.

9/5/89   Ease of masculine and feminine and some verb forms.

10/31/89   I feel as if something is happening with my verbs. There are a whole bunch that are now automatic (except perhaps in the future; viz. *ekra – I will read*). . . . There's another group of verbs that I'm actively working on: Either I try to produce and I'm understood and/or corrected or I want to produce but can't so avoid or say in English. Then there's another group – generally on a higher level of Hebrew – that I recognize but have never thought of using (*to give a ride to – lehasiya –* P5 *hifil:* second time encountered in two weeks).[14]

Many of the journal entries focused on verbs because these were felt to be central to the learning process, the lexical item that carried a large part of the semantics of the Hebrew sentence. At this time too (11/2/89) there was an awareness of how the passive *binyanim* fit into the language. Because the more common verb forms had become automatized, attention could be devoted to the less common *binyanim* (e.g., passives *pual* and *hufal*) and then to the production of verbs in different persons and in different tenses (especially the future). This increase in flexibility in using the different grammatical and semantic forms of the verb reduced reliance on the production of unanalyzed wholes.

In January 1990, during a very intensive period of ulpan study (5 hours daily), a list was made of verbs that were being worked on that were not

14 Although difficulty with the future is mentioned here, it is difficulty with a more complex form of the future that is referred to, one where the third consonant is morphophonologically problematic. The implication is that more regular forms of the future are not as problematic.

just simple *binyan paal*. The list included instances of both successful and problematic production of certain forms along with an explanatory comment. Examples of successful production included forms considered easy to learn (*hitpael*), forms derived from known nouns (especially *hifil*), unanalyzed wholes (mostly participles), and words used frequently (examples from all the *binyanim*). Examples of problematic production included particle selection, the future, imperatives, confusion between *binyanim* (e.g., *to rent from* – *paal* versus *to rent to* – *hifil;* transitive *hifil* versus intransitive *nifal*), and specialized verbs (e.g., *wear hat, wear shoes* – each an entirely different verb root from the root for *wear clothes*).

Following this period of intense, conscious focusing on the production of verbs in speech, a greater fluency in production was noticed along with increased attempts to produce the passive *binyanim* of *pual* and *hufal*. This seemed to suggest that a third stage of language development was beginning wherein forms of the less common *binyanim* would be refined and the irregular forms in the more common *binyanim* would be sorted out.

The learner awareness expressed in these journal entries enabled the identification of approximately three stages in the acquisition of Hebrew verbs. The stages are, of course, somewhat overlapping since not all forms in any one category can be learned at the same time. The trend, however, was as follows: That which was produced at one stage had been noticed at an earlier stage. That which was produced easily was once noted as problematic. That which was noted as being worked on would eventually be noted as known at a later time. These different awarenesses would recur each time there was an item that was noticed in the input or that was needed for production. They are what might be referred to as *phases* of development (Karmiloff-Smith, 1986, p. 165): steps that are passed through repeatedly for each element being learned. Insights about phases of learning were also noted in the section on self-assessment of verbs, whereby learners passed through phases of not recognizing, recognizing, and finally producing the verbs. The insights about stages of learning, however, became most apparent in the journal entries themselves.

## Discussion

The combined research methodology of language production data and journal entries greatly facilitated the investigation of the process of vocabulary learning. The unique situation in which the language learner served as subject for the research enabled continuous refinement of the methodology throughout the study. The extensive journal entries on specific language items, on language production and processing, and on general issues of language learning and teaching provided an extraordinarily rich source of data both for answering research questions and for posing new questions for future research. The research questions posed at the beginning of this study are addressed in the sections that follow.

## Accounting for production

The first question posed was, To what can successful productive vocabulary use be attributed? A summary of the success of production as measured by each of the data elicitation tasks appears in Figure 6. Success or failure in the production of verbs in Hebrew seems to revolve around the patterning of the verb form. Morphophonologically regular forms result in relatively more successful production; morphophonological irregularity leads to avoidance.

The critical role of phonology in acquiring verbs in Hebrew can also be deduced from journal entries that indicated that production seemed to lag significantly behind initial comprehension. Spontaneous production of a particular verb pattern following a one- to two-year latent period seems to suggest that production was stalled until a minimal number of instances of the form had been perceived in input. Once the underlying morphophonological pattern had been extracted from all the instances perceived, a threshold was reached wherein the pattern could then be applied to the whole array of roots (whose meaning was known) and thus result in a significant increase in production. This threshold was reached earlier for verbs in *paal* (as it is the most frequent *binyan* and is the first one taught) and for *piel* (rather frequent, the second *binyan* taught, and highly productive due to innovations). Because of the lower frequency of the verbs in the less common *binyanim*, threshold was reached later and thus the forms took longer to acquire. Forms with problematic phonology (i.e., complications in one of the root consonants or vowels) were learned even later, due to avoidance.

This influence of phonology on the acquisition of verbs seems to derive from the fact that meaning resides not only in the root but also in the vowel-consonant alterations of the various *binyanim*. This influence of phonology might not have been apparent had the study focused on a wide array of vocabulary items. Nevertheless, the question that must be asked at this point is whether this influence of phonology plays a part in the acquisition of verbs only (where acquisition of a system is involved) or if it plays a part in all vocabulary acquisition.

As noted earlier, the nouns in Hebrew follow their own patterns (mishkalim) wherein a three-consonant root combines with prefixes and/or

| Data elicitation instrument | Success |
|---|---|
| Oral storytelling & interview | 50% from learning/input<br>50% from phonological generalization |
| Formal lecture | limited success; avoidance due to phonological factors |
| Self-assessment | more successful if regular; less successful if irregular (especially morphophonologically) |

*Figure 6    Summary of successful production in three types of data elicitation tasks.*

suffixes, which carry their own meaning. There is nothing to suggest, therefore, that the pattern of acquisition of the nouns in Hebrew should be any different from that of the verbs. The adjectives too are often based on the same three-consonant roots as the verbs, with the adverbs in turn derived from the adjectives by the addition of a prefix /b-/. Outside the realm of Hebrew, preliminary research by Kelly (1992) reports on a study where retention of vocabulary over time was better when the material was presented both visually and aurally than when it was studied only visually. It is likely, therefore, that the acquisition of all lexical items in any language can be enhanced by introducing an oral component that focuses on recurring language patterns.

## Stages of development

The second question posed for this study was what stages in vocabulary development could be identified. By definition, a stage entails particular stretches of time in which qualitative changes have occurred in the underlying organization (Karmiloff-Smith, 1986, p. 164). In attempting to determine stages in verb acquisition in Hebrew, the journal entries were quite helpful in pinpointing the time and nature of such changes. As such, three major stages in the acquisition of Hebrew verbs could be ascertained: (1) more common, more regular *binyanim,* present and past tense; (2) less common *binyanim,* more irregular forms, future tense; and (3) least common *binyanim,* most irregular forms. Although a stage cannot definitively be defined until it has been passed, two additional stages might also be postulated at this time. (See Figure 7.)

Again, focusing on the verb system made it possible to identify stages of development because the verbs could be classified in several ways (e.g., *binyanim,* tense, regularity of phonology). The items seemed to fall into each stage naturally. There seemed to be no other order in which they

| | |
|---|---|
| Stage 1: | most common *binyanim* (*paal, piel*) and distinctive *hitpael*; regular forms; present and past tense |
| Stage 2: | less common, more difficult *binyanim* (*hifil, nifal*) regular forms; irregular forms more common *binyanim*; future tense |
| Stage 3: | least common *binyanim* (passive *pual, hufal*); more irregular forms all *binyanim* |
| Stage 4: | irregular forms, all tenses, all *binyanim*; clarification of *pual, hufal*; passives |
| Stage 5: | native speaker-like mastery of the entire system |

*Figure 7   Stages in the acquisition of Hebrew verbs.*

could have appeared. With so many demands on the attention of the language learner, the fact that an item was noticed and began to be worked on meant that the attention was freed up from other, more pressing, matters. At each stage, certain forms would be noticed that had "never been heard before" – though this was assuredly not the case. For example, the unanalyzed wholes of *pual* and *hufal* were only noted as noticed in 9/88 – though surely they appeared in the input previously.

## Improving production

The third question asked was how to make vocabulary production even more successful. Even if the stages of vocabulary learning just described seem to be fixed – (in support of Ellis's (1986) summary of the literature) – it may be possible to improve production by improving the rate of production (Ellis, 1986). Evidence in the journal entries seems to suggest that the rate of acquisition by this learner may have been faster than normal. Some reports on comments made by friends, colleagues, and teachers were later recorded in the journal:

10/26/89   Everyone says how good my Hebrew is, including teacher at ulpan where I had been studying [we had become friendly, though she was never my teacher] who said that my Hebrew was natural, without mistakes, without heavy American accent.

12/5/91   Two people from the university administration marveled at the level of my Hebrew – given the fact that I've only been in the country 2½ years.

Praise often followed use of a verb structure that was apparently slightly in advance of the overall proficiency level at the time of production. Here are three comments of this nature:

1/17/90   No sooner had I said two sentences and used the verb form for *needed to* [*hictaraxti* – a more advanced form apparently],[15] than a bilingual speaking friend said my Hebrew had indeed improved.

1/26/90   As soon as I said to service man visiting that the rain was getting stronger [*mitxazek* – a more advanced form apparently], he said that I speak Hebrew beautifully [*yofi*]. That he didn't think I spoke so well (I imagine from my halting Hebrew on the phone).

12/5/91   A university administrator admitted she is quite pleased with my level of Hebrew, and knows many people in the country a lot longer who, in situations warranting *if . . . had* [*lu* – word signaling counterfactual conditional] would instead use the simple if [*im* – word signaling the regular conditional].

To what can this perhaps more-than-successful production be attributed? The journal entries showed that input was always being noticed and that serious attempts were made to receive appropriate instruction. In classroom situations, the learner expressed appreciation when the teacher presented something that helped explain the verb system (e.g., relationship between active and passive *binyanim;* passives). Similarly, satisfaction was felt when something that had been brought up in class was noticed in the input. For example, while attending a lecture that was either boring or not comprehensible because of the high level of the Hebrew, an attempt was made to write down language forms that were heard in the input that were being worked on at the time. At the beginning, it was forms that were recognized but not understood or able to be produced; another time it was *hifil* verbs or *hitpael* verbs; another time nominals formed from verb roots; another time passives (*nifal, pual,* and *hufal*). It seemed as if the co-occurrence of opportunity in both the input and the formal learning situation greatly facilitated the mental processing, an advantage articulated by Spolsky in the Formal Language Learning-Teaching Condition (1989, p. 200). It was as if the more work done in a particular area, the more those items were noticed elsewhere. Encountering the language in multiple situations led to significantly greater processing of the language and concomitantly facilitated learning.

## Conclusions

This study has attempted to account for the acquisition of vocabulary – particularly the verbs – by an adult learner of Hebrew. Stages of development have been ascertained; factors influencing the rate of development have been suggested. The nature of the methodology used in the study has

15  I have since learned that *hictaraxti* is a form created by nonnative speakers of Hebrew to force a distinction between *needed to* and *was supposed to,* both represented by *hayiti carix/c'rixa* in standard Hebrew.

allowed for insights that might otherwise not have been obtained. Despite claims of the lack of generalizability in case studies, the task is not to generalize to other case studies but to a theory (Yin, 1989, p. 44). Consequently, issues of theoretical interest that surfaced in the study can serve as data for theory development. The issues of most relevance to vocabulary acquisition from this study can be subsumed under the following topics: (1) confluence of opportunity and need to produce; (2) oral model and automaticity; and (3) unanalyzed wholes and avoidance.

## Confluence of opportunity and need to produce

A key to the success of the language learner seemed to be the extensive employment of awareness – the focusing of attention on all aspects of the language to be learned. The two major sources of language for the focusing of attention were instruction and language input itself (oral or written, other-generated or self-generated). Regardless of the source, once an item entered conscious attention, the more likely it was to be noticed again. The more noticing was done, the more noticing was generated. Noticing appeared to increase geometrically. With learning taking place both in the classroom and in the natural environment, a condition of *confluence of opportunity* resulted, whereby an item noticed in one source was then more likely to be noticed in a different source – where it had not previously been noted. Of course, a single appearance of an item was no guarantee that noticing would be triggered elsewhere, but once a threshold number of items appeared, the item entered awareness and multiple opportunities reinforced the awareness.

One of the strongest triggers for noticing seemed to be the need to produce in the language. It raised an awareness unlike anything raised by simple input. When trying to produce the language, unsuccessful attempts to retrieve vocabulary items set off a signal to pay attention to any information that might provide the missing item. Recurrent instances of unsuccessful retrieval might even result in an active search for the item (in a dictionary or by consulting a native speaker, for example), which would result in the input being comprehensible, to the point, and answering a need. Although such a search might have to be repeated, the constellation of factors of need, awareness, and search contributed significantly to the possibility that the input would be attended to.

## Oral model and automaticity

The acquisition of verbs in Hebrew requires not only the acquisition of the semantics of the verb (based in the triconsonantal root) but also the morphology (for indicating person, number, tense, and meaning variations), and the phonology (interacting with morphological and semantic variants). Success in learning the semantics of the root alone, therefore, is no guarantee of success in learning all the possible variants. The study clearly showed, however, that acquisition was aided where an oral model for a particular form was provided. Continual appearance of this oral model in the input resulted in the learner's having been exposed to a threshold number of instances, which facilitated the internalization of the underlying phonological form. This internalization of the underlying model then contributed to success in verb production, wherein novel forms were created by incorporating known semantic roots into the acquired underlying model.

Automaticity resulted from repeated attempts at production: Each attempt at retrieval served as a prime for each successive attempt. The first attempt at creative construction was crucial particularly in serving as self-generated input for future production attempts. Thereafter, the more attempts at production, the more opportunities for retrieval, and the quicker the response was likely to be. Thus, verbs created just once were more easily produced at each successive attempt. This automaticity applied both to the retrieval of the semantic root itself and to retrieval of the underlying morphophonological verb form.

## Unanalyzed wholes and avoidance

Two means of language production include the production of unanalyzed wholes or the creative construction of language according to rules. In this study a great deal of data was presented showing that verb production in the early stages consisted primarily of unanalyzed wholes. Even in cases where verbs reflected person and number agreement, the further modifications required for different tenses were often not mastered until much later on.

The production of unanalyzed wholes was only one manifestation of production caused by lack of knowledge. Another major manifestation of insufficient knowledge was the production of forms that may have been correct, in and of themselves, but were probably much simpler than the forms required by the situation. This avoidance of more advanced forms was a deliberate production strategy that permeated all aspects of vocabulary production (viz., semantics, morphology, and phonology). Primary evidence for this practice was found in the journal entries on everyday speech production and in the journal entries accompanying data from the elicitation instruments. These data regarding the extent of avoidance (particularly due to phonological complications) were obtained only as a result of the extensive learner introspections produced in the journal entries. A study based solely on language production data by definition could not have revealed such avoidance strategies.

# Implications

The richness of the diary as a source of information on language processing reaffirms its usefulness as a source of data for case study research. The
fact that many insights would not have been available to the researcher
had the researcher not also been the language learner confirms the usefulness of this design in contributing to theory development.

Some research questions that derive from the insights of this study are:

1. a. What combination of confluence of opportunity (formal learning
      versus naturalistic contexts; oral versus written input) works best?
   b. What combination of language production activities (teacher-
      generated versus learner-generated) works best?
2. a. What is the threshold number of instances that a learner must
      encounter orally in order for a recurring pattern to be internalized?
   b. How much practice is needed for the production of an item to be
      considered automatic?
3. a. At what point is an item that is produced considered a creative
      construction rather than an unanalyzed whole (i.e., where un-
      analyzed whole is considered a form previously encountered by the
      learner in exactly the same form as the form produced)?
   b. How can information about avoidance be utilized to improve
      instruction?

Although the lexical data for this research consisted only of verbs, the
similarity of the nominal system and the derivation of adjectives from the
verbal forms indicate that the conclusions could apply to the acquisition
of any vocabulary items. It has always been known that vocabulary learning is facilitated by input factors such as frequency and saliency. Learner
introspections here have identified several other factors that facilitate
vocabulary acquisition: the presence of oral models, confluence of opportunity, and the need to produce. It has been shown that unanalyzed
wholes make up a significant portion of production until an item is
completely mastered, and that avoidance is a significant production
strategy – undetectable except through an introspective study such as this
one. If these points of avoidance can more easily be identified in the
language learning situation, then learning can be maximized by capitaliz-
ing on the need to produce. If vocabulary acquisition passes through
certain immutable stages, and only the rate of acquisition can be influenced, then the best approach seems to be oral input models in a variety
of contexts with monitoring of avoidance when required to produce the
language. Being provided with a lexical item at the point of need may just
be the key to maximizing vocabulary acquisition.

# References

*ACTFL Proficiency Guidelines.* (1986). Hastings-on-Hudson, NY: American Council on the Teaching of Foreign Languages.

Bailey, K. M. (1983). Competitiveness and anxiety in adult second language learning: Looking *at* and *through* the diary studies. In H. W. Seliger and M. L. Long (Eds.), *Classroom oriented research in second language acquisition* (pp. 67–103). Rowley, MA: Newbury House.

Barnard, H. (1971). *Advanced English vocabulary.* Rowley, MA: Newbury House.

Berman, R. (1978). *Modern Hebrew structure.* Tel Aviv: University Publishing Projects.

    (1982). Verb-pattern alternation: The interface of morphology, syntax, and semantics in Hebrew child language. *Journal of Child Language, 9,* 169–191.

Chafe, W. (Ed.) (1980). *The pear stories: Cognitive, cultural, and linguistic aspects of narrative production.* Norwood, NJ: Ablex.

Ellis, R. (1986). *Understanding second language acquisition.* Oxford: Oxford University Press.

Firestone, W. A., & Dawson, J. A. (1988). Approaches to qualitative data analysis: Intuitive, procedural, and intersubjective. In D. M. Fetterman (Ed.), *Qualitative approaches to evaluation in education: The silent scientific revolution* (pp. 209–221). New York: Praeger.

Gass, S. M. (Ed.). (1987). *Studies in second language acquisition. Special issue: The use and acquisition of the second language lexicon, 9,* 128–262.

Huckin, T., Haynes, M., & Coady, J. (Eds.). (1993). *Second language reading and vocabulary learning.* Norwood, NJ: Ablex.

Karmiloff-Smith, A. (1986). Stage/structure versus phase/process. In I. Levin (Ed.), *Stage and structure: Reopening the debate* (pp. 164–190). Norwood, NJ: Ablex.

Kelly, P. (1992). Does the ear assist the eye in the long-term retention of lexis? *IRAL, 18,* 137–145.

McLaughlin, B. (1987) *Theories of second-language learning.* London: Edward Arnold.

Meara, P. (Ed.). (1983). *Vocabulary in a second language: Bibliography.* London: Centre for Information on Language Teaching and Research.

    (1987). *Vocabulary in a second language.* Vol. 2. London: Centre for Information on Language Teaching and Research.

Meisel, J., Clahsen, H., & Pienemann, M. (1981). On determining developmental stages in natural second language acquisition. *Studies in Second Language Acquisition, 3,* 109–135.

Nation, I. S. P. (1982). Beginning to learn foreign vocabulary: A review of the research. *RELC Journal, 13,* 14–36.

Nation, I. S. P., & Coady, J. (1988). Vocabulary and reading. In R. Carter and M. McCarthy (Eds.), *Vocabulary and language teaching* (pp. 97–110). London: Longman.

Nation, P., & Carter, R. (Eds.). (1989). *Vocabulary acquisition,* AILA Review, 6. Amsterdam, NL: Association Internationale de Linguistique Appliquée.

Patton, M. Q. (1980). *Qualitative evaluation methods.* Beverly Hills, CA: Sage.

Rivers, W. (1979). Learning a sixth language: An adult learner's diary. *Canadian Modern Language Review, 36,* 67–82.

Spolsky, B. (1989). *Conditions for second language learning: Introduction to a general theory.* Oxford: Oxford University Press.

Tarmon, A., & Uval, E. (Eds.). (1978). *Hebrew verb tables.* Jerusalem: Tamir.

Uveeler, L., & Bronznick, N. M. (1980). *HaYesod, Fundamentals of Hebrew.* Jerusalem: Feldheim Publishers.

Wesche, M., & Paribakht, T. S. (1993). Assessing vocabulary knowledge: Depth vs. breadth. Paper presented at 1993 AAAL Conference, Atlanta, GA, April 16–19.

White, P. (1980). Limitations on verbal reports of internal events. *Psychological Review, 87,* 105–112.

Yin, R. K. (1989). *Case study research: Design and methods.* Applied Social Research Methods Series, vol. 5. Newbury Park, CA: Sage.

# 6 Reading and vocabulary development in a second language

## A case study

William Grabe and Fredricka L. Stoller

## Introduction

Researchers in reading seldom have the opportunity to experience, as adults, an extended period of time learning to read. Although it is virtually impossible to have such an adult experience in one's first language, it is possible to find oneself in such a fortuitous situation in a second language (L2) context. This situation arose for the first author of this chapter when he spent 5 months in Brazil in 1990. Since he was not a speaker or reader of Portuguese, he took that opportunity to learn to read in Portuguese. This paper is a report of that case study, the outcomes after 5 months, and the records and reflections on the experience. As a case study, this report cannot make claims for statistical generalizations. There are, however, a number of important methodological advantages and research insights to this type of case study that cannot easily be explored experimentally (McCormick, 1993; Neuman & McCormick, 1995).

As a research methodology, a small number of published case studies document the learning of a second or foreign language and second language (L2) teacher education (Bailey, 1980, 1983; Porter, Goldstein, Leatherman, & Conrad, 1990; Schmidt & Frota, 1986; Schumann, 1980; Schumann & Schumann, 1977; see Bailey, 1990, for a review of diary studies in teacher education). Few case studies, however, specifically address the development of L2 reading and vocabulary skills (see Parry, 1993). The research reported here represents an effort to explore L2 reading and vocabulary development through such a methodology. The case study was designed with the following objectives in mind: (1) to analyze the development of reading abilities in a second language, (2) to consider the relationship between reading development and vocabulary acquisition, (3) to explore the relationship between reading development and general comprehension processing (i.e., the comprehension processes

Acknowledgment and thanks to the following members of the PUC-Rio faculty for participating in and contributing to this study: Beatriz Maria Fortes Figueiredo, Ines de Kayon Miller, Lucia Pacheco de Oliveira.

involved in both reading and listening), and (4) to examine the relationship between reading development and overall L2 language acquisition.

Like many case studies, this one involved the use of multiple sources of evidence (i.e., a set of systematic reading routines and listening routines, journal keeping, and a number of evaluation procedures), all converging on the same set of issues (Yin, 1989, 1993). As a result of follow-up analyses, it is possible to make observations on L2 reading development, vocabulary acquisition, comprehension development, and overall language acquisition.

## Language learning background of case study subject

Before going to Brazil, Bill, the subject of this study, had had a number of language learning experiences, though none was particularly successful; Bill retained little from these experiences and characterized himself as a somewhat poor language learner. His first two language learning opportunities involved instruction in two Romance languages, specifically Spanish and French. He studied Spanish from 1968 to 1970 in an American university, but in subsequent years he never used Spanish in any reinforcing contexts. He learned French while in the U.S. Peace Corps from 1973 to 1976 and could use French to function adequately in the host country. The French learned abroad, and a reading course in an American university in 1977, placed his French at a third-year college level at the time of taking the reading course. Five years later, in 1982, Bill passed a university reading exam in French. Since then, he has neither read nor spoken French. At the time of the case study, neither language was active, and the actual number of still-remembered vocabulary items was quite small. Despite the fact that Bill had some passive knowledge about Romance languages from these two language learning experiences, it was assumed, at the onset of the case study, that these languages would not have a major impact on Bill's learning of Portuguese. Nonetheless, it was recognized that the existence of Romance language cognates would make reading comprehension in Portuguese more accessible for him (Holmes & Ramos, 1993). Bill also studied three non-Romance languages: Moroccan Arabic, Chinese, and Navajo. None of these learning experiences was particularly successful, and Bill claims very little remaining knowledge in any of these languages.

In addition to these language learning experiences, Bill had lived overseas a number of times before going to Brazil. He lived in England for 5 months in 1971, Morocco for 3 years from 1973 to 1976, and China for 1 year from 1980 to 1981. Because of these overseas experiences, it is fair to say that he was sufficiently adaptable to living in other countries that the culture shock expected from living in Brazil would not severely influence his efforts to learn Portuguese.

Bill went to Brazil on relatively short notice. As a result, he did not spend more than approximately 20 hours on self-instruction in Portuguese before departure, and at no time did he have access to a native or nativelike speaker of Portuguese. Upon arrival in Brazil, Bill was a true beginner in Portuguese; he knew very few words, had never heard Portuguese spoken by native speakers, and had no formal instruction in the language. Because Brazilian colleagues and friends whom Bill met during the first few weeks in Brazil all had excellent knowledge of English, he had few pressing needs for Portuguese initially. As it turned out, he had little need for productive use of Portuguese (spoken or written) for the entire 5-month stay.

## The language learning context of the study

Bill lived in Brazil for 5 months (March–August 1990) during which he conducted university classes in English at Pontificia Universidade Catolica do Rio de Janeiro (PUC-Rio) and gave lectures in English around the country to Brazilian English teachers. In most professional and social contexts, Bill was exposed to more English than Portuguese. During his first week in Brazil, he stayed in a Brazilian home in which all members of the family spoke good English. He then moved into an apartment where he lived by himself for the duration of his stay in Brazil.

Within 5 days of arriving in Brazil, Bill enrolled in a 5-week intensive Portuguese course at the Instituto Brasil-Estados Unidos (IBEU); the course met 10 hours per week (from 10 to noon, Monday through Friday). Because the intensive course had started before he enrolled, Bill missed the first week of class. He also missed the last week of the 5-week course because of professional commitments. Based on a review of the notebook and materials used in what turned out to be a 3-week course, it is estimated that Bill learned the basic tenses and basic sentence structures of Portuguese. In addition, he learned approximately 170 verbs and more than 500 vocabulary items overall; a number were English cognates or were recognized from Spanish.

## Beginning to read in Portuguese

On his second day in Brazil, Bill first began looking at the *Journal do Brasil,* a major Brazilian newspaper, although he could not actually read the news stories. He paged through the newspaper during the first week and tried to listen to TV news. After 2 weeks, he focused his attention on the Portuguese course, reading the textbook and casually reading the newspaper for an hour. During this time, he began watching a popular drama series nightly on TV; he continued to watch the series every night throughout the entire 5-month period. After 4 weeks in Brazil, Bill had to take a 5-day trip out of country. On his return, he decided not to begin the second intensive course at IBEU but to focus intensively on learning to read Portuguese. This decision reflected his professional interests as well as the research interests of a number of members of the PUC-Rio faculty. It also represented a goal that Bill felt was attainable within his 5-month stay in Brazil.

## Specific learning methodology from week 5 to week 21 (end of 5-month stay)

Beginning with week 5, Bill began a daily routine of reading Portuguese 3–4 hours per day. (See Figure 1 for a summary of routines.) His primary focus for each day's reading was the daily newspaper, *Journal do Brasil*. His basic routine for each day was to read the first page of the newspaper by (*a*) selecting the more interesting news articles, (*b*) reading those articles while underlining all unknown words on the first page of the paper, (*c*) looking up all the underlined words in a large hard-bound English-Portuguese dictionary, and (*d*) rereading the articles for comprehension. The words that were looked up were listed on a yellow pad; when the list filled the page, Bill would stop looking up words for that day. (On average, during the 80 days during which records were kept, Bill looked up 40 words per day. In total, he looked up 3,148 words during the intensive reading time; some of the words were looked up multiple times.) After reading the rest of the front page without looking up words, Bill continued to read the entire paper without underlining or looking up any other words.

This procedure usually took 2–3 hours per day. There were a number of advantages and motivations for this procedure. First, it allowed Bill to keep abreast of both Brazilian and international news on a daily basis. In addition, the stories often continued over a number of days, recycling vocabulary and allowing him to call upon a knowledge frame from the previous day. The stories were also often reinforced by nightly TV news programs that Bill watched regularly, beginning week 5. Furthermore, Bill was able to follow Brazilian sports and became an avid reader of the sports page, not only for American basketball scores, but also to follow the topics surrounding the Brazilian soccer team and the World Cup games. Finally, a major advantage of the newspaper was that front-page articles were short and fairly easy to comprehend; a three-paragraph story, with simple sentences and many names, led to a fairly successful reading experience. Consequently, Bill felt a sense of accomplishment with newspaper reading early on in the case study.

It should be noted that once he began the systematic reading routine, Bill realized that newspaper editorials were much more difficult to read than either front-page or sports news stories. Consequently, editorials became regular reading, with intensive look-up sessions, only during the last 2 months of Bill's stay in Brazil.

He made the decision to have a regular procedure for looking up a set of words each day in order to provide focused vocabulary input for some part of each day. Not only did it structure some part of the reading, but it also gave Bill some sense of which words he was forgetting and which he was able to remember. Finally, it provided an ongoing record of changes in the words he learned as well as a record of overall vocabulary acquisition for later analysis.

In addition to the morning newspaper reading, Bill began to read (1) Portuguese comic books from week 5 on (Mickey Mouse and Donald Duck seemed to be highly readable); (2) a Portuguese grammar book, written predominantly in English, which included simple readings and vocabulary in each short chapter; (3) *Veja*, a weekly newsmagazine, from week 8 on, and (4) other magazines and newspapers on occasion. Longer materials, such as simplified short stories or novels, proved to be too difficult to read in Portuguese. For the first 5 weeks of the study, Bill did not use a dictionary for reading materials other than the first page of the *Journal do Brasil*.

Beginning week 10, when Bill began traveling more extensively in Brazil and the normal reading routine was not always possible, he began to use a small pocket dictionary with other reading materials, particularly *Veja*. To continue the more systematic encounters with a subset of Portuguese vocabulary (e.g., the looking up of words from the front page of the newspaper), he felt that a certain number of words looked up in the pocket dictionary while reading *Veja* would be a workable substitute for the newspaper routine on each travel day. Bill normally read 2 hours per travel day.

It is important to note that he spent a large part of reading time without underlining and the intensive looking up of unknown words. Since much of the reading did not involve an active examination of vocabulary, but rather depended on extensive reading exposure, the theory underlying Bill's vocabulary development was that many exposures of differing intensities would gradually lead to a large recognition vocabulary (e.g., McKeown & Curtis, 1987; Nagy, 1988; Nagy, Anderson, & Herman, 1987).

Apart from the reading procedures followed on a daily basis, Bill attempted to watch a TV drama series and news broadcasts nightly. The purpose of this additional exposure was to see whether continual exposure to Portuguese vocabulary and reading comprehension improvement would lead to better listening comprehension (Sticht & James,

1984). At issue was whether or not reading comprehension would lead to a more general comprehension ability in either modality (aural or visual). The inclusion of the nightly news was intended to tap many of the similar topics read in the morning newspaper. It was expected that the listening comprehension skill would improve, with a slight time delay, as reading comprehension improved. Since Bill had 3 weeks of formal Portuguese instruction, he was familiar with letter-to-sound correspondences in Portuguese and was able to connect spoken words to written words.

The reading and listening routines described above were the controlled sources of Portuguese input in this study. As one might expect, there was considerable oral Portuguese in the background environment. On occasion, as Bill's Portuguese improved, he used Portuguese for daily routines such as transportation, shopping, and getting information. His spoken Portuguese, however, at no time matched his reading knowledge, nor did he make any systematic attempt to learn to be a good speaker of Portuguese (cf. Schmidt and Frota, 1986, for such an attempt). It should be noted that while reading and listening to Portuguese over the course of the study, Bill also read an English-language newspaper, the *International Herald Tribune,* and a weekly newsmagazine, *Newsweek,* on a regular basis.

Beginning the fifth week, Bill also began to make frequent entries in a journal in order to record daily language exposure, consider language learning difficulties, speculate on his own language learning progress, and contemplate larger language learning issues (e.g., the role of formal grammatical analysis, the usefulness of a dictionary, the role of cognates in written and oral communication, the ebb and flow of language learning, the influence of frustration on language learning, and the need for incidental exposure to language).

## Evaluative methodology used in the study

Three main sources of data were designed to be evaluated as part of the study. First, all front pages of the newspaper and all look-up vocabulary lists were retained for later analysis. The lists were used to examine which words were seen as persistent problems (based on the number of times each word was looked up), which sorts of words Bill was regularly exposed to in the newspaper genre (as opposed to vocabulary that might be more prominent in other genres), and which words were looked up only once or twice (e.g., because of less frequent vocabulary exposure or the particular salience or importance of the vocabulary item).

A second source of evaluation was Bill's regular (but subjective) journal entries concerning his exposure to, and learning of, Portuguese. Besides providing a detailed record of Portuguese language exposure during each

Weeks

| Sources | 1 | 2 | 3 | 4 | 5 | 6 | 7 | 8 | 9 | 10 | 11 | 12 | 13 | 14 | 15 | 16 | 17 | 18 | 19 | 20 | 21 |
|---|---|---|---|---|---|---|---|---|---|---|---|---|---|---|---|---|---|---|---|---|---|
| *Formal instruction* | | | | | | | | | | | | | | | | | | | | | |
|   Intensive Portuguese instruction | | X | X | X | | | | | | | | | | | | | | | | | |
| *Systematic reading routines* | | | | | | | | | | | | | | | | | | | | | |
|   Casual "reading" of the newspaper | X | | | | X | | | | | | | | | | | | | | | | |
|   Daily newspaper routine (2–3 hours/day) | | | | | X | X | X | X | X | X | X | X | X | X | X | X | X | X | X | X | X |
|   comic books (occasional) | | | | | X | X | X | X | X | X | X | X | X | X | X | X | X | X | X | X | X |
|   Portuguese grammar book, written predominantly in English | | | | | X | X | X | | | | | | | | | | | | | | |
|   Weekly newsmagazine *Veja* | | | | | | | | X | X | X | X | X | X | X | X | X | X | X | X | X | X |
|   Newspaper editorials | | | | | | | | | | | | X | X | X | X | X | X | X | X | X | X |
| *Systematic listening routines* | | | | | | | | | | | | | | | | | | | | | |
|   TV news broadcasts on an informal basis | X | X | | | | | | | | | | | | | | | | | | | |
|   Nightly popular TV drama series | | | X | X | X | X | X | X | X | X | X | X | X | X | X | X | X | X | X | X | X |
|   Nightly TV news broadcasts | | | | | X | X | X | X | X | X | X | X | X | X | X | X | X | X | X | X | X |
| *Reflections on Portuguese* | | | | | | | | | | | | | | | | | | | | | |
|   Journal entries | | | | | X | X | X | X | X | X | X | X | X | X | X | X | X | X | X | X | X |

Figure 1   *Sources of Portuguese input.*

day, the journal commentary also raised a number of larger language learning issues. The commentary allowed Bill to reflect on each day's readings and specific pieces of language or language use that caught his attention, speculate on his language learning progress, and consider specific language learning problems he was encountering.

A third source of evaluation was a battery of objective tests given to Bill by three members of the Letras faculty at PUC-Rio. At the end of months 2–5 (in approximately 1-month intervals), Bill was given a vocabulary test, a reading comprehension test (Portuguese to English translation test), a listening comprehension test, and a cloze test. The listening comprehension test was given to see whether more general language comprehension would follow reading comprehension even though Bill's listening exposure to understandable language was fairly limited. The cloze test was seen as a measure of overall language learning. Since there were no ready-made measures of Portuguese suitable for the purposes of the study, these measures were developed by PUC-Rio faculty specifically for this study.

## Testing Procedures

*Vocabulary tests.* The vocabulary tests were created by PUC-Rio faculty, who selected 800 content-words, in a pseudorandom fashion, from a Portuguese junior high school reader. These words were then randomly sorted into four groups of 200 words. Bill was given one of the 200-word lists at the end of months 2–5 and had 30 minutes to write an English synonym for each word that he thought he knew or was willing to take a guess on (see Riegel, 1970, cited in Coady, 1993). This testing procedure was effective because it permitted the testing of a large number of vocabulary items, it allowed for the evaluation of vocabulary (junior-high level) determined to be at the right level of difficulty, and it was easy to create. In grading the tests, each item was evaluated on a 0–3 scale (cf. Leung & Pikulski, 1990):

0 = no recognition of the word meaning or incorrect response;
1 = a general, but vague, sense of the word meaning;
2 = a good sense of the meaning of the word but not the best meaning or the meaning that a native speaker would provide;
3 = the most appropriate meaning of the word; a semantically and morphologically correct answer, parallel to a native speaker response.

*Reading comprehension tests.* The reading comprehension tests involved translations of passages, approximately 400–500 words in length, from junior high school textbooks. Bill was given 30 minutes to translate as much of the passage as possible into English, without a dictionary. The translations were scored holistically by two evaluators who assigned up to 100 points per test. The evaluators also provided a written commentary describing Bill's abilities, strategies, problems, and improvement on each test.

*Listening comprehension tests.* The listening comprehension tests were created by compiling 3 minutes' worth of TV and radio news broadcasts. Male and female voices were interspersed on each test, though a change of voice on the tape did not necessarily represent a new news story. Often two or three voice segments were combined, referring to the same news story. Bill listened to the tape three times. The first time, he could not stop the tape but could make any notes he wanted. The second time, he was simply to identify how many different news stories had been included on the tape and then give as accurate a written rendering of the information on the tape as possible (in English). He was permitted to stop the tape as frequently as needed but could not reverse the tape to listen again. Bill then listened to the tape a third time and answered a set of written comprehension questions prepared by the examiners in English. The questions required him to identify the main idea of each news story in addition to details, location, place, character identification, and so on. Again, Bill could stop but not reverse the tape. Three scores were assigned for each test: The first depicted the number (and percentage) of stories identified correctly as a percentage of the total number of stories on the tape; the second characterized the number and percentage of accurately summarized news items; the third represented the number and percentage of correctly answered comprehension questions.

*Cloze tests.* The cloze tests were created by using passages from Portuguese junior high school textbooks. Each passage had an intact opening sentence, 43–50 blanks (i.e., 50, 43 48, 50 for tests 1–4, respectively) created by random deletion (every seventh word), and an intact final sentence. Bill had 30 minutes to complete each of these tests. Cloze responses were scored as semantically and morphologically appropriate (one point), semantically acceptable but with a morphological and/or spelling error (½ point), or semantically incorrect (no points). Since there was only one subject taking these tests, there was less concern for maintaining reliability across test scores and greater concern for examining the nature of each item that was answered. The cloze tests were the only tests in the battery of exams that required Bill actually to produce Portuguese.

## Results from battery of tests

*Vocabulary tests.* Results of the vocabulary tests showed that Bill's vocabulary acquisition (i.e., vocabulary he learned well) doubled from months 2 to 5. As can be seen in Table 1, Bill correctly identified approximately

TABLE I. VOCABULARY TEST RESULTS

| Test | | Number and percentage of vocabulary items in each score category | | | | Total points earned/total points possible |
|------|---|------|------|------|------|-----------|
| | | *0* | *1* | *2* | *3* | |
| Test 1 | % | 59.5 | 5.0 | 10.0 | 25.5 | |
| | N | 119 | 10 | 20 | 51 | 203/600 |
| Test 2 | % | 53.0 | 6.5 | 6.5 | 34.0 | |
| | N | 106 | 13 | 13 | 68 | 243/600 |
| Test 3 | % | 55.0 | 4.5 | 2.5 | 38.0 | |
| | N | 110 | 9 | 5 | 76 | 247/600 |
| Test 4 | % | 42.0 | 3.5 | 5.0 | 49.5 | |
| | N | 84 | 7 | 10 | 99 | 324/600 |

*Note:* Total number of vocabulary items on each test was 200.

Grading scale: 0 = no recognition of word meaning; 1 = a general, vague sense of word meaning; 2 = a good sense of the meaning of the word but not the best meaning or the meaning that a native speaker would provide; 3 = the most appropriate meaning of the word (parallel to a native speaker response).

Test 1 was administered on May 2, 1990; Test 2 on June 6, 1990; Test 3 on June 29, 1990; Test 4 on August 3, 1990.

25% of the words on the first test, whereas in the final test he identified approximately 50% of the words correctly. Overall scores also showed a marked improvement, with increases from month to month. On the first test, Bill received a score of 203 out of 600 (34%). On the final test, he received a score of 324 out of 600 (52%). The most dramatic increases occurred between the first and second tests, with an increase of 40 points, and the third and fourth tests, with an increase of 77 points.

The largest vocabulary gains were actually made in the movement of words from the completely incorrect category (a score of 0) to the completely correct category (a score of 3). On the first test, 59.5% of Bill's responses were judged to be incorrect (0 points each), whereas 25.5% were correct and parallel to a native speaker's response (3 points each). On the fourth test, only 42% of his responses fell into the 0 category, whereas 49.5% were judged to be 3. The number of words judged to be partially correct, with a score of 1 or 2, decreased between the first and fourth tests.

*Reading comprehension tests.* Results of the reading translation tests show that Bill's reading comprehension improved dramatically during the 4 months of testing. As indicated in Table 2, the first month's translation was rated as 30% accurate and the final month's translation was rated as 90% accurate. The evaluators' comments note a movement from sen-

TABLE 2. READING COMPREHENSION (TRANSLATION) TEST RESULTS

| Test | Holistic evaluations by two graders, % |
|------|----------------------------------------|
| 1 | 30 |
| 2 | 60 |
| 3 | 80 |
| 4 | 90 |

*Note:* Test 1 was administered on May 3, 1990; Test 2 on June 6, 1990; Test 3 on June 30, 1990; Test 4 on August 2, 1990.

tence level translation with many errors and obvious guessing strategies to a much more accurate translation that reflects the idiomaticity of the original piece. On the final test, evaluators noticed that Bill was no longer strictly tied to sentence-by-sentence comprehension; his last translation not only captured the essence of the text as a whole but it also reflected the style of the original author. The only notable errors on the final test were due to false cognates.

*Listening comprehension tests.* Results of the listening comprehension tests show a marked improvement in Bill's listening comprehension. (See Table 3.) Although Bill had few difficulties identifying the actual number of news stories included on each tape, the results of the first test indicate that, after 2 months in Brazil, he had problems comprehending any aural information beyond simple and highly predictable main topics. Bill's summaries indicated that he understood only 40% of the information and the comprehension tests revealed a 20% comprehension rate. Yet, by the end of month 3, results reveal that Bill's listening comprehension improved greatly for news information. Brief summaries of the stories were 62.5% accurate and comprehension scores jumped from 20% to 51.4%. This progress in listening comprehension continued in the last 2 months as Bill provided more accurate summaries (100% and 75% for tests 3 and 4, respectively) and more complete comprehension (80.5% and 84.1% for tests 3 and 4, respectively). The anomaly in listening comprehension progress, specifically on the summarizing task in tests 3 and 4, may have been due to an overestimation of Bill's listening comprehension abilities; the PUC-Rio faculty included a purposefully tricky splicing of two closely related stories on test 4. The inclusion of this news item may have contributed to Bill's poorer performance on the summarizing task on test 4.

*Cloze tests.* Results of the cloze tests (see Table 4) verify a number of observations recorded in Bill's journal. Scores on the cloze tests remain relatively uniform throughout the study (i.e., 44%, 46.5%, 43.7%, 35%). Even assuming a "bad day" on Bill's part during the final test, it is apparent that the cloze test did not tap the same language skills as those

TABLE 3. LISTENING COMPREHENSION TEST RESULTS

| Test | | Number and % of news items correctly identified | Number and % of accurately summarized news stories | Number and % of correctly answered comprehension questions |
|---|---|---|---|---|
| 1 | % | 91.6 | 41.6 | 20.0 |
| | score/total | 11/12 | 5/12 | 7/35 |
| 2 | % | 75.0 | 62.5 | 51.4 |
| | score/total | 6/8 | 5/8 | 18/35 |
| 3 | % | 100.0 | 100.0 | 80.5 |
| | score/total | 8/8 | 8/8 | 29/36 |
| 4 | % | 100.0 | 75.0 | 84.1 |
| | score/total | 8/8 | 6/8 | 37/44 |

*Note:* Test 1 was administered on May 2, 1990; Test 2 on June 7, 1990; Test 3 on June 29, 1990; Test 4 on August 3, 1990.

TABLE 4. CLOZE TEST RESULTS

| Test | Score/total possible | % |
|---|---|---|
| 1 | 22/50 | 44.0 |
| 2 | 20/43 | 46.5 |
| 3 | 21/48 | 43.7 |
| 4 | 17.5/50 | 35.0 |

*Note:* Items were scored as semantically appropriate (1 point), partly appropriate (½ point), or wrong (0 points).

Test 1 was administered on May 11, 1990; Test 2 on June 9, 1990; Test 3 on July 1, 1990; Test 4 on August 3, 1990.

measured by the vocabulary, reading, and listening tests. Even accounting for partially correct responses, Bill was completely wrong (0 points) approximately half the time on each test (50%, 48%, 50%, 60%).

## Results from an analysis of subject's vocabulary lists

There were approximately 80 days in which Bill looked up and recorded unfamiliar vocabulary words from the first page of the newspaper onto a yellow pad. At the time of writing, words from the first 5 weeks of intensive reading had been compiled (N = 899) and analyzed. As indicated in Table 5, the words that were looked up most often were nouns and verbs; 49% of the words looked up were nouns or relative pronouns;

TABLE 5. NUMBER AND PERCENTAGE OF WORDS LOOKED UP BY
GRAMMATICAL CATEGORY

| Grammatical category | N | % |
|---|---|---|
| Nouns and relative pronouns | 443 | 49 |
| Verbs and participles | 315 | 35 |
| Adjectives | 84 | 9 |
| Adverbs and adverbial phrases | 43 | 5 |
| Prepositions | 14 | 2 |

*Note:* Calculations are based on the 899 words looked up in the first
5 weeks of the subject's daily reading routine.

TABLE 6. NUMBER AND PERCENTAGE OF WORDS LOOKED UP
MULTIPLE TIMES, BY GRAMMATICAL CATEGORY

| Grammatical category | N | % |
|---|---|---|
| Nouns and relative pronouns | 82 | 48 |
| Verbs and participles | 72 | 42 |
| Adjectives | 5 | 3 |
| Adverbs and adverbial phrases | 8 | 5 |
| Prepositions | 4 | 2 |

*Note:* Calculations are based on the 899 words looked up in the first
5 weeks of the subject's daily reading routine.

35% of the words looked up were verbs or participles. Of these 899
words, 171 were looked up multiple times (from two to six times). As
indicated in Table 6, the majority of words that were looked up more
than once were nouns (48%) and verbs or participles (42%).

## Results from an analysis of journal commentary

Bill maintained a journal in which he recorded his daily exposure to and
use of Portuguese. This journal was also used to record observations and
comments about the language learning process over the course of 5
months. Bill's decision to keep a journal was strongly influenced by
Schmidt and Frota (1986), who report on Schmidt's learning experiences
in Brazil based in large part on journal entries. Bill's observations, although different in focus, represent a useful replication of the Schmidt
and Frota study in that the case study reported here also examines the
extent to which extensive input, without a significant formal instruction
component, leads to the development of L2 reading abilities.

The journal comments that have most relevance to this paper fall into two categories, those that offer insights on the learning of new vocabulary and those that reflect on the enhancement of reading comprehension.

*Learning of new vocabulary.* In a large number of journal entries, Bill commented on the progressive nature of the development of word knowledge. Interestingly, Bill's observations are not so different from claims made by research on the development of word knowledge in L1 contexts (Beck & McKeown, 1991; Beck, McKeown, & Omanson, 1987). In order to summarize Bill's observations, it is convenient to present them as seven types of word knowledge. First, he noticed that there were words that were totally unfamiliar to him; these were words that he had never seen and did not understand. Second, he identified words with which he sensed a degree of familiarity. The words falling into this category were those that he had read before, and thus recognized, but he could not recall their meaning. Third, there were words that he felt he had never seen before, but that must have been in his environment because once he looked up the words and learned them, he noticed them everywhere (in the newspaper, on store fronts, etc.). The words falling into this category were usually fairly common words, making Bill think that he had probably been exposed to them before. For some unknown reason, he had not noticed them and thus had not looked them up. Fourth, there were familiar and understandable words that he had looked up at an earlier time and retained. Fifth, there were other generally familiar and understandable words for which, at a certain point in time, Bill felt a need for better, more accurate meanings. It seems that Bill was initially content with one meaning and later noticed that an alternative, more refined, definition might be more appropriate in a given context. These words were then stored as having multiple meanings. Sixth, there were words that Bill knew had multiple meanings. However, when he recognized the need for a less common meaning, he could access only the most common meaning. Words that sometimes fell into this category were cognates, though it was the minor, noncognate meanings that he had difficulty accessing while reading. Seventh, there were words that had multiple meanings; for these, Bill could access the most appropriate meaning at the time of reading.

Bill made other observations about the role of cognates in reading. He was surprised that his knowledge of French and Spanish, though limited, did not help him recognize Portuguese cognates initially. As Bill's reading abilities improved and his vocabulary increased, he noticed that cognates were more easily recognized in written form, though they continued to be difficult to recognize in speech.

Throughout the journal, Bill commented on the usefulness of dictionary consultation for vocabulary learning. Initially, he wrote that it would be impossible to comprehend any reading passage – with his extremely limited vocabulary – without some use of the dictionary. Toward the end of the journal (and case study), when he felt that he had reached a comfortable level of comprehension while reading the newspaper, he contemplated weaning himself away from dictionary use. Nonetheless, he decided to continue referring to the dictionary when he encountered unfamiliar lexical items because he appreciated the prolonged and focused contact with new words that dictionary consultation afforded him. In a sense, dictionary use provided the subject with an "accuracy anchor," a sense that he clearly knew the meaning of some of the words he encountered (cf. Hulstijn, 1993; Luppescu & Day, 1993). In addition, he felt that the conscious thought involved in deciding whether or not to look up a word was useful for vocabulary retention.

Bill was puzzled by the relative learning difficulties of different sets of lexical items, particularly those words that needed to be looked up only once and those that required not only multiple exposures but also multiple dictionary consultations. Bill commented that some words just "never seem to stick." He found it necessary to occasionally review lists of looked-up words and create a master list of 50–60 words, which he designated as "key" words. Bill wondered whether the words he was having difficulty remembering could be more easily remembered if he actively engaged in Portuguese conversation (cf. Schmidt & Frota, 1986).

Toward the end of the study, Bill stated that he had finally developed a basic vocabulary and a formal newspaper vocabulary that facilitated newspaper reading. However, he felt that he was missing a range of vocabulary, lexical items that fit somewhere in between these two sets of vocabulary. Limiting himself to the newspaper genre might have contributed to this gap. On a similar note, Bill noted that editorial writing was distinct from the news story genre. Although he developed some facility reading editorials, he shied away from editorials focusing on local issues because they were full of unfamiliar acronyms and required extensive background knowledge. When reading editorials on human interest topics, general economics, and world events, Bill experienced more success.

*Enhancement of reading comprehension.* Through an analysis of journal entries, it becomes apparent that Bill felt that his reading comprehension was enhanced when he could (1) recognize the conjugated forms of familiar verbs, (2) distinguish between transition words and nouns or verbs, (3) identify different forms of a familiar root word, and (4) realize that in certain contexts a cognate may have a minor, noncognate meaning. Bill also commented on the role of guessing the meaning of unfamiliar words and the impact of guessing on reading comprehension. He felt that high levels of frustration develop when a reader relies solely on guessing the meaning of unfamiliar lexical items; readers have a need to know that certain word meanings are correct so that they can continue reading with some level of confidence.

## Discussion

The goals of the study were to explore the extent to which extensive reading practice without formal instruction would promote reading ability and vocabulary development in Portuguese. Since listening comprehension is assumed to be closely associated with reading comprehension (Palmer, MacCleod, Hung, & Davidson, 1985; Sticht & James, 1984), it was also useful to examine the extent to which listening comprehension would develop along with reading, even though Bill made minimal effort to speak and listen interactively in Portuguese. The cloze measure, as a general language proficiency measure, was also included in an effort to understand the relation between reading and vocabulary development, and overall language proficiency.

*Development of reading abilities.* With respect to the development of reading abilities, it is clear that Bill made reasonably good progress learning to read with the primary input being extensive reading and bilingual dictionary use. Given that the L2 of the study was not very different from Bill's L1, and given Bill's prior, though limited, exposure to other Romance languages, the strategy of learning to read by reading newspapers was a successful one; reading extensively in a not-too-dissimilar second language contributed to an improved reading ability. Using this learning strategy in other L2 situations, such as learning to read Japanese or Hebrew, would almost certainly lead to a different outcome because of differences in script and syntax as well as a lack of cognates (cf. Altman, Chapter 5, this volume).

In this situation, the newspaper as text was a good reading source for learning to read (see also Kyongho & Nation, 1989). It provided much information of interest to Bill; the reading was purposeful and was not overly frustrating; and the newspaper permitted the use of a large network of background knowledge from previous days, from TV, and from English-language newspapers. The study also points out the need for motivation in learning to read. As is evident from Bill's intense and consistent routine, learning to read involves a belief that reading practice is important and a willingness to tolerate delayed gratification.

As a second observation on the reading comprehension results, it appears that reading newspapers is quite different from reading novels and short stories. Even the transition from front-page news to the editorial page required 2 months of reading practice. At the end of 5 months, a short story still proved to be too difficult for Bill to read. Thus, the genre of reading materials can have a major influence on reading performance, and one should not assume that reading extensively in one genre will prepare students for reading well in other genres (cf. Wodinsky & Nation, 1988). In particular, Bill noted that he was missing what he called "in-between" vocabulary for the other genres. In reading newspapers, the descriptive vocabulary and the nouns and verbs marking actors and actions were all grounded in real events in the near present time. Fiction, in contrast, involves more elaborate scene setting and descriptions of characters in a manner not found in newspapers. The words used for these fiction purposes were words that Bill, in effect, bypassed by reading only newspapers and news magazines. Thus, large sets of vocabulary that might be introduced through the reading of fiction and/or in formal instruction were missing from Bill's reading recognition vocabulary. These missing sets of words, it is argued, create a serious problem for a reader who suddenly switches reading genres.

The success of this study also supports the usefulness of a good bilingual dictionary for learning vocabulary and for reading comprehension. Unlike the assertions of many second language teachers and teacher trainers, a bilingual dictionary is an important resource if used appropriately. Bill's observations coincide strongly with those of Luppescu and Day (1993). In their study of 293 Japanese university students, they found that dictionary use improved students' learning of vocabulary. Yet, because dictionary use led to occasional learner confusion, learners need practice in using a dictionary appropriately. Although the case study being described here is quite different, Bill's observations coincide strongly with those of Luppescu and Day. The dictionary led to much vocabulary acquisition, though its use slowed down the reading process, and at times the dictionary entries were confusing. Common words with many meanings required some ambiguity tolerance and a recognition that such words would have to be looked up again when they reappeared in the newspaper. One additional point that can clearly be suggested from the case study is that the dictionary not only improved vocabulary learning but also contributed to increased reading comprehension.

Bill appreciated the support he gained from using the dictionary. Frequently, he felt that too much guessing led to great frustration. Perhaps, for adults, there are times when it is important to know that a word is understood accurately. The dictionary provided this "accuracy support."

*Development of vocabulary.* Many issues and observations specifically related to vocabulary deserve comment. First, results suggest that, at least with Bill, words do not remain a long time in vague or partially known transition stages. The results of the vocabulary measure indicated that there were fewer words in the in-between categories at the end of the study than at the beginning. We might have speculated the reverse: as more words are encountered, more will fall into a vaguely known category and be sorted out at a much later time as they become encountered more often (cf. Parry, 1993). This does not appear to have been the case with Bill. Instead, the sharp increase in vocabulary learning appeared to be through complete learning of basic meanings (a kind of automaticity; cf. Segalowitz, Poulsen, & Komoda, 1991; Stanovich, 1990).

Although it may be true that L1 readers have many partially known words simply because their overall vocabularies are so large, the same observation could not be made in this L2 case study. The vocabulary ability measure used in this study may not have been sensitive enough to "find" partially known words; however, given the large number of words encountered over 5 months of reading, one would have expected that even the testing measure used in this study would reveal partial knowledge of words. It may be that the extensive use of the dictionary facilitated the transfer of many words from a non-known state to a well-known state in a fairly rapid period of time.

A second observation about vocabulary involves the large number of words that were looked up several times. This is not unusual with words that have multiple meanings. There were many instances, however, when words were not confusing, abstract, or polysemous; they were simply words that Bill could not remember or that he was unsure of (cf. Luppescu & Day, 1993). Some words in particular, such as *recursos, cobrar,* and *exigir,* were repeatedly looked up but not readily remembered. We have no good explanation for this phenomenon, but we believe that it is common among L2 learners. Each learner seems to encounter some set of words that just will not be remembered. The reverse also seems to be true. In many instances, a word was finally noticed and remembered. It seems that such words then reappeared a number of times throughout Bill's reading over the next few days. The notions of attending and awareness, as discussed by Schmidt (1990; 1993; Schmidt & Frota, 1986), provide a good possible explanation for this phenomenon and its role in language learning. Finally, Bill learned some words after just one or two uses of the dictionary. We have no good explanation for this phenomenon either, though we generally accept the notion that some words are involved in a "fast mapping" in word acquisition (de Villiers & de Villiers, 1992).

A third general observation on vocabulary learning is directed at assertions made for the usefulness of word families or base words that provide meanings for various derived words. Goulden, Nation, and Read (1990), for example, argue that many words should be seen as a single lexical family of words for purposes of estimating vocabulary size. For them, lexical forms related by inflectional and derivational affixation do not represent different words. The implication is that many studies of vocabulary size are overestimated, and if vocabulary sizes are smaller than believed, then various types of vocabulary instruction become more relevant than some researchers assume.

Bill's experience, however, was quite different from the assumptions proffered by the "word family" position. In the case study, many words were recognized as related in some way, but that did not guarantee an appropriate meaning. In fact, many times Bill was well aware that a basic meaning was not appropriate for a specific derived word. It was apparent to him that the meaning of many derived words could not be determined from some other meaning of the word. Native speakers can look at sets of apparently related words and assume a connectedness, but the learner does not have sufficient language resources to do this; in many cases, Bill knew that a different meaning was intended in the text, and the alternative meaning of the word had to be looked up.

A fourth observation with respect to vocabulary learning involved the relative importance of vocabulary and structure for learning to read. It is clear that learning to read requires some knowledge of structure and grammar, though how much knowledge is necessary is not clear. Bill's experience was that a basic knowledge of structure was important; this included being able to recognize a verb by familiar conjugation suffixes and sorting out common irregular verb forms from similar-looking short grammatical words. Beyond the level of such a distinction, however, the finer points of grammar were usually unnecessary. (See Ulijn & Strother, 1990.)

If Bill knew who was being referred to by the grammatical subject of the sentence and recognized an adverbial that marked the time of the event, that was sufficient for most reading comprehension. A careful comprehension of all the possible conjugations of a verb was not important knowledge for reading. What was more crucial for comprehension was a continuous supply of new vocabulary (see also Bossers, 1992; Coady, 1993; Ulijn, 1981, cited in Huckin & Bloch, 1993). This matches well with what our own ESL students say. Students who enter L2 classes typically have the right intuition when they think that learning a language is all about learning words. This appeared to be particularly true of Bill's experiences in this study. Although it is possible to present specific counterexamples for reading in which grammatical information is critical, typically with scientific information, the overwhelming majority of texts he read did not require a detailed knowledge of Portuguese structure.

A fifth and final comment on vocabulary learning can be drawn from the evidence collected in the daily vocabulary lists. An examination of the words looked up every day revealed that Bill looked up more nouns and verbs than adjectives, adverbs, and prepositions. This reflects the greater importance of referential and content information over the need for grammatical information. Furthermore, it is the nouns and verbs that most typically carry unrelated, or only loosely related, multiple meanings (e.g., *portaria* could mean governmental decree, front entrance, reception desk, or entrance; *recolher* could mean to withdraw from circulation, to guard, or to take care of). For this reason, Bill may have felt the need to look up many of the nouns and verbs multiple times. It seems that he did not know whether a simple meaning for a noun or verb would apply or whether other meanings were intended in specific news stories. In fact, on many occasions, he looked up words multiple times to be sure that there were no other good alternative meanings to those he already knew. Perhaps this multiple look-up strategy finally accounted for the "automaticity" of many words on the vocabulary tests; that is, the greatest vocabulary gains were not in recognizing more words vaguely, but in recognizing more words exactly as native speakers recognize them.

*Relationship between listening comprehension and reading abilities.* Two comments deserve mention from the results of the listening comprehension tests. First, it seems apparent that listening comprehension followed closely along with reading comprehension in its development; that is, as Bill's reading comprehension improved, so did his listening comprehension. Since Bill made no specific effort to develop his L2 speaking skills and did not engage extensively in oral interaction in Portuguese, the cause of this progress is most likely extensive reading and vocabulary development, in combination with regular TV listening almost every evening. It would seem from this case study that reading and listening comprehension support each other, and that strong development in reading comprehension will assist the development of listening comprehension. This outcome coincides with the assertion that there may be some generalizable comprehension mechanism that can be developed by improving reading skills (Hoover & Gough, 1990; Jackson & McClelland, 1979; Palmer et al., 1985; Sticht & James, 1984). Furthermore, it is a plausible speculation that a strongly developed listening comprehension ability will assist reading comprehension if the learner already possesses appropriate basic literacy skills. It is interesting to note, in this regard, that words read were often recognized in the nightly TV news, but that recognizing words in reading after hearing them on TV was extremely rare. The bias from reading to listening in this study was most likely due to the particular learning procedures used.

Second, it was apparent to all concerned in this research that the tests of listening comprehension measured only abilities to understand a specific genre. At no time during the 5-month case study was Bill able to understand Portuguese conversations, lectures, directions, and so on, in any way that matched the comprehension abilities shown in listening to news stories. It seems, then, that genre exposure is also a critical factor in both reading and listening development (cf. Martin, 1989). The news genre, in this study, was well suited to Bill's learning needs (and interests); both oral and written news stories are short, use simple sentences, repeat vocabulary often, and provide familiar schemata for the learner. An interesting question that cannot be answered by this study is when (and if) such genre-specific skills would expand and transfer into good comprehension of other spoken and written genres.

*Cloze procedures as a measure of L2 reading development.* A general comment is necessary with respect to the cloze measure used in the study. It is obvious from Table 4 that this measure did not follow the trend of all the other measures taken. It quickly became apparent to the subject that the cloze measure was not an appropriate measure of second language reading development. Two possible explanations can be given to account for the cloze results. If we assume that the cloze test procedure is not a measure of L2 reading, which it does not appear to be in this case, then the cloze procedure may represent a measure of overall L2 language proficiency. It is true that Bill did not significantly improve his L2 spoken language abilities over the 5 months, and he did not improve his ability to comprehend ongoing face-to-face conversations. These may be seen as indicators of little progress in overall language proficiency. However, such an analysis does not take into account Bill's marked improvements in reading and vocabulary, as well as his improvements in listening comprehension over familiar and controlled domains.

A second view of cloze procedures, as commonly practiced, is to see them as measures of production skills. It is readily apparent that Bill did not significantly improve his production skills in Portuguese after completing the 3-week intensive language course. It may be the case that, because many L2 analyses of cloze testing procedures do not separate learners' reading skills from production skills, cloze results appear to be good measures of overall L2 language development. The results of this case study, however, lead us to believe that cloze procedures may be more accurately seen as measures of productive L2 language proficiency. Although it is difficult to generalize from a case study, there are strong indications that the cloze-as-production measure is the most reasonable way to account for Bill's lack of progress on the battery of cloze measures used in this study.

## Conclusion

There is always the danger in a case study of succumbing to the temptation to generalize. We recognize that the role of case studies in research is not to validate strong general claims but rather to suggest avenues for research and raise questions about commonly accepted assumptions. Trying to keep these constraints in mind, we would like to summarize the results of this study in terms of a few important issues in L2 reading and vocabulary research.

First, the case study supports Coady's (1993) call for research toward a theory of L2 vocabulary acquisition. When considering vocabulary learning, notions such as "receptive" versus "productive" vocabulary knowledge are too simple, and even the notion of core, or "nuclear," vocabulary needs to be reconsidered in light of this study. Many vocabulary items that may be "nuclear" for a particular genre or set of genres may not be as central in other written genres. For example, many common descriptive adjectives useful in fiction may be marginal in news stories. Instead, a more comprehensive set of proposals for vocabulary development needs to be devised. Coady (1993) suggests a more complex set of patterns for L2 vocabulary development. The results of this study provide additional information that should be useful for such a theory.

Second, the use of a bilingual dictionary in a consistent and appropriate manner would appear to have a positive impact on vocabulary learning and reading development. This finding coincides with Luppescu and Day (1993) on the potential effectiveness of a bilingual dictionary for vocabulary acquisition. Of course, we recognize that the approach used in this study was an intensive one and involved a highly motivated learner. Additional studies that explore different types of dictionary use over time for L2 learning might help to clarify the effectiveness of dictionaries as L2 language learning resources.

Third, the study raises rather direct questions about the use of standard cloze tests as measures of L2 reading ability. It should first be noted that a modified multiple-choice cloze might have been a more appropriate measure of comprehension since it would have required recognition rather than production. Despite the fact that this case study involved a single subject, the findings raise the question of whether standard cloze procedures may be more appropriate as measures of productive language abilities than of comprehension language abilities.

Fourth, this study suggests that learning to read in a second language centrally involves learning words. Vocabulary knowledge has long been recognized as a strong correlate of reading ability. This study suggests that reading and vocabulary are reciprocally causal, a not surprising conclusion, but one that is useful to reiterate (cf. Stanovich, 1986). In short, it is nice to be able to report that reading improves vocabulary knowledge and vocabulary knowledge supports reading development.

Finally, this study strongly suggests that reading and vocabulary abilities will develop as a result of extensive reading practice. In this study, extensive reading resulted in improved vocabulary, reading, and listening comprehension. This finding supports a number of recent studies that argue for the importance of extensive reading (Elley, 1991; Krashen, 1989), in particular the recent work of Stanovich and his colleagues (Cunningham & Stanovich, 1991; Stanovich & Cunningham, 1992; Stanovich & West, 1989; West & Stanovich, 1991; West, Stanovich, & Mitchell, 1993). Perhaps most important, this case study argues that an effective way to develop language abilities over time is through extensive reading.

# References

Bailey, K. M. (1980). An introspective analysis of an individual's language learning experience. In R. Scarcella & S. Krashen (Eds.), *Research in second language acquisition: Selected papers of the Los Angeles Second Language Research Forum* (pp. 58–65). Rowley, MA: Newbury House.

(1983). Competitiveness and anxiety in adult second language learning: Looking *at* and *through* the diary studies. In H. W. Seliger & M. H. Long (Eds.), *Classroom oriented research in second language acquisition* (pp. 67–103). Rowley, MA: Newbury House.

(1990). The use of diary studies in teacher education programs. In J. C. Richards & D. Nunan (Eds.), *Second Language Teacher Education* (pp. 215–226). New York: Cambridge University Press.

Beck, I., & McKeown, M. G. (1991). Conditions of vocabulary acquisition. In P. D. Pearson, R. Barr, M. L. Kamil, & P. Mosenthal (Eds.), *Handbook of reading research* (vol. 2, pp. 789–814). White Plains, NY: Longman.

Beck, I., McKeown, M. G., & Omanson, R. C. (1987). The effects and uses of diverse vocabulary instructional techniques. In M. G. McKeown & M. E. Curtis (Eds.), *The nature of vocabulary acquisition* (pp. 147–163). Hillsdale, NJ: Lawrence Erlbaum.

Bossers, B. (1992). *Reading in two languages: A study of reading comprehension in Dutch as a second language and in Turkish as a first language.* Rotterdam: Drukkerij Van Driel.

Coady, J. (1993). Research on ESL/EFL vocabulary acquisition: Putting it in context. In T. Huckin, M. Haynes, & J. Coady (Eds.), *Second language reading and vocabulary learning* (pp. 3–23). Norwood, NJ: Ablex.

Cunningham, A. E., & Stanovich, K. E. (1991). Tracking the unique effects of print exposure in children: Associations with vocabulary, general knowledge, and spelling. *Journal of Educational Psychology, 83,* 264–274.

de Villiers, P. A., & de Villiers, J. G. (1992). Language development. In M. Bornstein & M. Lamb (Eds.), *Developmental psychology: An advanced textbook* (pp. 337–418). Hillsdale, NJ: Lawrence Erlbaum.

Elley, W. (1991). Acquiring literacy in a second language: The effect of book-based programs. *Language Learning, 41,* 375–411.

Goulden, R., Nation, P., & Read, J. (1990). How large can a receptive vocabulary be? *Applied Linguistics, 11,* 341–363.

Holmes, J., & Ramos, R. G. (1993). False friends and reckless guessers: Observing cognate recognition strategies. In T. Huckin, M. Haynes, & J. Coady (Eds.), *Second language reading and vocabulary learning* (pp. 86–108). Norwood, NJ: Ablex.

Hoover, W. A., & Gough, P. B. (1990). The simple view of reading. *Reading and Writing, 2,* 127–160.

Huckin, T., & Bloch, J. (1993). Strategies for inferring word-meaning in context: A cognitive model. In T. Huckin, M. Haynes, & J. Coady (Eds.), *Second language reading and vocabulary learning* (pp. 153–178). Norwood, NJ: Ablex.

Hulstijn, L. H. (1993). When do foreign-language readers look up the meaning of unfamiliar words? The influence of task and learner variables. *Modern Language Journal, 77*(2), 139–147.

Jackson, M. D., & McClelland, J. L. (1979). Processing determinants of reading speed. *Journal of Experimental Psychology: General, 108*, 151–181.

Krashen, S. (1989). We acquire vocabulary and spelling by reading: Additional evidence for the input hypothesis. *Modern Language Journal, 73*(4), 440–464.

Kyongho, H., & Nation, P. (1989). Reducing the vocabulary load and encouraging vocabulary learning through reading newspapers. *Reading in a Foreign Language, 6*(1), 323–335.

Leung, C. B., & Pikulski, J. J. (1990). Incidental learning of word meanings by kindergarten and first-grade children through repeated read aloud events. In J. Zutell & S. McCormick (Eds.), *Literacy theory and research: Analyses from multiple paradigms* (pp. 231–239). Chicago, IL: National Reading Conference.

Luppescu, S., & Day, R. R. (1993). Reading, dictionaries, and vocabulary learning. *Language Learning, 43*(2), 263–287.

Martin, J. (1989). *Factual writing.* New York: Oxford University Press.

McCormick, S. (1993). Single-subject experimental research: Rationale, tenets, and basic designs. In D. J. Leu & C. K. Kinzer (Eds.), *Examining central issues in literacy research, theory, and practice* (pp. 131–139). Chicago, IL: National Reading Conference.

McKeown, M. G., & Curtis, M. (Eds.). (1987). *The nature of vocabulary acquisition.* Hillsdale, NJ: Lawrence Erlbaum.

Nagy, W. (1988). *Teaching vocabulary to improve reading comprehension.* Urbana, IL: National Council of Teachers of English.

Nagy, W., Anderson, R., & Herman, P. (1987). Learning word meanings from context during normal reading. *American Educational Research Journal, 24* 237–270.

Neuman, S. B., & McCormick, S. (Eds.). (1995). *Single-subject experimental research: Applications for literacy.* Newark, DE: International Reading Association.

Palmer, J., MacCleod, C. M., Hung, E., & Davidson, J. E. (1985). Information-processing correlates of reading. *Journal of Memory and Language, 24*, 59–88.

Parry, K. (1993). Too many words: Learning vocabulary of an academic subject. In T. Huckin, M. Haynes, & J. Coady (Eds.), *Second language reading and vocabulary learning* (pp. 109–129). Norwood, NJ: Ablex.

Porter, P. A., Goldstein, L. M., Leatherman, J., & Conrad, S. (1990). An ongoing dialogue: Learning logs for teacher preparation. In J. C. Richards & D. Nunan (Eds.), *Second language teacher education* (pp. 227–240). New York: Cambridge University Press.

Schmidt, R. W. (1990). The role of consciousness in second language learning. *Applied Linguistics, 11*, 129–158.

(1993). Awareness and second language acquisition. In W. Grabe et al. (Eds.), *Annual Review of Applied Linguistics, 13. Issues in Second Language Teaching and Learning* (pp. 206–226). New York: Cambridge University Press.

Schmidt, R. W., & Frota, S. N. (1986). Developing basic conversational ability in a second language: A case study of an adult learner of Portuguese. In R. R. Day (Ed.), *Talking to learn: Conversation in second language acquisition* (pp. 237–326). Rowley, MA: Newbury House.

Schumann, F. E. (1980). Diary of a language learner: A further analysis. In R. Scarcella & S. Krashen (Eds.), *Research in second language acquisition: Selected papers of the Los Angeles Second Language Research Forum* (pp. 51–57). Rowley, MA: Newbury House.

Schumann, F. E., & Schumann, J. H. (1977). Diary of a language learner: An introspective study of second language learning. In H. D. Brown, R. H. Crymes, & C. A. Yorio (Eds.), *On TESOL '77: Teaching and learning English as a second language* (pp. 241–249). Washington, DC: TESOL.

Segalowitz, N., Poulsen, C., & Komoda, M. (1991). Lower level components of reading skill in higher level bilinguals: Implications for reading instruction. *AILA Review: Reading in two languages, 8,* 15–30.

Stanovich, K. E. (1986). Matthew effects in reading: Some consequences of individual differences in the acquisition of literacy. *Reading Research Quarterly, 21,* 360–407.

(1990). Concepts in developmental theories of reading skill: Cognitive resources, automaticity, and modularity. *Developmental Review, 10,* 72–100.

Stanovich, K. E., & Cunningham, A. E. (1992). Studying the consequences of literacy within a literate society: The cognitive correlates of print exposure. *Memory and Cognition, 20,* 51–68.

Stanovich, K. E., & West, R. (1989). Exposure to print and orthographic processing. *Reading Research Quarterly, 24,* 402–433.

Sticht, T. G., & James, J. H. (1984). Listening and reading. In P. D. Pearson, R. Barr, M. L. Kamil, & P. Mosenthal (Eds.), *Handbook of reading research* (vol. 1, pp. 293–317). White Plains, NY: Longman.

Ulijn, J. M., & Strother, J. B. (1990). The effect of syntactic simplification on reading EST texts as L1 and L2. *Journal of Research in Reading, 13*(1), 38–54.

West, R., & Stanovich, K. E. (1991). The incidental acquisition of information from reading. *Psychological Science, 2,* 325–330.

West, R., Stanovich, K. E., & Mitchell, H. R. (1993). Reading in the real world and its correlates. *Reading Research Quarterly, 28,* 34–50.

Wodinsky, M., & Nation, P. (1988). Learning from graded readers. *Reading in a Foreign Language, 5*(1), 155–161.

Yin, R. K. (1989). *Case study research: Design and methods* (rev. ed.). Newbury Park, CA: Sage.

(1993). *Applications of case study research.* Newbury Park, CA: Sage.

# PART III:
# EMPIRICAL RESEARCH

In contrast to the qualitative, hypothesis-raising research of Part II, the studies in Part III single out certain variables for more controlled investigation. The main variables include the cognitive skills involved, the type of lexical unit being learned, and the method of instruction employed.

Chapter 7, by Lynne Yang, reports on a study of the acquisition of L2 vocabulary under controlled experimental conditions. Three cognitive skills were measured over the course of learning: conscious word translation, word recognition, and semantic priming. Twenty-nine monolingual speakers of English were taught a miniature artificial L2 in a controlled laboratory setting, using computerized tutorials over a 5-week period. The three tests were administered periodically over the learning period, for both the L2 and L1 (control) vocabulary. The results suggest a different time course for each of the three developing skills. Conscious translation ability developed most rapidly. In contrast, automated skills at both the meaning level (semantic priming) and the phonological level (word recognition) lagged considerably behind. This is consonant with cognitive studies of the development of automaticity. The results do confirm, however, that real changes at the cognitive level can occur during a relatively short learning period; indeed, at the end of this 5-week learning period, the manner of processing of L2 vocabulary for these learners began to approximate that of the L1 control.

Chapter 8, by Pierre (J. L.) Arnaud and Sandra J. Savignon, describes the passive knowledge of rare English words and complex English lexical idioms by 236 francophone learners at four levels ranging from first-year university majors to teachers in mid-career. Arnaud and Savignon used both multiple-choice tests and yes/no tests to estimate this knowledge, and they compared their results to those obtained with a control group of 57 native-speaking undergraduates. Although the most advanced learners (those having 10+ years of professional experience studying English) seem to have attained a nativelike competence with rare words, this was not quite the case for complex lexical units. The difficulty with complex lexical units may be due to the fact that they most commonly occur in speech rather than writing, and EFL learners have relatively little exposure to speech, especially in interactive mode.

Arnaud and Savignon suggest that many second language learners are unaware of the nature of complex lexical units; they therefore encourage a pedagogy that provides explicit instruction in this area. They note also that low-frequency (rare) words are important in reading comprehension, and thus should not be left to guesswork. In general, they argue that more attention should be given to long-term vocabulary teaching at advanced levels, especially the teaching of rare words and complex lexical items. This study provides support for any teaching methodology that advocates giving explicit attention to oral vocabulary and complex lexical units (for example, the Lexical Approach, as described in Chapter 13) or to low-frequency lexis in reading (as in Chapters 2, 6, and 8).

Chapter 9, by T. Sima Paribakht and Marjorie Wesche, examines the effect of reading activities and explicit vocabulary teaching on the incidental learning of vocabulary. In an experimental study, Paribakht and Wesche hypothesized that extensive reading plus vocabulary instruction will be significantly better than extensive reading alone. The subjects were thirty-eight young adults from a variety of L1 backgrounds in an intermediate-level ESL course. Half of the subjects did vocabulary exercises emphasizing salience, recognition, manipulation, interpretation, and production, in addition to extensive reading. The other subjects did no vocabulary exercises but instead did extra reading. Paribakht and Wesche used both self-reports and performance evaluations to determine vocabulary knowledge. They found that "while reading for meaning appears to produce significant results in vocabulary acquisition, such reading supplemented with specific vocabulary exercises produces greater gains." The difference was both qualitative and quantitative. The findings of this study reinforce those of the studies presented in Chapters 2 and 7, and they support pedagogies that combine extensive reading and explicit instruction, as exemplified in Chapters 11 and 12.

# 7 Tracking the acquisition of L2 vocabulary

## The Keki language experiment

Lynne Yang

## Introduction

Reported here are the first results of an experimental study of the acquisition of a second language in the laboratory under controlled conditions. The overall project aimed at tracking the time-course of the acquisition of a specially-designed artificial language. The acquisition of both lexicon and grammar was tracked through repeated tests over a 5-week instruction period. Some of the tests involved cognitive tasks, while others involved more natural linguistic performance tasks. In this paper I report the results of the acquisition of the lexicon.

Most applied linguistic studies in the area of second language vocabulary focus on instructional method, and test conscious lexical competence in or out of communicative context.[1] While I used one conscious lexical translation task, the bulk of my study involved testing the development of two subconscious – automated – cognitive skills: (1) word recognition; (2) semantic priming. The impetus for my use of these cognitive tasks does not come from studies of second language acquisition,[2] but rather from two lines of cognitive-psychological work on the fluent processing of native vocabulary.

The first line of cognitive research concerns the recognition of word forms. Sieroff and Posner (1988) and Sieroff, Pollatsek and Posner (1988) have shown that the recognition of habituated, native word forms is

This research was conducted as part of the author's doctoral research. The author would like to thank Tom Givón for his contributions to earlier versions of this paper. Without his guidance and assistance, this work would not have been possible. Valuable advice on the design and implementation of the study was provided by Michael Posner, Morti Gernsbacher, Linda Forrest, Bruce McCandless, Paul Compton, Will Goodwin and Russell Tomlin. The technical assistance of Ruth Rush, Marina Tuckett, Shu-sen Yang, Zhu Qin and Ian Valentine are gratefully acknowledged. The research presented here was supported by a grant from the William M. Keck Foundation.
1 See Nation (1990), Carter (1987), Carter and McCarthy (1988), Gairns and Redman (1986), inter alia.
2 For a good review of the history of cognitive psychological research on bilingualism, see Keatley (1992).

automatic and does not demand attention. This contrasts with the recognition of nonhabituated nonsense letter strings, which is attention-demanding. We have reproduced these results previously in a study of second language learners (Givón, Yang & Gernsbacher, 1990). It was shown there that monolingual English speakers read Spanish vocabulary in an attention-demanding manner, essentially the same way as nonsense letter strings. After 2 years of Spanish instruction, the reading of Spanish words by native English speakers begins to approximate the automated, attention-free manner in which they read their native English vocabulary. Related neurocognitive studies have demonstrated that the fluent, automated reading of habituated native vocabulary involves activity in the left-occipital visual area of the brain. In contrast, reading nonhabituated nonsense letter strings involves activity in the visual attention center on the right side of the brain (Petersen, Fox, Posner, Mintun & Reichle, 1988; Posner & Carr, 1991; Posner, Sandson, Dhawan, & Shulman, 1989).

The second line of cognitive research involves the automatic activation of conceptual nodes along lexical-semantic networks. Within this line, experiments such as those of Swinney (1979) have shown that multiple senses of the same word are activated automatically, instantaneously and subconsciously during the first 200 milliseconds of word reading. Only at 250 msec following the presentation of the word form does the effect of the clausal context begin to manifest itself, leading to the suppression of contextually inappropriate senses, and to the final conscious access to only one contextually-appropriate sense. In a different vein, experiments on semantic priming (cf. Morton, 1969; Neeley, 1990) have demonstrated that a perceived word form does not activate only its own specific meaning, but also potentially many related meanings. Put another way, by activating a node in the lexical-semantic network, one also activates, automatically and subconsciously, connected nodes.

What I demonstrate here by the use of cognitive performance tests is not altogether surprising: The development of conscious knowledge of lexical meaning of novel foreign vocabulary may follow a rather different time-course than the acquisition of a fully-automated cognitive processing of foreign vocabulary. This applies to both automatic word recognition and the automatic activation of semantic networks (semantic priming). Further, among the two, the development of automated word recognition may be an important prerequisite for the development of automated semantic activation.[3]

---

3 It has been suggested (cf. Brown & Haynes, 1985; Haynes & Carr, 1990) that the automated process of word recognition is a good predictor of reading comprehension and new vocabulary acquisition from context in second language learning.

# Design of the overall experiment

## Overview

The overall experiment was conducted as a 5-week computer-controlled instructional laboratory environment. A group of twenty-nine monolingual American English speakers spent 2 hours a day, 5 days a week learning a specially-constructed language. Their performance was tested periodically over the course of the instruction period. The experiment as a whole was designed to test the hypothesis of *cognitive competition* between the acquisition of vocabulary and grammar. Briefly, it had been suggested (Givón, 1990) that in the early stages of language acquisition – both L1 and L2 – the processing of vocabulary and grammar are pitted against each other in competition for limited attentional resources.[4] In the early stages of that competition, the vocabulary tends to win, for both cognitive and adaptive/pragmatic reasons.[5] The early stages of both L1 and L2 acquisition are thus characterized by the acquisition of a pregrammatical – pidgin – communicative mode.[6]

## Subjects and instruction

In order to test the competition hypothesis, the subject pool of twenty-nine paid volunteers, all university of Oregon undergraduates, was divided into two groups. In group 1 (pidgin group), the introduction of grammar was delayed until after the first two weeks (20 hours) of instruction. In group 2 (grammar group), grammar was introduced from the very start. The subjects in both groups studied the language 2 hours a day, 5 days a week over the course of 5 weeks, for a total of 50 hours of instruction. The communicative tasks, total hours of study and mode of

4 For attention as a limited-capacity mental resource and the contrast between attended and automated processing, see Posner and Boies (1971), Posner and Warren (1972), Posner and Snyder (1974), Schneider and Shiffrin (1977) and Schneider (1985), inter alia. For discussion of grammar as an automated language-processing device, see Givón (1979, ch. 5; 1989, ch. 7), Blumstein and Milberg (1984), Lieberman (1984) and Schnitzer (1989).

5 Cognitively, generalizing on the lexical meanings is an easier, more concrete task, as compared with generalizing on the much more abstract communicative functions of grammar. Pragmatically, one can communicate with lexical vocabulary but no grammar (pidgin), but communication by grammar without vocabulary is contentless.

6 In L2 acquisition there is also evidence of natural pidgin ("simplified") input (cf. Clyne, 1977; Ferguson, 1975; Long, 1981; Meisel, 1977; Selinker, 1972). For the natural pidgin-first stage in second language acquisition, see Selinker (1972), Bickerton and Givón (1976), Schumann (1978a, 1978b, 1984, 1990), Anderson (1979), Givón (1979) and Bickerton (1981), inter alia. Strong suggestions for an early pidgin-like stage in child language can be seen in Bloom (1973), Limber (1973), Keenan (1974, 1975), Scollon (1976), Slobin (1977) and Givón (1979), inter alia.

computer-controlled instruction were identical for the two experimental groups. The only difference between the two groups was the presence versus the absence of grammar in the target language input.

## The experimental Keki language

Practical constraints limited the amount of time that volunteer subjects could spend – daily as well as overall – on learning the second language. For several reasons, it was decided to teach a specially-constructed miniature L2, with a controlled limited vocabulary of sixty-seven nouns, verbs and adjectives, and a deliberately-constructed minigrammar. Preliminary results from an earlier pilot study indicated that the size of the language constructed would permit learners to fully automate the processing of vocabulary in the limited instructional time.[7]

The choice of an artificial over a natural second language was motivated by the following considerations:

a. Making the target language syntactically and morphotactically maximally different from English
b. At the same time adhering to a highly universal semantic and pragmatic organization that does not vary much from that of English
c. Ensuring that none of the subjects had any prior exposure to the language
d. Eliminating phonological complexity and morphophonemic irregularity as variables in the study, since they are irrelevant to the purpose of the experiment and slow down learning

The functional – semantic and pragmatic – organization of Keki is highly universal, and its morphosyntax is typologically common and natural, even as it is maximally differentiated from English. Technically an artificial language, Keki is nonetheless, both functionally and typologically, an unmistakable natural language.

The drawbacks of using a miniature artificial language include reducing the validity of the experimental results in terms of application to natural language learning, and possibly diminishing the motivation of the learners. In our judgment, these considerations did not override the considerable advantages of using a constructed language. The learning of artificial languages under controlled conditions has been demonstrated previously.[8] And my own results certainly demonstrate the acquisition of both conscious competence and covert cognitive skills.

---

7 The acquisition of grammar was not piloted.
8 See Reber (1967), McLaughlin (1980). All these artificial languages had arbitrary grammars constructed randomly through Markov-chains. In this they all differ radically from the Keki grammar, which was designed to resemble the grammar of a natural language.

## The Keki language

The experimental language Keki has sixty-seven lexical words (nouns, verbs and adjectives). Typologically, Keki is a rigidly-ordered SOV nominative-accusative language with suffixal morphology, unmarked subject and object, and postpositionally-marked indirect (or obliques) arguments. The language exhibits obligatory subject agreement, two pronominal genders (animate, inanimate), and morphologically-marked tense-aspect, postpositions, definitization and pluralization. The grammatical constructions of Keki include:

a. active/direct voice
b. passive/de-transitive voice
c. yes/no questions
d. WH questions
e. negative clauses
f. verbal complement clauses
g. intransitive, transitive and bitransitive clauses
h. dative-shifted bitransitive clauses
i. nominal, adjectival and locative predicates
j. verb-clitic anaphoric pronouns
k. noun phrase conjunction

As noted earlier, one experimental group (pidgin) received no grammatical linguistic input for the first 2 weeks (10 days) of instruction. This difference pertained only to clauses, not to vocabulary. And further, one element of Keki grammar, the SOV word order, was preserved in the pidgin input. As illustrations of the difference between grammatical and pidgin input, consider:

1. Transitive direct-active clause (SOV)
   a. Grammatical input
      Menti-lo   prano-ze binde-mi-lo.
      Woman-the car-the   drive-PAST-she
      'The woman drove the car'
   b. Pidgin input
      Menti prano binde
      Woman car   drive
      'The woman drove the car'
2. Passive (de-transitive) clause
   a. Grammatical input
      prano-ze   menti-lo-na   binde-za-mi-ze
      car-the   woman-the-by drive-PASS-PAST-it
      'The car was driven by the woman'

    b. Pidgin input
       prano menti binde
       car   woman drive
       'The car was driven by the woman'
3. WH question
    a. WH question
       ze-ki   tanti-lo luti-lo-la fune-mi-lo?
       it-WH   man-the   boy-the-to give-PAST-he
       'What did the man give to the boy?'
    b. Pidgin input
       ki tanti luti fune?
       WH man   boy give
       'What did the man give to the boy?'
4. Negation and complementation
    a. Grammatical input
       noti-lo   sasi-lo kale-la   beme-mi-ka-lo
       girl-the dog-the sit-COMP say-PAST-NEG-she
       'The girl didn't tell the dog to sit'
    b. Pidgin input
       Ka noti sasi kale beme
       NEG girl dog sit say
       'The girl didn't tell the dog to sit'
5. Pronominalization
    a. Grammatical input
       kale-la   lo-beme-mi-lo
       sit-COMP him-say-PAST-she
       'She told him/her to sit'
    b. Pidgin input
       kale beme
       sit   say
       'She told him/her to sit'

## Computer-controlled instruction

The language was introduced to the learners through computerized tutorials developed using *HyperCard* (TM).[9] The program allows the si-

---

9 *HyperCard* (TM) is a software authoring kit that facilitates the design of software applications that resemble professionally-designed Macintosh software (cf. Goodman, 1987; Laws, 1987). It is frequently used in the design of educational software. In the design of the Keki instructional materials, HyperCard made it possible to incorporate recorded audio materials, photocopied pictures and written texts into individual lessons and instructional tests. The student progresses through the materials of a packaged lesson unit by clicking the mouse buttons. These buttons may release sequenced language materials (words, sentences), auditory input or pictures, in whatever combinations. Or they may release questions and check the accuracy of

multaneous presentation of pictorial, written and auditory materials. During the early stages of instruction, written Keki materials were reinforced by the simultaneous presentation of the spoken language and appropriate pictorial materials. This fully-controlled mode of instruction was chosen to ensure an identical instructional environment for all subjects in the experiment. All subjects were exposed to the same words, clauses and short episodes, the same number of times, including the schedule of practice and testing. The variation in attitude, energy level and subtle personal approach that are characteristic of human instructors was thus eliminated.

I readily concede that by gaining a definite measure of experimental control, one inevitably incurs some losses. The use of computerized tutorials presents problems in areas such as (*a*) limited communicative context; (*b*) no human interaction; and (*c*) potential loss of motivation. I attempted to compensate for these drawbacks by making the computer-driven learning tasks as interactive as possible.

After comparing the two experimental groups (pidgin versus grammar) on the three lexical acquisition measures, I found no significant differences between the two groups in two of the meaning-related measures – word translation and semantic priming. The third measure, word recognition, showed a general speed advantage for the grammar group over the pidgin group. But this advantage showed up in the same magnitude in the subjects' recognition of English words as in their recognition of Keki words. Early in the experiment, there was also the expected advantage – in both subject groups – of English word recognition over Keki word recognition. This advantage disappeared toward the end of the experiment, so that the subjects' reaction to Keki words was just as fast as their reaction to English words. Still, the grammar group's speed advantage persisted to the end with both Keki and English words.

## Measuring vocabulary acquisition

### *Preliminary review*

Kroll and Curley (1988) found that novice bilinguals may rely on the semantic network of word associations already extant in their first language to facilitate lexical access in the second language. In contrast, more expert bilinguals can understand second language vocabulary directly, without mediation through their first language translation equivalencies.

answers vis-à-vis correct responses. HyperCard has limited interactive capabilities, which I chose not to use. My decision was motivated by the need to keep the instruction identical for all subjects. The only individual variable introduced was in the student-controlled rate of release of the sequenced instructional material within the same 1-hour packaged lesson.

In their experiments, Kroll and Curley presented novice and expert English-to-German bilinguals with a picture-naming task and a word-translation task. They found that the novices were significantly faster at the translation task than at the picture-naming task. The experts, on the other hand, showed no significant reaction-time differences between the two tasks. Kroll and Curley then argue that there is a shift during second language vocabulary acquisition, from a strategy of comprehending L2 words by first accessing L1 equivalents, to a strategy of direct lexical access in L2.

Kroll and Scholl (1992) showed an asymmetry in the directionality of both translation and semantic-priming tasks. Translation L1-to-L2 was significantly slower than L2-to-L1. Further, semantic priming of L2-by-L1 was stronger than that of L1-by-L2. They then suggest that the connections between a bilingual's two languages include both conceptual and lexical (i.e., word-form) links, but that the strength of the connections differs for the two languages. Lexical links L2-to-L1 may be stronger than L1-to-L2.[10]

The studies reviewed above look at lexical access among bilinguals from a cross-sectional perspective. The present study tracked the longitudinal development of lexical skills acquired from ground zero.

# Word translation

## Methods

### STIMULI

Forty Keki vocabulary items and their English translation equivalents were used as stimuli in this task.

### STIMULI PRESENTATION

Two blocks of paired translation equivalents were presented. One block presented pairs in which the first word was English and the second was Keki. The other block presented pairs in the opposite order. The order of block presentation was counterbalanced across subjects. Within an individual block, each target word was followed by its translation equivalent twice and twice by words that were unrelated in meaning. For example, the Keki target word "bakso" was presented twice followed by its correct English equivalent "table." In the other two presentations, "bakso" was followed in one case by the English word "cat," and in the other by "stand." In 50% of the instances, thus, the two words matched in meaning, and in 50% they did not. The order of presentation was semiran-

---

10 Kroll and Scholl (1992) suggest that this is especially true when the second language is acquired after childhood.

domly distributed in such a way that none of the target words was repeated within a span of twenty target words.

An individual trial consisted of the following steps:

1. First a single asterisk (*) was presented for 500 msec in the center of an Apple Macintosh IIci computer screen in order to direct the subject's attention to the location at which the words would be presented.
2. The asterisk was replaced by a target word, which was presented for 250 msec.
3. After the first word disappeared, the screen remained blank for an interval of 100 msec.
4. The second word appeared on the screen following the interval and remained on the screen until the subject made a response.

Trials were separated from each other by 2-second intervals.

## Procedure

Subjects were asked to read a set of instructions and to complete ten practice trials before beginning the experiment. They were told that they would see a series of pairs of English and Keki words presented one word at a time. Their task was to read each pair of words and determine if the two had the same meaning or not. They were told that the first word would be in one language and the second word would be in the other language. They were also told, prior to beginning the experiment, the order of block presentation. They thus knew that all pairs in a particular block would be presented in the same order. Subjects were instructed to indicate their choice by pressing a computer key labeled Y for "yes, they have the same meaning" and N for "no, they do not have the same meaning." Subjects were encouraged to respond as quickly and as accurately as possible. The task was administered at three points in time along the developmental continuum: after 5 days of instruction (10 hours; 1 week), after 10 days (20 hours; 2 weeks) and after 24 days (48 hours; 4.8 weeks).

Reaction times were measured from the time the second word appeared on the screen until the time the subject hit the yes/no key. Both reaction times and accuracy were recorded for each test item. Only results from the trials in which the pair had the same meaning were analyzed, and only cases in which the subject responded correctly were used in determining mean reaction times for each subject.

## Results

The mean percent correct responses for word translation in both directions – Keki to English and English to Keki – are represented graphically in Figure 1.

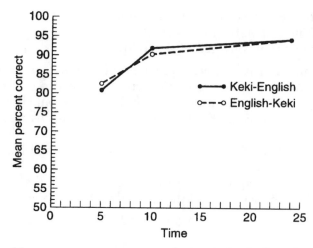

*Figure 1    Mean percent correct translation in both directions over time.*

As can be seen from Figure 1, the learning curves flatten out at about 10 days (20 hours; 2 weeks) of instruction. No measure was taken at the very beginning of the study, but it can be safely assumed that performance must have been at *zero* level. Given the binary task, mere random guessing should have averaged out at 50% accuracy *zero*-level performance.

A repeated measures analysis of variance comparing percent accuracy for both orders over time revealed that there was no significant difference between the two directions of translation – English to Keki versus Keki to English. The main effect of improved accuracy over time was significant in both directions of translation – but only up to the first 10 days (2 weeks; 20 hours) (F 2, 54 = 48.779; p < .0001). There was no significant improvement from then on to the end of the experiment (24 days; 5 weeks; 48 instruction hours). Put another way, the learning curve as measured by translation accuracy flattened out after 20 hours of instruction time. Performance did not improve significantly after that.

The reaction-time results for the translation tasks are represented graphically in Figure 2.

There was a clear improvement over time in translation speed (reaction times) in both directions of translation. Unlike the accuracy results, the improvement in performance was significant (in both orders) all the way to the end of the experiment (5 weeks; 24 days; 48 hours) (F 2, 54 = 33.054; p < .001). What is more, the RT measure reveals significant differences between the two directions of translation: The English-to-Keki (L1 to L2) translation was performed consistently faster than the Keki-to-English (L2 to L1) translation (F 1, 271 = 5.282; p < .0295).

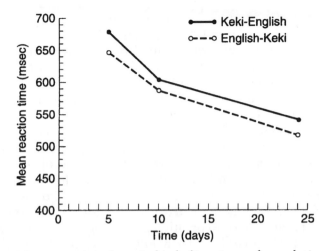

*Figure 2    Mean reaction times in both directions of translation over time for the word-translation task.*

There was no significant interaction between the two main effects; that is, the increased translation speed over time was the same for both directions of translation.

## Discussion

Word translation is a *conscious* skill. My results suggest that the subjects' accuracy – conscious knowledge – at this task developed more rapidly than their speed. Improvement in translation accuracy in both directions flattened out after 10 days (20 hours) of instruction. In contrast, translation speed continued to improve significantly all the way to the end of the instructional period. Thus, while the measurement of a more conscious aspect of performance may reveal no further learning, the measurement of more covert aspects of cognitive skill – in this case RTs – reveals continued improvement in translation speed. The acquired capacity is performed faster, and thus presumably more skillfully and with increased automaticity. As we shall see, this is borne out by the time-course of other cognitive measures.

   The significant reaction-time effect I found in the direction of translation – English-to-Keki (L1 to L2) translation consistently faster than Keki-to-English (L2 to L1) translation – is the exact opposite of the one reported by Kroll and Scholl (1992). I suspect that the different results may be due at least in part to differences in methodology, and that these results in fact make excellent cognitive sense. First, the overall range of RTs in my experiment was roughly between 500 msecs and 700 msec.

The first word of a stimulus-pair in our experiment was presented for only 250 msec, followed by a 100 msec interval before the presentation of the target word. There was thus a total of 350 msec available to the subjects for processing the first word. With such a short time frame, it may well be that subjects were still processing the first word when the second word appeared. Kroll and Scholl (1992) did not measure performance under such extreme time pressure.

Second, Swinney's (1979) data suggest something on the order of 250–300 msec needed for completion of the processing of a *well habituated* native-language word. My experimental time frame of 350 msec for processing the first word thus allowed sufficient time for processing when the English word was presented first (English-to-Keki translation). But when the Keki word was presented first (Keki-to-English translation), presumably its unconscious cognitive processing is likely to be slower, since it is less habituated. In other words, the system processing the L2 vocabulary at either the word-recognition or semantic-activation end (or both) is not yet fully automated. The fact that translation RTs in both directions continue to improve to the very end of the instruction period supports this interpretation. The consistently slower RTs of L2-to-L1 translation (Keki-to-English) thus reflect the incomplete acquisition of full automaticity of word processing.[11]

## Semantic priming

### Preamble

The classic semantic priming effect for individual words is based on the notion of mental representation of the lexicon as a network of connected nodes. When a word form is activated by either hearing or reading, not only is the word's own mental-lexical node activated, but so are *connected* nodes of words that are semantically closely related to it (Morton, 1969; Neeley, 1990). When subjects are asked to read two words in a row and perform a lexical decision task on the second word, they tend to perform faster on processing the second word when the first word is semantically related, as compared to when the two words are unrelated (Meyer & Schvaneveldt, 1971).[12] Tracking the development of semantic priming in L2 target words, as compared to semantically identical L1 targets, is thus an important measure of L2 lexical acquisition, in that it

11  I would predict that with a longer interstimulus time and thus less cognitive stress, my results would have fallen closer in line with those of Kroll and Scholl (1992).

12  Thus, for example, if one sees the word *doctor,* the mental nodes for *nurse, hospital, sick,* and so on, may become activated along with the mental node for *doctor.*

presumably tracks the increasing automaticity in processing recently-acquired L2 vocabulary.

Kroll and Scholl (1992) suggest that words in different languages are connected to the *same* semantic mental network. This assumption needs careful substantiation, since the lexical-semantic organization of a language reflects its cultural world view, and cultures may differ substantially in the way they organize human experience, at least in some subdomains.[13] In the case of Keki, however, I deliberately designed its vocabulary to closely echo English semantic structure. Nothing in the Keki instructional input thus contradicts the native English learner's reasonable null hypothesis that Keki and English share the very same lexical-semantic structure.[14] With this reasoning, I chose to prime both English and Keki target words with English prime words.

Another important reason for priming both Keki and English target words with English prime words was the need to reduce, at least to some extent, the effect of another automated cognitive skill – word recognition. As one can see below, the development of Keki word recognition continues to the end of the experimental period. Priming Keki target words with English prime words thus removes the effect of imperfect Keki prime-word recognition. It is of course true that the effect of imperfect Keki target-word recognition remains. This component of Keki word processing is likely to be most significant in measuring semantic priming during the early test periods.

The final reason for choosing to prime Keki target words with English prime words was that the vocabulary of Keki was rather limited – sixty-seven words mapping a rather limited cultural universe. It would have been nearly impossible to find enough related and unrelated prime words for all the target words on the Keki list.

13 The extreme cultural relativity commonly ascribed to Whorf (1956) is probably too strong a position, at least as far as grammatical-pragmatic structure is concerned. It is much easier to demonstrate such cultural relativity in the lexical-semantic organization of experience. The opposite extreme assumption, that of full "underlying" semantic universality (cf. Katz, 1978), is in fact an assumption about full cultural universality, thus a completely human-universal world view. This extreme assumption is equally unsupported by comparative cross-cultural facts (Givón, 1989, ch. 9). To the extent that the cultures of the L1 and L2 used by Kroll and Scholl (1992) were substantially different, chances are that the assumption of full identity of semantic-mental networks was less warranted than in our study.

14 There is no reason to assume that this null hypothesis is not the universal modus operandi in early L2 acquisition. The extant (native) lexical-semantic network is all L1 speakers have to go on at time zero of L2 acquisition. Until the input begins to contradict this hypothesis in an intrusive enough fashion (i.e., high enough frequency of adaptively-important instances), the null hypothesis of semantic identity between L1 and L2 clearly remains the most economical learning strategy. One has to assume, further, that the effect for Keki should be *zero* at the very start of instruction, when the subjects did not know the meaning of Keki words.

## Methods

### STIMULI

Two matched lexical decision tasks were constructed, one with 40 English target words, the other with 40 Keki target words. The two lists were made of paired translation equivalents. The English list served as a baseline to gauge the semantic-priming effect in the subjects' native language. Each pair of target words – one English, the other its translation equivalent in Keki – were primed by the same English prime word.

Each target was preceded once with a semantically-related English prime word, and once with an unrelated English prime word. Half the targets were primed first by a related prime word, the other half first by an unrelated prime word. For each English and Keki target word, a matching nonword was constructed according to two criteria:

1. The nonword had to be a phonologically possible word in the language, and in fact be orthographically fairly similar to the real Keki or English target word.
2. The nonword could not have close sound correspondences (e.g., rhyming) to the prime word with which it was primed.

Within a block of trials, the two primes were also presented one time each with the nonword corresponding to the target word (i.e., English or Keki).

## Procedure

The stimuli were presented separately in two experimental blocks, each containing 160 trials. One block consisted of English primes and Keki target words. The other block consisted of English primes and English target words. The English primes used for both blocks were the same, and the English target words were matched in meaning to the Keki target words.

Subjects were asked to view a computer screen on which two words were flashed one at a time, at the same location on the screen. The subjects were told to read the words as they came on the screen, and then to determine if the second – target – word was or was not a word in Keki or English, respectively. The effect of priming was measured in terms of the reaction time to this lexical decision task. Since word pairs were presented in separate language blocks, the subjects knew what type of word versus nonword they were asked to judge (English or Keki).

Before performing the main experiment, subjects were asked to read a set of instructions and to perform ten practice trials. An individual trial began with a fixation asterisk, which flashed briefly at the center of the computer screen. The prime word was presented then at the same centered location for 250 msec. A brief time interval of 17 msec followed. The target word then appeared on the screen at the same centered location, and remained there until the subject responded by pressing a specified key on the computer keyboard. The keys indicated the subjects' decision about the lexical status of the word – *Y* for "yes" and *N* for "no." Following a response, the next trial began after an additional 500 msec. Both response times and accuracy scores were recorded.

The English-English block was administered 4 times: before instruction began, after 5 days (10 hours; 1 week), after 10 days (20 hours; 2 weeks), and after 24 days (48 hours; 5 weeks). The English-Keki block was administered 3 times: after 5 days (10 hours, 1 week), after 10 days (20 hours, 2 weeks), and after 24 days (48 hours, 5 weeks) of instruction. Only trials where the target was a real English or Keki word, and where the subject responded correctly, were used in the analysis of reaction times.

## Results

The results of the semantic priming tests are expressed graphically in Figure 3.

Mean reaction times for all subjects were compared at 3 points in time – 5 days, 10 days, 24 days – for English and Keki targets primed by both related and unrelated words using a Repeated Measures Analysis of Variance. There was a significant main effect for time ($F\,2, 48 = 34.287$, $p < .0001$), a significant main effect for target type ($F\,1,24 = 87.253$, $p < .0001$) and a significant main effect for prime type ($F\,1,24 = 105$, $p < .0001$). There was also a significant interaction between time and target type ($F\,2, 48 = 13.072$, $p < .0001$), and between target type and prime type ($F\,1,24 = 5.763$, $p < .0245$). There was no significant interaction between time and prime type. There was also no significant interaction between the three factors combined: time, prime type and target type.

The main effect of decreasing RTs over time reflects subjects' improved skill with practice. The main effect for target type reflects the overall speed advantage in lexical decision about English words over Keki words. But, as can be seen in Figure 3, this advantage is much more pronounced at the early stage of L2 learning, and tapers off toward the end. The main effect for prime type represents the priming effect itself, i.e., the processing advantage of related over unrelated prime words. This effect is remarkably stable over time (hence the lack of significant interaction). The time stability of the priming effect, and its essentially-identical level for English and Keki targets, are represented graphically in Figure 4.

The interaction between time and target type represents a significantly different rate of improvement (decreased RTs) over time in the recogni-

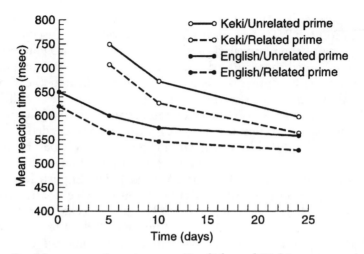

*Figure 3    Mean reaction times to English and Keki targets primed by related and unrelated English words.*

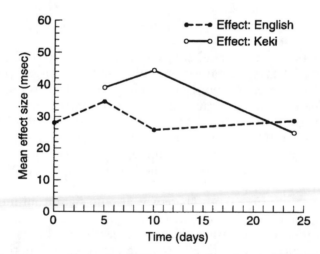

*Figure 4    Mean effect size (RTs to unrelated primes, RTs to related primes) for English and Keki target words over time.*

tion of Keki words versus English words. The smaller improvement in English word-recognition RTs over time presumably reflects the effect of *experimental habituation* (rather than lexical learning). The faster rate of improvement in Keki RTs must, on the other hand, reflect the combination of two distinct time-dependent developments:

1. the experimental habituation effect (as in English)
2. real learning of Keki vocabulary

The lack of significant interaction between time and prime type suggests, as noted above, that the main priming effect is the same for English and Keki. The lack of significant interaction between time, target type and prime type suggests that the main priming effect remains stable over time for both Keki and English. This constancy of the priming effect is reflected in Figure 4.

Since the RTs for Keki targets decrease significantly faster than those for English targets, we decided to assess some more specific differences between the two RT curves through 5 post-hoc comparisons.[15] For these comparisons, the RTs for related and unrelated primes were pooled together. The change in RTs between day 5 and day 10 was not significant for English but significant for Keki (F 1,48 = 48.418, p. < .0001). The change in RTs between day 10 and day 24 (end time) was again not significant for English, but remained significant for Keki (F 1,48 = 6.201, p. < .0162), albeit at a lower level. Thus, the habituation effect in English was only significant up to day 5 of the experiment (10 hours), while the learning effect in Keki remained significant to the end of the experiment.

By the last test date (day 24), the subjects' RTs to English targets were still significantly shorter (faster) than their RTs to Keki targets (F 1,48 = 18.41, p < .0001). Thus, the absolute gap between English and Keki word-recognition performance indeed decreased over time (cf. Figure 3). But the subjects' word-recognition skills in Keki by the end of the experiment still had not caught up with their word-recognition skills in English.

## Discussion

This experiment was not designed to discriminate between alternative models of the bilingual lexicon – shared versus separate semantic networks.[16] What my results do suggest is that learners can access the lexical-semantic network of nodes and associations via their second language vocabulary relatively early in the development of second language vocabulary, certainly when the semantic structure of the L2 lexicon is not at obvious variance with that of the L1 lexicon. By the end of the first 5 days of instruction (10 hours) under such nonvariance conditions, the same absolute magnitude of the semantic priming effect – RT to unrelated prime minus RT to related prime – is observed in both Keki and

---

15  The Bonferoni technique was used to control family error rate for post hoc comparisons: .05/5 = alpha level, p. < 0.1.
16  As Keatley (1992) notes, "there is no grand consensus in current research on the nature of bilingual memory."

English. This effect remains stable in both languages to the end of the experiment (cf. Figure 4). The subjects have apparently concluded, by the end of 10 hours of instruction, that Keki could be effectively represented by the very same lexical-semantic network that represented English. This is probably the most reasonable null hypothesis in early L2 acquisition.[17]

The difference in absolute level of RTs between English and Keki is largest at the early stage of the experiment (5 days) and shrinks gradually toward the end (24 days). But even then the RT values remain significantly higher (slower) for Keki target words as compared to English words. Taken together, the two results suggest that the time-course for establishing semantic networks for L2 vocabulary is very different from the time-course of developing L2 word recognition. The former – at least under the condition of cross-cultural semantic similarity – proceeds rapidly, perhaps guided by a strong null hypothesis of nondistinctness. The latter proceeds much more slowly.

Because the priming effect is the same for English and Keki by the end of 5 days of instruction, the improvement in RTs for Keki targets from day 5 through day 24 cannot be attributed to improvement in the efficacy of semantic networks. The effect of experimental habituation in English was found to be not significant beyond day 5. One could therefore tentatively conclude that the continuing significant improvement in RTs to Keki words must represent a net effect of improved word-recognition skills. This conclusion is indeed borne out by the next test.

# Word recognition

## Preamble

Cattell (1887) was the first psychologist to report that people were faster at recognizing written words than at recognizing written nonword letter strings. Reicher (1969) showed that when subjects were given the task of deciding if a given letter was present in a previously displayed string of letters, they were much faster if the string of letters formed a meaningful word. This suggests that words are recognized as unitary chunks, while strings of letters are scanned serially.

Sieroff and Posner (1988), Sieroff et al. (1988), and Posner et al. (1989) have shown that the visual recognition for familiar words by normal fluent adults proceeds in a different manner and at a different brain location than the visual recognition of unfamiliar letter strings. Familiar –

17 See again footnote 14.

habituated – words are processed automatically at a nonattentional location of the prestriated left-side posterior visual area of the brain. In contrast, unfamiliar words – such as nonsense letter strings – are processed in an attended manner at the right-side posterior visual attention brain site.

In a previous study (Givón et al., 1990) we used the visual attention (left-right cuing) measures of Sieroff and Posner (1988) and Sieroff et al. (1988) to study L2 (Spanish) vocabulary acquisition. We showed that prior to instruction, subjects processed L2 vocabulary in the same attention-demanding manner as they did nonsense letter strings. After two years of instruction, subjects processed L2 vocabulary approximately in the same unattended (automated) fashion as they did habituated L1 (English) words. The word-recognition measure we used here was designed to further probe the time-course of the development of automated Keki word-recognition skills.

## Methods

### STIMULI WORD LISTS

The stimuli lists included 40 Keki words 4–6 letters long, 40 English words of roughly matching length, and 40 Keki-like nonwords of roughly matching length. The English words were matched in length to the Keki words, and were all everyday words of high use-frequency. The Keki-like nonwords were matched in length – and were orthographically similar to – the real Keki words. The Keki-like nonwords also followed the Keki canonical word form of C(C)VC(C)V.

### STIMULI PRESENTATION

Stimuli appeared as black letters on a white background of a Macintosh RGB computer screen. Subjects viewed the display binocularly and were instructed to fixate initially on the center of the screen. Subjects were asked to view pairs of words that were presented briefly (87 msec) one after the other and then to determine if the two words (or letter strings) were the same or not. The first word in a pair was presented in lowercase letters, and the second in uppercase letters. Word pairs were presented randomly so that all three word lists were intermixed. For each word in the 3 word lists, 4 pairs of stimuli were presented: In two of the pairs, the two words were identical. In the other two pairs, the second word (or nonword) differed from the first by one letter – a vowel in one case, a consonant in the other.

## Procedure

Subjects were asked to read a set of instructions, which included a set of practice trials for each word type (English words, Keki words, Keki nonwords). Each individual trial was presented in the following manner:

1. A fixation point (a single asterisk) was flashed in the center of the screen for 500 msec.
2. Following the fixation point, a word in lowercase type was flashed on the screen for 87 msec.
3. This word was then followed by a mask – a row of 10 uppercase Xs that remained on the screen for 1 sec.
4. Following the mask, the second word – either the same or different – was flashed on the screen for 83 msec.
5. The second word was then followed by the same kind of mask as the first, and for the same duration.
6. Subjects were instructed to decide whether the second word was the same as or different from the first, and to respond as quickly and as accurately as possible by pressing a key labeled *S* for "same" or *D* for "different."
7. The subjects' choices were recorded and their reaction times (in msecs) were measured from the time the second word first appeared on the screen.
8. After a response was made, the word "Ready" appeared on the screen and remained there until the subject pressed the space bar, with his or her other hand, to continue.
9. Periodically during the 480 trials, subjects were instructed to take a 2-minute break. However, they were allowed to take more frequent breaks if necessary.

The word-recognition test was administered 4 times over the course of the 25-day learning period: prior to the beginning of instruction, after 5 days (10 hours), after 10 days (20 hours), and after 24 days (48 hours). Only trials in which the pair of words was the same, and in which the response was correct, were included in the analysis of RTs.

## Results

The mean reaction times for the word-recognition test over the experimental period, for Keki-like nonwords, real Keki words and English words, are plotted graphically in Figure 5.

The mean reaction times for all subjects were compared at all points in time for the three word types, using a Repeated Measures Analysis of Variance. There was a main effect for time (F $3,81 = 38.831$; p $< .0001$),

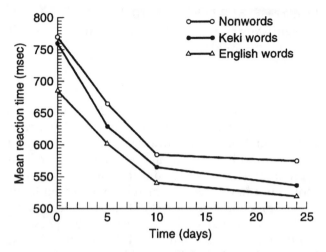

*Figure 5 Mean reaction times to English, Keki and nonwords over time in word-recognition matching task.*

a main effect for word type (F 2,54 = 74.708; p < .0001), as well as an interaction between time and word type (F 6,162 = 7.678; p < .0001).

At time *zero*, before beginning Keki instruction, the subjects processed Keki words and Keki-like nonwords identically, with no significant difference in speed. But the subjects processed both Keki words and Keki-like nonwords significantly more slowly than English words (mean RT = 760 msec versus mean RT = 680 msec, respectively). And this difference was statistically significant (KvE F 1,54 = 41.0l2, p. < .0001).[18]

After 24 days of Keki instruction, the pattern of similarities and differences was reversed. There was now no significant difference between the subjects' RTs to English and Keki words. But their RTs to both English and Keki words were now significantly faster (lower) than their RTs to Keki-like nonwords (nonwords versus English: F 1,54 = 78.7, p < .0001; nonwords versus Keki: F 1,54 = 40.596, p < .0001).

The rate of decrease in RTs over time for English words closely parallels that for Keki-like nonwords, presumably reflecting in both cases experimental task habituation. But for Keki words, the rate of decrease in RTs is significantly greater, presumably reflecting the effect of both habituation and lexical learning.

For Keki-like nonwords, there was no significant decrease in RTs after the first 10 days of instruction (2 weeks). For both English and Keki,

18 A total of 9 means comparisons were made as post hoc analyses. The Bonferoni technique (alpha = .05/number of comparisons made) was used to control for family error rate. An effect was thus considered significant if p < .0055.

however, the decrease of RTs between 10 days (2 weeks) and 24 days (5 weeks) was significant (English: F  1,54 = 16.72, p < .0003; Keki: F  1,54 = 36.505, p < .0001).

## Discussion

These results suggest that in the course of L2 instruction, learners can develop their L2 word-recognition skills to a level that approximates their L1 word-recognition skills. Toward the end of the instruction period my subjects recognized Keki words in the same rapid, accurate and presumably automatic fashion as they did their native English vocabulary. This effect could not have been due merely to increased familiarity with possible orthographic patterns of Keki. This is so because the subjects' RTs to Keki-like nonwords – all orthographically possible in Keki – remained significantly slower than their RTs to either English or meaningful Keki words. (It is of course possible that the lack of further improvement in processing speed of Keki-like words is due to less practice.) Although no significant improvement in RTs to Keki-like nonwords occurred after 10 days, the RTs to meaningful Keki words (and to English words) continued to show significant improvement till the end of the experiment (24 days).

It remains to be answered why the RTs to English words also continued to improve (although at a slower rate than the Keki RTs) till the end of the experiment. Ideally, one would expect those to level off at the same point in time (here 10 days) as those for Keki-like nonwords. On the face of it, this conflicts with the behavior of English words in the semantic priming experiment. However, the two tasks – lexical-status decision versus similarity decision – were different.

The continued improvement in the RTs to meaningful Keki words supports our finding in the semantic-priming experiment. The improvement in word-recognition skills in Keki continued in both cases till the end of the experiment.

The acquisition of L2 word-recognition skills, up to the L1 level, seems to require a significant amount of exposure to L2 vocabulary. Haynes and Carr (1990) found that learners did not master the L2 writing system easily and rapidly. Under the present experimental conditions, however, 48 hours of L2 instruction seem to have sufficed to remove all significant difference between L1 and L2 word-recognition skills. Visual matching skills have been shown to correlate with comprehension, and to predict the ability to learn new words from context (Brown & Haynes, 1985; Haynes & Carr, 1990). My findings thus have important implications for testing reading performance in both the first and second language classroom.

# General Discussion

## Methodology

Can the acquisition of a second language be studied profitably under controlled laboratory conditions, with an artificially-concocted L2? This question remained a nagging if silent companion as I conceived, designed and implemented this complex study. It has also been the gist of many critical comments I have received from worried, if well-meaning, colleagues. I think that I have demonstrated, at least to my own satisfaction, that the answer to this ancillary methodological question must be a resounding *yes*. Keki vocabulary – as well as other linguistic communicative skills – was indeed acquired under the rigorous and often artificial conditions that were imposed on instruction via machine-human interaction. What is more, my various measurements suggest that Keki vocabulary was acquired in a way that makes perfect sense for a natural language.

Semantic networks coded by Keki words are evidently activated by English prime words at the same level as the semantic networks coded by native English words. Skilled Keki word recognition approximates the subjects' performance in English word recognition. Explicit, attention-demanding types of knowledge were acquired much earlier than implicit, automated skills. All this is not to say that I recommend this experimental methodology as a regular venue for L2 instruction. The pragmatic constraints on such controlled conditions make this an unlikely proposition. What I have shown, I think, is that this is indeed an efficient, sensitive, meaningful research environment, one in which complex questions can be addressed in a controlled yet meaningful way.

## Explicit translation skills

The capacity to perform conscious, explicit translation was acquired early and showed no directional bias (L1-to-L2 versus L2-to-L1). After 10 hours (5 days) of instruction, the subjects performed at more than 90% accuracy, and the learning curve essentially flattened out. In contrast, performance speed continued to improve to the end of the experiment, and a significant directional bias was evident: Translation L1-to-L2 was consistently faster – to the very end – than translation L2-to-L1. Given the results of my two other measures, semantic priming and word recognition, I attribute the continuing improvement in translation speed to a continued improvement in Keki word-recognition skills, an improvement that remained significant to the very end of the experiment.

Improvement in semantic-network efficacy must be ruled out as an explanation. The priming experiment showed essentially the same level of priming effect in Keki at the end of the first week (10 hours) as for English.

In measuring translation skills, I thus tapped into two different cognitive skills: explicit conscious learning of conceptual meaning of word forms, a process that can be completed rather rapidly; and implicit, subconscious development of automated processing skills, which proceeds more slowly and gradually. Like other automated skills, this capacity requires repeated practice, hence the slower developmental curve.

The directional bias in the development of the second, automated skill reinforces this interpretation. The time allotted for translation-stimulus presentation – under the present experimental conditions, 350 msec – was just enough for recognition of the well-habituated English vocabulary, but clearly too taxing for the yet-emerging skill of Keki word recognition. In contrast, the presentation time for the second – matching – word in this task was not constrained, but rather controlled by the subjects' own response speed. Since Keki word-recognition skills continued to improve to the end of the experiment, the directional advantage that favored L1-to-L2 (English-to-Keki) translation remained all the way to the end.

## Semantic networks

I designed the semantic structure of Keki vocabulary to be fully compatible with the lexical-semantic structure of English. Under such conditions, I could prime both Keki and English target words with English prime words. This allowed me to bypass the effect of imperfect Keki word recognition, relevant at least in the early stages of instruction. But this choice also made it necessary to keep Keki lexical-semantic structure identical to that of English.

My results here again show the dual pattern of explicit knowledge versus implicit skills. The acquisition of semantic networks of concept activation, as measured by the priming effect, was essentially complete after the first 5 days (10 hours) of instruction. The priming effect in Keki – advantage of related over unrelated prime word – was by then identical to that in English, and remained at the same level throughout the experiment. I interpret this to mean that once the subjects had acquired the rudimentary – and conscious – connections between Keki word forms and conceptual nodes, the very same lexical-semantic network was accessed by Keki vocabulary as by same-meaning English vocabulary.

On the other hand, the absolute reaction-time values for Keki lexical decision in this test – in priming by both related and unrelated primes – continued to improve till the end of the experiment, and only began to approximate the absolute RTs of English after 25 days (28 hours of instruction). I ascribe this again to the slow acquisition of automated Keki word-recognition skills, a process that continued to the end of the experiment. Further, it may be that the *lexical decision task* used in the semantic priming test ("Is it a word or not a word in Keki?") is cognitively more difficult than the *word-matching task* used in the word-recognition test ("Is the second word identical to the first word?").

By choosing to make Keki semantically nondistinct from English, I left an interesting theoretical issue moot: Are the semantic networks of L2 identical to the extant networks of L1? What my results suggest is that under conditions where the two cultures – C1 and C2 – share a very similar world view, L2 learners find it extremely easy to access the extant semantic networks by L2 translation-equivalent word forms.

The semantic similarity between languages – thus cultural world views – is most commonly a matter of degree. The semantic organization that underlies the more concrete, sensory-motor, spatiotemporal vocabulary is likely to be much more universal and culture-neutral. It is acquired by children of all cultures early and prelinguistically, and it serves as the early template for later linguistic-conceptual development.[19] Even in adulthood metaphoric extension of both lexical and grammatical meaning proceeds overwhelmingly from the more concrete to the more abstract.[20] This suggests that in some strong sense the more human-universal sensory-motor, spatiotemporal, early-acquired semantic network remains the common core of the mental lexicon of all languages.

The present experimental conditions could easily be adjusted to the controlled study of vocabulary acquisition under various conditions of semantic-network similarity versus contrast between L1 and L2. Under the starkest conditions of semantic dissimilarity, I would predict that the learners' null hypothesis – expected at least in the early stages of acquisition – will remain the assumption that the two languages share their semantic networks. Thus semantic priming of L2 targets by L1 primes may reveal a U-shaped time curve: first efficient (if erroneous) priming, then inefficient priming, finally a reestablished efficient priming, as the semantic networks of L2 get sorted out and established as *distinct* from those of L1.

## Word recognition

My results here reconfirm earlier findings that the acquisition of word recognition involves a shift in both the mode and the neurological loca-

19 See Carter (1974); Slobin (1973, ed. 1985); H. Clark (1970), E. Clark (1972a, 1972b).
20 See Lakoff and Johnson (1980); Lakoff (1987); Heine, Claudi and Hünnemeyer (1991).

tion of processing – from slow attended processing on the right-posterior side of the brain, to skilled automated processing on the left-posterior side of the brain.[21] Prior to instruction, the word-recognition skills of my subjects with Keki and Keki-like words were statistically identical. By the end of the instruction period, the subjects' skills with Keki words were statistically indistinguishable from their skills with English words. Further, unlike conscious translation and unlike semantic priming, the improvement in the subjects' word-recognition skills continued to the very end of the instructional period.

I interpret the time-course of the Keki word-recognition performance to involve two distinct components: (1) experimental habituation; (2) word-recognition skill acquisition. The first component is evident in the time-course of both the Keki-like nonwords and the English words. The first flattens out by the end of week 2 (10 days). The second seems to flatten out the same way, but the small increment from week 2 (10 days) to week 5 (24 days) is statistically significant. In contrast to both, the improvement in Keki word-recognition skills continues visibly and significantly to the very end.

There are two ways to interpret the discrepancy between the time-course of English and Keki-like nonwords. One may ascribe it to the effect of *added practice:* The subjects experienced the Keki-like nonwords only four times, during tests. In contrast, both the English and the Keki words were presented to the students repeatedly through the instructional period. Alternatively, one may suggest that word recognition is not a purely perceptual skill, but rather is acquired – universally – under conditions of *word meaningfulness.* Language learners are not merely habituated to legitimate (versus illegitimate) possible letter strings, but to legitimate letter strings associated with *stable meaning.* The more rapid termination of the experimental habituation phase with Keki-like nonwords – as compared to English real words – can thus be ascribed to lack of such "semantic incentive." My data give us no grounds for choosing between these two alternative explanations.

Cognitively as well as neurologically, one can factor out lexical access into (at least) three distinct components:

1. automated visual word recognition at the left-posterior prestriate visual location
2. connection from left-posterior word forms to the phonologically-labeled semantic node in the left-frontal semantic-lexical center.[22]

---

21  See again Sieroff and Posner (1988); Sieroff et al. (1988); Peterson et al. (1988); Posner et al. (1989); Posner and Carr (1991); Givón, Yang and Gernsbacher (1990).
22  See Petersen et al. (1988), Posner et al. (1989), and Posner and Carr (1991) for support for the left-frontal location of the semantic lexicon.

3. activation of closely-associated semantic nodes via the network of connections

If my second – preferred – interpretation proves to be valid, what my results suggest is that components 1 and 2 in the course of real lexical acquisition are *inseparable;* they become habituated (automated) *in tandem.*[23] So that "to acquire automated word-recognition skills" means not only to learn to recognize automatically a letter sequence as "phonologically belonging to the language," but also to establish a habituated automatic connection between the perceived letter sequence in the left-posterior visual location and a habitually-associated left-frontal location in the semantic lexicon.

The status of habituation versus nonhabituation of phonologically-possible nonsense letter strings remains somewhat murky. Sieroff and Posner (1988) and Sieroff et al. (1988) found that English-like nonsense sequences behaved – with respect to left/right cuing – like English words but unlike phonologically impossible (non-English) nonsense letter sequences. The results cited by Givón, Yang, and Gernsbacher (1990) support those earlier findings with a slight modification: Letter sequences that are phonologically impossible as English (and Spanish) words are indeed processed by monolingual English speakers in an attention-demanding fashion. But unfamiliar Spanish words, all phonologically *possible* in English,[24] are *also* processed by monolingual English speakers in an attention-demanding fashion. After two years of studying Spanish, bilingual English speakers now processed Spanish vocabulary in the same attention-free fashion as their native English words.

## Conclusion

To the extent that our earlier results in the Spanish study are indeed valid, they reinforce my contention that acquiring an automated visual word-recognition capacity involves not only the habituated detection of legitimate word forms, but also – in tandem – the automated connection of those posterior perceptual targets to stable, habituated anterior semantic locations.

Word forms have two characteristics that lend them to – indeed beg for – automated processing:

1. They are largely arbitrary, at least in their relation to lexical meaning.[25]

23 A similar suggestion was made in Reicher (1969).
24 Spanish has a much simpler phonological structure, so that most Spanish words are also possible as English words (but not vice versa).
25 Purely phonological constraints on word structure are much less arbitrary vis-à-vis speech perceptual and speech production needs.

2. They are cross-linguistically different, with very scant carry-over from one unrelated language to another.

In contrast, lexical-semantic networks (and communicative-pragmatic structure) are rather different:

1. They are much more closely motivated by adaptive experience.
2. They reveal more universal characteristics, and thus carry over well from one language (and culture) to the next.

In second language acquisition, under the null-hypothesis condition of rough semantic identity between L1 and L2, the main task of vocabulary acquisition is *not* to establish a new semantic network, since the extant native one remains valid. Rather, the task is to habituate the two coupled processes of word recognition:

1. automated recognition L2 word forms
2. automated, stable connection between posterior word forms and their corresponding anterior semantic targets

In this experiment, I found that semantic priming – indicative of connectivity in the anterior semantic network itself – was intact very early. This was reflected in the rapid establishment of accurate conscious translation and semantic priming. It was the word-recognition skill, presumably both components, that lagged behind and continued longer to benefit from instruction. This relationship between the components of the word-processing system is rather natural. The fact that it revealed itself in our experiment in such a fashion reinforces my conviction that what I tracked here was indeed real, natural language learning.

## References

Anderson, R. (1979). Expanding Schumann's pidginization hypothesis. *Language Learning, 29,* 105–120.

Bickerton, D. (1981). *Roots of language.* Ann Arbor, MI: Karoma.

Bickerton, D., & Givón, T. (1976). Pidginization and syntactic change: From SOV and VSO to SVO. In S. Stever, C. A. Walker, & S. S. Mufwene (Eds.), *Papers from the Parasession on diachronic syntax* (pp. 9–39). Chicago: Chicago Linguistics Society.

Bloom, L. (1973). *One word at a time: The use of single-word utterances before syntax.* The Hague: Mouton.

Blumstein, S. E., & Milberg, W. (1984). Automatic and controlled processing in speech/language deficits in aphasia. Paper presented at the Symposium on Automatic Speech, Minneapolis, MN.

Brown, T. L., & Haynes, M. (1985). Literacy background and reading development in a second language. In T. H. Carr (Ed.), *The development of reading skills* (pp. 19–34). San Francisco: Jossey-Bass.

Carr, T. H. (Ed.). (1985). *The development of reading skills.* San Francisco: Jossey-Bass.

Carr, T. H., & Levy, B. A. (Eds.). (1990). *Reading and its development: Component skills approaches.* New York: Academic Press.

Carr, T. H., & Posner, M. I. (In press). The impact of learning to read on the functional anatomy of language processing. In B. de Gelder & J. Morais (Eds.), *Language and literacy: Comparative approaches.* Cambridge: MIT Press.

Carter, A. (1974). *The development of communication in the sensory-motor period: A case study.* Ph.D. diss., University of California, Berkeley.

Carter, R. (1987). *Vocabulary.* London: Allen & Unwin.

Carter, R., & McCarthy, M. (Eds.). (1988). *Vocabulary and language teaching.* London: Longman.

Cattell, J. M. (1987). Experiments on the association of ideas. *Mind, 12,* 68–74.

Clark, E. (1972a). On the child's acquisition of semantics in two semantic fields. *Journal of Verbal Learning and Verbal Behavior, 8,* 750–758.

(1972b). Some perceptual factors in the acquisition of locative terms by young children. *CLS, 8.* Chicago: Chicago Linguistics Society.

Clark, H. (1970). The primitive nature of children's relational concepts. In J. Hayes (Ed.), *Cognition and the development of language* (pp. 269–278). New York: John Wiley & Sons.

Clyne, M. (1977). Multilingualism and pidginization in Australian industry. *Ethnic Studies, 1,* 40–55.

Ferguson, C. (1975). Towards a characterization of English foreigner talk. *Anthropological Linguistics, 17,* 1–14.

Foss, D. J. (1969). Decision processes during sentence comprehension: Effect of lexical item difficulty and position upon decision time. *Journal of Verbal Learning and Verbal Behavior, 8,* 457–462.

Gairns, R., & Redman, S. (1986). *Working with words.* Cambridge: Cambridge University Press.

Givón, T. (1979). *On understanding grammar.* New York: Academic Press.

(1989). *Mind, code and context: Essays in pragmatics.* Hillsdale, NJ: Lawrence Erlbaum.

(1990). Natural language learning and organized language teaching. In H. Burmeister & P. L. Rounds (Eds.), *Variability in second language acquisition: Proceedings of the tenth meeting of the Second Language Research Forum* (pp. 61–84). Eugene: University of Oregon.

Givón, T., Yang, L., & Gernsbacher, M. A. (1990). The processing of second language vocabulary: From attended to automated word recognition. In H. Burmeister & P. L. Rounds (Eds.), *Variability in second language acquisition: Proceedings of the tenth meeting of the Second Language Research Forum* (pp. 345–364). Eugene: University of Oregon.

Goodman, D. (1987). *The complete HyperCard handbook.* New York: Bantam Books.

Haynes, M., & Carr, T. H. (1990). Writing system background and second language reading: A component skills analysis of English reading by native speaker-readers of Chinese. In T. H. Carr & B. A. Levy (Eds.), *Reading and its development: Component Skills Approaches* (pp. 375–420). New York: Academic Press.

Heine, B., Claudi, U., & Hünnemeyer, F. (1991). *Grammaticalization: A conceptual framework.* Chicago: University of Chicago Press.

Katz, J. J. (1978). Effability and translation. In F. Guenthner & M. Guenthner-Reutter (Eds.), *Meaning and translation* (pp. 191–234). London: Duckworth.

Keatley, C. W. (1992). History of bilingualism research in cognitive psychology. In R. J. Harris (Ed.), *Cognitive processing in bilinguals* (pp. 15–49). New York: Elsevier Science Publishing.

Keenan, E. O. (1974). Again and again: The pragmatics of imitation in child language. Paper read at the American Anthropological Association Annual Meeting, Mexico City, November.

(1975). Making it last: Repetition in child language discourse. *Berkeley Linguistics Society #1* (pp. 279–294). Berkeley: University of California.

Kroll, J. F., & Curley, J. (1988). Lexical memory in novice bilinguals: The role of concepts in retrieving second language words. In M. Gruneberg, P. Morris & R. Sykes (Eds.), *Practical aspects of memory*, vol. 2 (pp. 389–395). London: John Wiley & Sons.

Kroll, J. F., & Scholl, A. (1992). Lexical and conceptual memory in fluent and non-fluent bilinguals. In R. J. Harris (Ed.), *Cognitive processing in bilinguals* (pp. 191–204). New York: Elsevier Science Publishing.

Lakoff, G. (1987). *Women, fire and dangerous things: What categories reveal about the mind.* Chicago: University of Chicago Press.

Lakoff, G., & Johnson, M. (1980). *Metaphors we live by.* Chicago: University of Chicago Press.

Laws, K. (1987). *HyperCard 2.0*, v. 2 [computer program]. Cupertino, CA: Apple Computer.

Lieberman, P. (1984). *The biology and evolution of language.* Cambridge: Harvard University Press.

Limber, J. (1973). The genesis of complex sentences. In T. Moore (Ed.), *Cognitive development and the acquisition of language* (pp. 169–185). New York: Academic Press.

Long, M. (1981). Input, interaction and second language acquisition. In H. Winitz (Ed.), *Native language and foreign language acquisition, Annals of the New York Academy of Sciences*, 379, 259–278.

McLaughlin, B. (1980). On the use of miniature artificial languages in second language research. *Applied Psycholinguistics, 1,* 353–365.

Meisel, J. (1977). Linguistic simplification: A study of immigrant workers' speech and foreigner talk. In S. Corder & E. Roulet (Eds.), *The notions of simplification, interlanguages and pidgins, and their relation to second language pedagogy* (pp. 88–113). Geneva: Droz.

Meyer, D. E., & Schvaneveldt, D. E. (1971). Facilitation in recognizing pairs of words: Evidence of a dependence between retrieval operations. *Journal of Experimental Psychology, 90,* 227–234.

Morton, J. (1969). The interaction of information in word recognition. *Psychological Review, 76,* 340–354.

Nation, I. S. P. (1990). *Teaching and learning vocabulary.* New York: Newbury House.

Neeley, J. H. (1990). Semantic priming effects in visual word recognition: A selective review of current findings and theories. In D. Besner & G. Humphreys (Eds.), *Basic processes in reading: Visual word recognition* (pp. 264–336). Hillsdale, NJ: Lawrence Erlbaum.

Petersen, S. E., Fox, P. T., Posner, M. I., Mintun, M. & Reichle, M. E. (1988). Positron emission tomographic studies of the cortical anatomy of single-word processing. *Science, 240,* 1627–1631.

Posner, M. I., & Boies, S. W. (1971). Components of attention. *Psychological Review, 78*(5), 319–408.

Posner, M. I., & Carr, T. H. (1991). Lexical access and the brain: Anatomical constraints on cognitive models of word recognition. *American Journal of Psychology (Technical Report 91-5,* University of Oregon, Institute for Cognitive and Decision Sciences).

Posner, M. I., Sandson, J., Dhawan, M., & Shulman, G. L. (1989). Is word recognition automatic? A cognitive-anatomical approach. *Journal of Cognitive Neuroscience, 1*(1), 50–60.

Posner, M. I., & Snyder, C. R. R. (1974). Attention and cognitive control. In R. L. Solso (Ed.), *Information processing and cognition: The Loyola symposium* (pp. 669–681). Hillsdale, NJ: Lawrence Erlbaum.

Posner, M. I. & Warren, R. E. (1972). Traces, concepts and conscious constructions. In A. W. Melton & E. Martin (Eds.), *Coding processes in human memory* (pp. 25–43). Washington, DC: Winston & Son.

Reber, A. S. (1967). Implicit learning of artificial grammars. *Journal of Verbal Language and Verbal Behavior, 77,* 317–327.

Reicher, G. M. (1969). Perceptual recognition as a function of meaningfulness of stimulus material. *Journal of Experimental Psychology, 81,* 275–280.

Schneider, W. (1985). Toward a model of attention and the development of automatic processing. In M. I. Posner & O. Marin (Eds.), *Attention and performance XI* (pp. 475–492). Hillsdale, NJ: Lawrence Erlbaum.

Schneider, W., & Shiffrin, R. M. (1977). Controlled and automatic human information processing, I: Detection, search and attention. *Psychological Review, 84,* 1–66.

Schnitzer, M. (1989). *The pragmatic basis of aphasia.* Hillsdale, NJ: Lawrence Erlbaum.

Schumann, J. (1978a). *The pidginization process: A model for second language acquisition.* Rowley, MA: Newbury House.

(1978b). Second language acquisition: The pidginization hypothesis. In E. Hatch (Ed.), *Second language acquisition* (pp. 256–271). Rowley, MA: Newbury House.

(1984). Non-syntactic speech in Spanish-English basilang. In R. Anderson (Ed.), *Second languages: A cross-linguistic perspective* (pp. 355–374). Rowley, MA: Newbury House.

(1990). Extending the scope of the acculturation/pidginization model to include cognition. *TESOL Quarterly, 24,* 667–684.

Scollon, R. (1976). *Conversations with a one year old child.* Honolulu: University of Hawaii Press.

Selinker, L. (1972). "Interlanguage." *International Review of Applied Linguistics, 10,* 209–231.

Sieroff, E., Pollatsek, A., & Posner, M. I. (1988). Recognition of visual letter strings following injury to the posterior visual attention system. *Cognitive Neuropsychology, 5,* 427–449.

Sieroff, E., & Posner, M. I. (1988). Cuing spatial attention during processing of words and letter strings in normals. *Cognitive Neuropsychology, 5,* 451–472.

Slobin, D. (1973). Cognitive prerequisites to the development of grammar. In C. Ferguson & D. Slobin (Eds.), *Studies of child language development* (pp. 175–208). New York: Holt, Rinehart & Winston.

(1977). Language change in childhood and history. In J. MacNamara (Ed.), *Language, learning and thought* (pp. 185–214). New York: Academic Press.

(Ed.). (1985). *The crosslinguistic study of language acquisition,* vols. 1, 2. Hillsdale, NJ: Lawrence Erlbaum.

Swinney, D. A. (1979). Lexical access during sentence comprehension: (Re)Consideration of context effects. *Journal of Verbal Language and Verbal Behavior, 18,* 645–659.

Whorf, B. L. (1956). *Language, thought and reality.* Ed. J. B. Carroll. Cambridge: MIT Press.

# 8 Rare words, complex lexical units and the advanced learner

Pierre J. L. Arnaud and Sandra J. Savignon

## Introduction

It is often acknowledged in the language teaching community that native speaker-like competence is neither a very realistic nor necessarily a desirable goal for the average adolescent or adult foreign language learner. Some learners, however, do manage to attain a proficiency level at which it is difficult to distinguish their performance subjectively from that of native speakers. If this is rare in the case of pronunciation, receptive lexical performance more frequently displays apparent native characteristics. The research presented here was aimed at determining how "passive" knowledge of rare words and complex lexical units by advanced learners increases with level of study and eventually compares with that of native speakers.

## Passive vocabulary

It should be made clear at the outset what is understood here by "passive" knowledge. Many a paragraph in the literature is devoted to "what it means to know a word," but passive knowledge can best be described by considering what happens when an utterance is comprehended: Using phonetic clues present in the speech continuum, the phonological representation (*significant*) of a lexeme is accessed, which in turn permits access to the representation of its meaning (*signifié*). Whether this semantic representation leads to another, extralinguistic and more abstract "higher" representation or concept is relatively unclear at present in the

For help and advice, the authors are grateful to Daniel Serant (Université Claude Bernard-Lyon 1) and Jacques Aupetit (Université Lumière-Lyon 2); of course, any errors remain their own responsibility. They are deeply indebted to Tony Silva (Purdue University), who provided access to the native-speaker group. They also thank the anonymous teacher trainers at the Institut Universitaire de Formation des Maîtres de l'Académie de Lyon (IUFM) who volunteered to take part in the experiment. During the preparation of this article the first author was also part-time director of studies with the IUFM de l'Académie de Lyon.

semantic or psycholinguistic literatures (see, for instance, Cruse, 1988, and Segui and Beauvillain, 1988, respectively), but the ultimate aim of comprehension is that the hearer should form a representation of the speaker's communicative intent, not just of a juxtaposition of lexical and grammatical *signifiés*. This calculus of meaning is interactive (top-down and bottom-up) and it takes place automatically and unconsciously. A lexeme present in a subject's passive vocabulary is therefore one whose *signifié* can be accessed effortlessly and combined with the other *signifiés* encountered to form overall representations.[1] This notion of *passive vocabulary* is therefore close to those of *sight vocabulary* or *automated vocabulary* used by other authors (see, for example, Huckin, Haynes and Coady, 1993, pp. 219, 291).

## Rare words

Recent research by Goulden, Nation, and Read (1990) with improved methodology has led to an estimate of 17,000 word families for the vocabulary of an average native-English-speaking university student (a word family groups together a base-form and its derived forms). The L2 vocabularies acquired by secondary school learners are far inferior: For instance, Takala (1984) has found that the average "comprehensive-school" graduate in the Finnish school system has acquired a passive English vocabulary of approximately 1,500 words over seven years of study.

A passive vocabulary comprising the 2,000 most frequent words will cover 87% of the tokens in an average text (Nation, 1990, p. 16), and the consensus, well represented by Nation, is that these 2,000 words should be taught intensively, whereas infrequent words are not worth teaching as class time is limited. Instead, learners should be equipped with strategies for dealing with such words when encountered in a text. A number of objections can be raised, however. Engels (1968) stressed the fact that even though learning 3,000 words provides comprehension of 95% of occurrences, the remaining hundred thousand words – 113,000 head-words in Nation's (1990, p. 16) count – still pose a formidable problem. In addition to this argument, also presented by Honeyfield (1977), one can note that it is precisely those few tokens of rare types that carry the highest information load in any text, and therefore cause the most hindrance in the reading process when unknown. The situation is somewhat

---

1 A "passive" lexeme may or may not be available for production as well, or rather, it may be available for production in all, certain or no circumstances. It is a general observation that the active vocabulary is a subset of the passive whether in L1 or L2, but the relationship between the two is not well understood and merits more research (see, however, Meara, 1990; Melka Teichroew, 1989).

more favorable in speech comprehension where lexical variety is considerably reduced (Tripp, 1990) and some interaction may be possible, but lack of lexical knowledge still constitutes a major obstacle to comprehension.

Among the strategies generally recommended, guessing in context, on which there exists an extensive literature (see, for instance, Huckin, Haynes and Coady, 1993; Nation, 1990, pp. 160ff.), figures prominently. Guessing in context is not without its problems, however. First of all, it is, strictly speaking, a reading strategy, not primarily a vocabulary acquisition strategy, although its use involves semantic treatment of the input and therefore may facilitate incidental learning (Hulstijn, 1992). Experimental results, however, do not unanimously show such an effect of guessing on vocabulary retention (Mondria & Wit-de Boer, 1991). A second problem is that guessing may result in erroneous guesses (Haynes, 1984; Kelly, 1990; Laufer & Sim, 1985), making some later unlearning necessary. Kelly also remarks that "one stands the greater chance of succeeding the greater one's vocabulary!" In addition, when a rich context facilitates guessing, effortless access to the overall meaning of the passage may just prevent the acquisition of the lexeme (Nation & Coady, 1988). Kelly (1990) is in favor of the systematic learning of words beyond the most frequent ones and advocates the use of mnemonics, in particular the hookword method, and presents his experience of learning Polish words with it (Kelly, 1989). Generally speaking, the literature is comparatively poor on the subject of learning strategies for words beyond the first two or three thousand, outside the subject of mnemonics.

Knowledge of rare words is a valuable goal as it enables an L2 reader to access the meanings of utterances effortlessly and immediately, without having to devote too much energy to lexical guessing. There is a well-established link between the vocabulary difficulty and readability of texts (Nation & Coady, 1988), and, considering the learners' individual characteristics in L2 reading, there is a link between lexical proficiency and reading performance: Laufer (1992), correlating Israeli students' English vocabulary size estimates yielded by the Vocabulary Levels Test (Nation, 1990, pp. 261ff.) and the Eurocentres Vocabulary Tests (Meara & Jones, 1989) on one hand, and scores on two standardized reading tests on the other hand, has found that 3,000 word families (corresponding to approximately 4,800 words) corresponds to a threshold in reading ability. This in itself constitutes a serious argument in favor of the acquisition of massive doses of vocabulary by learners beyond the most frequent 2,000 or 3,000 words.[2] (See Laufer, Chapter 2, this volume.)

---

2 Rare words probably pose less of a problem in production, as the learner can usually resort to negotiation strategies in face-to-face interaction and to lexicographical aids

## Complex lexical units

Quantitative data on the learning or use of complex (or multiword) lexical units are less advanced than the data on simple units. One reason for this is that complex units are more difficult to trace in corpora as they take more different shapes in discourse the more complex they are (Arnaud & Moon, 1993; Moon 1992). The following data on units included in this study, kindly researched in the Oxford, Hector Pilot Corpus of British English (18 million words) by Rosamund Moon, may provide an idea of the discourse frequencies of complex lexical units (all variants are included):

| | |
|---|---|
| tongue-in-cheek | 31 occurrences |
| to take something in (one's) stride | 26 |
| a flash in the pan | 13 |
| to beat around the bush | 5 |
| it's all in the day's work | 1 |

Work on machine translation has shed some light on the number of complex units in a language: Research on French at the Laboratoire d'Automatique Documentaire et Linguistique has shown that there are more complex units than simple ones. For instance, there are 6,000 adverbial expressions compared with 2,000 adverbs, 300,000–400,000 compound nouns versus 80,000 simple nouns (reported in Chanier, Colmerauer, Fouqueré, Abeillé, Picard & Zock, 1993). The figure provided by Goulden et al. (1990) (see above) involved only simple units, and little is known on the number of complex units in native speakers' individual vocabularies. Arnaud (1992) has found, however, that the average French university student is able to recognize some 284 proverbs, and proverbs are but a drop in the phraseological ocean.

Complex lexical units are notoriously difficult to classify (Alexander, 1978; Gläser, 1988; Gläser, 1988; Kuusi, 1974) since several parameters, such as degree of fixedness, syntactic nature, idiomaticity and pragmatic function, are involved. These parameters are difficult to combine, and the emphasis may be laid on different ones depending on the purposes of the taxonomy. Thus, work on machine translation may favor syntactic and formal categorization (Danlos, 1988), while pedagogical considerations may lead to different communicative and/or pragmatic approaches (Sornig, 1988). Nattinger and DeCarrico (1992) have combined formal and

---

in written production – actual knowledge of words being naturally far preferable. Besides, it would appear from an L1 experiment that readers are not spontaneously very sensitive to the lexical richness of texts (Thoiron & Arnaud, 1992) and native speakers would certainly detect a nonnative through other clues before they became aware of the paucity of rare words in his or her productions.

functional considerations in their study of preconstructed units in discourse.

Idiomaticity is usually defined as the fact that the meaning of the complex unit does not result from the simple combination of those of its constituents. It is not, however, a simple parameter as many nonlexicalized co-occurrences (spontaneous syntagms) also have an overall meaning that is more than the sum of its parts (David, 1988), and there are various degrees of idiomaticity (Gläser, 1988), which are linked to the opacity or extinct nature of the metaphor that may be involved, or depend on how many of the components take part in the metaphor: *to jump the gun* is very idiomatic, *to jump the queue* less so. Most complex lexical units are idiomatic to some degree (Gläser, 1988).

Given their numbers, complex lexical units are omnipresent in discourse and the learner must not only acquire their canonical forms as in the case of simple units, but also the ability to recognize their exploited forms, such as "Hook, Lyne and Stinker," the title of a film review (*Newsweek*, 5/3/93, p. 54), or "Nothing fails like failure" (*CBS Evening News*, 12/7/93) (see Arnaud and Moon, 1993). Besides their numbers, another source of difficulty is that complex lexical units tend to have much longer *signifiants* than simple units, which might involve a greater memory load, although experimental results are not univocal on this point (Laufer, 1990). Finally, weakly idiomatic complex units such as *to have the last word* and complex units that have a close equivalent in the L1, such as *to grease someone's palm/graisser la patte à quelqu'un,* do not pose a decoding problem and therefore tend to pass unnoticed, which probably hinders their acquisition, as Marton (1977) remarked of collocations. For these reasons, the acquisition of a large stock of complex lexical units is necessary for the advanced learner's receptive competence but involves considerable difficulty (Alexander, 1985; Irujo, 1986).

Although all advanced learners cannot be expected to reach a nativelike vocabulary, the case of language teachers is different: One of their professional justifications is the proximity of their competence to that of native speakers.

## The study

Two questions are addressed in the present research: (1) How does the lexical knowledge of nonnative professional learners of English, that is, specialist students and teachers, improve with level of study? (2) Can they attain a nativelike level in their passive knowledge of rare words and complex lexical units?

# The tests

## Rare words

The rareness of lexemes is determined by means of frequency lists. In order to eliminate any bias toward British or American English, it was decided to use two equivalent frequency lists together: Kucera and Francis (1967), which rests on a corpus of 1 million tokens of American text published in 1961, and its British counterpart, Hofland and Johansson (1982), which was purposely collected on similar principles. Modern lexicography uses much larger machine corpora, but these are not readily accessible and the two lists mentioned are sufficient for the purpose of the study.

Since there is no standard definition of *rare*, it was decided that a lexeme would be considered rare if the corresponding family did not include more than six occurrences in the two lists taken together (i.e., three tokens per million), a family gathering together derivatives and the inflected forms that figure separately in these nonlemmatized frequency lists. A list was then assembled of "rare" items that were not transparent French cognates or whose meaning was not otherwise guessable from their form, given the passive nature of the vocabulary knowledge under investigation. Of course, at this frequency level, the proportion of latinate vocabulary (most of which is shared with French), internationalisms or scientific terms is considerable.

Given the available testing time and the testing format, sixty items were drawn at random from the resulting list and submitted to three native speakers of British English and three of American English, all teaching assistants in Lyons, who were required to cross out any item they might not know. This led to the elimination of a few words that were apparently more British or American, such as *bollard* or *furlough,* and their replacement with other words drawn at random from the original list. This, in addition to the fact that the list (see Appendix A) was specifically designed for the testing of French learners, makes it impossible to consider it an absolutely random sample of a specific frequency range, and no conclusion as to the vocabulary sizes of the subjects will be drawn.

There are two principal ways to test passive vocabulary, the checklist method and more traditional multiple-choice tests. The checklist method, or yes/no method (Meara & Buxton, 1987; Read & Nation, 1986), requires that the testees indicate whether or not they know the items on a list. Corrections for optimistic answers are possible if pseudowords are included in the list. This method has the advantage of allowing larger samples to be used than in the case of multiple-choice items, which are more time-consuming, but the latter method permits some verification of knowledge of meaning. It was retained for that reason. A key and three distractors were written for each word, using mainly vocabulary contained in the *Longman Defining Vocabulary* (Longman, 1987), but also obvious cognates. The use of French keys and distractors was precluded by the fact that native speakers were to take part in the study. The task was facilitated by the fact that lexemes in this frequency range tend to be monosemic. Two sample items are reproduced in Appendix B.

## Complex lexical units

No frequency list for complex lexical units is readily available and therefore rareness could not be taken into account. A list was compiled from the authors' personal files and collections like Cowie, Mackin and Mc-Caig (1983) and Heaton and Noble (1987). Since here too passive knowledge was to be tested, only idiomatic items were retained. In this category, many units are more or less equivalent in French and English: Chanier et al. (1993) list cases of correspondence, and quote a study by Freckleton (1985), who has found that some 80% of expressions around *to take* have an idiomatic equivalent in French, and of these 20% are word-for-word equivalents. In addition, many units include metaphors transparent for French speakers although they have no L1 equivalent, such as *to rub salt into the wound*. Only opaque idioms were included.

A syntactic-equivalence classification was retained: Each complex unit was classified under the type of syntagm it could substitute for: noun phrase (*a damp squib*), verb equivalent (*to make no bones about X*), adjectival, adverbial or prepositional phrase (*at a pinch, tongue in cheek*), predicates (*to bite the bullet*), and sentences (sayings: *the penny drops*). This classification does not exhaust all possible cases, such as some of Nattinger and DeCarrico's (1992) *sentence organisers,* but most of the ground is covered. From the original list of 166 complex units, 60 were drawn randomly, making sure that the initial proportions of categories were respected: the final list includes 14 noun-phrase equivalents, 7 verb phrases, 10 adjectival, adverbial or prepositional phrases, 25 predicates and 3 sayings (Appendix C).[3] After verification with the six American and British informants, which led to a few changes, keys and distractors, mainly in the form of paraphrases, were written (two sample items are reproduced in Appendix D).

---

3 Unfortunately, despite several verifications, one item was found to be missing from the final version at a stage when it was too late for correction. The scores on the complex units tests are therefore out of 59.

## Subjects and administration

Four groups of French advanced learners of English took part in the study. Group 1 was made up of 91 first-year students studying English at the Université Lumière, Lyons, France. These are specialist students, i.e., English is their main subject; they studied English for 7 years in secondary schools at the rate of 3 to 5 hours a week. Group 2 included 75 third-year students. Both groups took the two tests at 1-week intervals during normal class time. Group 3 was comprised of 36 teacher trainees at the Institut Universitaire de Formation des Maîtres de l'Académie de Lyon (IUFM). This is not the place to explain in great detail how French secondary schoolteachers are recruited and trained, but these students are graduates and have passed competitive examinations for the French Civil Service for which preparation takes an extra year of study. They are therefore in their fifth year of higher studies; in addition, most of them have spent a year in Britain or the United States as teaching assistants.[4] These students took the two tests in one session. Group 4 included 34 secondary schoolteachers who are part-time teacher trainers and advisers for the IUFM. Only subjects with more than 10 years' professional experience were asked to participate. The two tests were mailed out to all the IUFM teacher trainers, who were guaranteed anonymity, and the return rate was approximately two-fifths.[5] A group of 57 English native-speaking undergraduate students enrolled in English classes at Purdue University served as native controls. They took the two tests in one session.

## Results

Group statistics are presented in Table 1 and graphically in Figure 1.[6] The improvement of the learners' scores with level of study was examined by means of an ANOVA for repeated measures, with level as the independent variable and rare word and complex lexical unit scores as the dependent variables. Inspection of Table 1 shows that there are large differences in variance between the groups, and that the distribution of scores for

4 It should be noted that the French university system is highly selective, though not at entry point: Although anyone with a final secondary degree (*baccalauréat*) may enroll in a language department, there are examinations with high failure rates at the end of each academic year, so that graduates are the survivors of a long selection process. The students in groups 1 through 3 are therefore not strictly comparable in terms of general academic ability.
5 The return rate was actually higher, since the tests were mailed out to *all* the teacher trainers as we had no knowledge of their number of years in the profession.
6 The almost identical average scores of the native speakers on the two tests constitute a serendipitous outcome.

TABLE I. GROUP STATISTICS (ALL SS)

| Group | 1 | 2 | 3 | 4 | 5 |
|---|---|---|---|---|---|
| Rare words | | | | | |
| mean | 2.73 | 8.44 | 21.83 | 39.24 | 36.65 |
| s.d. | 2.83 | 5.31 | 9.10 | 10.59 | 9.57 |
| Complex units | | | | | |
| mean | 5.24 | 8.64 | 16.42 | 29.85 | 36.68 |
| s.d. | 3.90 | 4.70 | 8.54 | 9.93 | 9.05 |

Group 1: 1st-year students
   2: 3d-year students
   3: teacher trainees
   4: experienced teachers
   5: U.S. undergraduates

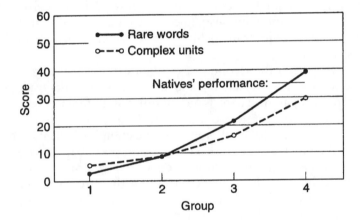

*Figure 1   Group means all Ss.*

group 1 (first-year students) is clearly nonnormal due to a floor effect. Since ANOVA is robust with respect to these departures from normal conditions provided the cells contain equal numbers of subjects (Guilford & Fruchter, 1978, p. 284; SPSS, 1988, p. B-158), samples of 34 Ss (the size of the smallest group) were randomly drawn from groups 1 (first-year students), 2 (third-year students) and 3 (teacher trainees), and the ANOVA performed on the corresponding statistics. The results appear in Table 2. The effects of level, type of items tested and their interaction are all highly significant. Pairwise comparisons also showed that the differences between rare word and complex lexical item scores are highly significant for groups 1 (first-year students), 3 (teacher trainees) and 4

TABLE 2. ANOVA FOR REPEATED MEASURES (34 SS PER GROUP)

| Source of variation | Sum of squares | d.f. | Mean squares | F | Significance |
|---|---|---|---|---|---|
| Between Ss | | | | | |
| Level | 36734.77 | 3 | 12244.93 | 122.63 | < 0.00001 |
| Within Ss | | | | | |
| Type of score | 463.34 | 1 | 463.34 | 30.26 | < 0.0001 |
| Interaction | | | | | |
| Level x type | 1751.95 | 3 | 583.98 | 38.14 | < 0.0001 |
| Explained | 38950 | | | | |
| Residual | 15202 | | | | |
| Total | 54152 | | | | |

(experienced teachers), but not for group 2 (third-year students) (F-values, respectively, 37.95, 15.45, 119.28 and .25). These statistics show, somewhat unsurprisingly, a continuous increase in the knowledge of the two lexical unit samples, but also, and more interestingly, that the acquisition of complex units trails behind that of single words, and the gap increases with time.

In order to answer the second research question, the average scores for groups 4 (experienced teachers) and 5 (American undergraduate students) were compared. There is no significant difference between the average scores on the rare word test (F = 1.24, p = .47; t = 1.18, p = .239 for 89 d.o.f.), but the 12% difference on the complex lexical units test is highly significant (F = 1.22, p = .51; t = -3.32, p = .001 for 89 d.o.f.). In other words, the most advanced learners in the experiment did not perform differently from the native controls on the rare words task (their mean score was actually higher, but not significantly so), but their performance was inferior in the case of complex lexical items.

## Discussion

The discussion will open on a warning note: Any kind of language assessment is performed at a cost. Our discussion of passive vocabulary in the Introduction implied that what is involved is knowledge of a procedural kind. Multiple-choice tests, however – or checklist tests, for that matter – constitute overtly metalinguistic tasks, which tend to tap declarative knowledge. They can only very imperfectly take into account the automatic nature of the processes at work in language comprehension and therefore only provide indirect assessment. This should not be lost sight of in the following.

The results of the American undergraduates serve as a reminder of a well-known fact: When we speak of native performance, we should never forget that this does not imply "perfect" mastery of the language. These native students' average scores were, after all, 61% in the case of rare words and 62% on the complex lexical units test.

The first research question was, *How does the students' lexical knowledge improve with their level of study?* The fact that the two graphs intersect can be simply attributed to the idiosyncrasies of the item samples in the two tests, there being a few more easy items in the complex units test. The very poor performance on both tests of the first-year students of group 1 comes as no surprise, given what we know of the vocabularies of European secondary-school graduates: It is at university that the acquisition of words beyond the first 2,000 really begins. In fact, these students may hardly be considered as advanced as far as lexical knowledge is concerned. The sheer number of words in the lower frequency ranges seems to constitute an obstacle to the acquisition of nativelike status through university studies, however, as even the teacher trainees in group 3 are way below their native counterparts: Their average score is only 60% of that of the American students for rare words. As stated earlier, they are in their fifth or sixth year of higher education, and they are due to take up classroom teaching at the end of their training year. The fact that scores are even lower in the case of complex units (45%) points at these as a major problem in the acquisition of English by nonnatives. This is confirmed by the results of the experienced teachers (group 4). Indeed, the second question addressed in this study was, *Can nonnatives reach nativelike proficiency with respect to rare word and complex lexical units?* The answer would seem to be *yes* in the first case and *no* in the second.

Two restrictions should be mentioned with respect to the comparison of native and nonnative scores, however. The native controls and the experienced teachers in group 4 are not exactly comparable; the former are undergraduates, the latter are middle-aged professionals. As vocabulary acquisition continues throughout life – although obviously at a far more moderate rate than in childhood – a strictly equivalent native control group of American secondary school teachers with at least 10 years' experience might have produced a different result. In addition, as we have seen, the teachers in group 4, who participated on a voluntary basis, were motivated individuals in a rather successful category of their profession, and therefore may have performed better than a random sample of teachers.

The main point of interest is that nativelike performance was attained in the case of rare words, not in that of complex lexical units. Although these teachers have all spent some time in English-speaking countries (typically, a 1-year period during their studies and many separate stays to a total of several months or years afterward), they live in a non-English-speaking country. It may be that constant exposure to the language is necessary for nativelike proficiency in the case of complex lexical units but not simple ones. Total amount of exposure to the language is the simplest explanation, but, as the study has shown, reduced exposure does not prevent the acquisition of a nativelike store of rare words, and additional causes must be found. If one examines what kind of exposure to English is available to teachers in France and sought by them, causes for the difference observed may appear. For instance, there is comparatively little occasion for the informal interaction with natives that takes place daily in an English-speaking country, and an important source of complex lexical units, in particular those at a low level of formality, may be lost. The main opportunity for exposure to oral English is noninteractive, and consists mainly of what English-speaking programs are shown on television, and these are few and far between. Although the British press is widely, if not inexpensively, available, teachers would tend to prefer the quality press to the so-called popular newspapers, which actually constitute a far richer source of complex units. Finally, literary fiction, to which many teachers are attracted by taste, may not provide them with much complex vocabulary. Naturally, those are generalizations that do not take individual situations into account. Lack of awareness of the nature and importance of complex units leading to reduced attention to them is another possible cause, which may combine with the other factors.

## Conclusion

The aim of specialist language departments is to bring their students as close as possible to the proficiency of native speakers. Very little specific vocabulary teaching takes place in such departments in France – or many other countries – at present: The students' results show that this should be systematically provided. This implies in turn that more reflection on long-term, large-scale vocabulary teaching methodology at advanced levels should be undertaken. The results of this study also confirm the idea that complex lexical units deserve special pedagogical attention, and that learners should have specific strategies to deal with them. (See Lewis, Chapter 13, this volume.)

These strategies, which would be of a metacognitive nature, could be of two kinds: awareness strategies and retention strategies. There is no a priori reason why strategies of the latter type should be different from those that have been described for lexical units in general, such as mnemonics, but awareness strategies involve some metalinguistic knowledge. Learners should know a complex unit when they see or hear one, and this in turn implies that we teach them some lexicological facts, such as the nature and categories of complex units, and their behavior in discourse. These suggestions, though not identical with the current movement toward the teaching of lexicalized chunks of language, represented, for instance, by Lewis (1993) or Nattinger and DeCarrico (1992), clearly go in the same direction.

## Appendix A: List of rare words tested

| | | |
|---|---|---|
| 1 hefty | 21 shank | 41 doe |
| 2 crony | 22 chime | 42 acorn |
| 3 buxom | 23 frazzled | 43 steed |
| 4 dunk | 24 blob | 44 askew |
| 5 girder | 25 hobnob | 45 cur |
| 6 garnet | 26 quagmire | 46 betrothal |
| 7 quandary | 27 cockroach | 47 rudder |
| 8 yolk | 28 lancet | 48 breeches |
| 9 oversight | 29 beseech | 49 bladder |
| 10 worsted | 30 chomp | 50 sludge |
| 11 squid | 31 contraption | 51 flunkey |
| 12 fad | 32 ladle | 52 smattering |
| 13 upshot | 33 zither | 53 whiff |
| 14 slush | 34 rickety | 54 cad |
| 15 elopement | 35 armadillo | 55 clout |
| 16 fluke | 36 gimlet | 56 hemp |
| 17 berate | 37 pew | 57 henchman |
| 18 cog | 38 guffaw | 58 pliers |
| 19 dollop | 39 furlough | 59 comely |
| 20 knead | 40 hearse | 60 puck |

## Appendix B: Two sample items from the rare words test

| quandary | A congratulations | knead | A burn |
|---|---|---|---|
| | B extortion | | B cut |
| | C refusal | | C press |
| | D dilemma | | D helper |

## Appendix C: List of complex lexical units tested

| | |
|---|---|
| 1 a busman's holiday | 6 a couch potato |
| 2 red tape | 7 a chip off the old block |
| 3 a red herring | 8 a flash in the pan |
| 4 a wet blanket | 9 a nest egg |
| 5 a sitting duck | 10 a hot potato |

11  the silver lining
12  the three R's
13  the last straw
14  a square peg
15  to lead someone up the garden path
16  to give someone a good hiding
17  to bring someone to heel
18  to give something a wide berth
19  to be at loggerheads with someone
20  to take something in stride
21  to set one's sights on something
(22: missing item)
23  wide of the mark
24  across the board
25  tongue in cheek
26  for a song
27  out of sorts
28  on/at the double
29  in the sticks
30  by dint of
31  on a shoestring
32  when the chips are down
33  to ring a bell
34  to be on the wagon
35  to call it a day
36  to be up the creek
37  to be up in arms
38  to do a double take
39  to be out on a limb
40  to blow the whistle
41  to beat around the bush
42  to be sitting pretty
43  to break even
44  to bring up the rear
45  to bring the house down
46  to do time
47  to get cold feet
48  to pass the buck
49  to jump the gun
50  to kick the bucket
51  to paint the town red
52  to push up the daisies
53  to see eye to eye
54  to sit on the fence
55  to spill the beans
56  to take forty winks
57  to foot the bill
58  blood is thicker than water
59  his/her goose is cooked
60  it's all in the day's work

## Appendix D: Two sample items from the complex lexical units test

to be on the wagon
    A  to exploit prostitutes
    B  to be sure to happen
    C  to be a poor artist
    D  not to drink

for a song
    A  not seriously
    B  with little money
    C  without real cause
    D  for fun

# References

Alexander, R. (1978). Fixed expressions in English: A linguistic, psycholinguistic, sociolinguistic and didactic study. *Anglistik und Englishchunterricht, 6,* 171–188.
 (1985). Phraseological and pragmatic deficits in advanced learners of English. *Die Neueren Sprachen, 84*(6), 613–621.
Arnaud, P. J. L. (1992). La connaissance des proverbes français par les locuteurs natifs et leur sélection didactique. *Cahiers de Lexicologie, 60*(1), 195–238.
Arnaud, P. J. L., & Moon, R. (1993). Fréquence et emplois des proverbes anglais et français. In C. Plantin (Ed.), *Lieux communs, topoï, stéréotypes, clichés* (pp. 323–341). Paris: Kimé.
Chanier, T., Colmerauer, C., Fouqueré, C., Abeillé, A., Picard, F., & Zock, M. (1993). *Modélisation informatique de l'acquisition des expressions lexicales en langues secondes.* Communication présentée au 9ème colloque international sur l'acquisition des langues, St.-Etienne, 13–15 mai 1993.
Cowie, A. P., Mackin, R., & McCaig, I. R. (1983). *Oxford dictionary of current idiomatic English.* Vol. 2: *English idioms.* Oxford: Oxford University Press.
Cruse, D. A. (1988). Word meaning and encyclopedic knowledge. In W. Hüllen & R. Schulze (Eds.), *Understanding the lexicon: Meaning, sense and world knowledge in lexical semantics* (pp. 73–84). Tübingen: Niemeyer.
Danlos, L. (Ed.). (1988). Les Expressions figées. *Langages, 90.*
David, J. (1988). Tous les prédicats ne meurent pas idiots mais nul n'est à l'abri. In G. Gréciano (Ed.), *Europhras 88: Phraséologie contrastive. Actes du colloque international, Klingenthal/Strasbourg, 12–16 mai 1988* (pp. 75–82). Strasbourg: Université des Sciences Humaines, Département d'Etudes Allemandes (1987).
Engels, L. K. (1968). The fallacy of word-counts. *IRAL, 6*(3), 213–231.
Flieller, A., Delesmont, P., & Thiébaut, E. (1992). La mesure des compétences lexicales: Effet des instruments utilisés. *L'Année Psychologique, 92,* 365–392.
Freckleton, P. (1985). *Une Comparaison des expressions du français et de l'anglais.* Doctoral diss. Université Paris 7.
Gläser, R. (1988). The grading of idiomaticity as a presupposition for a taxonomy of idioms. In W. Hüllen & R. Schulze (Eds.), *Understanding the lexicon: Meaning, sense and word knowledge in lexical semantics* (pp. 264–279). Tübingen: Niemeyer.
Goulden, R., Nation, P., & Read, J. (1990). How large can a receptive vocabulary be? *Applied Linguistics, 11*(4), 341–363.
Guilford, J. P., & Fruchter, B. (1978). *Fundamental statistics in psychology and education.* New York: McGraw-Hill.
Haynes, M. (1984). Patterns of perils of guessing in second language reading. In J. Handscombe, R. A. Orem & B. P. Taylor (Eds.), *On TESOL '83: The question of control* (pp. 163–176). Washington, DC: TESOL.
Heaton, J. B., & Noble, T. W. (1987). *Using idioms: A learner's guide.* New York: Prentice Hall.
Higa, M. (1965). The psycholinguistic concept of 'difficulty' and the teaching of a foreign language vocabulary. *Language Learning, 15*(3/4), 167–179.

Hofland, K., & Johansson, S. (1982). *Word frequencies in British and American English*. Bergen: Norwegian Computing Centre for the Humanities.

Honeyfield, J. (1977). Word frequency and the importance of context in vocabulary learning. *RELC Journal, 8*(2), 35–42.

Huckin, T., Haynes, M., & Coady, J. (1993). *Second language reading and vocabulary learning*. Norwood, NJ: Ablex.

Hulstijn, J. H. (1992). Retention of inferred and given word meanings: Experiments in incidental vocabulary learning. In P. J. L. Arnaud & H. Béjoint (Eds.), *Vocabulary and applied linguistics* (pp. 113–125). Basingstoke: Macmillan.

Irujo, S. (1986). A piece of cake: Learning and teaching idioms. *ELT Journal, 40*(3), 236–242.

Kelly, P. (1989). Utilization of the hookword method for the learning of Polish vocabulary: A personal investigation. *ITL: Review of Applied Linguistics, 85/86*, 123–142.

(1990). Guessing: No substitute for systematic learning of lexis. *System, 18*(2), 199–207.

Kucera, H., & Francis, W. N. (1967). *Computational analysis of present-day American English*. Providence, RI: Brown University Press.

Kuusi, A. L. (1974). An approach to the categorisation of phrases. *Proverbium, 23*, 895–904.

Laufer, B. (1990). Ease and difficulty in vocabulary learning: Some teaching implications. *Foreign Language Annals, 23*(2), 147–155.

(1992). How much lexis is necessary for reading comprehension? In P. J. L. Arnaud & H. Béjoint (Eds.), *Vocabulary and applied linguistics* (pp. 126–132). Basingstoke: Macmillan.

Laufer, B., & Sim, D. D. (1985). Taking the easy way out: Non-use and misuse of contextual clues in EFL reading comprehension. *English Teaching Forum, 23*(2), 7–10.

Lewis, M. (1993). *The lexical approach: The state of ELT and a way forward*. Hove, England: Language Teaching Publications.

*Longman dictionary of contemporary English* (2d ed.). (1987). London: Longman.

Marton, W. (1977). Foreign vocabulary learning as problem no. 1 of language teaching at the advanced level. *Interlanguage Studies Bulletin, 2*(1), 33–57.

Meara, P. (1990). A note on passive vocabulary. *Second Language Research, 6*(2), 150–154.

Meara, P., & Buxton, M. (1987). An alternative to multiple-choice vocabulary tests. *Language Testing, 4*(2), 141–154.

Meara, P., & Jones, G. (1989). *Eurocentres vocabulary test 10 KA*. Zurich: Eurocentres.

Melka Teichroew, F. J. (1989). *Les Notions de réception et de production dans le domaine lexical et sémantique*. Bern: Peter Lang.

Mondria, J.-A., & Wit-de Boer, M. (1991). The effect of contextual richness on the guessability and the retention of words in the foreign language. *Applied Linguistics, 12*(3), 249–267.

Moon, R. (1992). Textual aspects of fixed expressions in learners' dictionaries. In P. J. L. Arnaud & H. Béjoint (Eds.), *Vocabulary and applied linguistics* (pp. 13–27). Basingstoke: Macmillan.

Nation, I. S. P. (1990). *Teaching and learning vocabulary.* New York: Newbury House.

Nation, I. S. P., & Coady, J. (1988). Vocabulary and reading. In R. Carter & M. McCarthy (Eds.), *Vocabulary and language teaching* (pp. 97–110). London: Longman.

Nattinger, J. R., & DeCarrico, J. S. (1992). *Lexical phrases and language teaching.* Oxford: Oxford University Press.

Read, J., & Nation, I. S. P. (1986). Some issues in the testing of vocabulary knowledge. Paper presented at the LT+25 Symposium, 11–13 May 1986, Quiryat Anavim, Israel.

Segui, J., & Beauvillain, C. (1988). Modularité et automatisme dans le traitement du langage: L'exemple du lexique. In P. Perruchet (Ed.), *Les automatismes cognitifs* (pp. 13–25). Liège: Mardaga.

Sornig, K. (1988). Idioms in language teaching. In W. Hüllen & R. Schulze (Eds.), *Understanding the lexicon: Meaning, sense and word knowledge in lexical semantics* (pp. 280–290). Tübingen: Niemeyer.

*SPSS/PC+ V2.0 base manual* (1988). Chicago: SPSS.

Takala, S. (1984). *Evaluation of students' knowledge of vocabulary in the Finnish Comprehensive School.* Reports from the Institute of Educational Research. University of Jyväskylä, no. 350.

Thoiron, P., & Arnaud, P. J. L. (1992). Quelques aspects de la perception de la richesse lexicale. *Cycnos* (Nice), *8*, 33–47.

Tripp, S. D. (1990). The idea of a lexical meta-syllabus. *System, 18*(2), 209–220.

# 9 Vocabulary enhancement activities and reading for meaning in second language vocabulary acquisition

T. Sima Paribakht and Marjorie Wesche

## Introduction

The long-neglected issue of vocabulary acquisition is currently receiving attention in second language pedagogy and research – reflecting the importance always accorded it by learners. But it is still far from clear how learners acquire vocabulary or how it can best be taught. Reading comprehension processes may offer some clues. There is considerable evidence from first language studies that extensive reading for meaning leads to vocabulary acquisition over time, and indeed that reading probably accounts for most L1 vocabulary expansion beyond the first few thousand words in common oral usage. Second language research on this issue is sparse, but what there is indicates that extensive reading programs are generally more effective than systematic vocabulary instruction using decontextualized exercises (see, for example, Elley and Mangubhai, 1983; Krashen, 1989). The process by which "incidental" acquisition through reading occurs is slow, however, and there is no way to predict which words will be learned, when, nor to what degree. The question remains as to whether instructional intervention could support the process and make it more directed and efficient. The classroom experiments reported here attempt to do this, using instructional procedures designed to increase the salience and cognitive processing of targeted words encountered by L2 students in reading texts. These experiments track the acquisition of these words using a recently developed instrument, the Vocabulary Knowledge Scale (Paribakht & Wesche, 1993; Wesche & Paribakht, forthcoming).

This research was made possible through a grant from the Social Sciences and Humanities Research Council of Canada. We are very grateful to the participating teachers, Rhoda Diebel, Catherine Read and Dorothy Roberge, and to their students, to our research assistants Judith Holman and Louise Jasmine, to Doreen Bayliss for the statistical analysis, to Jean-Luc Daoust for data processing, and to Beatrice Magyar for word processing and formatting of tables.

174

# Learning vocabulary incidentally through reading

Research in L1 reading indicates that direct vocabulary instruction can-not account for a significant proportion of the words learners acquire, and that the major way in which vocabulary knowledge is increased is by learning through context (Nagy, Herman & Anderson, 1985; Nation & Coady, 1988). Although aural language experience is important, written language normally contains a higher proportion of difficult or low-frequency (unfamiliar) words; thus reading is normally the major vehicle for continued vocabulary acquisition in literate L1 learners. Nagy et al. (1985) concluded from their studies of school children reading in L1 that this learning is incremental and depends on repeated exposure. They estimated the probability of learning a new word from context after just one exposure as between 5% and 10%. Studies of the relationship be-tween L2 reading practice and vocabulary gains indicate that increasing the amount of reading where learners are motivated and focused on meaning leads to measurable vocabulary acquisition (Elley & Man-gubhai, 1983; Ferris, 1988; Kiyochi, 1988, cited in Krashen, 1989; Pitts, White & Krashen, 1989). Hulstijn (1992) demonstrated incidental learn-ing and retention of word meanings in an L2 use situation, although retention from a single encounter was quite low. Long-term results from meaning-focused L2 instructional programs such as immersion also indi-cate that aspects of new vocabulary knowledge (e.g., word recognition and understanding in context) can be gained through pedagogy that emphasizes the global comprehension of meaning (Genesee, 1987; Harley, 1988). Again, however, progress is slow and haphazard, and meaning-based language use activities are not necessarily sufficient for internalization of all the lexico-semantic-syntactic features and relation-ships that underlie accurate production in the L2 (Lyster, 1990; Swain, 1988). These studies all point to a role for reading processes in vocabu-lary acquisition, but an unpredictable one, and not necessarily the most effective. How it works is also not clear. As pointed out by Nation and Coady, "the very redundancy or richness of information in a given con-text which enables a reader to guess an unknown word successfully could also predict that the same reader is less likely to learn the word because he or she was able to comprehend the text without knowing the word" (1988, p. 101). Jenkins, Stein and Wysocki (1984, p. 769), for their part, note that "learning from context is still a default explanation."

How might reading comprehension lead to the acquisition of new vocabulary knowledge? Even though the process appears laborious and uncertain, a better understanding of it would provide a starting point for attempts to enhance its effectiveness. Reading theory tells us that reading comprehension involves complex interaction between reader and text in which the reader uses information from the surrounding text and from other knowledge sources to verify and elaborate the mental textual representation. Different levels of text comprehension can involve differential analysis of unfamiliar or partially known individual words, corresponding to the kinds of knowledge involved in "knowing a word." It is reasonable to think that the amount and kinds of cognitive processing required will be related to the "depth" of comprehension of unfamiliar words attempted by the reader, and will help determine the internalization of new knowledge about them, with deeper processing leading to more acquisition. Such a link is suggested by Hulstijn's (1989) experiments, in which the *retention* of words learned incidentally from context was greater than that in which inferential clues such as multiple-choice synonyms were provided, a finding he attributed to the greater "mental effort" required.

Other recent research on incidental learning of vocabulary in context has looked at how unfamiliar word meanings are learned, and whether contextual cues or strategy training can lead to more effective inferencing. Saragi, Nation and Meister (1978, p. 76) found that repeated exposure positively influences L1 vocabulary learning, but that the relationship is considerably complicated by other factors (e.g., meaningfulness of the context, similarity of other words in the L1). Their study suggested that the minimum number of repetitions for new words to be learned through reading is around ten. Furthermore, for guessing the meaning of an unknown word in context, clear clues are needed. Research on L1 vocabulary learning through reading indicates that certain kinds of textual features aid vocabulary learning. Specifically, texts in which key concepts and the relations between them are thoroughly explained lead to measurable gains in the acquisition of new word meanings (Herman, Anderson, Pearson & Nagy, 1987). On the other hand, Bensoussan and Laufer's (1984) research found that many of the target words in a text for adult ESL readers had no contextual cues to meaning, and that even when present, such cues did not always help guessing. Hulstijn (1989, p. 8) found that learners were more likely to infer an incorrect meaning of an unknown L2 word in a text when no cue to its meaning had been given than when a cue was present; thus cues may at least help prevent misguesses. But Bensoussan and Laufer (1984) concluded that word guessability was less a function of using the context than of learners applying "preconceived notions" about the meaning of a word or phrase, which they identified as the most frequent cause of incorrect guessing. In their study, wrong guesses occurred more frequently than correct and approximate guesses. Also important was their finding that the most popular reaction of their ESL student subjects to unknown words appeared to be to ignore them. Paribakht and Wesche (1993) likewise concluded from introspective ESL student data about how they dealt with unknown words in reading texts that most of them ignored such words unless reading comprehension questions specifically required that they be understood.

It appears from the above that successful incidental vocabulary learning through reading depends on the presence of a number of factors. Learners must attend to new words, and clear cues to their meanings and relationships must be present. Other text features, such as redundant presentation of given words and the learners' previous knowledge (such as partial knowledge of the word, of similar words or cognates), also play a role. The kinds of words to be learned and the clarity of their reference influence the ease of learning as well; thus, for example, concrete nouns are likely to be learned more quickly than discourse connectives. Ultimately, in some sense, the amount and variety of cognitive processing undertaken by the learner in dealing with unfamiliar vocabulary items will determine gains in knowledge; however, exactly what this consists of is not well understood.

## Contextualized reading-related activities for vocabulary development

It appears from research on incidental vocabulary acquisition that if systematic development of L2 vocabulary is desired, it cannot be left to the students themselves. They cannot be expected to "pick up" substantial or specific vocabulary knowledge through reading exposure without guidance. Given the limitations of decontextualized vocabulary instruction, the question for L2 pedagogy is whether L2 vocabulary acquisition can be enhanced through instructional intervention in the context of meaningful language use. Specifically, can tasks be designed that will increase the effectiveness of vocabulary learning through reading practice?

## The study

### Purpose

Several classroom experiments were undertaken to explore the role of various vocabulary instruction techniques based on reading texts for vocabulary learning by university ESL students.

### Research question

The main question addressed was whether reading comprehension plus vocabulary enhancement exercises led to more effective acquisition of selected vocabulary items than did an equal amount of learning time spent on reading additional texts that incorporated the same words, and the extent to which each instructional method was effective.

Hypotheses deriving from this question were:

H1. Students will gain in their knowledge of target words found in the reading texts through reading plus vocabulary instruction activities but also through reading alone.
H2. Given the same amount of time devoted to the two treatments, gains for the reading plus vocabulary instruction will be greater.
H3. Vocabulary gains will be both quantitative (reflected in the number of words known to some degree versus not known) and qualitative (increased "depth" of knowledge of given words).
H4. Gains in the reading plus vocabulary instruction will be greater for content words (nouns and verbs) than for discourse connectives.

In addition to these hypotheses, the following question was explored: Did students and teachers perceive the vocabulary activities as useful, and if so, which ones were seen as most and least useful, and why?

## Setting

The studies took place in the context of the comprehension-based ESL program offered to beginning and intermediate students at the bilingual University of Ottawa's Second Language Institute. The comprehension-based curriculum consisted of four one-semester courses and responded to a university graduation requirement of high-level reading and listening skills in the second language of instruction (French or English) for Arts and Social Sciences students. The subjects were young adults from a variety of L1 backgrounds in the fourth-semester course in this series. The course content was thematically organized, and authentic reading and listening texts and related exercises and discussion constituted the core L2 input to learners.[1] Exercises ranged from text comprehension to the practice of specific reading and listening skills (e.g., identifying the main idea, inferencing, skimming and scanning). Six themes were used for instructional purposes during the 39 hours of class contact during a semester course. Half the class time per week (i.e., 2 hours) was used for reading related activities, and the remaining time was used for listening

---

1 These materials come from a variety of sources (magazines, newspapers, radio broadcasts, etc.) and cover a wide range of topics of interest to university students (e.g., fitness, media, environment). Normally no changes are made to the original forms of these materials. However, certain criteria (e.g., length, cueing level, density of information) are used for the choice of materials appropriate for different proficiency levels. The nature of comprehension tasks based on these materials also varies depending on the proficiency level of students (see Paribakht & Raymond, 1992, and Paribakht, Read & Burger, 1992, for more details).

practice. There was no systematic grammar instruction. Oral and written production was encouraged but not forced, and students were not evaluated on it.

## Instructional treatments

In order to compare students' vocabulary acquisition from reading texts in enhanced (i.e., Reading Plus vocabulary instruction) and unenhanced (i.e., Reading Only) conditions, the same students were exposed to each of the two instructional treatments. Subjects thus served as their own controls.

In the Reading Plus (RP) treatment students read selected texts (a total of four) on two themes and answered the accompanying comprehension questions. They then did a series of vocabulary exercises based on the target words from these main readings.

In the Reading Only (RO) treatment students likewise read selected texts (a total of four) on two themes, and answered the accompanying comprehension questions. Instead of doing vocabulary exercises, however, after reading each main text they read a supplementary text composed to present again the target words from the main text. The aim was to further expose students to the target words through reading.

## Vocabulary test

The Vocabulary Knowledge Scale (VKS) had previously been developed by the researchers to distinguish stages in learners' developing knowledge of particular words (cf. Paribakht & Wesche, 1993; Wesche & Paribakht, forthcoming). This instrument uses a 5-point scale combining self-report and performance items to elicit self-perceived and demonstrated knowledge of specific words in written form. The scale ratings range from total unfamiliarity, through recognition of the word and some idea of its meaning, to the ability to use the word with grammatical and semantic accuracy in a sentence (see Figure 1). Learners are presented with a list of target words and asked to indicate their level of knowledge for each, and, for self-report levels III–IV, to demonstrate this knowledge. VKS scale differences are large enough to be self-perceived yet small enough to capture gains during relatively brief instructional periods.[2]

VKS scoring accepts self-reported word knowledge of categories I and II for scores of 1 and 2, and requires a demonstration of knowledge for

---

2 The VKS scale is not intended to go beyond the ability to use the words in initial contextualized production, for example, to tap knowledge of additional word meanings, or derivational, paradigmatic, semantic and other relationships and networks.

```
┌─────────────────────────────────────────────────────────┐
│                                                           │
│  Self-report                                              │
│  categories                                               │
│                                                           │
│  I            I don't remember having seen this word      │
│               before.                                     │
│                                                           │
│  II           I have seen this word before, but I don't   │
│               know what it means.                         │
│                                                           │
│  III          I have seen this word before, and I think   │
│               it means _____ . (synonym or     │
│               translation)                                │
│                                                           │
│  IV           I know this word. It means _____ .    │
│               (synonym or translation)                    │
│                                                           │
│  V            I can use this word in a sentence: ____ .   │
│               (Write a sentence.)                         │
│               (If you do this section, please also do     │
│               Section IV.)                                │
│                                                           │
└─────────────────────────────────────────────────────────┘
```

*Figure 1     VKS elicitation scale – self-report categories.*

higher scores. The possible scores for a word on this instrument and their relationship to the self-report categories are given in Figure 2.

As is illustrated in Figure 2, wrong responses in self-report categories III, IV or V will lead to a score of 2. A score of 3 indicates that an appropriate synonym or translation has been given for self-report categories III or IV. A score of 4 is given if the word is used in a sentence demonstrating the learner's knowledge of its meaning in that context but with inaccurate grammar (e.g., a target noun used as a verb: "This famous player announced his retire."), or a mistakenly conjugated or derived form is given (e.g., "losed" for "lost"). A score of 5 reflects both semantically and grammatically correct use of the target word, even if other parts of the sentence contain errors.

A reliability estimate for the VKS was established through test-retest administration of a word list (N = 32) to 93 students at 6 different proficiency levels in the 1992 ESL summer school program. The resulting Pearson correlation was .89 for scores on the 24 content words, and .82 for scores on the 8 discourse connectives, indicating that the instrument can elicit acceptably reliable responses.

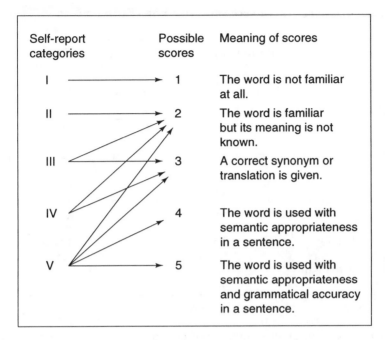

*Figure 2    VKS scoring categories – meaning of scores.*

## Pilot study

A pilot study was carried out with one class (N = 17) in the fall of 1992 to field-test the materials and procedures. The materials covered four themes with two main reading texts each and four supplementary reading texts for the RO treatment. Pretests consisted of 77 RP treatment and 61 RO treatment words, including discourse connectives, nouns, verbs, adjectives and adverbs. The original word lists included all non-French cognates in the main texts that were judged as challenging for these intermediate-level students by experienced teachers.

Paired t-tests on the pre-post data for the ten students who were able to complete all tests revealed significant gains on the RP treatment word list scores for nouns alone (p < .01) and for total vocabulary (p less < .05). The gain score for verbs alone approached significance (p < .06), while no significant gain was shown on the RP treatment discourse connectives (N = 10). There were no significant gains of any kind on the RO treatment word list (see Table 1). This limited evidence suggested that vocabulary enhancement techniques were effective in increasing the acquisition of

TABLE I. PILOT STUDY: VOCABULARY GAINS FOR READING PLUS AND READING
ONLY TREATMENTS

| | Reading Plus (N = 10) | | | Reading Only (N = 8) | | |
|---|---|---|---|---|---|---|
| Vocabulary measures | Target words | Pre | Post | Target words | Pre | Post |
| Nouns | 14 | 30.7 (6.5)[e] | 38.9[b] (6.1) | 20 | 48.7 (8.3) | 52.9 (5.1) |
| Verbs | 19 | 41.7 (9.4) | 48.8[c] (7.2) | 20 | 54.9 (9.6) | 49.8 (4.7) |
| Discourse connectives | 10 | 27.4 (6.6) | 27.9 (5.3) | — | — | —[d] |
| Total vocabulary (including discourse words, adjectives and adverbs) | 77 | 108.8 (22.4) | 127[a] (19) | 61 | 141.0 (25.6) | 142.8 (13.9) |

Significant differences are based on paired t-tests.
[a]$p \leq .05$; [b]$p \leq .01$; [c]$p \leq .06$
[d]There was an insufficient number of discourse words for separate analysis.
[e]Standard deviation

selected content words. A larger study of this phenomenon was thus
undertaken.

# Main study

The main study was carried out in the winter of 1993 with two ESL
classes at the same level as the pilot study.

## Subjects

Subjects in the main study were thirty-eight young adult students from a
variety of L1 backgrounds (e.g., French, Arabic, Chinese) in two sections
of the fourth semester (intermediate-level) comprehension-based ESL
course. The same subjects were exposed to both treatments, i.e., acted as
their own controls.

## Vocabulary exercises

Exercises for words in the RP treatment were developed (Paribakht &
Wesche, forthcoming) in the following way. A compendium of exercise

types was collected through an extensive examination of L2 vocabulary teaching textbooks. These exercises were then grouped into five distinct categories, representing a hypothesized hierarchy of mental processing activity, as follows:

## SELECTIVE ATTENTION

This exercise category uses different techniques to draw the learner's attention to the target word. Its aim is to ensure that students "notice" the target word, thought to be the first stage in acquisition of the word (cf. Gass, 1988). It is often used as an advance organizer, and is the least demanding exercise type for the learner. Examples include:

- Boldfacing, italicizing, circling, underlining, colouring or other visual signalling of the target words in the reading text.
- Providing students with a list of target words in the beginning of a text and asking them to read the list and notice where the words appear in the text. A variant is to have them underline the target words every time they appear in the text.

## RECOGNITION

In recognition exercises all necessary elements are provided and the learners are asked only to recognize the target words and their meanings; thus they require only partial knowledge of the target vocabulary items. Examples include:

- Matching the target word with a definition or synonym (usually more definitions or synonyms than words are provided).
- Recognizing the meaning of the target word from a multiple choice of meanings.
- Choosing the correct picture after seeing or hearing the target word.
- Choosing the right word to label a picture.
- Seeing or hearing the target word in the L2 and giving its equivalent in L1.

## MANIPULATION

Manipulation exercises involve rearranging and organizing given elements to make words or phrases, drawing on students' knowledge of morphology and grammatical categories. Examples include:

- Giving derivations of words (i.e., changing the grammatical category of the target word, such as from noun to adjective, or from verb to noun).
- Using stems and affixes to construct words.

INTERPRETATION

Interpretation involves analysis of meanings of words with respect to other words in given contexts (i.e., collocations, synonyms and antonyms). Examples include:

- Finding the odd word in a series of collocationally related words.
- Understanding the meanings and grammatical functions of the target word in the text (i.e., in a given context) and recognizing words or phrases that could be substituted in the text.
- Classifying words according to their discourse functions (e.g., discourse connectives classified by type – cause and effect, contrast, addition).
- Multiple-choice cloze exercises.
- Guessing the meaning of target words in context.

Our analysis of vocabulary exercise types in textbooks revealed that most text-based written exercises are of the interpretation type.

PRODUCTION

These exercises require the learner to produce the target words in appropriate contexts. Examples include:

- Open cloze exercises.
- Labelling pictures.
- Answering a question requiring the target word.
- Seeing or hearing the L1 equivalent or an L2 synonym and providing the target word.
- Finding the mistake in idiom use in a sentence and correcting it.

Production exercises, which require recall and reconstruction of words, are the most demanding type.

Further classification of the collected exercise types was done according to the following features:

- Identification of the *stage in reading* in which the exercise can be used (i.e., before, during or after reading a text).
- The *linguistic basis* of the exercise (i.e., whether it is primarily based on the visual/phonological or grammatical form of the word, on its meaning, or both).
- The *medium of presentation* of target words (i.e., their use in a written or an oral text).
- The *language skill(s)* required of the learner for completion of the exercise (i.e., speaking, reading, writing, listening or a combination of these).

Once the vocabulary teaching techniques were analyzed and grouped, exemplary techniques from different categories that could be used with reading texts were selected. Vocabulary exercises were then developed for the target words in the RP treatment. Three vocabulary exercises were used for each target word, that is, students worked at least three times with each word in addition to encountering it while reading the main texts.

## Selection of target texts and words

The four themes used in the pilot study were again used for instructional treatments in the study, two for the RP treatment (media and environment) and two for the RO treatment (fitness and biological revolution). Since the same subjects were exposed to both treatments, it was necessary to use different themes for each. The themes and texts were selected carefully, based on the previous experience of participating teachers and the researchers, to balance for student background knowledge, interest and text difficulty. Each theme comprises two main reading texts used in both treatments (see Figure 3 for details).

Target nouns, verbs and discourse connectives to be learned were selected from the main texts. These vocabulary items were of medium to high difficulty (i.e., with the most "learning potential"), as demonstrated in the pilot study, and had been screened to exclude French cognates with the help of a bilingual native speaker of French, since cognates present special learning characteristics and are generally easy for students in a bilingual context (Duquette, 1993; Tréville, 1993). There were a total of 28 RP target content words (12 nouns and 16 verbs), and 30 (12 nouns and 18 verbs) for the RO. In addition, 10 discourse connectives were selected for the RP, so that intratreatment differences in the development of knowledge of different categories of words could be explored. (The RO texts contained an insufficient number of discourse connectives of appropriate difficulty levels to warrant inclusion.) (See Figure 3 for details and Appendix A for the list of target words.)

As a result of the pilot study, the number of target words, and consequently the number of vocabulary exercises used with the corresponding four RP main reading texts, was reduced, and the exercises were refined in a number of ways to ease their administration, require less class time and increase their effectiveness. The RO vocabulary items were used in composing four supplementary texts for the treatment. See Figure 3 for a breakdown of themes, texts and vocabulary items.

## Treatments

*Reading Plus treatment.* In the RP treatment students read the selected texts and answered the accompanying comprehension questions at home.

**Treatments**

| | Reading Plus treatment | | | Reading Only treatment | | |
|---|---|---|---|---|---|---|
| Themes | Media | Environment | Reading Plus word totals | Fitness | Biological revolution | Reading Only word totals |
| Main texts | a. Violence on TV<br>b. Grade 6 Kids | a. Rachel Carson<br>b. Acid Shock | | a. Medics for fitness<br>b. Physical activity | a. Surrogates<br>b. Cloning | |
| Instructional treatment | Vocabulary exercises | Vocabulary exercises | | Supplementary texts:<br>aa. I was an Olympic athlete<br>bb. Eating disorders | Supplementary texts:<br>aa. Women and fertility<br>bb. Teenage clone | |
| Target words Nouns | 5 | 7 | 12 | 6 | 6 | 12 |
| Verbs | 8 | 8 | 16 | 9 | 9 | 18 |
| Total content Words | 13 | 15 | 28 | 15 | 15 | 30 |
| Discourse connectives | 7 | 3 | 10 | 0 | 0 | 0 |

*Figure 3  Themes, texts and target words.*

These were assigned as homework because classroom completion of the tasks would have been too time-consuming. The comprehension exercises were then corrected in class. This was followed by in-class completion of the vocabulary exercises for the given text, to control for the time spent, and to ensure the completion of tasks according to the instructions. These exercises were then corrected in the class.

*Reading Only treatment.* In the RO treatment, students also read the main texts and answered the accompanying comprehension questions at home, followed by correction in class.

Instead of vocabulary exercises, however, this was followed by the reading of the relevant supplementary texts and completion of comprehension exercises in class. These texts had been specially composed to present new information on the RO themes (i.e., fitness, biological revolution), using the target words. In this way the students were exposed to the target words again through reading and subsequent completion of comprehension exercises. These activities required approximately the same amount of class time as the vocabulary exercises used in the RP treatment.

Gains in students' vocabulary knowledge were measured using the VKS and a record of their marks was kept for all comprehension and vocabulary exercises in both treatments.

## Analyses and findings

Data analyses and their results are reported for each hypothesis.

H1. Students will gain in their knowledge of target words found in the reading texts through reading plus vocabulary instruction activities but also through reading alone.

To measure vocabulary gains in target vocabulary knowledge in the two treatments (RP and RO), t-tests for correlated data were calculated on preinstruction and postinstruction scores. These are presented by treatment in Table 2 for target nouns and verbs separately and summed (total content words), and for discourse connectives (for the RP treatment only). T-test results showing gains by theme within treatment are given in Appendix B.

As is apparent from Table 2, highly significant gains ($p < .001$) were achieved by students in *both* treatments for all categories of target words. The t-tests carried out by theme (Appendix B) revealed the consistency of this overall pattern for content words (a minor discrepancy being the lower significance level ($p < .01$) for verbs in the RO "Fitness" theme). The gain in discourse connectives on the RP "Environment" theme was not significant – perhaps attributable to the fact that only three target

TABLE 2. OVERALL VOCABULARY GAINS FOR READING PLUS AND READING ONLY
TREATMENTS[a]

| Variables | Reading Plus | | | Reading Only | | |
|---|---|---|---|---|---|---|
| | N | Pre | Post | N | Pre | Post |
| Nouns | 31 | 47.2 | 69.5[b] | 27 | 45.0 | 61.2[b] |
| Verbs | 31 | 45.9 | 65.0[b] | 27 | 51.6 | 60.1[b] |
| Total content words | 31 | 46.4 | 66.9[b] | 27 | 48.9 | 60.6[b] |
| Discourse connectives | 33 | 51.8 | 64.2[b] | | | |

[a]Significant differences are based on t-tests for correlated data.
[b]= p < .001

TABLE 3. MANOVA REPEATED MEASURES COMPARISONS OF
PRE- AND POSTVOCABULARY SCORES, READING PLUS AND READING
ONLY TREATMENTS

| Effect | Multivariate F | P |
|---|---|---|
| Group | 4.50 | .007 |
| Time | 94.74 | .000 |
| Group by time | 11.88 | .000 |

| Variable | Univariable ANOVA follow-ups<br>Group time |
|---|---|
| Nouns | Reading Plus > Reading Only |
| Verbs | Reading Plus > Reading Only |
| Total content | Reading Plus > Reading Only |

words were involved, while there was a highly significant gain on the seven discourse connectives in the RP "Media" theme. These findings provide support for Hypothesis 1; both treatments produced significant gains for all categories of words.

H2. Given the same amount of time devoted to the two treatments, gains for the Reading Plus vocabulary instruction will be greater.

MANOVA repeated measures analysis was carried out to determine comparative treatment effects. For this purpose the subjects were treated as two separate groups for the units in which they had received the RP versus the RO instruction. The results are reported in Table 3.

It can be seen from the Multivariate F for Group by time that for content words (nouns and verbs separately and summed), the RP treatment brought significantly greater gains than the RO treatment (p < .000). Hypothesis 2 is supported by these data. It was not possible to make such a comparison for discourse connectives since they were only studied in the RP units.

H3. Vocabulary gains will be both quantitative (reflected in the number of words known to some degree versus not known) and qualitative (increased "depth" of knowledge of given words).

Analyses of individual pre- and postresponses for each word were grouped to reveal patterns of target word knowledge before and after instruction for the two treatments. These are presented in Table 4 and the accompanying bar graphs (Figures 4–8).

Gains involved movement from "not known" (1–2) to "known" (3–5) scoring categories and incrementally within these groupings. In Table 4 it may be seen that all categories of words showed quantitative gains (i.e., the number of words in categories 3–5). Table 5 shows that the percentage of target nouns in categories 3–5 increased from 25% before instruction to 65% after instruction for the RP treatment, and from 26% to 50% for the RO treatment. Similarly, target RP treatment verbs in the "known" categories were 22% before instruction and 55% afterward, while RO treatment verbs were 33% before and 44% afterward. While 29% of the target discourse connectives in the RP treatment received scores of 3–5 before instruction, 50% did so following instruction.

These gains for different word categories in RP and RO treatments are summarized in Table 6. It is shown that there was a 40% increase in the number of nouns known after the treatment for the RP group and a 24% increase for the RO group. Gains in the knowledge of verbs were 33% for the RP group and 11% for the RO group. The increase in knowledge of discourse connectives was 21% for the RP group. It is evident, therefore, that quantitative gains in vocabulary knowledge were greater for the RP treatment than for the RO treatment.

As for qualitative differences, Figures 4–7 illustrate patterns of movement across word knowledge categories for both treatments. These patterns appear to be similar for nouns and verbs. It is also evident that while there are dramatic decreases in category 1 (words never seen) for both word categories in both treatments, many of these unknown words appear to have moved to category 2 (recognition level knowledge) for the RO treatment, while substantially more have moved to higher categories (i.e., 3, 4 and 5) for the RP treatment. In other words, many learners in the RP treatment seem to have passed the recognition level of target words and to have achieved greater depth in their knowledge of these words. These findings thus provide support for H3.

H4. Gains in the Reading Plus vocabulary instruction will be greater for content words (nouns and verbs) than for discourse connectives.

TABLE 4. FREQUENCY DISTRIBUTIONS OF PRE- AND POSTVOCABULARY SCORES, READING PLUS AND READING ONLY TREATMENTS

### Reading Plus treatment

| Variable | No. of words | Time | VKS scoring category | | | | | Total group score |
|---|---|---|---|---|---|---|---|---|
| | | | 1 | 2 | 3 | 4 | 5 | |
| Nouns | 12 | Pre | 21% (69) | 54% (175) | 10% (31) | 5% (15) | 10% (34) | 324 |
| | | Post | 3% (11) | 32% (104) | 19% (62) | 11% (35) | 35% (112) | |
| Verbs | 8 | Pre | 24% (104) | 54% (235) | 9% (39) | 2% (8) | 11% (46) | 432 |
| | | Post | 3% (12) | 41% (179) | 18% (79) | 9% (39) | 28% (123) | |
| Total content words | 28 | Pre | 23% (173) | 54% (410) | 9% (70) | 3% (23) | 11% (80) | 756 |
| | | Post | 3% (23) | 37% (283) | 19% (141) | 10% (74) | 31% (235) | |
| Discourse markers | 10 | Pre | 14% (34) | 57% (57) | 10% (26) | 1% (3) | 18% (49) | 270 |
| | | Post | 3% (9) | 46% (46) | 11% (30) | 3% (9) | 36% (98) | |

### Reading Only treatment

| Variable | No. of words | Time | 1 | 2 | 3 | 4 | 5 | Total group score |
|---|---|---|---|---|---|---|---|---|
| Nouns | 12 | Pre | 29% (93) | 45% (147) | 10% (34) | 3% (9) | 13% (41) | 324 |
| | | Post | 4% (12) | 46% (149) | 14% (46) | 13% (41) | 23% (76) | |
| Verbs | 9 | Pre | 20% (98) | 47% (226) | 9% (46) | 3% (16) | 21% (100) | 486 |
| | | Post | 4% (21) | 52% (252) | 10% (47) | 7% (34) | 27% (132) | |
| Total content words | 30 | Pre | 24% (191) | 46% (373) | 3% (25) | 3% (25) | 17% (141) | 810 |
| | | Post | 4% (33) | 50% (401) | 11% (93) | 9% (75) | 26% (208) | |

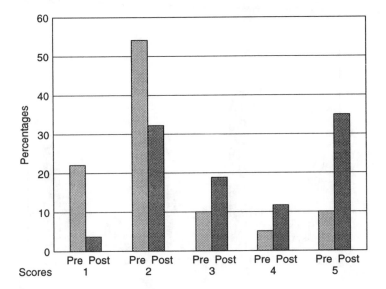

*Figure 4   Nouns: Score frequency distributions for Reading Plus treatment.*

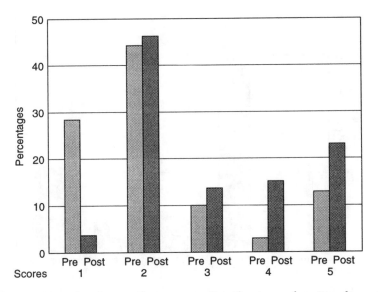

*Figure 5   Nouns: Score frequency distributions for Reading Only treatment.*

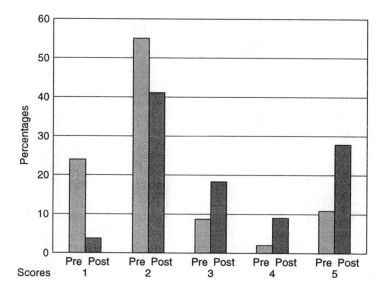

*Figure 6   Verbs: Score frequency distributions for Reading Plus treatment.*

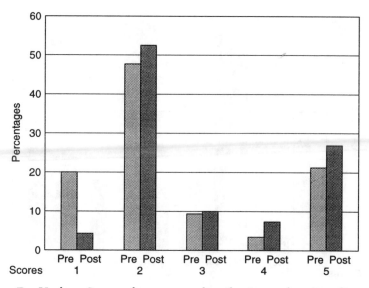

*Figure 7   Verbs: Score frequency distributions for Reading Only treatment.*

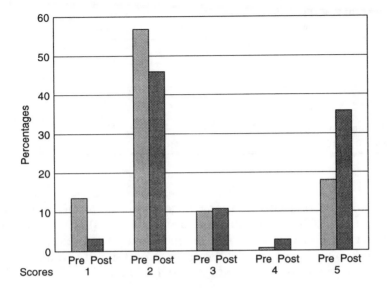

*Figure 8   Discourse connectives: Score frequency distributions for Reading Plus treatment.*

TABLE 5. FREQUENCY DISTRIBUTIONS OF PRE- AND POSTVOCABULARY SCORES FOR NOT KNOWN AND KNOWN CATEGORIES, READING PLUS AND READING ONLY TREATMENTS

*Reading Plus treatment*

| Variable | Time | Category<br>*Not known<br>(1–2)* | *Known<br>(3–5)* | *Total* |
|---|---|---|---|---|
| Nouns | Pre | 75% (244) | 25% (80) | 324 |
|  | Post | 35% (115) | 65% (209) |  |
| Verbs | Pre | 78% (339) | 22% (93) | 432 |
|  | Post | 44% (191) | 55% (241) |  |
| Total content words | Pre | 77% (583) | 22.9% (173) | 756 |
|  | Post | 40.5% (306) | 59.5% (450) |  |
| Discourse connectives | Pre | 71% (230) | 29% (78) | 270 |
|  | Post | 49% (133) | 50% (137) |  |

*Reading Only Treatment*

| Variable | Time | Not known | Known | Total |
|---|---|---|---|---|
| Nouns | Pre | 74% (240) | 26% (84) | 324 |
|  | Post | 50% (161) | 50% (163) |  |
| Verbs | Pre | 67% (324) | 33% (162) | 486 |
|  | Post | 56% (273) | 44% (213) |  |
| Total content words | Pre | 69.6% (564) | 30.4% (246) | 810 |
|  | Post | 53.6% (434) | 46.4% (376) |  |

TABLE 6. PERCENTAGE OF WORDS MOVING FROM "NOT
KNOWN" TO "KNOWN" CATEGORIES FOR EACH TREATMENT

| | Treatments | |
|---|---|---|
| Words | RP, % | RO, % |
| Nouns | 40 | 24 |
| Verbs | 33 | 11 |
| Total content words | 36.6 | 16 |
| Discourse connectives | 21 | — |

Table 6 indicates that while percentage of gains for total content words
was 36.6% (40% for nouns and 33% for verbs), it was 21% for
discourse connectives in the RP treatment, indicating relatively greater
gains in knowledge of content words than of discourse connectives (see
also Figure 8). H4 is confirmed by these findings.

Did students and teachers perceive the vocabulary activities as useful, and
if so, which ones were seen as most and least useful, and why?

In addition to testing the main hypotheses of the study, the question of
the learners' and teachers' perceptions of the vocabulary activities used in
the RP treatment was explored. Through the use of a questionnaire at the
end of the instructional period, students were asked to rate the usefulness
of vocabulary activities on a 5-point scale and state their reasons for their
ratings. They were also asked to give the approximate number of vocabulary items they thought they had learned, and react to the appropriateness
of the amount of time they had spent on the vocabulary exercises.

The questionnaire was based on the Acid Shock text and the vocabulary exercises developed for that text,[3] which included the following:

A. Read word list and notice the same words in the text (selective
   attention).
B. Match word list with list of definitions (recognition).
C. Find words in the text and match them to definitions (interpretation).
D. Replace words with target words from text (interpretation).
E. Classify connectives by type (interpretation).
F. Unscramble words to form sentences (production).

3 Note that the manipulation exercise type is not represented in this list because it was
  not used with this text. After the pilot study, it was necessary to delete a number of
  target words, which resulted in deleting some of the exercises developed for them.
  Manipulation type exercises were, however, used with other experimental texts, e.g.,
  "Violence on TV." It should also be noted that it is not possible to use manipulation
  exercises with all words.

Analysis of the responses to the questionnaires showed that, in general, students found the vocabulary exercises helpful and useful, and were satisfied with the kinds and numbers of the exercises used. In fact, some students checked all exercises as useful and others did not check any as not useful. Overall, however, exercises of kinds B and C were consistently rated as more useful than the others. The analysis produced the following order of usefulness: B, C, D, A, F and E.

Students' comments on the relative usefulness of the exercise types revealed that they found exercises B and C most useful because they helped them remember the target words and drew their attention to their meanings. Some students commented that exercises D and F helped them learn how to use the target words in appropriate contexts, and that exercise F went beyond vocabulary and helped them to practice grammar as well. Although it was seen as least useful overall, some students commented that exercise E helped them clarify and learn the meanings of discourse connectives, or that exercise A helped them with locating and remembering the target words.

Negative comments on the exercises were mainly related to their being too time-consuming or difficult. Students' comments also revealed that whether they like the text content and the text type on which the exercises are based is more important to them than the exercise types. They seemed to link the success of the exercises and their usefulness to the interest level of the text and consequently to the usefulness of the target words themselves.

When asked what percentage of the target vocabulary items students thought they had learned, students' estimates ranged from 30 to 100%, averaging 65%. Teachers estimated that students learned about 60% of the target words. Furthermore, the majority of students (56%) found the number of exercises appropriate, while 34% perceived them as too many and 3% thought there were too few.

Teachers commented that they had altered their attitudes toward vocabulary exercises as a result of the project. Students' comments and ratings, although at times inconsistent and contradictory, can provide some insight into the effectiveness and efficiency of vocabulary exercises. It may, therefore, be worthwhile to pursue this line of study, perhaps by using a more focused questionnaire in the context of a lesson that includes exercises, together with think aloud procedures while learners do them.

## Discussion and conclusions

The results of this study indicated that both instructional treatments (Reading Plus and Reading Only) resulted in significant gains in learners' vocabulary knowledge, but that the RP treatment led to greater gains. Although some gains were expected from the RO treatment, it is interesting to see that these gains are as high as they are. It should be remembered, however, that the readings were thematically related and the supplementary texts ensured that target words were presented several times in different meaningful contexts. Furthermore, each reading text in the study was followed by a series of comprehension questions, and answering them may have involved attending to and understanding the meanings and functions of certain target words. These gains may then be partially attributable to the effects of redundant presentation and doing the comprehension exercises. This may make a difference compared to reading that only involves understanding the general meaning of a text, as is often the case in the "real world" reading situations. Learners often ignore the meanings of unknown words, unless they are essential for achieving the desired level of text comprehension. This strategy, although justifiable for general reading practice and increasing reading speed, is not ideal for vocabulary enrichment over a limited instructional period. Only a few words may require more than passing attention, and even then recognition knowledge of them may be sufficient in most cases.

The results of this study indicate that learners in the RO treatment acquired some words but that their knowledge of many of these words tended to stay at the recognition level. In the RP treatment, however, learners learned more words and their knowledge of many of these words reached higher levels over a period of 1 semester (3 months). In other words, focused vocabulary instruction based on theme-related reading texts and using a variety of techniques has shown greater effectiveness than reading comprehension alone for learning selected vocabulary.

Given previous research findings (cited earlier) and the results of this study, it seems reasonable to explain the significant but different gains shown in the two treatments in the same way. Both treatments provided – although to differing degrees – redundant exposure to target words, varied and meaningful contexts of use that furnished indications of their meanings and of their lexico-semantic-syntactic relationships, and tasks calling for different kinds and levels of text processing involving these words. The reason for the better success of reading followed by vocabulary exercises may be that these exercises ensured learner attention to specific vocabulary items and required learners to analyze and understand the meanings and functions of target words through different tasks. Both the amount and variety of mental processing required may have influenced the likelihood of learners acquiring more knowledge of particular words.

The findings of this study also suggest that within the RP treatment, content words were acquired more readily than discourse connectives. One can only speculate that content words relative to discourse connectives have clearer referents, which may make their acquisition somewhat easier.

In conclusion, although reading for meaning appears to produce significant results in vocabulary acquisition, such reading supplemented with specific vocabulary exercises produces greater gains for the targeted words. This suggests that although instruction makes a difference, more focused instruction is desirable when the learning period is limited and specific vocabulary outcomes are sought.

# Appendix A: Target vocabulary items for each text

*Violence on TV*

| | | |
|---|---|---|
| although | a display | retaliation |
| to arouse | to express | a screen |
| because | in fact | seldom |
| behaviour | to get rid of | since |
| childhood | however | to turn on |
| to desensitize | network | whereas |
| disapproval | on the other hand | |

*Grade 6 kids*

| | | |
|---|---|---|
| to advise | to draw pictures | to loosen |
| to be aware of | experiment | to make sure |
| ceiling | to find out | mind |
| crafts | to give up | moreover |
| to cut down | grip | though |
| despite | to hit upon | |
| to draw | huge | |

*Rachel Carson*

| | | |
|---|---|---|
| bitter | landmark | sea |
| to blend | masterpiece | shore |
| chemical | mosquito | to spray |
| crusade | out-of-doors | stream |
| to draft | powerful | wildlife |
| editor | to praise | to wipe out |
| to enroll | to retire | woods |

*Acid Shock*

| | | |
|---|---|---|
| coal | lethal | to raise |
| decay | to melt | to release |
| event | perhaps | to sink |
| fuel | in order to | to trigger |
| to last | otherwise | while |
| layer | to point out | |

*Surrogates*

| | | |
|---|---|---|
| to allow | to go through with | trial |
| barren | to occur | to undergo |
| on behalf of | to spot | to uphold |
| custody | surrogate | |

*Cloning risks*

| | | |
|---|---|---|
| afterwards | involvement | a test-tube baby |
| although | long-standing | threat |
| to avoid | to lose | to wonder |
| child-rearing | obviously | yet |
| clone | prior to | |
| for the sake of | to provide | |

*Fitness*

| | | |
|---|---|---|
| ailment | guideline | in pain |
| average | to heal | to recognize |
| besides | healthy | strange |
| to break down | jogger | to train |
| cramp | label | weight |
| to deal with | to lay siege | while |
| disease | to limp | wound |
| emergency | in the meantime | |
| field | out-of-condition | |

*Physical activity*

| | | |
|---|---|---|
| amount | to follow | to take hold |
| brisk | hard | time-frame |
| to exhaust | heart rate | work out |
| to fade away | however | |
| fitness | to stay | |

## Appendix B: Vocabulary gains by themes for reading plus and reading only treatments[a]

| Treatment | Theme | Variable | N | Pre | Post |
|---|---|---|---|---|---|
| Reading Plus | Media | Nouns | 33 | 51.6 | 69.2[b] |
| | | Verbs | 33 | 47.0 | 66.0[b] |
| | | Total content words | 33 | 48.9 | 67.2[b] |
| | | Discourse connectives | 33 | 50.0 | 64.6[b] |
| | Environment | Nouns | 31 | 44.3 | 68.9[b] |
| | | Verbs | 31 | 45.0 | 63.8[b] |
| | | Total content words | 31 | 44.5 | 66.1[b] |
| | | Discourse connectives | 33 | 56.7 | 63.3 |

| Reading | Biological | Nouns | 27 | 39.0 | 57.0[b] |
| Only | revolution | Verbs | 27 | 46.7 | 56.7[b] |
| | | Total content words | 27 | 43.6 | 56.9[b] |
| | Fitness | Nouns | 27 | 51.0 | 65.3[b] |
| | | Verbs | 27 | 56.4 | 63.6[b] |
| | | Total content words | 27 | 54.3 | 64.4[b] |

[a]Significant differences are based on t-tests for correlated data.
[b]$p < .001$

# References

Bensoussan, M., & Laufer, B. (1984). Lexical guessing in context in EFL reading comprehension. *Journal of Research in Reading, 7*(1), 15–32.

Duquette, L. (1993). *Étude sur l'apprentissage du vocabulaire en contexte par l'écoute d'un dialogue scénarisé en français langue seconde.* Québec: CIRAL.

Elley, W., & Mangubhai, F. (1983). The impact of reading on second language learning. *Reading Research Quarterly, 19,* 53–67.

Ferris, D. (1988). Reading and second language vocabulary acquisition. Unpublished paper. Department of Linguistics, University of Southern California.

Gass, S. (1988). Second language vocabulary acquisition. *Annual Review of Applied Linguistics, 9,* 92–106.

Genesee, F. (1987). *Learning through two languages.* New York: Newbury House (HarperCollins).

Harley, B. (1988). Accounting for patterns of lexical development in a classroom L2 environment. Manuscript. Toronto: OISE, MLC.

Herman, P., Anderson, R., Pearson, P., & Nagy, W. (1987). Incidental acquisition of word meaning from expositions with varied text features. *Reading Research Quarterly, 22*(3), 263–284.

Hulstijn, J. H. (1992). Retention of inferred and given word meanings: Experiments in incidental vocabulary learning. In P. J. L. Arnaud & H. Béjoint (Eds.), *Vocabulary and applied linguistics* (pp. 113–125). Basingstoke: Macmillan.

Jenkins, J. R., Stein, N. L., & Wysocki, K. (1984). Learning vocabulary through reading. *American Educational Research Journal, 21*(4), 767–787.

Krashen, S. (1989). We acquire vocabulary and spelling by reading: Additional evidence for the input hypothesis. *Modern Language Journal, 73*(4), 440–463.

Lyster, R. (1990). The role of analytic language teaching in French immersion programs. *Canadian Modern Language Review, 47*(1), 159–176.

Nagy, W., Herman, P., & Anderson, R. (1985). Learning words from context. *Reading Research Quarterly, 20,* 233–253.

Nation, I. S. P., & Coady, J. (1988). Vocabulary and reading. In R. Carter & M. McCarthy (Eds.), *Vocabulary and language teaching* (pp. 97–110). London: Longman.

Paribkaht, T., & Raymond, P. (1992). The implementation of the comprehension-based approach: The University of Ottawa experience. In R. Courchêne, J. Glidden, J. St. John & C. Thérien (Eds.), *Comprehension-based second language teaching/L'enseignement des langues secondes axé sur la compréhension*. Ottawa: University of Ottawa Press, 281–296.

Paribakht, T., Read, C., & Burger, S. (1992). A comprehension-based curriculum: Objectives, materials and evaluation. In G. Irons & T. Paribakht (Eds.), *Make changes – make a difference* (pp. 29–56). Toronto: Éditions Soleil.

Paribakht, T., & Wesche, M. (1993). The relationship between reading comprehension and second language development in a comprehension-based ESL program. *TESL Canada Journal, 11*(1), 9–29.

(Forthcoming). Enhancing vocabulary acquisition through reading: A hierarchy of text-related exercise types. To appear in the *Canadian Modern Language Review.*

Pitts, M., White, H., & Krashen, S. (1989). Acquiring second language vocabulary through reading: A replication of the Clockwork Orange study using second language acquirers. *Reading in a Foreign Language, 5*(2), 271–275.

Saragi, T., Nation, I. S. P. & Meister, G. F. (1978). Vocabulary learning and reading. *System, 6,* 2:72–78.

Swain, M. (1988). Manipulating and complementing content teaching to maximize second language learning. *TESL Canada Journal, 6*(1), 68–83.

Tréville, M.-C. (1993). *Rôle des congénères interlingaux dans le développement du vocabulaire réceptif.* Québec: CIRAL.

Wesche, M., & Paribakht, T. S. (Forthcoming). Assessing L2 vocabulary knowledge: Depth versus breadth. To appear in B. Harley (Ed.), *Studies in vocabulary learning.*

# PART IV:
# PEDAGOGY

Whereas the preceding chapters focus on the acquisition side of vocabulary study, the chapters in Part IV concentrate on teaching. Jan H. Hulstijn leads off with a discussion of mnemonic methods. Drawing on the literature and on personal experience as both a teacher and a learner, he argues that keyword mnemonics are a useful supplement to guessing from context. The use of mnemonics accords with generally accepted principles of vocabulary learning and teaching, such as an avoidance of rote learning, an avoidance of context-free learning, and the need for elaboration and rehearsal. Hulstijn argues that a theoretical basis for the approach can be found in the concept of spreading activation, and he notes that we remember concrete words better than abstract ones. The final part of his essay is devoted to practical guidelines for vocabulary learning and teaching, including how to develop metacognitive awareness (cf. Chapters 4–6), how to use nonvisual verbal mediators, how to use mnemonics in language production, and how to use rehearsal techniques.

James Coady next argues that proficient second language users acquire most of their vocabulary knowledge through extensive reading. For beginners, however, this presents a problem: How can they learn words through extensive reading if they don't have enough words to read extensively? Coady proposes that this dilemma can be overcome in two stages. First, learners should be given explicit instruction and practice in the 3,000 most common words in the language, to the point of automaticity (Laufer makes a similar recommendation in Chapter 2). Second, they should then be allowed to engage in reading tasks they find enjoyable. Of critical importance is the careful selection of reading materials: Drawing on Krashen's Input Hypothesis, Coady urges curriculum designers to adopt an approach in which there is comprehensible input, adequate and supportive feedback, and, above all, material that the learner finds interesting.

In Chapter 12, "Teaching vocabulary," Paul Nation and Jonathan Newton discuss the selection, sequencing, and presentation of vocabulary in second language learning programs. Nation and Newton recommend teaching vocabulary according to descending order of importance; high-frequency general words, high-frequency academic words, technical terms, low-frequency words. And, like Coady, they advocate different pedagogical approaches for the different types of words: direct teaching for high-frequency vocabulary, indirect teaching (i.e., incidental learning) for low-frequency vocabulary. In all cases, however, Nation and Newton encourage use of a variety of communicative activities, especially those involving depth of processing; and they provide extensive description and discussion of such activities. They also give considerable attention to "fluency activities" and "richness activities," both of which help develop quick lexical accesses, while at the same time urging caution in the use of semantic fields, antonyms, and other associative activities.

In Chapter 13, Michael Lewis introduces the Lexical Approach, which broadens the notion of lexical item to include lexico-grammatical chunks of language. Indeed, Lewis defines lexical items as "socially sanctioned independent units," and he identifies and describes four different types: words and polywords; collocations; institutionalized utterances; and sentence frames or heads. He gives special emphasis to institutionalized utterances, or highly conventionalized locutions such as "If I were you, I'd _____." Because of their fixedness, he considers such sentences to be lexical items and argues that they, rather than grammar, should form the basis of language learning programs. In the second half of the chapter, Lewis describes the methodology that can be used to develop such an approach, including an extensive variety of sample exercise types.

As noted by Zimmerman in Chapter 1, the Lexical Approach gives much more emphasis to oral vocabulary than do other approaches of recent years. This is due in part to the fact that ordinary spoken language contains a higher proportion of fixed expressions than does written language. In Chapter 8, Arnaud and Savignon observe that even advanced EFL learners often are slow to master such expressions (what they call "complex lexical units") because they lack exposure to L2 speech. Their research clearly underscores the need for a vocabulary learning pedagogy, such as that described in Lewis's chapter, in which lexico-grammatical chunks of language are explicitly taught.

# 10 Mnemonic methods in foreign language vocabulary learning
## Theoretical considerations and pedagogical implications

Jan H. Hulstijn

## Introduction

I would like to begin this chapter with a personal experience, one that will probably be recognized by many readers as familiar. English is a foreign language for me. (Throughout this chapter, I will use the abbreviation L2 both for second and for foreign language.) I consider myself an advanced learner of that language. I receive great amounts of input in written form (professional literature) and oral form (radio, TV), but almost every day I read or hear some unfamiliar words. When I deem a new word important, I first make an attempt to infer its meaning from the context, I then look it up in my dictionary in order to check my inference, and finally I write the word down in a notebook, together with its context. Yet, I tend to forget the meaning of most of the words thus processed soon afterward. The next time I come across one of them, I remember having seen it and looked it up, I sometimes remember the context in which it originally appeared, but I cannot retrieve its meaning. I feel very annoyed, consult my dictionary once again, but take no further measures in order to better anchor the word in memory.

Why is it that I couldn't remember the word's meaning the second time? What was wrong with my infer + look up + write down strategy? The most likely answer to these questions is that I might have done enough for immediate comprehension but not enough for retention over time. More precisely, I had not done enough to firmly link the word's form with its meaning. There is empirical evidence in the literature that inferring a word's meaning from the context, checking one's inference by consulting a dictionary, and writing the word down in a notebook (or, better yet, on an index card, or in a computerized personal L2 database) fosters an elaborate processing of the word and therefore facilitates its retention in memory (Huckin & Haynes, 1993; Nation, 1990; Schouten-Van Parreren, 1989). However, this procedure offers no guarantee for the retention of the link between the word's form and its meaning. It is only sometimes the case that such a link constitutes itself spontaneously, without a conscious effort on the learner's part. This is usually called "incidental" vocabulary learning (Hulstijn, 1989, 1990, 1992, 1993; Nagy, Anderson, & Herman, 1987). Quite often, however, learners need to intentionally learn words in order not to forget them. When they find a word very difficult to learn and remember, they might be well advised to apply a mnemonic technique, such as the keyword method (discussed later in this essay), which helps to facilitate the linking of a word's form with its meaning. However, as we will see, the keyword method has its critics, and it seems that it is not well known and seldom practised in L2 instruction.

The main aim of this chapter is to strike a balance between opponents and proponents of the keyword method and other mnemonic techniques. It will be argued that, on the one hand, the keyword method should not be seen as a substitute for the inferring technique, but as a helpful addition. On the other hand, it must be acknowledged that the keyword method and other mnemonics often cannot be applied (simply because a suitable mediating word cannot be found) and that therefore its usefulness should not be overestimated.

## Chapter organization

In this chapter, some examples of the keyword method will be given first. Research on the keyword method will be reviewed. Then some possible reasons for the fact that it is seldom applied in the classroom are given. The following two sections deal with the psycholinguistic literature on the bilingual mental lexicon and the role of imagery in memory. From this perusal of the literature it is concluded that there are no theoretical reasons to suspect the keyword method of playing an inhibiting role. On the contrary, its role is a facilitating one. In the final section, some practical guidelines for vocabulary learning and teaching are provided, giving both the inferring technique and mnemonic techniques their proper place.

## The keyword technique: Some examples

The keyword method comprises three stages: (1) an L1 or L2 word, preferably referring to a concrete entity, is chosen based on acoustic and/ or orthographic similarity with the to-be-learned L2 target word; (2) a strong association between the target word and the keyword must be constructed, so that the learner, when seeing or hearing the target word, is reminded immediately of the keyword; (3) a visual image must be constructed combining the referents of the keyword and the target word, preferably in a salient, odd, or bizarre fashion in order to increase its memorability. As Kasper (1993, p. 250) points out, "the important point to remember is to stress that the students concentrate on remembering the image of the interaction between the keyword and the foreign word. It is also important to make each image as unique as possible and to use a different keyword for each word." Here are some examples:

- An English learner of German, trying to remember the meaning of *Raupe* ("caterpillar") could associate *Raupe* with the English word *rope* (sound similarity), and construct a mental image representing a caterpillar stretched out in more than its fullest length (exaggeration helps!) on a rope.
- An English learner of French, trying to remember *paon* ("peacock"), might use the word *pawn* as mediator, imagining a chess board on which all pawns look like peacocks.
- French *ruisseau* ("brook," "gutter"); English keyword: *rust*. Mental picture: rust-coloured water streaming in the gutter of a narrow street.
- French *soupape* ("valve"). English keyword: *soup*. Mental picture: a valve from which a tall fountain of tomato soup spouts into the mouths of some mechanics. Alternative verbal mediator phrase: "to soup up an engine."
- French *vis* ("screw"). English keyword: *to vise,* or *a vise* (in American English).
- French *brancard* ("stretcher"). English keyword: *branch*. Mental picture: an improvised stretcher made of two long tree branches with which members of an expedition group carry a wounded colleague.
- French *colombe* ("dove," "pigeon"). English keyword: *Columbus*. Mental image: Columbus standing on the foredeck of his ship, like Noah on his ark, with a pigeon in the air coming from the as yet invisible American coast.
- Three examples cited from Kasper (1993): (1) Spanish *payaso* ("clown"). English keyword: *pie*. Think of a clown throwing a pie at his friend. (2) Spanish *llega* ("to arrive"). Keyword: *leg*. Mediating sentence: "The *payaso* 'arrives' at the circus on one 'leg.'" (3) Spanish *pequeño* ("small"). Keyword: *pecan*. Mediating sentence: "The 'small' *payaso* ate a bag of 'pequeño' nuts."

Note that in the mediating sentences of examples (2) and (3) the earlier learned Spanish word *payaso* is used, not the English word "clown."

If possible, keywords should be taken not from L1 but from L2 vocabulary with which the L2 learner is already familiar: An ESL learner familiar with *duck* could use this word as a keyword for the target word *decoy*. Using rhyme as a mnemonic is often a better technique within the L2 than across languages; for example, the target word *reel* can be remembered with the rhyming sentence "A reel is like a wheel."

When it is impossible to find a concrete keyword, other mediating words based on sound similarity may help out:

- French *fâché* ("angry"); English keyword: *fascist*. Linking sentence: "A fascist makes me 'fâché.'"
- French *se blottir* ("to crouch," "to nestle"). English keyword: *to blot out*. Linking association: "*Se blottir* makes me think of *to blot out*. When you want to blot out a serious error, you feel so ashamed that you would like to make yourself invisible and crouch away."
- French *serment* ("oath"). English keyword: *sermon*. Linking association: "a sermon about Saint Peter, who swore three times that he didn't know who Jesus was."
- An ESL learner may learn the target word *barb* with the aid of the L2 carrier sentence "A barb is barbaric!"

Sometimes only one or a few letters or sounds can be used to link the L2 word with its L1 equivalent:

coin = corner
anéantir = to annihilate
béclage = closing with bars, chains, etc.
ébouriffer les cheveux = to ruffle your hair
feutre = felt
selle = saddle

# Research on the keyword method

Investigations on the effectiveness of the keyword method were first conducted by Atkinson (Atkinson, 1975; Atkinson & Raugh, 1975). The keyword method became well known through the many studies of Levin and Pressley (summarized in Pressley, Levin and McDaniel, 1987).

## Summary of reviews

A critical but mainly positive evaluation of the method and a discussion of some questions that remain to be answered can be found in Cohen (1987) and McLaughlin Cook (1989). McLaughlin Cook, who reviewed the literature on visual and verbal mnemonics in general (not limited to the keyword method), pointed out that mnemonic techniques may be less suitable for children and mentally handicapped people. It has not been sufficiently shown that they are able to spontaneously and independently apply mnemonics. McLaughlin Cook further concluded that there is little evidence that verbal mnemonics are less effective than imagery mnemonics. One important issue needing further investigation is whether subjects will cease to use mnemonics when instruction to do so is no longer provided. This point will be taken up in the practical guidelines at the end of this chapter.

The most thorough review of the keyword literature and a discussion of a number of issues of contention are found in Cohen (1987). His verdict on the keyword method is mainly positive, although some questions remain open for further investigation (pp. 57–58):

- How well can learners use mnemonics under time pressure during oral conversation?
- What is the lag time involved when a mnemonic device is being used? Perhaps it will cost a speaker more time to retrieve a word from memory via a mnemonic device than the listener is willing to wait.
- Research is needed over longer periods of time (longer than 1 week, as in laboratory studies conducted so far), focusing on the role that mnemonic devices actually play on a daily basis. When does the keyword "drop out," such that the learner does not even remember it?
- A description is needed of the trial-and-error process of self-generated associations, in an effort to learn more concerning efficient ways of generating such associations.

## Review of recent investigations

Since the publication of the reviews just summarized, investigations were carried out by Desrochers, Gélinas and DeRoy Wieland (1989), Desrochers, DeRoy Wieland and Coté (1991), Moore and Surber (1992), Levin, Levin, Glasman and Nordwall (1992), Ellis and Beaton (1993a, 1993b) and Hogben and Lawson (1994). These studies will be briefly reviewed in this section. (Other recent studies will be mentioned later in this chapter.)

Desrochers et al. (1989, 1991) applied the keyword method to the learning of the grammatical gender of German nouns by substituting the concepts of a woman, a man and an inanimate object for the feminine, masculine and neuter genders, respectively. It was found that instructing English and French learners of German to recode the gender tag and to include its representation into an interactive mental image along with the referent of the German noun facilitated the recall of genders. This effect was more pronounced in the case of French learners of German than in the case of English learners of German, perhaps because native speakers of English are less familiar with grammatical gender than are native speakers of French.

Moore and Surber (1992) had American first-year, second-year and third-year students of German (L2) learn a list of twelve L2 nouns and twelve L2 verbs with concrete, imageable meanings under one of three conditions. In the Keyword condition, Ss were given an L1 translation as well as a keyword for each L2 target word. In the Context condition, Ss were given, for each L2 target word, the L1 translation and three L2 sentences containing the target word (written in upper case). They were instructed how to attend to contextual clues. Subjects in the Control condition were given only the L1 translation of each L2 target word. Subjects in all conditions were told that they would be tested afterward both on an English test in which they would have to provide the L1 translations of the L2 words, and on a German sentence completion test in which they had to fill in the missing German word that would fit the context. Three weeks later, identical but unannounced delayed posttests were administered. (No mention is made of pretests to assess to what extent Ss were already familiar with the target words prior to the learning phase.) Overall, there were no significant differences between the three groups on the English immediate and delayed posttests, although the second-year students in the Context condition performed significantly better than those in the Control condition on both the immediate and the delayed posttest. On the German tests, there was a significant overall main effect for treatment. Among the first-year and second-year students, Keyword and Context groups performed significantly better than the Control groups, but no significant differences were obtained between Keyword and Context groups. Interpreting their results, Moore and Surber speculate that "by the third year it may be that students have developed their own strategies to the point where an additional intervention does not help and might possibly interfere" (1992, p. 292). Furthermore, they find it surprising that students in the Context condition were not superior to those in the Keyword condition, even on the German test, a task that would seem to favor the Context learning activity. The following study to be reviewed (Levin et al., 1992), however, did find the keyword method to be superior to a contextual method.

Levin et al. (1992) compared the keyword method, using verbal and visual cues, with the more conventional context method, using only verbal cues. In the latter method, the target word (e.g., the pseudoword *gunnel,* meaning "fish") was embedded in a carrier sentence ("The pole broke when the powerful gunnel took the bait"). In the keyword method, the target word was associated with a similar sounding word, *gun,* and a picture was shown in which the fisherman's pole had the appearance of a gun. Four experiments were conducted. In all four experiments, subjects in the keyword condition performed better than subjects in the contextual condition, even on a posttest in which subjects had to fill in the target words in new sentences, not previously encountered. These experiments are important because this study compared the keyword method with the effects of a method in which target words were embedded in meaningful contexts, whereas in previous research, Levin and associates had compared the keyword method with the learning of isolated target words (paired-associate learning).

Ellis and Beaton (1993a, 1993b) conducted a psychometrically "clean" laboratory experiment using native speakers of English who had no knowledge of German. They had to learn a number of German words, e.g. *Sperre* ("barrier"). Subjects, who worked individually on a computer, were divided into four treatment groups. Two groups learned the target words with the keyword method: the Noun Keyword Group was given a noun (*sparrow*) as keyword (Imagine a SPARROW on a station BARRIER). The Verb Keyword Group was given a verb (*spare*) as keyword (Imagine you SPARE a penny at a station BARRIER). The Repetition Group had to learn the target words in a traditional rote fashion with their L1 equivalents (*Sperre* = "barrier") by constant repetition. Subjects in the Own Strategy Group were instructed to use their own strategies to learn the target words with their L1 equivalents. Two of the many research findings are worth mentioning in the present context. First, it was found that subjects in the two non-keyword conditions (Repetition and Own Strategy) used various types of mnemotechnics (e.g., using a rhyming word, possibly referring to a concrete concept). That is why performance of all four subject groups was almost equally good in the receptive posttest, in which subjects had to provide the L1 equivalent of the target words (e.g., translate *Sperre* into "barrier"). Second, performance in the productive posttest (i.e., translate "barrier" into *Sperre*) was much lower than in the receptive posttest, again across all four groups. These results suggest (1) that mnemonic techniques may be effective learning facilitators, (2) that university students participating in a laboratory experiment often spontaneously apply mnemonic techniques (not the keyword method exclusively, but a whole range of formal and semantic associations), and (3) that such subjects tend to apply these linking techniques in one direction only, i.e., to get from the L2 word to its L1 equivalent (for later receptive use) rather than from L1 word to L2 target word (for productive use).

The last recent empirical study to be reviewed here was conducted by Hogben and Lawson (1994). They offered keyword training to thirty-two Australian high school learners of Italian (L2) who had already received three years of L2 instruction. Half of them were additionally trained in making other associative links to help them remember new words. Thus, students trained in the Standard Keyword (SK) method were compared with students trained in the Multiple Elaboration (ME) method. Overall, students in the ME group outperformed those in the SK group on all immediate posttest measures but not in the delayed tests, administered after 2 weeks. The authors conclude that even experienced L2 learners at high school level can benefit from strategy training and that, therefore, there may be no grounds for the concerns raised by Levin, Pressley, McCormick, Miller and Shriberg (1979), that the keyword method might not be as successful with older, more cognitively experienced students as with younger, less cognitively mature elementary school students.

## Why does the keyword method seem to have so little appeal?

It seems that the keyword method is only rarely used in the instruction of foreign languages, at least in the Western world (Kasper, 1993; Oxford & Crookall, 1990, p. 19). In handbooks on foreign or second language instruction and in books on vocabulary teaching, the keyword method is either not mentioned at all (Morgan & Rinvolucri, 1986) or only marginally (Nation, 1990, p. 166; Taylor, 1990, p. 68; Wallace, 1982, p. 62). Similarly, textbooks on memory research pay little (Baddeley, 1990, p. 190) or no (Schwartz & Reisberg, 1991) attention to the keyword method.

One obvious reason why the keyword method has attracted little attention is that it can be successfully applied with only a minority of vocabulary items, i.e., with words referring to objects that can be perceived visually.[1] Furthermore, it is true that the keyword method is less effective for the production of L2 words than for their comprehension (reception). Yet these reasons, valid as they are, do not explain sufficiently why the keyword method is seldom advocated by teachers or textbooks. Why ban a powerful technique from the classroom only because it has limited application possibilities? My impression, obtained from in-service teacher-training courses, is that the most important reason is that teachers (and textbook authors), if not entirely ignorant of the keyword method, find it an "odd," "unnatural" technique, "not serious enough." Input in L2 language courses must be as authentic as possible, embedded in situations of quasi-natural communication. How can one, under such circumstances, possibly associate a target word (*paon*) with a keyword (*pawn*) whose meaning does not share any features with the meaning of the target word? These or similar arguments may well form the reason why the keyword method is seldom advocated in L2 classes. In the following sections I will try to show that the keyword method, temporarily using a somewhat "unnatural" mediator, does not at all stand in the way of "natural," "authentic," communicative L2 instruction.

## L2 words in the bilingual lexicon

What sort of conception should we form of "words" in the "mental lexicon," i.e., the memory system in which knowledge of a vast number of words, accumulated in the course of time, has been stored? A proper

---

1 Some authors (e.g., Kasper, 1993) claim that the keyword method can be successfully applied with abstract words too, but research has shown that its effect is significantly smaller when applied to abstract rather than concrete words (Johnson, 1985).

definition of "word" in the mental lexicon should account for the fact that language users store information, be it more or less complete, on a wide variety of word characteristics, such as orthography, phonological structure, pronunciation, morphological structure, syntactic characteristics, as well as various sorts of semantic information (literal, idiomatic, pragmatic and other meanings). Most theorists agree that it is impossible to draw a clear borderline between lexical knowledge and encyclopedic knowledge, and that therefore the mental lexicon cannot be regarded as an information module stored separately from other kinds of knowledge in long-term memory (Aitchison, 1987; Lakoff, 1987; Levelt, 1989). Furthermore, most theorists agree that words in the mental lexicon should not be regarded as clear-cut entities (Meara, 1992). This opinion is based on the fact that word knowledge may only be partially available at a given time, as in the "tip-of-the-tongue phenomenon." It is also possible that one may know a word form but not be familiar with its meaning; one may even have invented a concept but not (yet) have a word form for it.

For a long time researchers have wondered how L1 words and L2 words are stored in the mental lexicon (for a review, see De Bot, 1992). Are they located in a single store (the extended system hypothesis), in separate stores (the dual system hypothesis), or are similar words, such as cognates, stored in a common store and language-specific words in separate stores (the tripartite hypothesis)? Or is it the case that, although all words are located in a single store, the subset of L1 words are more strongly associated with each other than with those of the L2, as if L1 words and L2 words constituted two relatively separate "families" within the entire "community" of words (the subset hypothesis)? Most theorists nowadays support the subset hypothesis (De Bot, 1992; see also De Bot, Paribakht & Wesche, 1995), and, as we shall see, this has important consequences for an appraisal of the keyword technique.

The concept of spreading activation allows us to conceive of the mental lexicon as a dynamic system. For instance, two words may first be stored in an entirely unassociated fashion. Later they may be linked via only one formal or semantic feature, and still later via more features. Furthermore, the strength of all these associations may differ, and the strength of each individual association may increase, and even decrease, over time.

The concept of spreading activation gives us a new perspective on the debate, originating from Weinreich's seminal work on bilingualism (1953), over whether the relationship between L1 and L2 words should be seen as conceptually coordinate, subordinate or separate (De Groot, 1992, 1993; Hamers & Blanc, 1989, p. 10; Kroll & Sholl, 1992; Schreuder & Weltens, 1993). It may well be that an English speaker who has just embarked on the learning of French as a foreign language, wanting to express the French word for the concept war, can retrieve the French word *guerre* only via the native equivalent *war*. With increasing proficiency and fluency, however, this learner may reach a stage in which *guerre* can be accessed directly from the concept war. In a stage of even further mastery of the foreign language, the meaning of *guerre* may obtain conceptual features not shared by the meaning of L1 *war*. To draw this illustration of the dynamic nature of the mental lexicon even further, one could imagine that this learner enters a fourth stage, deciding to follow a course for conference interpreters. In situations of fast translation, this learner might then end up linking the two words *guerre* and *war* directly with each other, hardly even accessing the concepts at all.

## A psycholinguistic defense of mnemonic methods

What is the relevance for the keyword method of recent views on the mental lexicon outlined in the previous section? Let us assume that a learner decides to use the keyword method when she or he has noticed that the connection between form and meaning of a to-be-learned L2 word has not taken place spontaneously. The learner now links form and meaning of the word to be learned via the form of a similar-sounding other word, while constructing a salient, odd or bizarre visual image. It is crucial to note that the association via this bizarre mediator, whose meaning would not bear any relation whatsoever to that of the target word under normal circumstances, is meant to exist only temporarily. Thus, this bizarre, "unnatural" association may soon decay (i.e., the strength of the association may decrease substantially), after it has helped to establish a direct association between the target word's form and meaning. The notion of a dynamic and flexible mental lexicon in which many types of connections coexist (formal and semantic, within and across languages, with increasing and decreasing strengths) allows for a temporary beneficial role of mediators. As has been demonstrated by Crutcher (1992), keyword mediators thus do not permanently stand in the way of the forming of direct links between a target word's form and meaning.[2]

Few people would object to applying a keyword mnemonic when trying to commit to memory the (difficult) name of a person just encountered for the first time. In that case too, the keyword is not meant to live forever, but only has to serve temporarily. Of course, learning L2 vocabulary involves much more than committing names to memory. Learning a word (in L1 or L2) may be seen as an incremental process. The keyword method does not claim to offer a substitute for this entire process of adding all semantic and formal features to a node in the mental lexicon. It

2  In a series of three experiments, Crutcher (1992) provided support for direct L1-word access after extended retrieval practice: Keyword mediation declined dramatically and L1 word retrieval became significantly faster over time, although the keyword mediators continued to influence the retrieval process covertly.

functions only to help establish *one* of the necessary links in the *initial* phases of this process.

## Why do we remember concrete words better than abstract words?

According to the conventional formulation of the keyword method, one should try to find a keyword with a concrete meaning; that is, the keyword should refer to objects in the real world that one can see (or feel or hear). This recommendation rests on the claim that one can better remember concrete concepts (e.g., *TABLE*) than abstract concepts (e.g., *Peace*). In the psycholinguistic literature, it has been consistently found that subjects perform better on concrete words than on abstract words, in laboratory tasks such as paired associate learning, word recognition, free recall of words, lexical decision and pronunciation (Nelson & Schreiber, 1992). Nelson and Schreiber offered four alternative hypotheses to explain these concreteness effects. Two of these are structural hypotheses, assuming either that concrete words are associated with a smaller number of other words than abstract words, making them easier to recall, or, alternatively, that concrete words have larger and more densely connected sets, making them easier to recall than abstract words. Nelson and Schreiber claim that they have been able to falsify both of these (mutually incompatible) structural, quantitative hypotheses.

The two remaining hypotheses are qualitative in nature. The *imaginability hypothesis* (associated, but not exclusively, with the work of Paivio, 1976, 1986) assumes that subjects are more likely to generate images for concrete than for abstract words. According to Paivio, semantic memory consists of two separate but interconnected subsystems, a subsystem of verbal concepts and a subsystem of visual concepts. Abstract words are associated with the verbal system only. Concrete words are associated with both. The additional visual storage of concrete words gives them their edge over abstract words in recognition, recall and lexical decision tasks. (Whether images are stored as virtual photographs, in a spatiovisual fashion, or somehow as codings of verbal propositions, is an issue that, according to Anderson (1978), may never be answerable. See also Schwartz and Reisberg (1991, pp. 490–492).

Finally, the *context availability hypothesis* assumes that contextual information, associated with the contexts in which words have been encountered, is more accessible for concrete than for abstract words. Nelson and Schreiber cannot choose between these two qualitative explanations, imaginability and context availability.

Schwanenflugel, Akin and Luh (1992; see also Schwanenflugel & Akin, 1994), however, tried to investigate to what extent imagery and context availability influenced recall of concrete and abstract words independently. They found that, when rated context availability (prior contextual knowledge) was controlled, subjects still recalled concrete words better than abstract words. More important, no concreteness effects were found in relatively easy tasks but concreteness effects were found in relatively difficult tasks. On the basis of these findings, the authors argue that "imagery is used strategically only when prior contextual knowledge does not seem sufficient to enable task performance. . . . If a person is given a list of unrelated words or a series of unrelated sentences to recall, this may be seen as a difficult task for which calling on imaginal information might help beyond the simple retrieval of prior knowledge" (p. 103).

## Implications of concreteness effects for the keyword method

The conclusion of Schwanenflugel et al. may help us to assess the potential relevance of the keyword method in L2 instruction. It shows that visual information may not be necessary or effective on many occasions, but may be very effective when subjects find their task difficult to accomplish. Trying to commit to memory the meaning of an L2 word that has been found difficult to remember, may well be just such a task in which imagery may prove to be effective.[3]

## Summary

Three conclusions can be drawn from the previous sections. First, there are no reasons to ban the keyword method and similar mnemonics from the classroom. They are perfectly compatible with principles of vocabulary teaching that the L2 teaching profession has adopted in the last decades:

- New vocabulary items should not be presented in isolation (i.e., only with their L1 equivalent, and without a verbal L2 context) and should not be learned in rote fashion.

3 Crowston (1993) even argues that the advantage that the keyword method has over paired-associate learning may be due to the fact that the keyword method requires an elaborative processing of verbal and conceptual information, not necessarily to the fact that part of this information is visual in nature. Thus the success of the keyword method cannot be interpreted as straightforward evidence for Paivio's dual coding hypothesis. In line with this interpretation, Kasper and Glass (1988) have suggested that the keyword method facilitates recall by inducing learners to process item-specific information.

- New vocabulary items should be presented in a meaningful context (preferably authentic or quasi-authentic contexts, preferably offering enough clues to allow learners to successfully infer their meaning).
- Learners should elaborate on a new word's form and meaning in order to facilitate retention.

The keyword and other mnemonic methods should not substitute for these principles of contextual learning, but they must be added to the contextual method when necessary and applicable (Hall, Wilson & Patterson, 1981, p. 357). In short, as Stevick (1993) has said, imagination and memory are friends, not enemies.

Second, in contrast to behavioristic thinking about forty years ago (when Weinreich's influential book appeared), modern psycholinguistic theories of bilingualism do not see a subordinate organisation as inferior to or detrimental to the construction of a compound or coordinate organisation, nor should the establishment of a temporary, indirect link between the target word's form and meaning via a mnemonic mediator be seen as inhibiting or detrimental to the efficiency with which nodes in a lexical network can be accessed.

Third, visual information may not be necessary or effective on many occasions, but using imagery appears to be effective when subjects find their task difficult to accomplish, in particular when a word's form and meaning do not happen to associate easily.

## Practical guidelines

Modern foreign language pedagogy stresses the importance of teaching students appropriate learning and studying strategies (Brown, 1994; Oxford, 1989). Older students should and can be made responsible for their own vocabulary learning (Meara, 1993, p. 288). In the beginning, as well as during the language course, we must discuss with our students how they go about learning the language. As a teacher of Dutch to literate adults learning Dutch as a second language, I have found it extremely useful to:

- Talk with students about their expectations concerning their language study before and during the language course;
- Administer tests for various skills and subskills at regular intervals;
- Have them compare their test results with their expectancies;
- Evaluate with them their language learning strategies.

This procedure includes a discussion of vocabulary learning techniques. Students always favourably receive the lesson devoted to mnemonics. They talk about their frustrations in learning and remembering thousands of words. They appreciate sharing with each other the memory tricks they use. Based on this experience, I offer the following practical guidelines.

*Introductory lesson.* In the introductory lesson about vocabulary learning, ask your students to mention examples of words they have learned spontaneously, incidentally. Then ask them why they think these words have been retained in memory without their conscious effort to learn and remember them. (Usually the words mentioned have occurred frequently and/or in the context of everyday life, offering the opportunity to establish a rich set of connections to other nodes in the mental lexicon.) Then ask them to give some examples of word forms whose meaning they have had to look up several times, words they have had particular difficulty learning and remembering. Help them to become aware of the fact that they have not forgotten the forms of these words, nor their meaning, but the link between form and meaning. Point out to them that it is necessary to find a mediator between the two.

Then discuss various mnemonics. Do not limit this discussion to the keyword method only. Research has shown that multiple elaboration techniques are better than a single keyword technique (Hogben & Lawson, 1994). The techniques students mention themselves invariably include:

- Forming an association with an L1 or L2 word similar in sound and meaning (e.g., true cognates);
- Decomposing a morphologically compound word (especially helpful with "transparent" compounds, i.e., compounds whose meaning can easily be derived from their constituent parts);
- Forming associations with familiar words based on some sort of sound similarity (e.g., rhyme);
- Forming nonverbal sound associations (e.g., the noise made by objects, animals or humans, associated with various sorts of affective responses of pleasantness, unpleasantness, etc.).[4]

Genuine examples of the keyword technique are seldom mentioned, which underscores its unfamiliarity. Give some examples of this method, and ask students to apply the technique on a few words. Give them some words with concrete meanings first, and then some words with abstract meanings. They will then discover how difficult it often is to come up with keywords satisfying both requirements, i.e., (1) form similarity and (2) a semantic characteristic allowing for the establishment of a salient (preferably bizarre), sensory (mostly visual) mediating link with the

---

4 In an experiment with German adult learners of Russian, Weise (1990) found that, when choosing mediating keywords, learners paid more attention to their phonetic similarity with the target words to be learned than to their potential value for establishing semantic cues.

meaning of the target word. Emphasize that using mnemonics in general, and using the keyword method in particular, (1) is often not necessary, because more natural links between form and meaning have established themselves in their memories, and (2) is often not possible, because a suitable keyword cannot be found. Students should thus become aware of both the values and the limitations of these techniques.

Time spent on a confrontation with the vocabulary learning problem in such a metacognitive way is time well spent, provided that we give students (1) the opportunity to relate the contents of such a lesson to their personal word learning experiences, and share their experiences with others, and (2) some examples of the various mnemonic techniques and the opportunity to apply the techniques successfully on at least some of the test words we provide them. (This implies that we must have ready an adequate keyword solution to at least some of these test words.)

*Mnemonics in courses for intermediate and advanced learners.* It should be noted that the associations made by inexperienced L2 learners who have just embarked on a beginners' course in a language linguistically unrelated to their mother tongue are of necessity of a much more restricted variety than the associations made by intermediate or advanced learners. The latter learners have a much broader knowledge base at their disposal, containing more candidates (words, derivational and compositional morphemes within the L2) for potentially successful associations with new words to be learned.

It is therefore especially worthwhile to talk about vocabulary learning techniques with students at intermediate and advanced levels. Two additional advantages accrue from discussing these matters with students at higher proficiency levels. First, it is these students especially who feel the vocabulary learning burden most pressingly, having to increase a limited elementary vocabulary of, say, 1,000 items to 5,000 items, or even to 10,000 items and beyond (Hazenberg & Hulstijn, 1996). Second, in the case of second (in contrast to foreign) language instruction, teachers often have little or no knowledge of the mother tongue(s) of their students. They therefore cannot offer their students helpful L1 keywords, nor can they evaluate with certainty the quality of L1 keywords brought forward by their students. However, intermediate or advanced students have enough L2 knowledge (1) to participate with profit in a metalinguistic group discussion on mnemonics, and (2) to form associations within the L2, rather than between L2 and L1.

*Procedures during the language course.* The introductory presentation and discussion of mnemonic techniques just outlined can be supplemented with the following procedure. At regular intervals, test your students on the words they have been instructed to learn and remember, preferably words they have encountered in collective reading or listening assignments. There are always some words that turn out to be difficult to remember for most students. Present these words once again and ask the students to proffer associations that facilitate retention. The collective imagination of a group of students together with their teacher will always be richer than the imagination of a single learner or of the teacher alone. Therefore, the whole group stands to profit from this procedure, which need not take more than a few minutes of class time.

Encourage your students to include the sometimes bizarre associations thus proffered when they write the words to be learned in their personal vocabulary notebooks or databases, along with the remaining information about the words (including useful verbal contexts).

Furthermore, it seems appropriate to encourage students first to come up with their own mnemonic solutions for word retention problems. Only if they cannot find solutions themselves should the teacher offer a mediator. However, the teacher must point out that students themselves must assess and evaluate the usefulness of the various mediators offered, since the target words must be embedded in individual mental lexicons with individually different words and different interword connections. Generally speaking, learners who must, for whatever reason, be labelled as being novices profit more from teacher-induced and less from self-generated solutions than experts (Hall, Wilson & Patterson, 1981; Wang & Thomas, 1992). And, as McLaughlin Cook (1989) has pointed out, a technique once introduced and successfully applied does not necessarily become a natural habit. It is therefore necessary to remind students of the use of mnemonics repeatedly.

It is important to note here, along with Cohen (1987) and Nation (1982, pp. 25–29), that, following this procedure, mnemonic techniques must not be used with all words, but only with words that have shown up as being particularly difficult.

*Nonvisual, verbal mediators.* When students cannot find a keyword meeting both requirements of formal similarity and an imaginable, semantic relationship, they could try to find a mediator bearing a semantic relationship in a nonvisual way. Example: *Embed* the target word *barb* in the carrier sentence "A barb is barbaric!"

When students cannot find any suitable formally similar mediator, they are left with the conventional technique of trying to remember the target word in a semantically salient context, and to commit this sentence intentionally to memory (Ellis & Beaton, 1993a, 1993b; Kelly, 1986; McLaughlin Cook, 1989). This procedure requires rehearsal. Embedding in a meaningful context alone is not enough for successful retrieval of the word's meaning when the word form is encountered in a new context, as was illustrated with the personal experience cited at the beginning of this chapter.

*Mnemonics for language production.* When one wants to learn a difficult word not only for reading or listening (receptive purposes) but also for speaking and writing (productive purposes), it is important to pay special attention to the usefulness of the keyword in arriving at the word's form when starting off from a concept or meaning. Additional measures must be taken to traverse the bridge in the opposite direction, a direction for which the bridge had not been constructed. Keyword method research has focused almost exclusively on its receptive function (e.g., helping learners to remember the meaning of *gunnel,* but not helping learners to remember the L2 word form for L1 *fish*). Perhaps the following jingle, cited by Keyser (1994) in her review of Harrison and Winters Welker's Spanish memory book (1993), could help English learners of Spanish remember both the meaning (receptively) and the form (productively) of the word *bailar* ("to dance"): "*Buy* larger shoes to *dance* in; buy smaller pants to prance in."

Let me add a personal experience here. I have come to learn many English words that were difficult to learn receptively (from form to meaning) by having been compelled to use them productively. When faced with expressing a certain concept in English, while writing an English article such as the present one, I look up the English word by using a Dutch-English dictionary, Webster's Thesaurus or Longman's Language Activator (starting off with a semantically related English word that I can think of). I then often recognize the desired word, as mentioned in these reference books, and use it in my writing. When I read or hear the same word later, I have no difficulty knowing what it means. This, then, seems to be another case in which L2 production may facilitate L2 comprehension (cf. Swain, 1985).

*Rehearsal.* It has been convincingly shown that even the use of a mnemonic mediator does not guarantee that L2 learners will remember an L2 word's meaning forever (Hogben & Lawson, 1994; Moore & Surber, 1992; Wang & Thomas, 1992). Rehearsal will remain necessary for the many words that L2 learners do not see or hear frequently enough through regular reading and listening. For these words, intentional rehearsal of the meanings and other relevant features (spelling, pronunciation, stress pattern, inflectional forms, grammatical gender, syntactic characteristics, etc.) remains the feat of the L2 learner wishing to become proficient in the L2. And as anyone knows who has tried to commit a great number of facts to memory, rehearsal at regular intervals is much more effective than massive rehearsal at infrequent intervals (Bloom & Shuell, 1981; Dempster, 1987). Each time learners rehearse a word, they should try to revive as many previously formed associations as possible, since an elaborative rehearsal technique has been proved to be much more effective than a maintenance rehearsal technique (Baddeley, 1990, p. 172).

# Conclusion

The aim of this chapter was to give mnemonic techniques their proper place in vocabulary learning. To quote from the concluding paragraph of Cohen's review article (1987, p. 59): "At a time when training of learners in language-learning strategies is gaining momentum . . . , it may be particularly fitting to determine whether strategies for remembering words have a role within such training. Such memory techniques would not be intended to replace the other approaches to vocabulary learning, but rather complement them by providing a link for facilitating retrieval of a second-language word or its native-language meaning."

The keyword technique is not at variance with modern insights in the bilingual mental lexicon nor with the contextual method in language pedagogy. The keyword and other mnemonic techniques should not replace the more natural, contextual methods fostering incidental learning. Instead, mnemonics, fostering intentional learning, should be used for words that, for whatever reason, have not been successfully acquired. Although the applications of mnemonic techniques are limited, their effect has been sufficiently proven. To some extent they can transform the vocabulary learning task from uninspired drudgery into newfound delight.

# References

Aitchison, J. (1987). *Words in the mind: An introduction to the mental lexicon.* Oxford: Basil Blackwell.

Anderson, J. R. (1978). Arguments concerning representations for mental imagery. *Psychological Review, 85,* 249–277.

Atkinson, R. C. (1975). Mnemotechnics in second-language learning. *American Psychologist, 30,* 821–828.

Atkinson, R. C., & Raugh, M. R. (1975). An application of the mnemonic keyword method to the acquisition of a Russian vocabulary. *Journal of Experimental Psychology: Human Learning and Memory, 104,* 126–133.

Baddeley, A. (1990). *Human memory: Theory and practice.* Hove, England: Lawrence Erlbaum.

Bloom, K. C. & Shuell, T. J. (1981). Effects of massed and distributed practice on the learning and retention of second-language vocabulary. *Journal of Educational Research, 74,* 245–248.

Brown, H. D. (1994). *Teaching by principles: An interactive approach to language pedagogy.* Englewood Cliffs, NJ: Prentice Hall.

Cohen, A. D. (1987). The use of verbal imagery mnemonics in second-language vocabulary learning. *Studies in Second Language Acquisition, 9,* 43–61.

Crowston, D. J. (1993). Imagery mnemonics for foreign language vocabulary as evidence of dual coding theory: An alternative view. In J. Chappell & M.-T. Claes (Eds.), *Proceedings of the 1st International Congress on Memory and*

*Memorization in Acquiring and Learning Languages,* 1991 (pp. 79–95). Louvain-la-Neuve, Belgium: Centre de Langues à Louvain-la-Neuve et en-Woluwe.

Crutcher, R. J. (1992). The effect of practice on retrieval of foreign vocabulary learned using the key-word method. Ph.D. diss., University of Colorado, Boulder. Dissertation Abstracts International B: Sciences and Engineering, 53/6, 1992, 3187-B.

De Bot, K. (1992). A bilingual production model: Levelt's 'Speaking' model adapted. *Applied Linguistics, 13,* 1–24.

De Bot, K., Paribakht, T. S., & Wesche, M. (1995). Modelling lexical processing in a second language: Evidence from ESL reading. Paper presented at the American Association for Applied Linguistics (AAAL) Annual Conference, Long Beach, CA, March 25–28.

De Groot, A. M. B. (1992). Bilingual lexical representation: A closer look at conceptual representations. In R. Frost & L. Katz (Eds.), *Orthography, phonology, and meaning* (pp. 389–412). Amsterdam: Elsevier.

(1993). Word-type effects in bilingual processing tasks: Support for a mixed representational system. In R. Schreuder & B. Welten's (Eds.), *The bilingual lexicon* (pp. 27–51). Amsterdam & Philadelphia: John Benjamins.

Dempster, F. N. (1987). Effects of variable encoding and spaced presentations on vocabulary learning. *Journal of Educational Psychology, 79,* 162–170.

Desrochers, A., DeRoy Wieland, L., & Coté, M. (1991). Instructional effects in the use of the mnemonic keyword method for learning German nouns and their grammatical gender. *Applied Cognitive Psychology, 5,* 19–36.

Desrochers, A., Gélinas, C., & DeRoy Wieland, L. (1989). An application of the mnemonic keyword method to the acquisition of German nouns and their grammatical gender. *Journal of Educational Psychology, 81,* 25–32.

Ellis, N., & Beaton, A. (1993a). Factors affecting the learning of foreign language vocabulary: Imagery keyword mediators and phonological short-term memory. *Quarterly Journal of Experimental Psychology, 46A,* 533–558.

(1993b). Factors affecting the learning of foreign language vocabulary: Psycholinguistic determinants. *Language Learning, 43,* 559–617.

Hall, J. W., Wilson, K. P., & Patterson, R. J. (1981). Mnemotechnics: Some limitations of the mnemonic keyword method for the study of foreign language vocabulary. *Journal of Educational Psychology, 73,* 345–357.

Hamers, J. F. & Blanc, M. H. A. (1989). *Bilinguality and bilingualism.* Cambridge: Cambridge University Press.

Harrison, W. F., & Winters Welker, D. (1993). *Spanish memory book: A new approach to vocabulary building.* Austin: University of Texas Press.

Hazenberg, S., & Hulstijn, J. H. (1996). Defining a minimal receptive second-language vocabulary for non-native university students: An empirical investigation. *Applied Linguistics, 17*(1).

Hogben, D., & Lawson, M. J. (1994). Keyword and multiple elaboration strategies for vocabulary acquisition in foreign language learning. *Contemporary Educational Psychology, 19,* 367–376.

Huckin, T., & Haynes, M. (1993). Summary and future directions. In T. Huckin, M. Haynes, & J. Coady (Eds.), *Second language reading and vocabulary learning* (pp. 289–298). Norwood, NJ: Ablex.

Hulstijn, J. H. (1989). Implicit and incidental second language learning: Experiments in the processing of natural and partly artificial input. In H. W.

Dechert & M. Raupach (Eds.), *Interlingual processing* (pp. 49–73). Tübingen: Gunter Narr.

(1990). A comparison between the information-processing and the analysis/control approaches to language learning. *Applied Linguistics, 11,* 30–45.

(1992). Retention of inferred and given word meanings: Experiments in incidental learning. In P. J. L. Arnaud & H. Béjoint (Eds.), *Vocabulary and applied linguistics* (pp. 113–125). Basingstoke: Macmillan.

(1993). When do foreign-language readers look up the meaning of unfamiliar words? The influence of task and learner variables. *Modern Language Journal, 77,* 139–147.

Johnson, C. W. (1985). Keywords and vocabulary acquisition: Some words of caution about words of assistance. *Educational Communication and Technology, 33,* 125–138.

Kasper, L. F. (1993). The keyword method and foreign language vocabulary learning: A rationale for its use. *Foreign Language Annals, 26,* 244–251.

Kasper, L. F., & Glass, A. L. (1988). An extension of the keyword method facilitates the acquisition of simple Spanish sentences. *Applied Cognitive Psychology, 2,* 137–146.

Kelly, P. (1986). Solving the vocabulary retention problem. *ITL Review of Applied Linguistics, 74,* 1–16.

Keyser, E. D. (1994). Review of Harrison & Winters Welker (1993). *Modern Language Journal, 78,* 565–566.

Kroll, J. F., & Sholl, A. (1992). Lexical and conceptual memory in fluent and nonfluent bilinguals. In R. J. Harris (Ed.), *Cognitive processing in bilinguals* (pp. 191–204). Amsterdam: Elsevier.

Lakoff, G. (1987). *Women, fire, and dangerous things: What categories reveal about the mind.* Chicago: University of Chicago Press.

Levelt, W. J. M. (1989). *Speaking: From intention to articulation.* Cambridge: Bradford & MIT Press.

Levin, J. R., Levin, M. A., Glasman, L. D., & Nordwall, M. B. (1992). Mnemonic vocabulary instruction: Additional effectiveness evidence. *Contemporary Educational Psychology, 17,* 156–174.

Levin, J. R., Pressley, M., McCormick, C. B., Miller, G. E., & Shriberg, L. K. (1979). Assessing the classroom potential of the keyword method. *Journal of Educational Psychology, 71,* 583–594.

McLaughlin Cook, N. (1989). The applicability of verbal mnemonics for different populations: A review. *Applied Cognitive Psychology, 3,* 3–22.

Meara, P. (1992). Network structures and vocabulary acquisition in a foreign language. In P. J. L. Arnaud & H. Béjoint (Eds.), *Vocabulary and applied linguistics* (pp. 62–70). Basingstoke: Macmillan.

(1993). The bilingual lexicon and the teaching of vocabulary. In R. Schreuder & B. Weltens (Eds.), *The bilingual lexicon* (pp. 279–297). Amsterdam & Philadelphia: John Benjamins.

Moore, J. C., & Surber, J. R. (1992). Effects of context and keyword methods on second language vocabulary acquisition. *Contemporary Educational Psychology, 17,* 286–292.

Morgan, J., & Rinvolucri, M. (1986). *Vocabulary.* Oxford: Oxford University Press.

Nagy, W. E., Anderson, R. C. & Herman, P. A. (1987). Learning word meanings from context during normal reading. *American Educational Research Journal, 24,* 237–270.

Nation, I. S. P. (1982). Beginning to learn foreign vocabulary: A review of the research. *RELC Journal, 13,* 14–36.

(1990). *Teaching and learning vocabulary.* New York: Newbury House.

Nelson, D. L., & Schreiber, T. A. (1992). Word concreteness and word structure as independent determinants of recall. *Journal of Memory and Language, 31,* 237–260.

Oxford, R. L. (1989). Use of language learning strategies: A synthesis of studies with implications for strategy training. *System, 17,* 235–247.

Oxford, R., & Crookall, D. (1990). Vocabulary learning: A critical analysis of techniques. *TESL Canada Journal, 7,* 9–29.

Paivio, A. (1976). Images, propositions, and knowledge. In J. M. Nicholas (Ed.), *Images, perception, and knowledge.* Dordrecht, NL: Reidel.

(1986). *Mental representations: A dual coding approach.* New York: Oxford University Press.

Pressley, M., Levin, J. R., & McDaniel, M. A. (1987). Remembering versus inferring what a word means: Mnemonic and contextual approaches. In M. G. McKeown & M. E. Curtis (Eds.), *The nature of vocabulary acquisition* (pp. 107–127). Hillsdale, NJ: Lawrence Erlbaum.

Schouten-Van Parreren, C. (1989). Vocabulary learning through reading: Which conditions should be met when presenting words in texts? *AILA Review, 6,* 75–85.

Schreuder, R., & Weltens, B. (1993). The bilingual lexicon: An overview. In R. Schreuder & B. Weltens (Eds.), *The bilingual lexicon* (pp. 1–10). Amsterdam & Philadelphia: John Benjamins.

Schwanenflugel, P. J., & Akin, C. E. (1994). Developmental trends in lexical decisions for abstract and concrete words. *Reading Research Quarterly, 29,* 250–264.

Schwanenflugel, P. J., Akin, C., & Luh, W.-M. (1992). Context availability and the recall of abstract and concrete words. *Memory and Cognition, 20,* 96–104.

Schwartz, B., & Reisberg, D. (1991). *Learning and memory.* New York: W. W. Norton.

Stevick, E. W. (1993). Imagination and memory: Friends or enemies? *Journal of the Imagination in Language Learning* (Jersey State College, Jersey City, NJ), *1,* 8–18.

Swain, M. (1985). Communicative competence: Some roles of comprehensible input and comprehensible output in its development. In S. M. Gass & C. G. Madden (Eds.), *Input in second language acquisition* (pp. 235–253). Rowley, MA: Newbury House.

Taylor, L. (1990). *Teaching and learning vocabulary.* New York: Prentice Hall.

Wallace, M. (1982). *Teaching vocabulary.* London: Heinemann.

Wang, A. Y., & Thomas, M. H. (1992). The effect of imagery-based mnemonics on the long-term retention of Chinese characters. *Language Learning, 42,* 359–376.

Wang, A. Y., Thomas, M. H., & Ouellette, J. A. (1992). Keyword mnemonic and retention of second-language vocabulary words. *Journal of Educational Psychology, 84,* 520–528.

Weinreich, U. (1953). *Languages in contact.* The Hague: Mouton.

Weise, G. (1990). Was haben Merkmalserkennung und -nutzung mit dem Lernerfolg zu tun? Eine Untersuchung zu kognitiven Aspekten des Fremdsprachenlexikerwerbs [What do feature recognition and use have to do with learning achievement? A study of the cognitive aspects of second language vocabulary acquisition]. *Deutsch als Fremdsprache, 27,* 103–109.

# 11  *L2 vocabulary acquisition through extensive reading*

James Coady

## L1 vocabulary acquisition

The incidental vocabulary learning hypothesis (Nagy & Herman, 1985) is based on research into how children learn vocabulary in their native language. It proposes that the vast majority of vocabulary words are learned gradually through repeated exposures in various discourse contexts. Proponents of this view claim that learners typically need about ten to twelve exposures to a word over time in order to learn it well. They observe that native speakers can learn as many as fifteen words per day from the ages two to seven and therefore conclude that direct instruction of vocabulary cannot possibly account for the vast growth of students' knowledge of vocabulary. Consequently, Nagy and Herman (1987) argue that teachers should promote extensive reading because it can lead to greater vocabulary growth than any program of explicit instruction alone ever could.

## L2 vocabulary acquisition

Following this same logic, it is argued that L2 learners who achieve advanced reading proficiency in a language will acquire most of their vocabulary knowledge through extensive reading rather than from instruction. For example, Krashen (1989), a leading proponent of extensive reading, argues that language learners acquire vocabulary and spelling most efficiently by receiving comprehensible input while reading. He claims that this results from the Input Hypothesis, i.e., successful language learning results from comprehensible input as the essential external ingredient coupled with a powerful internal language acquisition device. Krashen originally postulated the Input Hypothesis for oral language acquisition and in a recent study of oral vocabulary acquisition Ellis (1994) argues that it is "not comprehensible input but comprehended input that is important" (p. 481). Nevertheless, Krashen (1989) claims that the Input Hypothesis also applies to vocabulary acquisition by means of extensive reading.

Instead of more traditional pedagogical approaches to L2 vocabulary learning, Krashen, like Nagy and Herman, advocates massive quantities of pleasure reading in the students' own area of interest as well as large quantities of light, low-risk material that students are not tested on. In short, he believes that the Input Hypothesis is more efficient than other hypotheses; moreover, even if it were not, it is a much more pleasurable process.

## L2 vocabulary acquisition research

Krashen (1989) analyzes the results from 144 studies in his attempt to provide evidence for the superiority of the Input Hypothesis. But it is very important to note that all but three or four of these studies involved native speakers rather than L2 learners. Research that positively supports Krashen's claims as regards L2 vocabulary acquisition is still very limited.

For example, in the Pitts, White, and Krashen (1989) study, intermediate ESL students read the first two chapters of *A Clockwork Orange*. The subjects were tested 10 minutes after having spent 60 minutes reading the text. A control group, which did not read the text, was also tested on the nasdat (invented) vocabulary. A small, but statistically significant amount of vocabulary was acquired by the subjects in the experiment as compared to the control group.

Day, Omura, and Hiramatsu (1991) carried out a similar study with Japanese high school and undergraduate EFL students who read an adapted version of a story and then took a vocabulary test on some of the words in the story. The control group took only the vocabulary test with the result that the subjects who read the story knew significantly more vocabulary. Their proficiency level was not specified.

Dupuy and Krashen (1993) had third-semester students of French watch five scenes of a play on film and then read the next five scenes in French. They were then given a surprise vocabulary test on words in the text. The subjects performed significantly better than control subjects enrolled in another third-semester class who did not see the film or read the text.

### Research issues

There are some important issues, however, that these studies do not address. First and foremost, there appears to be a serious methodological problem with these studies; namely, the control groups were not given any exposure to the texts containing the target vocabulary. Accordingly, it is hardly surprising that the experimental groups demonstrated better knowledge of these words than did the control groups. Apparently the goal of these studies was simply to demonstrate that vocabulary learning can take place through exposure to texts. A more informative process would have been to ask the control groups to simply memorize the target words in whatever mode they wished within an identical time frame. This procedure, together with follow-up testing and so on, would have produced greater validity for these studies.

Second, most of the subjects in the studies under review appear to be at an intermediate level of FL instruction. We are left with the question of whether such gains would occur with students at either the very beginning or very advanced levels. For example, do actual beginners know enough vocabulary to read well enough to learn words in this manner?

Third, do such gains occur when control groups are given alternative cognitive enriching opportunities, for example, strategy instruction and mnemonic techniques? For example, Moore and Surber (1992) compared several types of vocabulary acquisition strategies and found that the keyword method and the context method were superior to no method. Moreover, Sanaoui (1995) found two distinct approaches to vocabulary learning in L2: Some adults are clearly capable of managing their own learning whereas others rely heavily on instructors' guidance to develop their lexical knowledge, and for such learners she recommends helping them to acquire processes for managing their own learning.

Fourth, do such gains persist through time, and do they do so with a significant advantage over strategy-oriented approaches to vocabulary learning such as memorizing words, using the keyword technique, and so on?

## Negative research evidence

There is also some negative evidence in the research literature. For example, in an explicit attempt to test the IH, Tudor and Hafiz (1989) set up a 3-month ESL extensive reading program using graded readers. Compared to a control group, the experimental group showed significant improvement in both reading and writing, especially writing. However, "the subjects' vocabulary base remained relatively unchanged" (p. 164). Moreover, in a subsequent study with adults in an EFL setting who also used graded readers, Hafiz and Tudor (1990) again found no significant vocabulary gain. Hulstijn (1992), in several studies of adult L2 learners, concluded that "the retention of word meanings in a true incidental learning task is very low indeed" (p. 122). Thus we are left with very mixed results from the research in support of Krashen's claims about L2 vocabulary acquisition through extensive reading alone.

## Comparing instruction and extensive reading by adults

On the other hand, Paribakht and Wesche (Chapter 9, this volume) investigated this question in a university setting with adults studying English for academic purposes. They found that while reading for meaning alone did result in significant acquisition of L2 vocabulary, direct instruction led to acquisition of even greater numbers of words as well as more depth of knowledge. Zimmerman (1994) found similar results. It is beyond the scope of this article to survey the components of such an instructional approach, but see, for example, Paribakht and Wesche (Chapter 9, this volume), Hulstijn (Chapter 10, this volume), Nuttall (1982), Nation (1990), and Cohen (1990).

## Comparing instruction and extensive reading by children

In contrast to the above studies with adults, Elley (1991) presents the results of nine different studies that exposed young children to a large range of high-interest illustrated storybooks in second language literacy oriented programs. Five parameters were common to all of the studies: immersion in meaningful texts, incidental language learning, integration of oral and written language, focus on meaning rather than form, and the fostering of high intrinsic motivation. There were rapid gains in reading and listening comprehension, which tended to remain stable over time. Moreover, Elley (1989) found that oral reading of stories to L2 elementary learners led to significant and long-term vocabulary acquisition. Elley concludes that these studies provide support for whole-language approaches and Krashen's Input Hypothesis.

But here again it is important to note that these results are with children, not adults. Some researchers claim that children acquire language in a significantly different manner than adults whereas others disagree strongly with such claims. In view of such controversy, results from studies on how children can acquire vocabulary cannot be extrapolated to adult acquisition in a simple and straightforward manner. For an introduction to this debate, see Clahsen, 1990; White, 1990; Klein, 1990; Larsen-Freeman and Long, 1991.

## Extensive reading of newspapers

A different kind of evidence can be seen in a diary study by Grabe and Stoller (Chapter 6, this volume), which describes an attempt to learn

Portuguese by extensive reading of mainly newspapers for at least 2 hours per day. Their theory was that "many exposures of differing intensities would gradually lead to a large recognition vocabulary." They concluded that reading and vocabulary abilities did develop as a result of extensive reading practice. Note, however, that the subject was a highly motivated adult learner who was very knowledgeable about successful language learning strategies. For more discussion on how to use newspaper articles for extensive reading, see Kyongho and Nation (1989).

# The beginner's paradox

Since the empirical evidence in support of incidental acquisition of vocabulary is somewhat ambiguous, it would seem that we must pay more serious attention to the problem facing those language learners who are beginners and who face a truly paradoxical situation. How can they learn enough words to learn vocabulary through extensive reading when they do not know enough words to read well? For a possible solution, let us adopt a somewhat pragmatic and pedagogical approach.

From a pragmatic perspective, it appears quite logical for beginning L2 language learners to put most of their emphasis on learning words. And yet most contemporary academic approaches to language learning place minimal importance on vocabulary learning and appear to assume that somehow words will be learned as a by-product of the other language activities (see Zimmerman, Chapter 1, this volume).

## Vocabulary threshold for reading comprehension

Laufer (Chapter 2, this volume) discusses the L2 vocabulary knowledge needed for minimal reading comprehension and concludes that "the turning point of vocabulary size for reading comprehension is about 3,000 word families." Since a word family contains a base form plus its inflected and derived forms (e.g., *find, finds, finder, findings*, etc.), this increases the total amount to about 5,000 lexical items. She claims that, upon reaching that lexical threshold, good L1 readers can be expected to transfer their reading strategies to L2. Moreover, she cites Nation and Coady (1988) concerning their claim that successful guessing in context occurs when about 98% of the lexical items in a text are already known. She points out that this implies knowing about 5,000 word families or about 8,000 lexical items. Presumably the reader would then be an independent learner capable of learning words through context in the same manner as L1 learners. But it is sobering to note how much vocabulary knowledge the learner must have in order to read at this level of independence and nativelike proficiency. We can now further appreciate the beginner's paradox: How does a beginner learn enough words to read with even modest comprehension at the threshold level of 3,000 word families, and, beyond that, an independent level of 5,000 word families?

## Low-frequency vocabulary problem

Another basic problem facing foreign language learners is that they typically have minimal opportunities for exposure to the target language, and especially the types of spoken language experiences that native speakers enjoy and that enable them to achieve at least the minimal vocabulary needed for reading. For example, a comparison of the Schonell, Meddleton, and Shaw (1956) count of spoken English and the Kucera and Francis (1967) count of written English would seem to indicate that written English contains twice as many word types as does spoken English. In other words, a great many words of low frequency are found only in writing and therefore, logically speaking, can only be learned by encountering them in that context. Therefore, another problem facing the L2 learner is that many low-frequency words can be learned only by reading.

## Vocabulary control movement

Historically, the most significant attempt to solve the beginner's paradox was the vocabulary control movement, which attempted to drastically limit the vocabulary found in learner texts (see Zimmerman, Chapter 1, this volume). The assumption behind this practice is that the task of acquiring the language is greatly eased by eliminating (insofar as possible) the burden of recognizing too many different word forms. In an effort to produce comprehensible material, hundreds of simplified versions of texts have been produced, usually by eliminating all words above a certain level of difficulty as determined by a list of the frequency with which words occur in the language in general (e.g., West, 1953). For example, Nuttall (1982) cites the vocabulary levels of some major series of British EFL readers where the vocabulary levels range from 300 to 3,500 words. Such simplified reading texts, typically known as graded readers, are discussed in more detail by Bamford (1984), Hill and Thomas (1988, 1989), and Thomas & Hill (1993), who review many of the hundreds of available titles. Also see Wodinsky and Nation (1988), Hedge (1985), Greenwood (1988), and Ellis and McRae (1991), who discuss various aspects of learning from graded readers.

## Use of authentic materials

However, use of such simplified texts has been greatly criticized because they are not seen as "authentic." Because the process of simplification involves rewriting, it tends to eliminate much of the normal syntactic and pragmatic usage of an ordinary text as well as its less frequent vocabulary. Critics of such texts (Huckin, 1983; Widdowson, 1979) claim that they do not prepare students for the "real" texts they will face all too soon. Instead they suggest that actual native speaker materials that have not been simplified should be used for pedagogy, and they would presumably extend this same claim to the materials being used for extensive reading. Also, many graded readers are poorly written, stilted in style, and actually dull to read. Thomas and Hill (1993) do report, however, that there has been some improvement in this respect.

Note that beginning native speaker readers are not expected to read difficult texts, e.g., literature, until they are at a more advanced state in their schooling. They are usually exposed to simplified readers and specially adapted pedagogical materials such as the popular boxes of reading materials from *Science Research Associates*. On the other hand, there is growing support in elementary language arts education in America for whole-language approaches, which strongly advocate the use of language considered more appropriate to children's level of linguistic and cognitive growth. Proponents therefore argue that young readers should be given authentic, well-written materials that are designed for their age level, e.g., Caldecott and Newberry award-winning books for children. For an application of this approach to TESOL, see Rigg (1991).

Accordingly, many proponents of extensive reading advocate the use of simplified materials for beginners, but readily admit that the goal must be to move as quickly as possible to more authentic native speaker texts. For example, Wallace (1992) argues for a more flexible interpretation of authenticity and concludes that "if we see authenticity as lying in the interaction between text and reader and not in the text itself, we need not hesitate to use specially written texts" (p. 81).

## Responses to the beginner's paradox

A partial and preliminary answer to the beginner's paradox can be found in Coady (1993), who adopts the view that there is a universal model of word identification that is the same across native and nonnative speakers of a language. The vocabulary acquired through the medium of reading by L2 language learners can be divided into at least three major developmental categories: those whose forms and common meanings are recognized automatically, irrespective of context (or sight vocabulary); those whose forms and meanings are to some degree familiar to the learner but are recognized only in context; and those whose meanings, and, often, forms as well, are unknown to the learner and whose meanings must therefore be inferred from the context, looked up in a dictionary, or left uncomprehended (also see Grabe & Stoller, Chapter 6, this volume).

The crux of this proposal for the moment is that sight vocabulary typically consists of medium- to high-frequency words that have been well learned through repeated exposure and, in all likelihood, explicit instruction (see Coady, Magoto, Hubbard, Graney, & Mokhtari, 1993). Accordingly, less frequent words will normally be learned through incidental contact in context (preferably with the help of some strategic training) via extensive reading, but only after a critical level of automaticity has been achieved with the high-frequency vocabulary. This would clearly imply that some pedagogical emphasis would have to be given to helping beginners learn the 3,000 most frequent words in such a manner that they become automatic in their recognition, i.e., sight vocabulary (see Laufer, Chapter 2, and Yang, Chapter 7, this volume). Moreover, other scholars have argued for the need for further instruction beyond this minimal level (see Arnaud & Savignon, Chapter 8, this volume, and Nation, 1990).

Coady (1979) argues that there is an interaction between background knowledge, linguistic knowledge, and ability to comprehend, i.e., process a text. Therefore a student can pick a text that is very high in interest and read it with pleasure and success even if the linguistic aspects of the text are quite advanced relative to the student's ability. In this case, the subject matter is reasonably well known already, or, if not, there is a great desire to acquire precisely this knowledge. Moreover, the basic vocabulary of the topic is probably well known in L1 and it is much easier to recognize the cognates in L2 because of this fact. Most important of all, though, is the fact that high motivation will typically enable the reader to succeed in comprehending a difficult text to a surprising degree. The converse is equally true. An uninteresting text, even when comprehended, is not as worthwhile a linguistic event and vocabulary acquisition is not nearly as effective.

## The Vicious/Virtuous Circle of L2 reading

But we are still left wondering how the beginner is to learn enough of the syntax, semantics, and pragmatics of the language to successfully comprehend the various materials involved in an extensive reading program.

From a pedagogical perspective, Nuttall (1982) has cleverly represented this problem in her proposal that many L2 readers are trapped in a Vicious Circle:

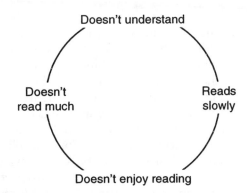

She claims that "It doesn't matter where you enter the circle, because any of the factors that make it up will produce any of the others" (p. 167). But she also proposes a Virtuous Circle that can enable one to escape from the Vicious Circle:

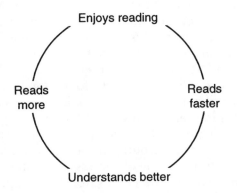

Basically, she proposes that to escape the Vicious Circle one must break the chain. Note that, for her, enjoyment and quantity of reading are paths to learning and pedagogical efforts in that direction are the most likely to succeed.

## Effective methods in extensive reading

In the literature on extensive reading there are some recurring parameters that appear to be effective methods for accomplishing this goal (Elley, 1991; Yu, 1993). It is important to note that under this approach there will be less emphasis on length of text, sentence length, or vocabulary/ new word density and more emphasis on reader interest, theme of text, match between reader's background knowledge and the text, and the linguistic/cultural authenticity of the text.

An overarching concern of this approach seems to be the necessity to construct an opportunity for students to choose materials that will enable them to read large amounts of material with successful comprehension, thereby letting the "natural learning ability" build vocabulary knowledge. Consequently, the reading curriculum must be structured in such a manner that there is comprehensible input, adequate feedback, encouragement, and, above all, material that the student is interested in reading.

Comprehensible input cannot be guaranteed in all cases, but some steps can be taken to increase its likelihood. For example, it is probably a good idea to test or assess learners' vocabulary knowledge in order to assist them in choosing appropriate texts for extensive reading. For further information on this point, see Nation (1990). Moreover, it is useful to be able to categorize the texts being used for extensive reading in terms of vocabulary difficulty in the case of simplified texts. But the most useful categorization will be by theme, topic, and genre so that students can find texts that they are interested in reading.

Feedback can be accomplished in a number of ways. Most proponents agree that there should be an absolute minimum of formal or traditional testing. A very practical method of checking on comprehension is to ask for short reviews, summaries, or responses to the stories. Teachers can have conferences with students and respond to their oral or written summaries. Indeed, Hafiz and Tudor (1990) found significant improvement in writing skills attributable to the summaries. Another technique is to encourage students to share the results of their reading with each other, for example, in small groups. The student should feel free to come to the teacher for assistance and encouragement when needed. But the best feedback will come from the joy of success in reading.

It is crucial that the teacher be a motivator in this approach. If students become discouraged and quit reading, there can only be one outcome. If, however, they can be supported and encouraged to persevere, there is every possibility of success.

The emphasis on using interesting texts leads to a rather obvious corollary. It is the students themselves who are best capable of choosing what interests them. Therefore, every effort should be made to enable them to select the texts themselves.

There is another important consequence of the claim that the texts must be interesting. Younger readers, for example, will tend to prefer a selection of romance novels, adventure stories, and more popular texts in the genres of science fiction, murder mysteries, and so on. See White (1979) and Reed (1985) for some interesting adolescent-level materials. Teachers are sometimes reluctant to use such materials in a school setting because they are not considered to be of literary value, i.e., not exemplars of good writing and high cultural values. But it is indeed the very linguistic and cultural complexity of such literary texts that makes them so difficult for the beginning reader. The text-interest principle is fundamental to this approach and must be followed for the method to succeed.

Finally, Nuttall (1982) gives a number of very practical suggestions on how a teacher can set up a collection of texts suitable for extensive reading, establish a continuous budget to support it, and find various ways to encourage students to use it.

# Conclusion

This chapter has attempted to provide some insights into the beginner's paradox and some ways to deal with it. The basic claim is that a great deal of L2 vocabulary is indeed learned through extensive reading and that extensive reading can be a means of solving the beginner's paradox. However, it was also pointed out that we need to help the beginners learn a relatively small number of highly frequent vocabulary words so well that they become automatic, sight vocabulary. Only with this fundamental competence will beginners be able to read independently and acquire the language in the natural manner that is assumed by so many pedagogical approaches today. In other words, instructional programs need to ensure that students know at least the basic 3,000 word families so that they can indeed acquire vocabulary incidentally through extensive reading.

Lewis asserts that "Language is not words and grammar; it is essentially lexical" (1993, p. 196). It is becoming increasingly apparent that we must enable students to learn and acquire a lexical base in order to achieve success in language learning. Extensive reading has a major role to play in that process.

# References

Bamford, J. (1984). Extensive reading by means of graded readers. *Reading in a Foreign Language*, 2(2), 218–260.

Clahsen, H. (1990). *The acquisition of syntax in children from 5 to 10*. Cambridge: MIT Press.

Coady, J. (1979). A psycholinguistic model of the ESL reader. In R. Mackay, B. Barkman, & R. R. Jordan (Eds.), *Reading in a second language* (pp. 5–12). Rowley, MA: Newbury House.

Research on ESL/EFL vocabulary acquisition: Putting it in context. In T. Huckin, M. Haynes, & J. Coady (Eds.), *Second language reading and vocabulary learning* (pp. 3–23). Norwood, NJ: Ablex.

Coady, J, Magoto, J., Hubbard, P., Graney, J., & Mokhtari, K. (1993). High frequency vocabulary and reading proficiency in ESL readers. In T. Huckin, M. Haynes, & J. Coady (Eds.), *Second language reading and vocabulary learning* (pp. 217–228). Norwood, NJ: Ablex.

Cohen, A. D., (1990). *Language learning: Insights for learners, teachers, and researchers*. New York: Newbury House.

Day, R., Omura, C., & Hiramatsu, M. (1991). Incidental EFL vocabulary learning and reading. *Reading in a Foreign Language, 7*(2), 541–551.

Dupuy, B., & Krashen, S. (1993). Incidental vocabulary acquisition in French as a foreign language. *Applied Language Learning, 4*(1), 55–63.

Elley, W. (1989). Vocabulary acquisition from listening to stories. *Reading Research Quarterly 24*(2), 174–187.

(1991). Acquiring literacy in a second language: The effect of book-based programs. *Language Learning, 41,* 375–411.

Ellis, G., & McRae, J. (1991). *The extensive reading handbook for secondary teachers*. London: Penguin.

Ellis, R. (1994). Factors in the incidental acquisition of second language vocabulary for oral input: A review essay. *Applied Language Learning, 5*(1), 1–32.

Greenwood, J. (1988). *Class readers*. Oxford: Oxford University Press.

Hafiz, F., & Tudor, I. (1990). Graded readers as an input medium in L2 learning. *System, 18*(1), 31–42.

Hedge, T. (1985). *Using readers in language teaching*. London: Macmillan.

Hill, D., & Thomas, H. (1988). Survey review: Graded readers. *ELT Journal, 42*(1), 124–36.

(1989). Survey review: Graded readers. *ELT Journal 43*(3), 221–31.

Huckin, T. (1983). A cognitive approach to readability. In P. Anderson, R. J. Brockmann, & C. Miller (Eds.), *New essays in technical and scientific communication: Theory, research and criticism* (pp. 90–108). Farmington, NY: Baywood.

Hulstijn, J. (1992). Retention of inferred and given word meanings: Experiments in incidental vocabulary learning. In P. Arnaud & H. Béjoint (Eds.), *Vocabulary and applied linguistics* (pp. 113–125). Basingstoke: Macmillan.

Klein, W. (1990). A theory of language acquisition is not so easy. *Studies in Second Language Acquisition, 12,* 219–231.

Krashen, S. (1989). We acquire vocabulary and spelling by reading: Additional evidence for the input hypothesis. *Modern Language Journal, 73*(4), 440–464.

Kucera, H., & Francis, W. N. (1967). *A computational analysis of present-day American English*. Boston: Houghton Mifflin.

Kyongho, H., & Nation, P. (1989). Reducing the vocabulary load and encouraging vocabulary learning through reading newspapers. *Reading in a Foreign Language 6*(1), 323–335.

Larsen-Freeman, D., & Long, M. (1991). *An introduction to second language acquisition research*. London: Longman.

Lewis, M. (1993). *The lexical approach: The state of ELT and a way forward*. Hove, England: Language Teaching Publications.

Moore, J., & Surber, J. (1992). Effects of context and keyword methods on second language vocabulary acquisition. *Contemporary Educational Psychology, 17,* 286–292.

Nagy, W., & Herman, P. (1985). Incidental vs. instructional approaches to increasing reading vocabulary. *Educational Perspectives, 23,* 16–21.

(1987). Breadth and depth of vocabulary knowledge: Implications for acquisition and instruction. In M. McKeown & M. Curtis (Eds.), *The nature of vocabulary acquisition* (pp. 19–35). Hillsdale, NJ: Lawrence Erlbaum.

Nation, I. S. P. (1990). *Teaching and learning vocabulary.* Rowley, MA: Newbury House.

Nation, I. S. P., & Coady, J. (1988). Vocabulary and reading. In R. Carter & M. McCarthy (Eds.), *Vocabulary and language teaching* (pp. 97–110). New York: Longman.

Nuttall, C. (1982). *Teaching reading skills in a foreign language.* London: Heinemann.

Pitts, M., White, H., & Krashen, S. (1989). Acquiring second language vocabulary through reading: A replication of the Clockwork Orange study using second language acquirers. *Reading in a Foreign Language, 5*(2), 271–275.

Reed, A. (1985). *Reaching adolescents: The young adult book and the school.* New York: Holt, Rinehart & Winston.

Rigg, P. (1991). Whole language in TESOL. *TESOL Quarterly 25*(3), 520–540.

Sanaoui, R. (1995). Adult learners' approaches to learning vocabulary in second languages. *Modern Language Journal, 79,* 15–28.

Schonell, F. J., Meddleton, I. G., & Shaw, B. A. (1956). *A study of the oral vocabulary of adults.* Brisbane: University of Queensland Press.

Science Research Associates. *Reading for understanding.* Chicago, IL.

*Reading laboratories.* Chicago, IL.

Thomas, H., & Hill, D. (1993). Survey review: Seventeen series of graded readers. *ELT Journal 47*(3), 250–267.

Tudor, I., & Hafiz, F. (1989). Extensive reading as a means of input to L2 learning. *Journal of Research in Reading, 12*(2), 164–178.

Wallace, C. (1992). *Reading.* Oxford: Oxford University Press.

West, M. (1953). *A general service list of English words.* London: Longman.

White, L. (1990). Second language acquisition and universal grammar. *Studies in Second Language Acquisition, 12,* 121–133.

White, M. (Ed.). (1979). *High interest easy reading for junior and senior high school students.* Urbana, IL: NCTE.

Widdowson, H. G. (1979). *Explorations in applied linguistics.* Oxford: Oxford University Press.

Wodinsky, M., & Nation, P. (1988). Learning from graded readers. *Reading in a Foreign Language, 5*(1), 155–161.

Yu, V. (1993). Extensive reading programs – how can they best benefit the teaching and learning of English? *TESL Reporter 26*(1), 1–9.

Zimmerman, C. B. (1994). Self-selected reading and interactive vocabulary instruction: Knowledge and perceptions of word learning among L2 learners. Ph.D. diss., University of Southern California, Los Angeles.

# 12 *Teaching vocabulary*

Paul Nation and Jonathan Newton

Designing the vocabulary programme of a course is similar to most examples of language course design. In addition to considering the situation in which the course occurs, it is necessary to decide what vocabulary will be selected for teaching, how it will be sequenced, and how it will be presented. In this review of vocabulary pedagogy, we will first look at these aspects of selection, sequencing, and presentation, and then explore in more detail two issues that have become a focus of recent research, namely, incorporating vocabulary development into communicative activities, and improving learners' access to vocabulary that has already been partly learned.

## Selection

There has been a long tradition of research into what vocabulary will provide the best return for learning. The majority of these pieces of research have been frequency counts, which have provided lists of the most frequent and widely used words of a language. Particularly for the early stages of learning a language, these studies have provided very valuable information. The often repeated finding of frequency counts has been that the most frequent 2,000 headwords account for at least 85% of the words on any page of any book no matter what the subject matter. The same words give an even greater coverage of spoken language. Focusing learners' attention on the high-frequency words of the language gives a very good return for learning effort.

Frequency and range, however, have not been the only factors that have guided the principled selection of vocabulary for teaching. Other factors include the ability to combine with other words, the ability to help define other words, the ability to replace other words, and other factors related to association and availability. These factors and others have been brought together in the notion of a 'core vocabulary' (Carter, 1986, 1987). West (1953) used some of these, but particularly frequency, range, and replaceability, in his classic *General Service List of English Words*, which contains 2,000 headwords with indications of their frequency and the relative frequency of each word's meanings.

# Sequencing

There are two sequences to look at here: first, the sequence of levels of vocabulary, and second, the grouping and ordering of words within a set of lessons.

A convenient division for the levels of vocabulary is shown in the accompanying table adapted from Nation (1990), and based on written academic text.

| Level | Number of words | Text coverage, % |
|---|---|---|
| High-frequency words | 2,000 | 87 |
| Academic vocabulary | 800 | 8 |
| Technical vocabulary | 2,000 | 3 |
| Low-frequency words | 123,200 | 2 |
| Total | 128,000 | 100 |

Clearly the 2,000 high-frequency words of English should receive attention first because without these it is not possible to use English in any normal way. These words deserve considerable time and attention. Once learners can use them, the decision as to which level to move to next depends on the use that the learners will make of English.

The academic vocabulary list (Nation, 1990; Xue & Nation, 1984) contains 800 headwords that are frequent in a wide range of academic texts, both in secondary or senior high school and in university, and in newspapers. Here are some examples of words from the academic word list: *abandon, alternative, comply, denote, element, evident.* If learners intend to do academic study or wish to read newspapers, then the academic vocabulary is the next level of vocabulary to teach. If, however, they intend to use English for social purposes, for occupations that do not require the reading of academic text, or for reading novels and popular magazines, the next level to move to is the low-frequency word level.

The division between high-frequency words and low-frequency words is arbitrary and researchers do not agree about where the division should be made, although they agree that the distinction can be most usefully made somewhere between the most frequent 1,500 words and the most frequent 7,000 words. Here are some examples of the more common low-frequency words: *bench, marble, thrill, brilliant, mess, circus, hug.* Less common low-frequency words include *gibbous, phytogeography, gybe, oppidan, telangiectasis,* and *yautia.*

Technical vocabulary has a very narrow range, that is, it is used within a specialized field. Within that field it may be reasonably common. It is likely that every field has its technical vocabulary or the equivalent. Academic fields like law, mathematics, chemistry, and philosophy clearly have technical vocabularies. It could also be argued that newspapers have their own technical vocabulary, such as the names of people, places, and organizations. Although this vocabulary changes rather rapidly, it does share several features with the technical vocabularies of, say, science. First, the names carry a lot of the message in a particular text. Second, it is often repeated within a text. Third, it may be defined in the text or be considered expected background knowledge for a reader. Technical vocabulary is best taught within the content area of the relevant subject and is usually not a useful focus in preparatory English classes. Grouping items within a lesson will be looked at later in this article in the section dealing with dangers in associative activities.

## Presentation

Academic and technical vocabulary lists can be used to make it easier for teachers and learners to treat these types of vocabulary in the same way as high-frequency vocabulary – namely, by learning these items directly through vocabulary exercises or individual learning. Because high-frequency words are relatively few in number, are essential for effective language use and give a very good coverage of text, each individual high-frequency word is worthy of attention by the teacher.

Because low-frequency words are many in number, can often be guessed from context if the high-frequency words are known, and occur very infrequently, each word does not deserve attention from the teacher, but strategies for coping with and learning these words do. These strategies include, in order of importance, guessing from context, using word parts to help remember word meanings, and using mnemonic and rote vocabulary learning strategies. Note that this approach is described from the teacher's point of view. As Kelly (1990) has pointed out, guessing is not a substitute for systematic learning of lexis. Both of these approaches – guessing and systematic learning – deserve attention from the teacher, particularly in terms of strategy development. It is at this point that the teacher's and the learner's interest may diverge. The teacher's main concern will be in the effective development of the strategies. The learner will be mainly concerned with the particular piece of learning that the strategies help.

The general principles for dealing with high- and low-frequency vocabulary have been described, but there are several ways that these principles can be put into practice. Generally, these ways can be described as direct and indirect. They are not necessarily alternatives and may complement each other.

In a direct approach to vocabulary teaching, explicit attention is given to vocabulary. There may be vocabulary lessons where periods of time are set aside for the study of vocabulary. There will certainly be explicit vocabulary exercises, which may include word-building exercises, matching words with various types of definitions, studying vocabulary in context, semantic mapping, and split information activities focusing on vocabulary. There may also be regular vocabulary testing and possibly assigned rote learning (see Nation, 1982, for a review of research on this topic). Time may be set aside for the learning of strategies and learners' mastery of strategies may be monitored and assessed.

In an indirect approach to vocabulary teaching, the teacher's concern for vocabulary learning will not be so obvious. The teacher may give consideration to incorporating vocabulary learning into communicative activities like listening to stories, information gap activities, and group work, although vocabulary will not often be the main learning goal of the activities. Learners would also be encouraged and guided to do substantial amounts of graded reading. Whenever problems with vocabulary occur in activities, these problems would be dealt with in a principled way. At times these problems may be used as an opportunity to focus explicitly on vocabulary development.

Both of these approaches require thought and planning on the part of the teacher. In an indirect approach, the teacher needs to ensure that learners are being exposed to material and activities that will expand their vocabulary in useful ways. In any language course it is worth looking at the opportunities for direct and indirect vocabulary learning to see that there is a systematic programme of vocabulary development.

In the next section, we will look further at the presentation of vocabulary to see how it can be incorporated both directly and indirectly into communicative activities.

## Learning through communicative activities

Communication activities have a well-established place within many language learning programmes. Although the range of types of such activities is large, all provide learners with opportunities to use language to do things and, in particular, to engage in meaningful interactive oral language production. Typically, their goal is to improve the fluency with which learners access their knowledge of the target language (Nation & Thomas, 1988; Ur, 1981). Other goals include developing confidence in social communication skills (Ladousse, 1983), dealing with the unpredictable nature of conversation (Ladousse, 1987), and improving grammatical accuracy (Rinvolucri, 1984).

Research carried out in recent years indicates that there may also be a role for vocabulary learning either as an incidental goal or as one of the primary goals of a communication activity.

In a study of the acquisition of mathematical vocabulary through the performance of split information activities by eleven- to thirteen-year-old students, Hall (1992) found that the vocabulary learning of students working on these interactive activities was greater than that of students working within a teacher-fronted arrangement with a reading focus. Figure 1 shows a sample task.

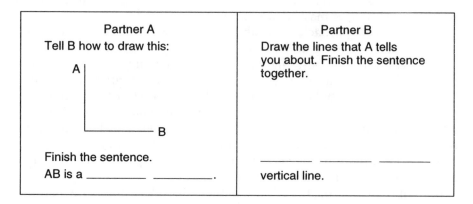

Hall concluded that split information activities 'can provide opportunities for talk . . . which increase both language knowledge and content knowledge'. Hall suggests that the requirement for spoken output in these activities and the generative use of new vocabulary items (their use in new contexts and in new structures) are the key factors leading to acquisition of these items.

Simcock (1993) studied learners' performance in ask-and-answer activities where students read a story in pairs and then respond to preset questions from their partners about the events in the story, responding as if they were the people in the story who had experienced these events. She found that new vocabulary encountered in the reading input for the activity was used productively and accurately by learners even when they were not being asked about these items by their partners. This suggests a role for incidental vocabulary learning when the learners' focus is primarily on meaningful performance of a communicative activity.

A study by Elley (1989) provided empirical evidence of incidental vocabulary learning for seven- to eight-year-olds involved in listening to stories in which there was repetition of the new words, illustrations of the words, and redundancy through context. Elley recorded gains of 15% where there was no explanation of the new words and 40% gains where explanation occurred. Although this result relates largely to listening, it also shows the acquisition of vocabulary in a context where attention is on meaningful communication and not on language itself.

Finally, a study by Newton (1993) investigated vocabulary gains through performance of two split and two shared information activities by two groups of four learners.[1] The learners' recognition of vocabulary in the tasks was pre- and posttested and full transcripts were used to analyse the negotiation of this vocabulary during task performances. Three key findings emerged from the study.

First, pretesting showed that many of the 111 words from the four tasks that were not known by at least one member of a group were known by some other group members. In other words, the combined group vocabulary was much greater than that of any one learner in a group. In group 1, for example, 38 words were recognised by all group members, 12 were not recognised by any group members, and the remaining 61 words were recognised by some members of the group but not the group as a whole. For these 61 words – the majority of unfamiliar words in the textual input – the learners within the group were clearly an important learning resource for each other.

Second, further positive evidence in support of this route to understanding of new vocabulary is seen in the negotiation of vocabulary in the performances. Of the 49 requests for word meaning made by learners in the course of performing the tasks, 29 were accurately dealt with by other learners within the group. Two were lost in the interaction and 11 resulted in repeating and spelling the word concerned, but without further information on meaning. Of the remaining 7 items, 5 required some level of supervisor prompting or assistance, and in only two cases did the learners provide inaccurate information. Overall, the learners negotiated unknown vocabulary successfully, thereby helping each other with the learning and use of this vocabulary.

Third, posttesting of the learners' ability to recognise and provide meanings for the vocabulary in the activities showed individual learning gains ranging between 10 and 20 words over the pretest scores for the two groups. This indicates that the learners made important first steps in acquiring new vocabulary through performing the four communication activities.

The research described in this brief review provides evidence for improved vocabulary recognition and use both indirectly, as a result of exposure to new vocabulary in a meaningful communicative context (Elley, 1989; Newton, 1993; Simcock, 1990), and directly as a result of communicative work on targeted vocabulary (Hall, 1992).

---

1  The split information tasks required interlocutors to exchange unique information each held in order to complete a diagram or table. The shared information tasks required interlocutors to discuss commonly held information in order to problem solve and rank various options.

## What are the features of communication activities that encourage vocabulary learning?

First, the face-to-face nature of communication in group activities can help speakers to set their speech to a suitable level for the particular listeners and to adjust it when listeners indicate a lack of understanding. Listeners can also help the speaker by pointing out items that he or she may not be using correctly. Thus learners involved in group work can get help from each other on the meaning of unfamiliar language, including vocabulary items they do not know. Through negotiation, learners can continue to get additional information on an unfamiliar item until they are satisfied that they understand it.

Second, communication activities generally provide a meaningful context such as a scenario for role play or an illustrated setting within which to encounter new vocabulary. This context may not only provide sufficient evidence for a learner to make a reasonable guess as to the meaning of unfamiliar items, but it also assists in the remembering of new items (Craik & Tulving, 1975) and in the networking of new knowledge within the learners' present knowledge structures (Anderson & Reder, 1979).

Third, there is a good chance learners will also be exposed to repeated use of the new items during the course of the activity. Furthermore, because the repetition occurs in a meaningful context, the durability of the learning of the new items is likely to improve.

Fourth, having encountered the new items, learners are likely to be required to use them productively in the activity. If this requires learners to use vocabulary in ways that are not rote repetitions of the way the vocabulary appeared in the input to the task, learning will be much greater (Hall, 1992).

Fifth, from a psycholinguistic perspective, group-based peer interaction typically provides a learning environment in which learners can make errors and express misunderstanding without the adverse effects of exposing their weakness to the whole class or to the teacher (Long & Porter, 1985).

To sum up, there are sound psycholinguistic and pedagogic reasons for using communication activities for improving learners' vocabulary knowledge. But whether and to what extent a learners' vocabulary knowledge will be extended through communication activities is dependent on certain features of the activities themselves. These features include the choice of vocabulary and its placement within the textual input for the activity, the teacher's and learners' strategies for arriving at the meaning of unfamiliar items, and the processing demands of the activity. By being aware of these features and the way they affect learners' responses to unfamiliar vocabulary, teachers can improve the quality of vocabulary learning that is likely to occur during performance of communication activities.

## The choice and placement of vocabulary in communication activities

Where the content matter for a task is provided in text form, there is clear evidence that learners spend time talking about vocabulary from this text rather than vocabulary generated by other learners (Newton, 1993). This finding provides us with good reason to take care with the choice and placement of vocabulary items in the printed input for an activity. The choice of a topic and the learners' proficiencies and needs are three primary factors that should determine what vocabulary goes into an activity.

The activity 'Making an Employment Decision' in the Appendix is an example of this principle. This activity was designed as part of a theme-based unit of study on employment for lower-intermediate learners in a university-based English proficiency course. Some of these learners were planning to go on to university study, but most were learning for a range of other purposes. The vocabulary included in the activity both reflects the content of the wider theme and provides for discussion of information relevant to those with an academic orientation (i.e., the names of qualifications), as well as for discussion of information relevant to those with a general community orientation (i.e., popular New Zealand sports, common occupations). For both groups there are also practice reading and saying long numerical figures.

When deciding on the best way to place vocabulary in an activity, there are a number of options to consider. Targeted vocabulary could be placed in instructions, diagrams, lists, a set of rules or criteria, or a description of a scenario. The following guidelines can assist placement.

First, instructions, as the way 'into' the activity, should be transparent, containing as little new vocabulary as possible. Unfamiliar vocabulary in the instructions may inhibit progress on the task and is not likely to receive the same depth of processing and recycling as unfamiliar vocabulary in the content of the task. For example, the activity in the Appendix involves reasonably complex operations, but the instructions have been written simply with few low-frequency words. Of the few potentially unfamiliar words for this particular group of learners, 'applicant' is covered in the initial discussion of the task and 'criterion/criteria' is pre-taught as a target vocabulary item.

Second, potentially unfamiliar vocabulary needs to occur where it is contextually meaningful. This increases the likelihood of the learner's making a successful guess at a word's meaning and encourages independence from dictionaries and the teacher. Options for contextual placement include labels in diagrams or illustrations, or within larger known categories such as a list of sports, or types of jobs or qualifications (such as those in the Appendix).

Finally, tasks should be selected in which the vocabulary will not cause undue strain or breakdown in the flow of task performance. Where difficult vocabulary exists, there are three options. First, vocabulary that is not important for the learners at their present level can be omitted in a revision of the task. This allows a focus on communicative intent rather than language form or meaning. But many tasks cannot be simplified without substantial effort.

Second, vocabulary that is useful and deserves attention can be pretaught in lessons leading up to performance of the task. This has the advantage of giving the learners opportunities to deepen their recall and productive skill during task performance using vocabulary that has previously been introduced in a controlled setting. However, preteaching takes time and may require learners to meet new items outside of a meaningful context.

Third, both important and less important vocabulary can be glossed in the task with either a definition, an example, a translation, or a picture. Glosses can save time since only the learners who do not know the items need refer to them. However, they may also deny the learners valuable opportunities to apply guessing strategies or to practice helping each other with word meaning. The choice made will depend on the content of the activity, the learning goal, and the constraints within which the teacher is working.

## Encouraging depth of processing through communication activities

The fact that learners spend time negotiating vocabulary items during performance of communication activities has already been discussed. However, the presence of unfamiliar vocabulary in a task will not automatically result in negotiation of these items. Newton (1993) found that of the 79 unfamiliar words in four communication activities performed by a group of learners, only 16 were subject to meaning-focussed negotiation. Most of this negotiation of word meaning occurred in the ranking/ discussion tasks rather than in the information exchange tasks.

The following extracts show the effect of the type of task on the content of negotiation.

Extract 1 is from a split information task in which learners must exchange information from their incomplete maps of a zoo in order to complete the maps. There is no requirement to understand the items in order to accurately transfer them.

*Extract 1*
S7    shed
S8    I don't know shed?
S7    s.h.e.d.    shed
. . .
S8    what's the meaning of said?
S6    what's a spell s m-?
S8    s.h.e.d.
S7    s.h.e.d.
S6    s.h.e.d.
S5    shed
S7    yeah ok I don't worry, we just write down
S6    and ?

Extract 2 is taken from a ranking/discussion task in which learners look at a zoo's organisation and development issues, work out why these cause problems, and then agree on appropriate changes to overcome these problems. To do this, learners must deal with each vocabulary item they do not know. The result is negotiation of the kind illustrated.

*Extract 2*
S7    do you know what is number nine?
S5    disco?
S7    yeah
S5    dolphins . . . you know dolphins? . . . dolphins yeah
S7    what animals that?
S5    yeah sometimes they show it in the performance
S8    like swimming pool
S5    yes
S8    yes
S5    swimming pool they jump up and they catch the
S8    ball
S7    just something fish?
S5    like a shark but they are not dangerous
S8    oh yeah its funny

In extract 1 learners were content to exchange items via spelling without successfully negotiating the meaning of the items. In extract 2, on the other hand, learners made an effort to help each other with meaning. The different treatment of unfamiliar vocabulary typified in these extracts is consistent with an analysis of overall negotiation of meaning in transcripts from the two tasks. This showed that 28 (or 17%) out of a total of

141 negotiating questions in the ranking activities were concerned with word meaning, and 26 (18%) with word form and perception. In the split information activities, on the other hand, only 5 (or .01%) out of a total of 326 questions were concerned with word meaning and 113 (35%) with perception.

These results provide clear evidence of a greater focus on word meaning in the ranking information activity and a greater focus on form in the split information activity. The key to these differences seems to lie in the depth of information processing of the two types of tasks. In the split task, information had to be accurately exchanged but was not used in any further decision making or problem solving. Information exchange required relatively superficial processing of task vocabulary. In the ranking task, however, learners had to evaluate the linguistic input provided in the activity and use it to make decisions and solve problems. These operations require deeper levels of comprehension (Bloom, 1956).

This finding is not intended to dismiss the use of split information activities since these have been shown to have two important advantages over ranking or open discussion activities: They generate much more overall negotiation (Doughty & Pica, 1986; Newton, 1993), and talk is much more evenly shared among all participants (Newton, 1993). We may wish, therefore, to consider ways of maintaining the split information dimension of a task, while also ensuring that a depth of information processing occurs. The activity in the Appendix is an attempt to do this.

In task 1 of the activity, learners are required to transfer information from the table. In task 2, the learners must then critically assess and rank this information according to a set of criteria. By incorporating these two types of performance into one activity, the learners are forced not only to be accurate and to concentrate on correct forms, but to undertake meaningful discussion of the information in the activity as well. This has the benefits of split activities – a large amount of negotiation and equal sharing of talk, as well as the benefits of the shared activities – a meaningful focus on content and vocabulary.

## Accessing existing vocabulary

Thus far we have focused on learning new vocabulary and the various approaches and factors that influence vocabulary expansion. It is one thing to learn new vocabulary; it is another to be able to access it quickly when it is required for use.

There are two ways vocabulary can be taught so that it can be readily accessed: (1) through fluency activities that provide a well-beaten path to an item, and (2) through richness activities that increase the syntagmatic and paradigmatic associations and networks, thus providing many points of access to an item. Let us look at each of these in turn.

# Fluency activities

Fluency activities have certain characteristics. (1) They may involve processing quite a lot of language. (2) They make limited demands on the language user; that is, they involve material that does not contain much unfamiliar language or many unfamiliar ideas. This allows the user to give most attention to the fluency goal. (3) They involve rehearsal of the task through preparation, planning, or repetition. (4) They involve some encouragement for the learner to reach a high rate of performance which requires that the activities reach a high level of automaticity. This encouragement may be in the form of limited time to do the activity or in some continuing record, such as a graph, of the result of the activity. The following fluency activities all make use of many of the features just described. Although vocabulary development is not their main goal, it is one of the subskills developed as a result of the activities.

1. Repeated reading (Dowhower, 1989) involves learners silently rereading the same text with the goal of reaching a faster speed or doing increasingly more difficult comprehension tasks.
2. The 4/3/2 technique (Maurice, 1983; Nation, 1989) requires the learners to repeat the same story or talk to three successive listeners with 4 minutes for the first telling, 3 minutes for the second, and 2 minutes for the third.
3. The best recording technique involves the learner repeatedly recording a talk in the language laboratory until the learner is satisfied that the best possible performance has been recorded.
4. The learners read a text to a high level of understanding and then work in pairs questioning each other about the content of the text.

Note that all of these fluency techniques can be based either on texts provided by the teacher or on material prepared by the learners. Using texts provided by the teacher allows the teacher to focus on particular vocabulary. Using learner-prepared texts ensures that the vocabulary is already known even though it may not yet be readily accessible.

# Richness activities

Activities that aim to increase the number of associations attached to a word can be of two types: those that establish syntagmatic relationships, and those that establish paradigmatic relationships. (Also see Lewis, Chapter 13, this volume.)

Syntagmatic relationships are those that associate a word with other words that can typically precede or follow it. For example, the word *fuel* can be preceded by words like *cost* (as in *the cost of fuel*), *alternative* (*alternative fuels*), *fossil* (*fossil fuels*). As a verb it may be followed by *inflation* (*fuels inflation*), *rumours* (*fuels rumours*), and can occur in the phrase *add fuel to the flames*. Activities that can be used to develop these relationships include the following.

1. *Collocation activities.* A typical collocation activity gets learners to match collocates with given items. For example, the learners have two lists of items that they must match up (Brown, 1974). As Brown (1974) and Rudzka, Channell, Putseys, and Ostyn (1981) show, there are many ways of devising collocation exercises. Collocation activities can also be done as group or class activities with learners drawing on their differing experience to suggest collocates for a given word. Collocation is related to the idea of a word having an underlying meaning. For example, the word *fade* has a range of uses. A colour may fade. A TV picture fades. Light fades. Music fades. Memories and feelings fade. Our looks fade (unfortunately!). A smile fades. Someone can fade into the background. These uses can be considered as several different meanings, and comparison with another language would often encourage such a division. However, if we look at all these uses we can see an underlying meaning that is common to them all. The underlying meaning is something like 'go slowly away until it is no longer there'. By looking for an underlying meaning we then regard the various uses as examples of different collocations rather than as different words. It is more economical in terms of learning and teaching, and more educational in terms of seeing how different languages organise experience in different ways to look for underlying meanings and develop collocational knowledge.

2. *Semantic mapping.* Semantic mapping (Stahl & Vancil, 1986) involves drawing a diagram of the relationships between words according to their use in a particular text. Semantic mapping has the effect of bringing relationships in a text to consciousness for the purposes of deepening understanding of a text and creating associative networks for words. Semantic mapping is best introduced as a collaborative effort between the teacher and the class.

3. *Dictation and related activities.* Nation (1991) has suggested that most value is gained from dictation activities when the dictation text contains known words used in unfamiliar ways. The nature of the

dictation activity is that it focuses learners' attention on the collocational relationships within dictated phrases.

Paradigmatic relationships are those that associate a word with others of related meaning. As Cruse (1986) shows, there is a wide variety of possible relationships, and these can be developed in matching and classification activities.

## Dangers in associative activities

It is worth remembering that the associative networks that exist for native speakers were gradually built up through normal language use. They were not established by learning opposites, by working through lists of near synonyms looking for differences, or by studying taxonomies of relationships (e.g., the young of deer are called fawns, the young of goats are called kids, etc.). In fact, research by Higa (1963) has shown that learning items together that are near synonyms, opposites, or free associates is much more difficult than learning unrelated items; that is, learning *hot* and *cold* at the same time makes learning more difficult, because many of the learners will mix the word forms and the meanings, and will be unsure after the lesson whether *hot* means 'hot' or *hot* means 'cold'. Similarly, learning items like *shrewd, sly, cunning, crafty,* or *sympathy, compassion, pity,* together results in more confusion than clarity and increases the difficulty of learning. The time for such activities is when all or all except one of the items in a group are largely familiar to the learners and they now need to clarify the distinctions between them. Interestingly enough, it is likely that the overlap of meaning and substitutability in use of such items is much greater than the differences between them; in short, they share a large number of semantic features and differ by only a few or even one.

## Conclusion

One purpose of this survey has been to show that vocabulary teaching incorporates a range of approaches and that vocabulary learning requires attention to a range of factors. If teachers are serious about their learners' vocabulary development, then there is a need for planning both on a broad scale in terms of goals and resources and approaches to achieve those goals, and within the scope of a particular language learning task. The research shows that teachers can have a major effect on learning. The challenge is to turn this research into classroom practice.

## Appendix: Making an employment decision

You are managers of a large computer business. Your task is to choose one of the following applicants for the position of Staff Welfare and Communications Officer. Four applicants have been interviewed for the job.

### Task 1: Exchanging information about the applicants

You have a table with information about the four applicants below. Information is missing from your table. Other members of your group have this missing information. Get this information and write it in the table. (The information is in a *different* order on the other tables.)

| Name | Lee, Gek Tay | | | |
|---|---|---|---|---|
| Occupation | Lawyer | Truck driver | Social worker | Electrician |
| Salary | | | | $29,000 |
| Qualifications | | | | Trade certificate |
| Languages | 1.<br>2. | 1.<br>2. | 1.<br>2. Korean | 1. English<br>2. |
| Marital status | | Unmarried | | |
| Age | | | 34 | 42 |
| Health | | High blood pressure | Very good | |
| Sports | 1.<br>2. | 1.<br>2. Chess | 1. Rock climbing<br>2. | 1. Rugby<br>2. |

### Task 2: Choosing the best applicant

Now you must decide together which applicant will get the job. Each of you has two or three different criterion about the most suitable applicant (see below). You must use all the criteria to make a group decision. Listen as each group member says his or her criteria. If the information in the table meets a criterion, put a tick (✔) beside that information in the table. Order the applicants according to the number of ticks they get. The applicant with the most ticks will get the job.

## Your criteria

The successful candidate should:

1. Have experience in work that requires communication skills.
2. Be under 32 years of age *if* unmarried.
3. Have earned no more than $40,000 in his or her previous job.

## References

Anderson, J. R., & Reder, L. M. (1979). An elaborative processing explanation of depth of processing. In L. S. Cermak & F. I. M. Craik (Eds.), *Levels of processing in human memory* (pp. 305–404). Hillsdale, NJ: Lawrence Erlbaum.

Bloom, B. S. (Ed.). (1956). *Taxonomy of educational objectives.* Handbook 1: *Cognitive domain.* New York: McKay.

Brown, D. (1974). Advanced vocabulary teaching: The problem of collocation. *RELC Journal, 5*(2), 1–11.

Carter, R. (1986). Core vocabulary and discourse in the curriculum – a question of the subject. *RELC Journal, 17*(1), 52–70.

(1987). Is there a core vocabulary? *Applied Linguistics, 8,* 178–193.

Craik, F. I. M., & Tulving, E. (1975). Depth of processing and the retention of words in episodic memory. *Journal of Experimental Psychology, 104,* 268–284.

Cruse, D. A. (1986). *Lexical semantics.* Cambridge: Cambridge University Press.

Doughty, C., & Pica, T. (1986). Information gap tasks: Do they facilitate SLA? *TESOL Quarterly, 20*(2), 305–325.

Dowhower, Sarah L. (1989). Repeated reading: Research into practice. *Reading Teacher, 42,* 502–507.

Elley, W. (1989). Vocabulary acquisition from listening to stories. *Reading Research Quarterly, 24*(2), 174–187.

Hall, S. (1992). Using split information tasks to learn mathematics vocabulary. *Guidelines, 24*(2), 72–77.

Higa, M. (1963). Interference effects of intralist word relationships in verbal learning. *Journal of Verbal Learning and Verbal Behaviour, 2,* 170–175.

Kelly, P. (1990). Guessing: No substitute for systematic learning of lexis. *System, 18*(2), 199–207.

Ladousse, G. P. (1983). *Speaking personally.* Cambridge: Cambridge University Press.

(1987). *Role play.* Oxford: Oxford University Press.

Long, M. H., & Porter, P. A. (1985). Group work, interlanguage talk, and second language acquisition. *TESOL Quarterly, 19*(2), 207–228.

Maurice, K. (1983). The fluency workshop. *TESOL Newsletter, 17,* 429.

Nation, I. S. P. (1982). Beginning to learn foreign vocabulary: A review of the research. *RELC Journal, 131*:14–36.

(1989). Improving speaking fluency. *System, 17,* 377–384.

(1990). *Teaching and learning vocabulary.* New York: Newbury House.

(1991). Dictation, dictocomp and related techniques. *English Teaching Forum, 29*(4), 12–14.

Nation, I. S. P., & Thomas, G. I. (1988). *Communication activities.* Occasional paper no. 13, English Language Institute, Victoria University of Wellington.

Newton, J. (1993). Task-based interaction among adult learners of English and its role in second language development. Unpublished Ph.D. thesis, Victoria University, NZ.

Rinvolucri, M. (1984). *Grammar games.* Cambridge: Cambridge University Press.

Rudzka, B., Channell, J., Putseys, Y., & Ostyn, P. (1981). *The words you need.* London: Macmillan.

Simcock, M. (1993). Developing production vocabulary using the "ask and answer" technique. *Guidelines, 15*(2), 1–7.

Stahl, S. A., & Vancil, S. J. (1986). Discussion is what makes semantic maps work in vocabulary instruction. *Reading Teacher,* 62–67.

Ur, P. (1981). *Discussions that work.* Cambridge: Cambridge University Press.

West, M. (1953). *A general service list of English words.* London: Longman.

Xue, Guoyi, & Nation, I. S. P. (1984). A university word list. *Language Learning and Communication, 3*(2), 215–229.

# 13 Pedagogical implications of the lexical approach

Michael Lewis

Language has traditionally been divided into grammar and vocabulary. Crudely, the former consisted of elements of the generative system of the language and the latter was the stock of fixed nongenerative 'words'. Recently, this analysis has been challenged and shown to be seriously misguided from both strictly linguistic and pedagogical points of view (Lewis, 1993; Nattinger & DeCarrico, 1992; Willis, 1990).

In fact, language consists broadly of four different kinds of lexical items, the constituent 'chunks' of any language. Each chunk may be placed on a generative spectrum between poles ranging from absolutely fixed to very free. Although it is true that traditional vocabulary is usually close to the fixed pole, and grammar structures are frequently close to the free pole, this fact obscures the vastly more numerous and in many ways more interesting items that occur nearer the middle of the spectrum. These items may be 'words', or 'structures' in traditional language teaching terms, but, as we will see, most typically they are lexical items of types not recognised in most teaching material.

Lexical items are socially sanctioned independent units. These may be individual words, or full sentences – institutionalised utterances – that convey fixed social or pragmatic meaning within a given community. This definition clearly entails that lexical items are dependent on agreement within a particular social group; what is a lexical item in American English may not be so in British English. Indeed, lexical items can be peculiar to social groups of many kinds: geographical, professional, or even family-, class- or age-based groups. Teenagers frequently use a whole range of lexical items that leave their parents' generation at a loss. Native speakers, in addition to words and grammar, have at their disposal a repertoire of multiword items that are, for certain purposes, treated as independent units. It is these items that have frequently been ignored.

Four fundamental types of lexical item may be identified:

Type 1 a. Word
       b. Polywords
Type 2 Collocations

Type 3  Institutionalised utterances
Type 4  Sentence frames or heads

Such an analysis is not unique. There is some overlap between categories and sometimes it is useful to consider a particular item as belonging to different classes for different analytical purposes. This is particularly the case when considering how such items may best be dealt with in the classroom.

## Words and polywords

Words have always been recognised as independent units. An utterance may change its meaning by the change of a single word (*Could you pass my pen/calculator, please?*) and single words may appear in speech or writing as fully independent items (*Stop, Sure!, Please.*). This category of lexical item has long been recognised in language teaching.

Polywords are but a small extension of this category. Although all lexical items except words consist of more than one word, the term 'polyword' is restricted here to those (usually short) phrases that have a degree of idiomaticity (*by the way, on the other hand*), and have usually appeared in even quite simple dictionaries.

## Collocations

Some pairs or groups of words co-occur with very high frequency, depending perhaps on the text-type of the data. Most typically this feature is associated with verb-noun and adjective-noun pairs (*to raise capital, a short-term strategy*), but it can apply to word groups larger than pairs, and to words from most grammatical categories. It will be noted that although the structures of highly frequent verb patterns have formed, and still form, a key element of most language courses, other highly frequent word patterns – which is precisely what collocations are – have usually been ignored or at best been seen as marginal to courses.

As Nattinger and DeCarrico (1992) pointed out, collocation is not equally powerful in both directions – *rancid* strongly suggests the collocate *butter*, whereas *butter* only weakly suggests *rancid*. Here the adjective is the 'key' word, carrying the most information content; most typically, the key word is a noun. This has important pedagogical consequences.

Multiword collocations are linear sequences: *to raise venture capital, to dissolve the mixture in water, to make a determined effort.* Typically, they are 3–5 words in length and are primarily concerned with referential content. There are obvious pedagogical advantages to ensuring both that students are aware of the word partnerships (the nontechnical term I prefer to 'collocation' for the classroom) and that when recording 'new vocabulary', students record together and in sequence those words that regularly occur in precisely that grouping. Too often students and teachers look for and record only the new words in texts. This is to misidentify the constituent chunks of the text in a way that is pedagogically unhelpful. The recognition, generation and effective recording of collocations are essential elements of the Lexical Approach.

## Institutionalised utterances

As the name suggests, these are more typical of the spoken than of the written mode. They tend to express pragmatic rather than referential meaning. They are all those chunks of language that are recalled as wholes and of which much conversation is made. In their influential paper, Pawley and Syder (1987) speculate that these items are vastly more numerous than has ever been accepted. The chunks may be full sentences, usable with no variation whatever but always with instantly identifiable pragmatic meaning (*I'll get it. It's nothing to do with me. There's a call for you.*), or sentence heads, which require another lexical item to provide a complete utterance (*If I were you, I'd wait*). This last utterance is interesting for it reveals the novelty within a lexical, rather than grammatical, analysis.

Traditionally, *If I were you, I'd wait* is a 'conditional' or even a 'subjunctive'. If asked which two 'bits' make up the utterance, teachers almost invariably make the division between clauses. But this is incorrect. We recognise that *If I were you* is ALWAYS followed by *I'd,* so the lexical boundary between chunks is after *I'd.* Similar utterances are *If I were you, I'd//go, get one, leave the car at home.* Notice that, under this analysis, the utterance is simply the base form *Go, Get one, Leave the car at home* preceded by a fixed chunk. Far from being a 'difficult structure', it is as simple as it could be.

Traditional grammar has led teachers to believe that because language items can be analysed in a particular way, it must be helpful to analyse them in that way. But language can be analysed in many ways – phonemes, syllables, morphemes or words. Different analyses are useful for different purposes. Misidentifying the chunks of which language consists has led to many pedagogical problems. In many cases the word is too small a unit and the sentence is too large. Furthermore, those sentences that are fully institutionalised utterances can be learned and used as wholes, without analysis, thereby forming the basis, not the product, of grammatical competence. This perception, extensively discussed by Nattinger and DeCarrico, turns much of what has traditionally been called 'grammar teaching' on its head.

Institutionalised utterances, most importantly those that have the form of a single fully grammaticalised sentence, should form a major element in the language input provided for students. Such language is the basis of natural language learning. Sadly, it is the very antithesis of the input provided by many language courses, most notably those with (overt or covert) behaviourist elements, which follow any version of the Present-Practise-Produce paradigm. Willis makes a very similar point in his *The Lexical Syllabus.* Fully contextualised (in the sense of occurring with relevant co-text in a natural situation) institutionalised utterances represent the lexical item-type in which most language courses are most deficient.

The precise problem that stimulated Pawley and Syder's original enquiry was why it was that many utterances produced by nonnatives, while not formally breaching the rules of well-formedness, were felt by native speakers to be unnatural. It is helpful to recall that not all *possible* sentences of English – i.e., those that are well formed according to the patterns of the language – are actual or even *probable utterances* of the language. Traditional grammar teaching concerned itself with all the possible sentences, believing that, in Chomsky's terms, performance derived from competence, a concept essentially based on the total corpus of possible sentences. In fact, acquisition appears to be based on induction from natural utterances in the learner's input that are heard, read and (at least partially) understood. Within this understanding it is clear that the input should be biased heavily toward high-frequency utterances, most of which will be fully or partially institutionalised.

Typically, institutionalised utterances are high on the 'Spectrum of Idiomaticity'. This does not mean they belong to that group of rather picturesque language items students and teachers frequently think of as idioms (e.g., *He threw in the towel; That's a whole new ball game*) but rather that the meaning of the whole is relatively nontransparent from the meaning of the constituent words. This in turn is because many institutionalised utterances contain a relatively high proportion of de-lexicalised words, such as *take, get* and *there,* which do not, in themselves, carry much meaning. Typical utterances of this kind are *I'll get it; There's not a lot you can do about it; We just can't keep on like this.* Ironically, within the Lexical Approach, de-lexicalised words have a very important part to play. The idiomatic nature of the wholes and the de-lexicalised nature of the component words is reflected in this list of archetypical utterances using *'ll:*

I'll give you a ring.
I'll be in touch.

I'll get back to you as soon as I can.
I'll be back in a minute.
I'll see what I can do.
You'll never get away with it.
It'll be all right.
It'll take time.
That'll do.
That'll be the day!
Nobody'll even notice.
There'll be hell to pay.
We'll see . . .

Although expressing instantly identifiable pragmatic meaning, and so of immediate use to learners, such language forms a relatively small part of the input in typical courses. Expressions like these deserve increased attention, both because of their immediate usefulness and because they provide input that is the basis for inductive acquisition of generalisable 'rules'. Additional emphasis on these institutionalised items must be accompanied by classroom strategies that make students more aware of lexical items, and provide ample opportunities for them to practice such language in the safety of the classroom.

## Sentence frames and heads

These are to a large extent the written equivalent of institutionalised utterances. They are those often large discourse features that allow us to decode complex written text. The frustration of reading a student's essay and thinking 'I know what you mean, but that's not the way to say (= write) it', is most frequently caused by the student's failure to use this type of lexical item. Some are comparatively short and easy (sequencers such as *secondly,* . . . *and finally*); some are sentence heads serving similar pragmatic purposes (*We come now to a number of important reservations* . . .); the largest represent those 'frames' that allow us to structure long passages of text, usually written (e.g., the essay), but sometimes spoken (the lecture or professional presentation). This type of lexical item remains outside the field of competence even of many native speakers; but it can be of great use to, for example, students of academic or professional English.

We have, then, four types of lexical item: the first two categories concerned principally with referential meaning, the latter two with pragmatic meaning. A balanced language programme will have to take account of all four types and, depending on the goals of the course, of the balance between them. Broadly, the categories equate to the traditional ones of Vocabulary (now Words and Collocations) and Function (now Institutionalised Utterance and Sentence Frame). Interestingly, no lexical item-type corresponds to such traditional structures as the present perfect, conditionals or the passive. Grammar in this sense is radically de-emphasised within the Lexical Approach.

## Methodology

Krashen and Terrell (1983) contend that 'we acquire language by under-standing messages'. If they are right, formal teaching may be of little benefit to the learner. Indeed, it may be counterproductive in that it frequently directs the learner's attention to individual words or gram-matical structures that, as we have seen, are not the fundamental compo-nents of the language. Although I am largely sympathetic to their view – I believe the structure of the language is acquired, as is the vast majority of a learner's lexicon – I believe that activities that raise conscious awareness of the lexical nature of language and its component chunks can aid acquisition. The claim is a modest one – conscious awareness of what constitutes a possible chunk provides learners with a tool that enables them to process input more effectively.

It must be stressed that the primary purpose of the activities is awareness-raising, rather than formal 'teaching'. Estimates of the mini-mum functional vocabulary for the learner vary widely, depending on technical factors such as what constitutes a 'word' or 'item', and different views of functional competence. Nobody, however, estimates lower than 20,000 separate items (and most estimates are much larger). If each item were formally taught, and took only 2 minutes of class time, and learning were 100% efficient, nearly 700 hours would be required for this element of the course alone. The truth is much closer to Krashen and Terrell's position than many teachers find comfortable – the types and quality of input must be carefully chosen, but we have less understanding of which items will be acquired, and thus retained for future use, than is usually acknowledged. Probably the best we can do is select input that is appro-priate and encourage a low-anxiety atmosphere conducive to acquisition.

Within the lexical approach, less attention will be paid to individual words and substantially less to traditional grammar structures; in con-trast, much more time will be devoted to ensuring that students are aware of the lexical items, particularly collocations, which carry much of the (referential) meaning in written text, and institutionalised utterances, which carry the meaning (in this case mostly pragmatic) of natural spo-ken text. Many of the activities will be of the receptive, awareness-raising kind. Teachers used to formal vocabulary teaching, using largely produc-tive practice, need to make an important change of emphasis, learning truly to value receptive practice.

# Practices in the Lexical Approach

Productive practices are possible. In some ways the exercise types resemble those of standard vocabulary or grammar teaching, although the linguistic focus is different. In the sample exercises only a few examples are given to illustrate the *type* of practice proposed; student materials would need longer exercises with more examples.

## Exercise type 1

In each of the following, one word does NOT make a strong word partnership with the word in capitals; which is the odd word?

1. HIGH season price opinion spirits house time priority
2. MAIN point reason effect entrance speed road meal course
3. NEW experience job food potatoes baby situation year
4. LIGHT green lunch rain entertainment day work traffic

Note that there is little dispute about the word in examples 1 and 2, while 3 and 4 may give rise to discussion and doubt. This is intentional – collocation is not a possible/impossible dichotomy, but likely/unlikely. Although students (and teachers) prefer certainty to uncertainty, an element of doubt is intrinsic to collocation. Care must be taken not to make this type of exercise confusing, but totally unambiguous examples should not be the sole target either.

## Exercise type 2

Choose from these words four that make *strong word partnerships* in business English with each of the verbs below.

| bill | presentation | invoice | discount | debt | lunch |
|------|--------------|---------|----------|------|-------|
| deal | calculation | mistake | service | message | expenses |

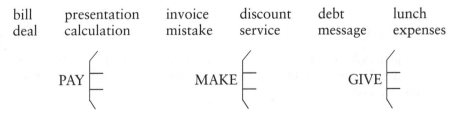

Use some of the word partnerships to say something about your own job.

Again notice the use of the phrase *strong word partnerships* in the instruction. Most partnerships are *possible;* the exercise raises awareness of *strong* or *very likely* partnerships.

## Exercise type 3

Complete the table with five adjectives and five verbs that form strong word partnerships with the noun VISIT.

| Verb | Adjective | (Key word) |
|------|-----------|------------|
| ———— | ———— |  |
| ———— | ———— |  |
| ———— | ———— | VISIT |
| ———— | ———— |  |
| ———— | ———— |  |

Note that this simple array is most useful at the size proposed here; smaller arrays are rarely sufficiently generative to be of pedagogical value, while larger ones are confusing to students. The words that are included in the array may be

a. Found from an accompanying source text.
b. Chosen from lists prepared in advance by the teacher.
c. Chosen from student suggestions.

In the last two cases the teacher must exercise careful judgement both of the possibility of the collocation and, more importantly, of its value to the student. 'Weak' adjectives (*big, new, nice*) rarely justify their place in the recorded array. Collocates should be selected for inclusion on the basis of their value in increasing the students' communicative power.

## Exercise type 4

Fill in the middle column with an adjective that is opposite in meaning to the word in the first column, but makes a correct word partnership with the word in column three.

| *Column 1* | *Column 2* | *Column 3* |
|------------|------------|------------|
| helpful |  | suggestion |
| efficient |  | system |
| careful |  | piece of work |
| safe |  | choice |

| Column 1 | Column 2 | Column 3 |
|----------|----------|----------|
| light    |          | green    |
| light    |          | suitcase |
| light    |          | rain     |
| light    |          | work     |

Note that the idea of 'opposites' is invalid unless confined to contextual or collocational opposites. Too often teaching oversimplifies this idea unhelpfully.

## Exercise type 5

His behaviour was very strange.
–Yes, very odd.

Her work is very careless.
–Yes, she's not careful at all.

Those roses are lovely.
–Yes, I like flowers around the house.

Everything seems to get more expensive all the time.
–Yes, especially food.

These examples, suggested by McCarthy (1991), show possible ways of agreeing, using synonyms, or antonyms, and with more general or more specific words. Recent work in discourse analysis suggests that 'lexical agreement' of this kind is typical of natural conversation (Pearson, 1986; Pomerantz, 1984). Oral exercises, resembling traditional grammar drills but with a freer choice of lexically appropriate responses like those above, provide excellent fluency practice.

## Exercise type 6

The first part of each sentence in List 1 can be completed with the group of endings given in List 2. Match the first parts with the endings.

| List 1 | List 2 |
|--------|--------|
| 1. I'm wondering | a. to concentrate. <br> to understand it but I can't. <br> to remember where I put them. |
| 2. I'm trying. | b. quite pleased with myself. <br> a bit off colour. <br> more confident than I did. |
| 3. I'm feeling | c. what I can about it. <br> nothing yet! <br> the best I can. |

4. I'm doing                 d. what we can do about it.
                                       if it will make any difference.
                                       if anyone else knows yet.

Can you think of a situation where you would say each of the twelve sentences? Choose *one* of them and write a short dialogue so that one of the people in the dialogue says *exactly* the sentence you have chosen.

## Exercise type 7

Rearrange the following to make natural sentences.

1. It two about hours TAKES.
2. How it long will TAKE?
3. You I what don't say seriously TAKE.
4. I'll to a have just chance TAKE.
5. I'll a the from station taxi TAKE.
6. Don't to home books forget your TAKE.
7. I more any can't TAKE!
8. Nobody the of your parents can place TAKE.

When you go on holiday, do you take a lot of photos? Of what people or places? What sort of souvenirs do you like to take home?

Are you the sort of person who:
a. takes responsibility    b. takes advice   c. takes risks?

Underline all the word partnerships with *take* in the examples.

Note that the rearrangement exercise is simplicity itself for the native speaker but comparatively difficult for learners. It is essential that the 'answers' be institutionalised utterances chosen as input appropriate to the particular group of learners. The 'conversation topics' are intended to introduce a more affective quality, while still focusing on collocates of the same de-lexicalised verb. The final underlining activity is important in checking that students really have correctly identified the chunks. This exercise type is useful for de-lexicalised verbs and nouns such as *thing, point, way*. Whether the keyword should be highlighted or not is a matter of taste (if it is not, many students simply do not notice that all the examples contain the same word).

## Exercise type 8

It must have been difficult.
–Difficult! It was absolutely impossible.

You must have been really fed up.
–Fed up! I was absolutely suicidal.

In pairs, make similar dialogues, using these expressions.

1. tired – exhausted
2. interesting – fascinating
3. dangerous – treacherous
4. surprised – astonished
5. irritated – furious
6. sure – certain
7. pleased – over the moon
8. expensive – a rip-off

When you speak your own language, are you the sort of person who says *I was quite pleased,* or do you prefer to say *I was absolutely over the moon?*

This resembles a traditional structure practice, but now focus is on the cross-turn lexical linking, which is typical of natural conversation. Synonyms (contextual) and hyponyms frequently provide the raw material for these exercises. Note also, the affective question. If students have to learn many thousands of lexical items, it is important that the classes also provide real opportunities for them to feel and to talk about their feelings.

## Exercise type 9

Complete the following by adding one word. Only one word is possible in each case. Make sure you know the *equivalent expressions* in your own language.

1. I've no idea where my bag is – it's just disappeared into . . . air.
2. We weren't expecting her. She just turned up out of the . . .
3. It's . . . time something was done about it.
4. It's a difficult . . . of affairs. I'm not sure what to do.
5. It might have been quicker to take the car . . . all.
6. He might have changed his job by now, . . . all I know.
7. Oh, no! I've spilled coffee all . . . the place.
8. Revise carefully, but . . . all, don't panic during the exam.

The Lexical Approach widens the concept of 'idiom' so that attention needs to be drawn to many natural phrases and whole sentences that were previously excluded from course materials. As the examples above indicate, both apparently meaning-carrying words (nos. 1–4) and de-lexicalised words (nos. 5–8) need to be considered. The idea of 'equivalent expressions' (rather than translations) is important in dealing with institutionalised utterances.

## Exercise type 10

Match each of these remarks with a response.

1. Would you like a cup of coffee?
2. Are you ready?

3. Have you got Jane's number there?
4. Everybody's worried about the situation.
5. Were you late last night?

a. I think so. Just a minute, I'll have a look.
b. No, we got there just in time.
c. Not just at the moment, thanks.
d. Oh, so it's not just me, then.
e. I will be in a moment. I'll just get my jacket.

This practice is in many ways typical of the Lexical Approach in that while providing an activity for the student, the most important pedagogical element is that the practice material itself provides valuable input, in this case the institutionalised replies.

## Exercise type 11

Answer briefly – and honestly!

1. Think of three jobs you do at home – what are they and where in your home do you do them?
2. Mention three public places or situations in your country where smoking is not allowed.
3. Think of two or three important ideas you have had in connection with your work or studies. Where did you get the ideas from?
4. Can you think of three ways you personally have made money without working?

Note that the answers for this type of exercise must be true, thus avoiding the random lexicalisation of practices of which Widdowson has complained. Most of the answers will be short phrases, and many of these, although not recognised as such by teachers, will be institutionalised: *In the kitchen, On public transport, From my parents, As Christmas or birthday presents.*

Of particular interest here is that the prepositional phrases are institutionalised and, as such, precisely the kind of learned wholes that provide the basis for, rather than being the product of, grammatical competence.

## Exercise type 12

Some fixed expressions are made with more than one word. Complete each of the phrases in List 1 with a word from List 2, then match the expressions to the word in List 3 that is more common in written English.

| List 1 | List 2 | List 3 |
|--------|--------|--------|
| 1. by and | then | a. occasionally |
| 2. in the long | away | b. immediately |
| 3. every now and | again | c. repeatedly |
| 4. time and | large | d. generally |
| 5. straight | run | e. eventually |

*Exercise type 13*

Some pairs or words can only be used in a particular order: *Ladies and gentlemen,* but not * *Gentlemen and ladies.* Make pairs from these words, find *equivalents* in your own language and use the English pairs in natural sentences.

| bread | now | rights | down | then | ins | back |
|-------|-----|--------|------|------|-----|------|
| forth | outs | butter | out | wrongs | there | here |

Although polywords and pairs represent only a minor part of the total lexicon, they should not be totally ignored.

# Recording formats

Too much teacher training is precisely that – preparing teacher activity. But it is the students who must learn and ultimately it is what they do that facilitates learning, in more or less efficient ways. Having recognised this, it is easier to see the importance of out-of-class activities.

Pre-class, the teachers' primary responsibility is the selection of high-quality input. Equally if not more important, however, is preparing students to make the best use of out-of-class activities such as independent reading or watching TV.

Stevick has memorably remarked, 'If you want to forget something, put it in a list', and all too often this is what students do with 'new words' – list them, and forget them. It is essential to develop students' skills in recording new lexical items they meet in or out of class in formats that are a positive aid to retention. In each case the physical formatting should mirror or highlight the real-world occurrence of the language.

*Format 1*

1. I'm so unfit. If I climb the stairs I'm completely          out of . . .
2. I couldn't steer the car at all. It was completely          out of . . .
3. I've repaid all the money I borrowed. At last I'm          out of . . .
4. There are none left, so you can't have one. You're          out of . . .
5. You certainly can't do that! It's          out of . . .

Note the alphabetical order of the answers, and the format, which highlights key expressions.

*Format 2*

| You can HAVE | lunch, a cup of tea, a plane to catch, a lot to do |
|---|---|
| PAY | an invoice, bill, expenses |
| PAY FOR | the tickets, lunch, a colleague |

See also the 5 adjective-5 verb-key noun box already referred to (exercise type 3).

*Format 3*

|  | emphasise |  |
|---|---|---|
|  | point out |  |
| I should | draw your attention to the fact | that |
|  | remind you |  |
|  | explain |  |

The precise formats vary, but the important point is that the recording formats should be designed to suit the collocations, institutionalised utterances, or sentence heads rather than simply listing items.

## Additional exercises

As with all language practice, not all useful lexical exercises lend themselves to the generalisation that is clearly possible with the types listed above. This is fortunate, for if the Lexical Approach is to work in the classroom, as well as promote language proficiency, it must also provide variety and enjoyment in class. Here are some activities that serve to indicate the range of possibilities that are consistent with the Lexical Approach.

1. Lexical Crosswords. The clues are lexical items, most typically utterances, with missing words. The answers to the crossword are in fact further clues to the utterances. The clues therefore represent valuable input.

2. In pairs or small groups, write a story. Your story must:
   a. Contain exactly 100 words – not one more or less.
   b. Not use any English word (including *a, the, is* and other easy words) more than once.

Once you have discovered some simple guidelines, this activity ensures lexically dense stories. The most effective tend to use incomplete sentences and 'de-grammaticalised dialogue-type' exclamations.

3. The teacher reads (or plays on tape) a story, chosen to include, for example, a number of expressions using a de-lexicalised verb such as *get, keep.* Students:
   a. Raise a hand (silently) each time they notice an expression containing the keyword (which keeps all involved and helps weaker students).
   b. Write down the expressions containing the keyword.

4. Jigsaw Dialogues. The lines of a dialogue are rearranged, either as a textbook exercise, or on strips of paper so that students can physically rearrange them on the table or walk around the room sorting themselves into the correct order. Students then read the dialogue in the correct order. It is important that the dialogue be written so that many of its turns are, or contain, institutionalised utterances.

5. Lexical Dominoes. A set of cards is prepared so each card is divided into like dominoes; on one half is written a noun, on the other a verb. Students draw a group of cards – say, 7 each – and take turns to add dominoes in the usual way. The two halves that touch must make a strong word partnership.

This can also be done with noun-adjective cards. The words may be chosen from a relatively small field such as the language for a particular job, or, by using a number of de-lexicalised words, particularly verbs, a more linguistically generative game can be constructed.

Many other activities with which teachers are familiar may be used within the Lexical Approach. What is important is the attitude the teacher takes toward the language of the input material. The two most essential changes to the teacher's mind-set are a willingness to search for, identify and direct attention toward the chunks of which all naturally occurring language consists, and, methodologically, a ready acceptance of the value of receptive, awareness-raising activities. Any classroom procedure that respects these two key principles has a valid contribution to make to a course informed by the Lexical Approach.

## References

Krashen, S., & Terrell, T. (1983). *The natural approach: Language acquisition in the classroom.* Oxford: Oxford University Press.

Lewis, M. (1993). *The lexical approach.* Hove, England: Language Teaching Publications.

McCarthy, M. (1991). *Discourse analysis for language teachers.* Cambridge: Cambridge University Press.

Nattinger, J., & DeCarrico, J. (1992). *Lexical phrases in language teaching.* Oxford: Oxford University Press.

270    *Michael Lewis*

Pawley, A., & Syder, F. (1987). Two puzzles for linguistic theory: Nativelike selection and nativelike fluency. In J. Richards & R. Schmidt (Eds.), *Language and communication* (pp. 191–226). London: Longman.

Pearson, E. (1986). Agreement/disagreement: An example of results of discourse analysis applied to the oral English classroom. *ITL Review of Applied Linguistics, 74,* 47–61.

Pomerantz, A. (1984). Agreeing and disagreeing with assessments: Some features of preferred/dispreferred turn shapes. In J. Atkinson & J. Heritage (Eds.), *Structure of social action* (pp. 57–101). Cambridge: Cambridge University Press.

Richards, J., & Schmidt, R. (Eds.). (1987). *Language and communication.* London: Longman.

Swan, M. (1984a). A critical look at the communicative approach. *English Language Teaching Journal 39*(1), 2–12.

(1984b). A critical look at the communicative approach. *English Language Teaching Journal 39*(2), 76–87.

Widdowson, H. (1991). Language awareness in language teaching education. Paper presented at International TESOL, New York, March.

Willis, D. (1990). *The lexical syllabus: A new approach to language teaching.* London: Collins ELT.

# PART V:
# SUMMING UP

In this concluding section, James Coady draws from the preceding chapters to construct general pedagogical guidelines for second language vocabulary learning. He begins by reviewing the reasons for neglect of vocabulary instruction in the past, and the main approaches being taken to remedy this problem. He then reviews a broad spectrum of empirical research on contextual acquisition, individual learning strategies, direct instruction, L2 vocabulary acquisition, collocations, reading, bottom-up processing, lexicon size, dictionary use, and general learning theory. Coady concludes by discussing the rationale for pedagogy that this research points to.

# 14 L2 vocabulary acquisition
## A synthesis of the research

James Coady

In Chapter 1 of this volume Zimmerman claims that "the teaching and learning of vocabulary have been undervalued in the field of second language acquisition (SLA) throughout its varying stages and up to the present day." Richards (1976) was one of the first scholars to alert us to the fact that vocabulary is typically neglected in foreign or second language instruction. He attributes this lack to the "effects of trends in linguistic theory," which at that time – the dusk of Structuralism and the dawn of the Chomskyan school of linguistics – was grammar- and sound-oriented. Levenston (1979) also criticized applied linguistics for its general neglect of vocabulary acquisition in favor of syntactic development.

Another factor contributing to the neglect of vocabulary can be seen in the observation by Sinclair and Renouf (1988, p. 143) that "it is exceptionally difficult to teach an organized syllabus of both grammar and lexis at the same time." In other words, it is very difficult to do two things at once. If one's syllabus is organized around grammar, then it will be unlikely that lexis can be focused on at the same time.

Moreover, Zimmerman reviews the history of language teaching methods in the first chapter of this volume and concludes that all of them pay some limited attention to vocabulary, but, with the possible exception of some newer approaches, e.g., Nattinger and DeCarrico (1992), and Lewis (Chapter 13, this volume), all emphasize other aspects of language learning far more than they do vocabulary. For another innovative approach, see Willis (1990).

In more recent times, Carter and McCarthy (1988) conclude that

although it suffered neglect for a long time, vocabulary pedagogy has benefited in the last fifteen years or so from theoretical advances in the linguistic study of the lexicon, from psycholinguistic investigations into the mental lexicon, from the communicative trend in teaching, which has brought the learner into focus, and from developments in computers. What is perhaps missing in all this is more knowledge about what happens in classrooms when vocabulary crops up. (p. 51)

An often-cited aphorism in teaching is that we tend to teach others in the same manner as we ourselves were taught. Zimmerman's survey would lead us to think that most second language learners have traditionally been taught by methods that gave minimal attention to vocabulary. Consequently, it seems reasonable to expect that most teachers will also continue to neglect vocabulary, whether it is because of the methods by which they have learned or the methods by which they are teaching.

In fact, a given teacher's attitude toward the role of vocabulary in language acquisition is the product of a number of factors. First, what was the teacher's personal experience of learning foreign languages and how did the method(s) the teacher experienced deal with it? Second, what is the teacher's metacognitive attitude toward vocabulary learning? Is it most effectively achieved through reading, spoken communication, memorizing words, and so on? Third, what is the teacher's knowledge of the research done on this issue? Fourth, what impact has the experience gained through teaching had on the teacher?

Let us consider some of the typical metacognitive attitudes that both teachers and students can hold toward the teaching/learning of vocabulary in a second or foreign language.

- In general, students feel that *words* are very important and are eager to learn them (Leki & Carson, 1994; Sheorey & Mokhtari, 1993).
- In contrast, teachers tend to feel that *words* are easy to learn – *grammar* is the challenge.
- Many teachers and scholars feel that teaching vocabulary is a low-level intellectual activity unworthy of their full attention.
- Both teachers and students feel that the productive areas of language use (speaking and writing) are much harder to achieve than the receptive areas of listening and reading.
- Almost all methodological approaches encourage both teachers and learners to assume that the skill of reading is transferred automatically from L1.
- Consequently, many teachers (and, as we will soon see, many scholars) seem to conclude that words are going to be learned naturally from reading and do not need to be taught.
- Therefore, it becomes much clearer why teachers do not see the need for vocabulary teaching in spite of the students' requests for it. Or, if the teachers do see the need for some vocabulary instruction, it is of a temporary, bridging nature until the students can do it on their own.

Notwithstanding the prior claims about the neglect of vocabulary, a number of teachers/scholars have published articles and books that advocate vocabulary instruction. The result is an extensive body of literature comprising a wide-ranging continuum of arguments, studies, and suggestions about the proper role of vocabulary instruction in language instruction. In view of the controversy surrounding this subject, this chapter proposes to delineate the various rationales and the evidence supporting them.

# Main approaches to L2 vocabulary instruction

This section identifies four main positions on the continuum of literature dealing with vocabulary instruction. Most of the scholars who have published on this question describe a widely varying number of approaches, methods, and techniques dealing with vocabulary instruction and/or acquisition. Nevertheless, in the following review the scholars being cited will be grouped according to a major emphasis found in their writings. In other words, although most of the scholars have typically proposed a much wider approach to vocabulary acquisition or instruction, this review will focus only on what might be described as a significant emphasis in their approach. For a fuller consideration of their views, see the works cited.

## Context Alone

The first position on the continuum is labeled Context Alone. It is on one end of the continuum and, in fact, proposes that there is actually no need or even justification for direct vocabulary instruction. This position is based on the claim that students will learn all the vocabulary they need from context by reading extensively, as long as there is successful comprehension (Krashen, 1989, 1993).

CONTEXTUAL ACQUISITION RESEARCH

Several studies have explored the acquisition through context hypothesis. Krashen (1989), for example, argues that we acquire vocabulary and spelling by reading. He first argues for the Input Hypothesis, which applies to reading as well as to oral language acquisition. It postulates that successful language learning results from comprehensible input as the essential external ingredient coupled with a powerful internal language acquisition device. Krashen then contrasts the Input Hypothesis (IH) with the Skill-Building Hypothesis (SBH) and the Output Hypothesis (OH). The Skill-Building Hypothesis (deductive learning) assumes that the learner consciously learns rules or items and gradually makes them automatic by drills and exercises. The Output Hypothesis (inductive) has one discovering rules or items in the course of language production and consciously confirming them by means of the feedback from successful communication. Krashen concedes that SBH and OH can lead to competence but the competence produced by SBH and OH is learned, whereas that of IH is acquired. In his 1989 article, Krashen analyzes the results from 144 studies in his attempt to provide evidence for the superiority of IH. However, it should be noted that only three of these articles are actually focused on L2 acquisition. In practice, he advocates massive quantities of pleasure reading in the students' own area of interest as well as large quantities of light, low-risk material that students are not tested on. In short, he believes that IH is more efficient than the other hypotheses; moreover, even if it were not, it is a much more pleasurable process.

Unfortunately, there has been ensuing debate about the distinction between IH and SBH or OH, with some scholars claiming that the situation is probably much more complicated than it first might appear to be. Ellis (1994), for example, has pointed out that attention is present in the case of both incidental and intentional learning and that this "distinction rests, somewhat uncomfortably, on a secondary distinction between focal and peripheral attention" (p. 1). Obviously, more research is needed.

Nagy and Herman (1984) and Nagy and Anderson (1984) argue that the number of L1 words that are learned by a child in elementary school is too enormous to rely on word-by-word instruction. Nagy, Herman, and Anderson (1985) then conclude from their experimental study that children indeed do learn large numbers of words by means of incidental learning from written context. They computed that the probability of learning a word from one encounter in context was only 15%, but they argue that if a child were to encounter 10,000 unknown words in a given period, he or she might learn 1,000–1,500 of them well enough to get the right answer on a multiple-choice vocabulary test. But there is not any comparable research for L2. It is not clear as to whether L2 learners can learn words at a similar rate and it is unlikely that they encounter 10,000 new words per year!

## Strategy Instruction

The second position on the continuum is called Strategy Instruction. The proponents of this approach also believe that context is the major source of vocabulary learning but they express some significant reservations about how well students can deal with context on their own. As a result, there is considerable emphasis on teaching specific learning strategies to students so that they can effectively learn from context. It is important to note that these scholars are typically dealing with advanced learners of English as a second language who need to use the language on a very advanced academic level. Consequently, their proposals must be considered as most appropriate for very advanced users of the language who, in general, already have some significant competence in the language.

Oxford and Scarcella (1994), for example, argue that it is crucial to teach students *explicit strategies* for learning vocabulary. They think that it is even appropriate at times to use some partially decontextualized activities. Some studies in support of this position will be cited later.

Another way to understand how this position differs from the first is to examine the domain of reading instruction in English for academic purposes where, for example, some scholars have argued that, for students with academic goals, no matter how intuitive the appeal, natural learning will not provide the literacy skills necessary for coping with academic demands (Carrell, Devine, & Eskey, 1988; Dubin, Eskey, & Grabe, 1986). They claim that, unlike oral language skills, academic literacy skills are not acquired naturally, but require instruction and training. For example, the subskills of summarizing a text, finding the main idea, and identifying rhetorical structures in a text all require some instruction.

The strategy instruction position, then, is similar to that of the proponents of teaching advanced literacy skills. It claims that the development of extensive vocabulary knowledge for advanced literacy purposes requires some direct instruction and strategy training, as well as extensive exposure to the language (usually through reading) (Huckin & Bloch, 1993; Parry, Chapter 4, this volume; and Williams, 1985).

STRATEGY RESEARCH

A number of scholars have argued that although there is a lot of individual variation across learners, teaching them vocabulary learning strategies is essential.

Ahmed (1989), in a study of some 300 Sudanese learners, found that good learners not only used more vocabulary learning strategies but also relied more heavily on different strategies than did poor learners. He also found some evidence of a progression in strategy as the learner became more experienced.

Oxford and Crookall (1990) examined a number of different techniques for teaching vocabulary and grouped them into fully, semi-, and de-contextualized. They concluded that not all students benefit equally from such techniques and that different ones may be appropriate to different students. They also concluded that incidental or indirect vocabulary learning through L2 use is essential for language development.

Cohen (1990) puts considerable emphasis on learning words through association, and particularly mnemonic techniques, because his research results have found that learners do not use such aids systematically and therefore need instruction.

Schouten-Van Parreren (1992, p. 94), in a study of Dutch students learning French, concluded that weak pupils should be helped to "master relevant vocabulary learning and reading strategies."

Ellis and Beaton (1993) investigated forty-seven students learning German and using Repetition, Keyword, or "Own" strategy conditions. They found that phonological and orthographic similarity of L2 to L1 was facilitative. The part of speech and the word's imageability were also strong determinants, particularly in the case of the keyword approach.

Oxford and Scarcella (1994) emphasize that, for most adult learners, direct vocabulary instruction is also beneficial and necessary. This is because students cannot usually acquire the mass of vocabulary they need just by meaningful reading, listening, speaking, and writing. For long-term retention and use of a large amount of vocabulary, additional support is usually helpful – the kind of support provided especially well by direct instruction. They compare their research-based approach with a traditional approach to L2 vocabulary development. In their approach, teachers carefully consider the words students need to know as determined by needs assessment. This is in comparison with the traditional method where vocabulary instruction is haphazard and teachers present words that students do not know. Oxford and Scarcella argue that learners should be taught how to continue to improve their vocabulary on their own by teaching them appropriate vocabulary learning strategies in contrast to simply letting students learn vocabulary in whatever manner they themselves may devise. They also advocate teaching vocabulary words through a variety of contextualized and partially decontextualized activities, and can even envision the use of decontextualized activities in some very limited situations.

Sanaoui (1995) identified two distinctive approaches to L2 vocabulary learning. Some adult students are clearly capable of independently and actively managing their own learning. Others are much more in need of assistance in order to develop adequate learning strategies and increase their self-awareness. A structured approach to vocabulary learning was more successful than an unstructured one regardless of level of instruction and type of instruction received.

Hulstijn (Chapter 10, this volume) argues that it is especially worthwhile to teach foreign language students how to use the keyword approach, particularly at the intermediate and advanced levels. This technique should be used for words that (for whatever reason) are not learned incidentally.

Parry (Chapter 4, this volume) carried out a longitudinal case study that demonstrates quite clearly how different cognitive strategies can have very dramatic impacts on the success or failure of particular students in terms of their acquisition of the vocabulary needed for authentic advanced academic textbooks.

Altman (Chapter 5, this volume) shows the importance of metacognitive awareness in the process of acquiring oral fluency. As she puts it, "Regardless of the source, once an item entered conscious attention, the more likely it was to be noticed again."

## Development plus Explicit Instruction

The third position on the continuum is *Development plus Explicit Instruction*. It argues for explicit teaching of certain types of vocabulary using a large number of techniques and even direct memorization of certain highly frequent items. There is significant emphasis in this approach on the explicit teaching of words at an early stage of acquisition, with the later stages being more context-based. It is based on an explicit rationale for vocabulary teaching derived from a research base (Coady, 1993; Nation, 1990, 1993; Nation & Newton, Chapter 12, this volume). It is again important to note that these scholars tend to come from a perspective different from those in other positions on the continuum. They are typically dealing with more elementary learners of English and, more often than not, in a non-English speaking environment, i.e., English as a foreign language. Accordingly, there is much more emphasis on the vocabulary skills needed by students at an earlier stage in their acquisition of the language.

For example, Nation argues that the 2,000 most frequent words should be learned as quickly as possible by the most efficient means possible, including direct teaching and learning and the use of graded readers. Coady emphasizes that these words should be learned to the point of automaticity. Nation proposes that students using a language for academic purposes should focus on academic or subtechnical vocabulary. They should then engage in extensive reading to build general word knowledge in tandem with materials in the field of specialization to improve the top-down skills of guessing in context and so on. See Nation (1993) for the research citations behind these proposals.

## L2 EMPIRICAL INSTRUCTIONAL RESEARCH

Two major studies found positive evidence in support of explicit vocabulary instruction in an ESL setting. The first, Paribakht and Wesche (Chapter 9, this volume), is a significant empirical study that argues that contextualized learning through reading is effective but that contextualized reading plus instruction is superior. Both the reading only and reading plus vocabulary treatments over a period of three months resulted in significant gains in vocabulary knowledge. But the experimental treatment (i.e., reading plus vocabulary) led to greater gains, which were quantitatively higher and qualitatively more advanced. Consequently, they concluded that although reading for meaning does contribute to vocabulary knowledge, a supplementary regime with specific vocabulary exercises produces more significant gains.

The second study is Zimmerman's 1994 dissertation titled "Self-selected reading and interactive vocabulary instruction: Knowledge and perceptions of word learning among L2 learners." She too found that systematic instruction can indeed result in students learning certain target words and in a manner superior to simply having them do free and assigned reading.

This dissertation tested the hypothesis that, when academically oriented L2 students are exposed to a combination of regular periods of self-selected reading and interactive vocabulary instruction, there will be significant increases in their knowledge of subtechnical vocabulary and significant changes in their perceptions of how words are learned. Perceptions of how words are learned were examined using questionnaires that included the ranking of six word-learning methods together with some open-ended questions.

A classroom-based study was conducted over 10 weeks with forty-five ESL students attending pre-university intensive English programs. The population was divided into three groups (interactive vocabulary plus self-selected reading, self-selected reading only, and no treatment). Knowledge of subtechnical vocabulary was examined using pre- and posttreatment multiple-choice and checklist tests, which were analyzed using covariate procedures.

The results suggested that 3 hours a week of vocabulary instruction accompanied by a moderate amount of self-selected and course-related reading led to significant gains in vocabulary knowledge, but not to significant changes in perceptions of how words are learned. Pre- and posttreatment questionnaires indicated that students in all groups rated classroom activities and reading as most helpful for vocabulary learning. Participants' comments about word learning suggest that academic students are aware of the complexity of word learning, and that they value help in using new words appropriately. Comments about reading suggest that, although most students considered self-selected reading to be helpful, there was a weak relationship between the amount of reading actually reported and the perception of reading as helpful. It appears that student enthusiasm for reading may be inhibited by time constraints, by the difficulty of selecting appropriate materials, and by limited reading proficiency. The results of this study suggest that reading is necessary but not sufficient for the learning of subtechnical vocabulary. It is argued that the most effective way of addressing the vocabulary needs of L2 academic students is through a combination of reading and interactive vocabulary instruction.

## Classroom Activities

The fourth position on the continuum emphasizes *Classroom Activities*. It advocates the teaching of vocabulary words along very traditional lines. These are best exemplified by a number of practical handbooks for teachers such as Allen's *Techniques in Teaching Vocabulary* (1983), Gairns and Redman's *Working with Words* (1986), Morgan and Rinvolucri's *Vocabulary* (1986), Taylor's *Teaching and Learning Vocabulary* (1990), and Nation's *New Ways in Teaching Vocabulary* (1994). These handbooks almost exclusively emphasize practical classroom activities without necessarily advocating a particular methodological approach. In other words, these activities could probably accompany almost any method. Consequently, teachers who are basing their teaching on these handbooks alone are not being asked to create or articulate an overall framework within which to make such practical classroom decisions. In short, these texts tend to present generic activities for vocabulary learning to teachers. The decision as to when teachers could or, even whether they should, use these activities would presumably come from the rationales proposed in the previous sections.

Allen (1983), for example, suggests that vocabulary is best learned when it is encountered in the classroom situation when the learner perceives a need for it. She categorizes students' general needs by the beginning, intermediate, and advanced levels of instruction. The major activities for beginners involve classroom-based communicative activities, e.g., pictures and games. On the intermediate level, small groups are given task work, simplified readings, and many activities. For advanced students she recommends dictionary work, morphological training, and comprehension work on reading passages. In short, teachers are presented with a mixture of contemporary communicative activities and traditional grammar-translation techniques for foreign language teaching.

# Other relevant areas of research

In the next section, six different areas of research will be examined. They are surveyed for their implications for pedagogy, which will be treated in the final section of the paper.

## L1 vocabulary acquisition research

The following research is cited in spite of the fact that it deals only with native speakers. The relevance of this research can be seen not only in the significant volume of studies cited, but also in the fact that they found that even native speakers can benefit from vocabulary instruction. If this is so, one could argue that L2 learners would benefit even more since they have so much less natural and incidental exposure to the language.

Stahl and Fairbanks (1986) conducted a meta-analysis of about seventy studies investigating the effects of vocabulary instruction on the learning of word meanings and on comprehension. The subjects were native speakers mostly on the elementary level, but some were at college level. Stahl and Fairbanks concluded that the following principles seem to underlie effective vocabulary teaching:

1. Providing learners with both definitional and contextual information about words
2. Encouraging learners to process information about words at a deeper level
3. Providing learners with multiple exposures to a word

Moreover, they concluded that the effects found on standardized vocabulary and comprehension measures are probably much closer to the actual effects than those of the study-specific passage comprehension measures. These effects, although smaller, are still significantly different from zero, indicating that vocabulary instruction does appear to have an effect on comprehension.

Klesius and Searls (1990) summarized another fifteen L1 studies looking at computer-assisted instruction (CAI), the keyword method with both arbitrary and semantically linked visual imagery, and writing activities. All methods were supported except arbitrary keyword, which was effective in the short term but not in the long term – not surprising considering that these are native-speaking children. For low-ability children, CAI and keyword semantically linked imagery were particularly effective.

## Collocational research

Several studies have found that multiword phrases are not learned well through ordinary language experience and suggest that there is a need for them to be learned explicitly.

Cowie (1992) found that a large number of familiar and stable collocations such as "make proposals" or "call for action" appear in newspaper writing. These must be known for receptive as well as productive language competence. Verstraten (1992) points out the need for information on fixed phrases to be included in learners' dictionaries. Moreover, Bahns and Eldaw (1993) argue that, for advanced students, collocations present a major problem in the production of correct English.

Arnaud and Savignon (Chapter 8, this volume) focused on low-frequency words and complex lexical idioms. They found that a group of thirty-four secondary school teachers of English with more than 10 years of experience could match university-level native speakers in their knowledge of low-frequency words but not idiomatic expressions. They conclude that constant exposure to the language is necessary to acquire idiomatic knowledge.

Lewis (1993; Chapter 13, this volume) cites recent research that has found that native speakers of a language utilize a large number of fixed and prepatterned phrases as they carry out the routines of normal spoken interaction. He then emphasizes that all languages utilize a wide range of expressions including words, polywords, multiword items, collocations, and institutionalized expressions. In his words, "Language consists of grammaticalised lexis, not lexicalised grammar" (1993, p. vi). He claims to embrace all of the assumptions of the communicative approach to language teaching, but he proposes that lexis must be the "organizing principle affecting both content and methodology" (p. 32). It is important to note that he is proposing a significantly different method of second or foreign language teaching. The methodological implications of his Lexical Approach (1993, pp. 194–195) are as follows:

- Early emphasis on receptive skills, especially listening, is essential.
- De-contextualized vocabulary learning is a fully legitimate strategy.
- The role of grammar as a receptive skill must be recognized.
- The importance of contrast in language awareness must be recognized.
- Teachers should employ extensive, comprehensible language for receptive purposes.
- Extensive writing should be delayed as long as possible.
- Nonlinear recording formats (e.g., mind maps, word trees) are intrinsic to the Lexical Approach.
- Reformulation should be the natural response to student error.
- Teachers should always react primarily to the content of student language.
- Pedagogical chunking should be a frequent classroom activity.

## Reading research

Some scholars argue that there is a need for students to quickly acquire a sizable basic vocabulary in order to comprehend successfully in reading. It is then suggested that this vocabulary base could be acquired more efficiently through some type of direct instruction.

Laufer (Chapter 2, this volume) argues that there is a lexical threshold for reading comprehension consisting of about 3,000 word families (approximately 5,000 words). She claims that even highly skilled readers in L1 who transfer their abilities cannot, generally speaking, read on task at the criterion of 70% comprehension unless they have such a lexical foundation.

Coady, Magoto, Hubbard, Graney, and Mokhtari (1993) found that explicit learning of the 3,000 most frequent words in English had a significant effect on reading comprehension. Their argument is that recognizing these words in a speedy and automatic manner provides more cognitive processing time.

Grabe and Stoller (Chapter 6, this volume) claim that extensive reading resulted in improved vocabulary, reading, and listening comprehension. Kirsner, Lalor, and Hird (1993) argue for "the importance of lexical training during the initial phase of second language learning" (p. 226).

Nation (1993) presents a rationale in the context of English for academic purposes for learning the 2,000 most frequent words first, followed by the University Word List and then focusing on repeated reading to integrate this core knowledge. For more specialized texts he emphasizes guessing in context and using definitions in context. Finally, he recommends extensive reading.

Coady (Chapter 11, this volume) points out that although most vocabulary is acquired through extensive reading, we must take into consideration the beginner's paradox; i.e., students must read in order to learn words but at the same time they must possess a minimal but critical mass of words in order to be able to read successfully.

## Bottom-up processing research

Several studies argue that students from different orthographic backgrounds will transfer these skills or lack thereof to L2 acquisition. Therefore teachers have to be aware of such potential handicaps in orthographic processing, phonological working memory, and word recognition. Presumably there should be some instructional emphasis on these skills.

Koda (Chapter 3, this volume) has found evidence that there are strong connections between the L1 orthographic knowledge of students and their L2 processing procedures. In particular she recommends that students be given metacognitive awareness of these processes and strategies for coping with deficiencies.

Yang (Chapter 7, this volume) found that the main task of vocabulary acquisition for adults at the earliest stages of L2 acquisition is not to establish a new semantic network but rather to achieve automated recognition of L2 word forms. And it was the word-recognition skill that lagged behind and continued longer to benefit from instruction.

Service and Craik (1993) claim that there are three main factors operating in the processing of new L2 vocabulary words into memory. First, to what degree are semantic associations available to link the new word to existing ones? Second, how easily can a phonological representation of the new form be created and maintained in working memory? Third, are there already existing similar phonological forms in long-term memory to support the learning? Their study found that children were superior on all of the new word learning tasks and that they seemed to rely less on their phonological representations than on their semantic associative ones, at least compared to a much older group of learners. See Laufer (Chapter 2, this volume) for more on this subject.

Finally, Perfetti, Zhang, and Berent (1992), in their examination of Chinese and English readers, conclude that for both phonology is an automatic part of reading, and they found evidence for phonological processing prior to meaning access. They conclude that phonological processes occur in reading in all writing systems because all writing systems reflect spoken language, not pictures.

## Lexicon size research

There is a significant disagreement in the literature over the total amount of vocabulary known by a university-educated native speaker, i.e., the target of English for academic purposes. These arguments are important because they tend to be a major determinant of a given teacher's philosophy about vocabulary instruction. For example, if one believes that educated university native speakers tend to know 50,000 to 100,000 words, then it is seems useless to try to teach a tiny subset of that amount. On the other hand, if one believes that university students tend to know about 16,000 base words, then teaching a thousand or so words does not seem like such a bad idea.

Nagy and Anderson (1984), for example, estimated that there are 85,533 word families in printed school English (grades 3–9). They counted as one word family semantically and morphologically related words such as *enthusiast, enthusiasts,* and *enthusiasm.*

In contrast, Goulden, Nation, and Read (1990) estimate that an average native-speaker English-speaking university student has a vocabulary of 17,000 word families (a base form and its derived forms).

D'Anna, Zechmeister, and Hall (1991) based their study on the *Oxford American Dictionary* (OAD), from which they eliminated proper names, archaic words, technical terms, and so on, in order to form a corpus of what they call functionally important words. They then asked their subjects to choose from a five-point scale how well they felt they knew a sample of almost 200 words from the OAD. They then extrapolated from these results and concluded that the average number of different words known by a university student is 16,785. Some further issues were explored in two follow-up studies, Zechmeister, D'Anna, Hall, Hall, and Smith (1993) and Zechmeister, Chronis, Cull, D'Anna, and Healy (1995). In the latter study the subjects were given multiple-choice tests to determine how accurate their self-rating was. They found that subjects typically overestimated their knowledge, particularly when there were difficult distracters. Moreover, they again extrapolated from their data that junior high students knew fewer words (9,684) than freshmen college students (16,679) and than older adults (21,252).

Meara (1996) discusses how difficult it is to carry out effective research on measuring the size of the lexicon and proposes the use of some standardized vocabulary tests which he has developed. They are simple to administer and remarkably sensitive to knowledge across a range of different frequency bands or a range of different specialist areas of lexis.

Further, he argues that as the lexicon grows, organization becomes a more significant factor than size. He therefore proposes a standardized measure of the relative organization of the lexicon. Finally, he feels that both measures together can be a method of assessing overall lexical competence.

## Dictionary instruction research

Several studies have found that many adult L2 learners systematically misinterpret dictionary entries and take much more time compared to nondictionary users with limited advantage gained.

Bensoussan (1983) found that subjects using dictionaries as a translation aid in a timed examination did not perform better than those without dictionaries. She concluded that the time used in dictionary searches is a significant variable.

Luppescu and Day (1993) found that students who used a dictionary did score better on a subsequent vocabulary test than those who did not. This would appear to demonstrate vocabulary learning from dictionary usage. However, they found that there are some trade-offs. The use of the dictionary results in a lower reading speed and may confuse the learner.

Nesi and Meara (1994) asked subjects to use dictionaries as an aid in writing sentences containing unfamiliar words. They found that many adult language learners systematically misinterpreted dictionary entries.

Grabe and Stoller (Chapter 6, this volume) found that using a bilingual dictionary in a consistent and appropriate manner was indeed beneficial for vocabulary learning and reading development.

# Implications for pedagogy

Let us now consider some implications for pedagogy that can be drawn from the research cited above. The contextual acquisition research does demonstrate that most vocabulary knowledge comes from meaningful language encounters. If the language is authentic, rich in content, enjoyable, and, above all, comprehensible, then learning is more successful. After all, this is the way native speakers acquire academic proficiency in a language, ideally speaking, albeit over the course of a number of years.

But second language learners who have to use a language for academic purposes soon find that they cannot learn the needed language skills fast enough and efficiently enough if they simply try to replicate the ordinary leisurely and time-consuming approach that a native speaker takes. Students find it very useful to be given strategies for improving their learning and to be made aware of both content and methodological goals and processes.

There are at least two recent and carefully carried out empirical studies (Paribakht & Wesche, Chapter 9, this volume, and Zimmerman, 1994) that found that although vocabulary learning certainly does take place through the presumed ordinary contextual approach, such learning can indeed be improved by adding formal instruction.

The L1 vocabulary acquisition research has shown that in spite of the fact that native-speaker children would not seem to need explicit vocabulary instruction, there is empirical evidence that it does help. Three main principles appear to underlie effective vocabulary teaching. First, learners should be provided with both definitional and contextual information about words. In the case of L2 learners, this could be related to their often-felt need for dictionary access. Second, learners should be encouraged to process information about words at a deeper level. Among L2 learners this could be reflected in the current emphasis on authentic communicative activities. Finally, learners need multiple exposures to words. This is certainly of even greater importance for L2 learners, who, in general, have had much less exposure to the language. Extensive reading is the most often cited remedy for this lack.

Some significant insights can be gained from the collocational research. For example, there are some complicated multiword expressions in every language that seem to necessitate explicit learning and contrived encounters in order to achieve significant fluency.

The research on reading in a foreign language emphasizes that comprehension of advanced, authentic, academic (AAA) texts demands significant skill in reading and, in particular, good knowledge of at least 5,000 words in L2. In addition, students with an L1 orthographic tradition significantly different from that of the L2 will almost certainly be challenged by this difference. It will also contribute to slow and inefficient word recognition, another skill that entails significant practice. Both of these skills are crucial prerequisites to efficient processing of AAA texts. They are therefore likely candidates for explicit instruction.

Depending on which body of research about the size of the lexicon is found to be more convincing, one might be persuaded that certain types of vocabulary are worth teaching, e.g. the University Word List. Moreover, several studies have found that many adult L2 learners systematically misinterpret dictionary entries and take much more time on reading tasks as compared to nondictionary users. Such limitations would suggest a need for more instruction in how best to use a dictionary.

## Conclusion

Words and phrases are essential to language learning. The only real issue is the best manner in which to acquire them. It seems clear that significant numbers of meaningful encounters with the target language will result in proficiency. If someone needs to achieve only small to moderate proficiency in the language without any time pressure, then the natural approach, whereby acquisition occurs through contextual use alone, would seem to be quite a reasonable suggestion.

If, however, students need to use a language for challenging academic purposes such as reading advanced, authentic, academic texts and, moreover, have only a limited amount of time in which to acquire the skills to carry out this task, then we can see a different type of approach being suggested in the literature. The proponents of the strategy approach are quite convincing in their claim that academically oriented students need help in order to improve their acquisition skills. Moreover, the studies by Paribakht and Wesche, and by Zimmerman, seem to demonstrate that systematic vocabulary instruction in addition to learning through reading is a more successful approach than simply learning through context alone. In sum, the research clearly suggests that students will benefit from such instruction.

# References

Ahmed, M. O. (1989). Vocabulary learning techniques. In P. Meara (Ed.), *Beyond words* (pp. 3–14). London: CILT.

Allen, V. F. (1983). *Techniques in teaching vocabulary.* Oxford, England: Oxford University Press.

Bahns, J., & Eldaw, M. (1993). Should we teach EFL students collocations? *System, 21*(1), 101–114.

Bensoussan, M. (1983). Dictionaries and tests of EFL reading comprehension. *ELT Journal, 37*(4), 341–345.

Carrell, P., Devine, J., & Eskey, D. (1988). *Interactive approaches to second language reading.* New York: Cambridge University Press.

Carter, R., & McCarthy, M. (Eds.). (1988). *Vocabulary and language teaching.* London: Longman.

Coady, J. (1993). Research on ESL/EFL vocabulary acquisition: Putting it all in context. In T. Huckin, M. Haynes, & J. Coady (Eds.), *Second language reading and vocabulary learning* (pp. 3–23). Norwood, NJ: Ablex.

Coady, J., Magoto, J., Hubbard, P., Graney, J., & Mokhtari, K. (1993). High frequency vocabulary and reading proficiency in ESL readers. In T. Huckin, M. Haynes, & J. Coady (Eds.), *Second language reading and vocabulary learning* (pp. 217–228). Norwood, NJ: Ablex.

Cohen, A. D. (1990). *Language learning: Insights for learners, teachers, and researchers.* New York: Newbury House.

Cowie, A. P. (1992). Multiword lexical units and communicative language teaching. In P. Arnaud & H. Béjoint (Eds.), *Vocabulary and applied linguistics* (pp. 1–12). Basingstoke: Macmillan.

D'Anna, C. A., Zechmeister, E. B., and Hall, J. W. (1991). Toward a meaningful definition of vocabulary size. *Journal of Reading Behavior, 23*(1), 109–122.

Dubin, F., Eskey, D., & Grabe, W. (Eds.). (1986). *Teaching second language reading for academic purposes.* Reading, MA: Addison-Wesley.

Ellis, N. C., & Beaton, A. (1993). Psycholinguistic determinants of foreign language vocabulary learning. *Language Learning, 43*(4), 559–617.

Ellis, R. (1994). Factors in the incidental acquisition of second language vocabulary from oral input: A review essay. *Applied Language Learning, 5*(1), 1–32.

Gairns, R., & Redman, S. (1986). *Working with words: A guide to teaching and learning vocabulary.* Cambridge: Cambridge University Press.

Goulden, R., Nation, P., & Read, J. (1990). How large can a receptive vocabulary be? *Applied Linguistics, 11*(4), 341–363.

Huckin, T., & Bloch, J. (1993). Strategies for inferring word meaning in context: A cognitive model. In T. Huckin, M. Haynes, & J. Coady (Eds.), *Second language reading and vocabulary learning* (pp. 153–176). Norwood, NJ: Ablex.

Kirsner, K., Lalor, E., & Hird, K. (1993). The bilingual lexicon: Exercise, meaning and morphology. In R. Schreuder & B. Weltens (Eds.), *The bilingual lexicon* (pp. 215–248). Amsterdam: John Benjamins.

Klesius, J. P., & Searls, E. F. (1990). A meta-analysis of recent research in meaning vocabulary instruction. *Journal of Research and Development in Education, 23*(4), 226–235.

Krashen, S. (1989). We acquire vocabulary and spelling by reading: Additional evidence for the input hypothesis. *Modern Language Journal, 73*(4), 440–464.

(1993). *The power of reading.* Englewood, CO: Libraries Unlimited.

Leki, I., & Carson, J. G. (1994). Students' perceptions of EAP writing instruction research. *International Review of Applied Linguistics, 24*(1), 69–75.

Levenston, E. (1979). Second language lexical acquisition: Issues and problems. *English Teachers Journal, 35,* 44–48.

Lewis, M. (1993). *The lexical approach: The state of ELT and a way forward.* Hove, England: Language Teaching Publications.

Luppescu, S., & Day, R. R. (1993). Reading, dictionaries, and vocabulary learning. *Language Learning, 43*(2), 263–287.

Meara, P., Malmkjaer, K., & Williams, J. (1996). *The dimensions of lexical competence* (pp. 35–53). New York: Cambridge University Press.

Morgan, J., & Rinvolucri, M. (1986). *Vocabulary.* Oxford: Oxford University Press.

Nagy, W. E., & Anderson, R. C. (1984). How many words are there in printed school English? *Reading Research Quarterly, 19*(3), 304–330.

Nagy, W. E., & Herman, P. A. (1984). Limitations of vocabulary instruction. (Tech. Rep. no. 326). Champaign: University of Illinois Center for the Study of Reading.

Nagy, W. E., Herman, P. A., & Anderson, R. C. (1985). Learning words from context. *Reading Research Quarterly, 20*(2), 233–253.

Nation, I. S. P. (1990). *Teaching and learning vocabulary.* Rowley, MA: Newbury House.

(1993). Vocabulary size, growth, and use. In R. Schreuder & B. Weltens (Eds.), *The bilingual lexicon* (pp. 115–134). Amsterdam: John Benjamins.

(Ed.). (1994). *New ways in teaching vocabulary.* Alexandria, VA: TESOL.

Nattinger, J. R., & DeCarrico, J. S. (1992). *Lexical phrases and language teaching.* Oxford: Oxford University Press.

Nesi, H., & Meara, P. (1994). Patterns of misinterpretation in the productive use of EFL dictionary definitions. *System, 22*(1), 1–15.

Oxford, R. L., & Crookall, D. (1990). Vocabulary learning: A critical analysis of techniques. *TESL Canada Journal, 7,* 9–30.

Oxford, R. L., & Scarcella, R. C. (1994). Second language vocabulary learning among adults: State of the art in vocabulary instruction. *System, 22*(2), 231–243.

Perfetti, C. A., Zhang, S., & Berent, I. (1992) Reading in English and Chinese: Evidence for a "universal" phonological principle. In R. Frost & L. Katz (Eds.), *Orthography, phonology, morphology, and meaning.* Advances in psychology, vol. 94. (pp. 227–248). Amsterdam: North-Holland.

Richards, J. (1976). The role of vocabulary teaching. *TESOL Quarterly, 10*(1), 77–89.

Sanaoui, R. (1995). Adult learners' approaches to learning vocabulary in second languages. *Modern Language Journal, 79,* 15–28.

Schouten-Van Parreren, C. (1992). Individual differences in vocabulary acquisition: A qualitative experiment in the first phase of secondary education. In P. Arnaud & H. Béjoint (Eds.), *Vocabulary and applied linguistics* (pp. 94–101). Basingstoke: Macmillan.

Service, E., & Craik, F. (1993). Differences between young and older adults in learning a foreign vocabulary. *Journal of Memory and Language, 32,* 608–623.

Sheorey, R., & Mokhtari, K. (1993). Reading habits of university ESL students. *TESOL Matters, 3*(2), 9.

Sinclair, J. M., & Renouf, A. (1988). A lexical syllabus for language learning. In R. Carter & M. McCarthy (Eds.), *Vocabulary and language teaching* (pp. 140–160). London: Longman.

Stahl, S. A., & Fairbanks, M. M. (1986). The effects of vocabulary instruction: A model-based meta-analysis. *Review of Educational Research, 56*(1), 72–110.

Taylor, L. (1990). *Teaching and learning vocabulary.* New York: Prentice Hall.

Verstraten, L. (1992). Fixed phrases in monolingual learners' dictionaries. In P. Arnaud & H. Béjoint (Eds.), *Vocabulary and applied linguistics* (pp. 28–40). Basingstoke: Macmillan.

Williams, R. (1985). Teaching vocabulary recognition strategies in ESP reading. *ESP Journal, 4,* 121–131.

Willis, D. (1990). *The lexical syllabus.* London: Collins COBUILD.

Zechmeister, E. B., D'Anna, C. A., Hall, J. W., Hall, C. H., & Smith, J. A. (1993). Metacognitive and other knowledge about the mental lexicon: Do we know how many words we know? *Applied Linguistics, 14*(2), 188–206.

Zechmeister, E. B., Chronis, A. M., Cull, W. L., D'Anna, C. A., & Healy, N. A. (1995). Growth of a functionally important lexicon. *Journal of Reading Behavior, 27*(2), 201–212.

Zimmerman, C. B. (1994). Self-selected reading and interactive vocabulary instruction: Knowledge and perceptions of word learning among L2 learners. Ph.D. diss., University of Southern California, Los Angeles.

# Author index

# Subject index

academic vocabulary, 239
acquisition, stages of, 86–91
Acquisition-Learning Hypothesis, 15
activation, spreading, 211
activities
   classroom, 280–1
   communication, 241–8
   out-of-class, 267
advanced learners, 157–73, 217
Affective Filter Hypothesis, 15
age differences, 228
alphabetic script, 44–5
anthropology, 56
Arabic, 43–4
artificial language, 128–30
ask-and-answer activities, 242
associative activities, 251
associative networks, 251
audio-lingual method, 10–12
authentic materials, 231
automated vocabulary, 158
automatic recognition, 23
automaticity, 93–4, 114, 117, 125–
   52, 284
avoidance strategies, 94–5
awareness raising, 260, 269

background knowledge, 30
beginner's paradox, 229–35
bottom-up processing, 284–5

Chinese, 45
classroom activities, 280–1
cloze tests, 106, 108–9, 117–9
COBUILD (Collins-Birmingham
   University International
   Language Database), 16
cognates, 111
cognitive strategies, 37

collocation, 6, 17, 256–7, 261–4
collocation activities, 250
collocational research, 282–3, 287
communicative language teaching,
   12–4
complex lexical units, 157–73
computational linguistics, 16
concreteness versus abstraction, 213
confluence of opportunity, 93
context availability hypothesis, 213
contextual clues, 2, 28–9, 31, 35
core vocabulary, 238
corpus analysis, 16
cross-linguistic studies, 37

deceptive morphology, 25
deceptive transparency, 2, 25–7, 31
de-lexicalised words, 258, 264, 269
depth of processing, 246–8
development, lexical, 125–56
diary studies, 72, 95
dictation, 250
dictionaries, bilingual, 6
dictionary use, 61–4, 101–2, 111–2,
   114–5, 119, 203, 219, 286–7
direct instruction, 174–200, 228,
   238–54, 274–5, 278–80, 287–8
Direct Method, 8–9

etymology, 6
exercises, vocabulary, 182–5, 194–7,
   261–9

false friends, 25
fluency activities, 248–9
French, 160–70
frequency counts, 58, 238
frequency lists, 7, 9, 14, 23–4, 158,
   162, 229–30

297

298     *Subject index*